Kuwait and Al-Sabah

Kuwait and Al-Sabah

Tribal Politics and Power in an Oil State

Rivka Azoulay

I.B. TAURIS

LONDON • NEW YORK • OXFORD • NEW DELHI • SYDNEY

I.B. TAURIS

Bloomsbury Publishing Plc

50 Bedford Square, London, WC1B 3DP, UK
1385 Broadway, New York, NY 10018, USA
29 Earlsfort Terrace, Dublin 2, Ireland

BLOOMSBURY, I.B. TAURIS and the I.B. Tauris logo
are trademarks of Bloomsbury Publishing Plc

First published in Great Britain 2020
This paperback edition published 2023

Cover design: Adriana Brioso
Cover illustration © Godruma/iStock
Cover background © Katsumi Murouchi/Getty Images

A catalogue record for this book is available from the British Library.

A catalog record for this book is available from the Library of Congress.

ISBN: HB: 978-1-8386-0505-6
        PB: 978-0-7556-5098-9
        ePDF: 978-1-8386-0506-3
        eBook: 978-1-8386-0507-0

Typeset by Integra Software Services Pvt Ltd.

To find out more about our authors and books visit www.bloomsbury.com
and sign up for our newsletters.

To Petite Chaya, your light will always shine in me

Contents

Acknowledgements

The research for this book could not have been accomplished without the institutional and human support I received between 2009 and 2014 as a PhD student at Sciences Po Paris. The first two years were financed by the Kuwait Foundation for the Advancement of Sciences (KFAS) within the Middle East Mediterranean Chair at Sciences Po Paris; an intellectual powerhouse for students of the region that regrettably ceased to exist today.

In Kuwait I owe my debt to the Center for Gulf Studies at the American University of Kuwait (AUK) and to Farah al-Nakib, who ran the Center while I was there. The Center hosted me, provided me with accommodation and connected me with international scholars on the region with whom I could share my research thoughts. Farah's collegiality and great knowledge of Kuwait's history were invaluable during my stay in Kuwait between October 2012 and January 2014.

Apart from these institutions, great debt goes to my two PhD supervisors – Gilles Kepel and Steffen Hertog – who assisted me in this long journey and offered their support. Gilles Kepel accepted me in his programme in 2007 and had faith in me while I was still a young student without much knowledge of the Middle East and the Arabic language. I will never forget those years at Sciences Po and in beautiful Paris, where I matured as a person in a very stimulating environment. Steffen Hertog is another excellent scholar who has been able to successfully combine empirical work on the Arabian Gulf with theoretical contributions to the field of political economy. Steffen tirelessly continued to supervise my work and is an exemplary mentor.

Many other academics have been dear friends and supporters along the way. My gratitude goes to George Irani, professor at the AUK. George has been the one who pushed me in 2012 – when I was already engaged in a full-time job with the ICRC – to finish my PhD and get the ticket to be part of the 'Club' at moments at which I was losing faith in the possibility of finishing. Mary Ann Tetreault was another academic of invaluable support. I have never been able to meet her in person and she sadly passed away just before I finished this book. I was introduced to Mary Ann in 2014 while in Washington DC. She was enthusiast about my work and it resulted in various calls and a series of email exchanges in which we talked more than academia. She has never been able to read the final draft, but I hope that this work will be a contribution to the field of Kuwait studies as she would have liked it to be.

Then there are my many friends who are also colleagues. In this regard, some deserve special mentioning. Many precious enduring friendships developed in Kuwait. Scott Weiner and Madeleine Wells are such dear friends who made me feel at home in Amman Street. The same holds for Claire Beaugrand and Zoltan Pall, whose friendship and intellectual support were crucial in the progression of this work.

Apart from these friends and colleagues, this study could not have been undertaken without the support and faith of the many Kuwaitis I interviewed since 2009, some of whom have become friends. Poet and scholar Muhammad al-Boghaili is a friend and offered his precious insights into Kuwait politics and Bedouin life at each moment I bothered him with my questions. Sami al-Khalidi has also been a great resource on Shi'a politics and has effortlessly helped me during my stay in Kuwait. Ahmad Bin Barjas' historical knowledge of Bedouin life and Kuwait provided a crucial source for my historical chapters and I owe him many debts. He effortlessly gave me his time throughout these years to answer my burning questions about Kuwait and Bedouin life. Many friends also made me feel at home and showed me Kuwait from the inside. Imane al-'Arbasch and Fatima Hammadi deserve to be mentioned specifically. Imane and Fatima made me discover Kuwaiti culture and the lives of Kuwaiti or better said Khaliji women.

I owe my gratitude to the editing board of Arabian Humanities and to my co-author Claire Beaugrand for allowing me to reproduce a large part of our previously published article in Part III of this book that deals with royal infighting and its impact on political life in Kuwait. The original article appeared under the title 'Limits of clientelism: elite struggles' fragmenting politics in Kuwait', *Arabian Humanities*, Vol. 4 (2015). Being able to use this work was of great importance in developing the argument of this book. I am similarly grateful to the editing board of Hurst Publishers for granting me permission to re-use many passages of my previously published chapter 'The Politics of Shi'i Merchants in Kuwait' in *Business Politics in the Middle East* (eds. S. Hertog, G. Luciani and M. Valeri, London: Hurst, 2013).

This book could not have been produced without the support of Bloomsbury Publishing House. Lester Crook was the first to read my manuscript and his faith in this work was invaluable. Sophie Rudland deserves special mentioning. As senior editor she has been very helpful throughout the journey of publication. My special thanks go out to Gogulanathan and Viswasirasini of Integra Software Services for their tireless efforts in editing this book and preparing it for publication.

One cannot undertake a work of such magnitude without the support of one's family and loved ones. I owe my inspiration to them and they all know what they mean to me. This work is for them as well.

Authoritarian regimes and the crucial role of the periphery

In the old order, the nobility lived on its estates.
In the new order, the state is the estate of the new nobility[1]

Tribal authority and the periphery in Kuwait

This is a book that unravels, via a historical approach, the nature of political authority in Kuwait's Al-Sabah Emirate. It argues that today's politics and regime–society relations are structured by a tribal authority system, in which the rulers co-opt groups at the periphery of power (in Kuwait's case the Shi'a minority and the *badu*) to counterbalance a powerful *in-group* – Kuwait's merchants – with whom the Al-Sabah historically shared power and kinship ties. This principle of rule has been described by late historian Ibn Khaldun (1332–1406) in his social history of Arabian dynasties and civilizations. In his *Muqaddimah* (Introduction), Ibn Khaldun argues that those who are capable of establishing dynasty are only those with tribal solidarity – an esprit de corps (*'asabiyya* in Arabic): social solidarity with lineage structuring power relations. According to his theory, rulers, once they have established themselves at the centre of power with the support of their own people, will rely on people outside the *in-group*, outside the inner *'asabiyya*, because the real threat stems from this *'asabiyya* that can always challenge the central elite status and seize power.[2]

'Asabiyya is a nebulous concept and can refer to different forms of social solidarity, depending upon social structures in a given society. In the case of Kuwait, this solidarity refers to kinship ties to the *Bani 'Utub* federation of founding families. It also refers to the traceability of one's lineage (*nasab*) to pure Arab tribes from *Najd* that were among the first families to settle in *Al-Kout* and because of this share an imagined identity of a diasporic community with its roots in Najd. Here both diasporic identity and the claim of purity of blood come together. Only this nucleus of old-settled *Najdi* merchant families – some of them part of the *Bani 'Utub* – found themselves on top of social and economic stratification in pre-oil Kuwait and today enjoy the privileges of having been granted exclusive prerogatives in the private sector as contractors and agents for foreign companies.

Those who found themselves out of this inner 'asabiyya of a Najdi elite were less threatening to the Al-Sabah being part of the periphery, in the sense that their externality to the inner elite – the nexus of rulers and merchants – has made them favoured allies for the Al-Sabah in the consolidation of their reign. In the case of Kuwait, these were the Shi'a minority and the *badu* whose support was crucial to the regime at various moments in time to counterbalance opposition from a Najdi elite, particularly during heydays of Arab nationalism.

During the consolidation of Kuwait as an oil state and until the Iraqi Invasion, this status quo upon which Kuwait's political order was built was not challenged. Merchants were granted the privileges of the private sector and the Al-Sabah the privileges of governance; an elite bargain in which the masses were upgraded as state-dependent middle-class actors and did not challenge the prerogatives of this inclusive elite. Yet, since the Invasion cracks have started to appear in this system and the two aspects of the regime's 'asabiyya have started to fragment: the coherence of the ruling elite and its ties to its periphery. The first trend is the rise of a young generation of *badu* in search of new modes of politics and better access to the state's resources; breaking away from previous clientelist modes of rule that relied upon tribal hierarchies mediated via elites as service deputies. This combines with a regime that increasingly faces the need to diversify its resources away from oil with mounting fiscal pressure and the unsustainability of its current social contract based upon a rentier bargain. The second trend has been the rise in elite rivalry within the Al-Sabah family since 2006 as a consequence of the breaking of the implicit rotation of power between the Al-Jabir and Al-Salim branches. This emboldened ambitious princes of the second generation to aspire to the throne one day.

The escalation of both trends in 2014 led to Emir to intervene often through the repression of dissent as previous modes of soft-authoritarianism proved ineffective to still popular anger and an increasingly cross-cutting opposition to corruption and austerity measures. This itself is a sign of a weakened regime's capacity to maintain social control and a fragmentation of the regime's 'asabiyya, both internally and in its ties to a restless periphery of mostly young tribesmen.

This social change takes place while Gulf monarchies face the challenge of reforming their economies anticipating a post-oil future and of preparing their youth population for a new social contract in which citizens will have to be inserted in productive sectors of the economy rather than in the inflated and highly inefficient public sectors. Although Kuwait's financial resources are abundant, the country has faced fiscal deficits since 2014/2015 (after consecutive years of fiscal surpluses) and will gradually have to initiate reforms to render its economy more productive and reduce the costs of its welfare regime. In January 2017 Kuwait launched its development plan 'New Kuwait', envisioning a radical shift from an oil-dependent economy. The diversification of the economy will require that the regime renegotiates and modernizes the monarchical pact and goes beyond its implicit agreement with the Najdi elite that has been granted the prerogatives of the private sector in exchange for giving up its entitlement to power-sharing. Diversifying the economy would need the participation of other citizens outside this elite, challenging the oligopolistic power of established merchant families. Consequently, economic diversification will ultimately lead to further democratize

Kuwait's political sphere and undermine the present system of authority upon which the Al-Sabah House has been established; a tribal authority system centred around 'asabiyya and relying on the support of the periphery. In order to become the regional and financial hub it aspires to be by 2035, the rule of law should apply equally to all citizens and transparency should be guaranteed in the state's dealing with society. The calls of the anti-corruption movement that crystallized in 2012 resonate strongly with this willingness from a large group within society to find new modes of politics and representation based upon a modern state of law and institutions (*dawla al-qanun wa al-mu'assasat*) rather than upon networks of privilege. Meanwhile, these same groups in society tend to oppose government measures aimed at diversifying the economy as it threatens the entitlements to which they got accustomed in the rentier state. Gradual awareness raising of the importance to make short-term sacrifices for long-term gains is therefore essential to make Kuwait future-proof with citizens embracing rather than resisting change via their parliamentary prerogatives.

The argument

While this is mainly a book about Kuwait, the core argument developed goes beyond Kuwait's case and argues that the support of the periphery is the condition sine qua non-Arab authoritarian regimes fragment and ultimately disintegrate. Understanding how regimes uphold this support as well as the factors which contribute to the fragmentation of patronage networks towards the periphery enables us to decipher deeper causes behind political order and political change in the Arab-Islamic context. In this regard, the two aspects of Khaldunian 'asabiyya apply to understanding the salience of some of these authoritarian regimes and the fragmentation of others. On the one hand, this refers to the coherence of the solidarity of the ruling elite. On the other hand, it refers to the capacity of the ruling elite to maintain the support of the periphery: those other friends or clients, not of the ruler's kin, who become essential allies in the ruler's aim to establish dynasty and consolidate reign.

The first aspect is the internal cohesion of the ruling elite, the regime's 'asabiyya and capacity to act as one bloc and maintain a certain balance between competing regime elites. This was one of the arguments developed by scholar Michael Herb (1999) in his book *All in the Family: Absolutism, Revolution and Democracy in the Middle Eastern Monarchies* explaining the survival or decline of Arab monarchies in the twentieth century. The author argues that the oil monarchies in the Arabian Gulf proved most successful in creating a form of power-sharing between ruling families that until today monopolize or dominate the highest state offices.[3] Consequently, ruling family members have a genuine interest in the preservation of monarchy and tend to work in support of the system.[4] Morocco, Jordan and Oman do not fit this classification and are according to Herb 'intermediate' cases in which ruling families dominate but not monopolize state institutions, allowing however for similar intra-family bargaining.[5] More importantly, this allows for the imbrication of the regime in society, omnipresent in different institutions, making it difficult for outsiders to overthrow the regime acting through these institutions. In the monarchies that fell in the 1950s and 1960s, ruling families were prohibited by constitution to occupy cabinet posts, argues Herb, and explains the fall of these one-man-dominated monarchies, in which the monarch had to deal with and balance powerful forces: the army, parliament, the parties and entrenched elites. Failing to balance these and a tendency for autocracy within the ruling circle precipitated the monarch's downfall.

A second aspect of Khaldunian theory of 'asabiyya relates to the ties between the ruling 'asabiyya and the periphery. While I argue that the periphery is a necessary factor for authoritarians' survival, I also contend that the nature of globalization since the 1990s – characterized by the communication revolution and neoliberalism – penetrated the lives of peoples of the periphery in a way that uprooted existing hierarchies and contributed to the fragmentation of previous forms of political patronage of authoritarian regimes. Neoliberal globalization was thus accompanied with the rise and sometimes revolts of the periphery throughout the MENA; the crucial pillar of minimal support to regimes.

Centre–periphery relations are broadly defined and refer to studies that relate to both the specific nature of Arabian civilization and solidarities and to societies that face sharp divisions between centre and periphery with the presence of strong peripheral communities, often rural and tribal ones. Periphery refers to close-knit communities governed by strong group solidarities, norms and hierarchies that have been less exposed to the disintegrative forces of industrialization and urbanization. Periphery opposes urban centres where group solidarities tend to be weaker as people mingle and adopt new identities based upon socialization in the marketplace. In this regard, the city refers to a place where community is mostly expressed in terms of association (*Gesellschaft*) whereas the periphery is characterized by stronger solidarities and a subjective sense of belonging (*Gemeinschaft*). Cities are linked to larger processes (such as industrialization, globalization) which create new forms of social relations and cohesion based upon mutual interdependence and a rational agreement. These concepts were first introduced by Ferdinand Tönnies and later extensively discussed by Max Weber, in a direct reaction to Tönnies in which Weber gave his own definition to the two terms, placing them in his wider conception of social change.[6] I find Weber's definition more convincing as he did not place a normative superiority in the Gesellschaft society and did not consider rationalized capitalism and democracy as inevitable outcomes of development. Weber moreover argued that his characterization was an ideal-type category and considered the possibility of both types of societies coexisting. The presence of hybrid political systems and societies today, with multiple forms of modernity, attests to Weber's point.

The periphery corresponds to the Gemeinschaft form of belonging and social solidarity, in which affection and tradition prime. Tribalism in the sense of extended kinship relations based upon a common ancestor is a particularly salient form of Gemeinschaft and the accompanying process of 'Vergemeinschafting'. Social hierarchies and solidarity tend to be strong in the periphery that is distant from the centre and that faces marginalization vis-à-vis the centre.

To uphold the support of the periphery, political regimes rely on patronage politics, mediated via local elites who are intermediaries and brokers between the regime and wider constituencies. Some conditions make the periphery more conducive to the salience of patronage politics. One of these is the relative closeness of family and tribal networks where social cohesion and group solidarity tend to be strong. Another condition relates to the relative marginalization from the political centre and its resources, making peripheral groups more in need of powerful people who can act as go-betweens for access to the centre's resources.

These local elites act as patrons for their constituencies, using their higher socio-economic status and access to the regime for persons of lower status, who in return offer support and assistance to the patron.[7] Transactions between a patron and his clients are in essence non-ideological and personalized, in which a certain dependency characterizes relations between the two parties. These patrons are regime-dependent, as opposed to the centrifugal power of notables in the case of a weak infrastructural state and strong local power centres. Studies on modernization and development in postcolonial states have pointed to the resilience of traditional identities coexisting with the presence of modern institutions and law. Neo-patrimonial regimes are regimes that combine the reliance on personalized forms of power as a mechanism of rule with a modern bureaucracy and rule of law and therefore strongly rely on their respective peripheries as a pillar of support.[8]

As urban centres tend to be the first exposed to outside influences and modern ideologies, they have historically been the first to challenge political centres. This happened in the 1920s throughout the Islamic world with urban notables rising up against political centres and their colonial backers. The legacy of Ottomanism furthermore had made the city the prime locus for politics – in the context of a weak infrastructural centre – while the periphery had largely been left to its own dynamics.

Tribal and rural populations – being relatively marginalized from the political centre and its forces of change – have together with minorities been crucial support groups for Arab authoritarians. Ethnic and religious minorities have been useful supporters of anti-democratic regimes and their colonial backers, as their minority status made them a lesser threat to the rulers. One can think of the 'Alawis and Sunnis in the case of colonial rule in Syria and Iraq, the Berbers and Jews in Morocco or the non-tribal *khadiris* in Saudi Arabia who have often been co-opted in high state functions as freeborn people who do not have a tribe to fall back on. The same holds for the Shi'a minority in Kuwait that has been a crucial support to the Al-Sabah at various moments in time.

In the context of state-building, regimes and their colonial backers resorted to local elites to leverage the regime's power. Some were made stronger, while others lost their power and sometimes new patrons were created. They all profited from newly available external resources, thereby changing the nature of local power relations. From here stems the observation of a nineteenth-century British naval officer named Slade on modernity, who noted that in the old order the nobility lived on its estates, but in the new order the state has become the estate of the new nobility.[9]

Postcolonial Arab states – the surviving monarchies and the republics that had been established following revolutions – tried to maintain the support of the periphery as a main pillar of rule, although both regimes did so in different ways. Social revolutions dethroning monarchies that were replaced by military dictatorships were all led by marginalized groups from the rural periphery. In these cases, monarchs backed by landed classes and foreign powers lost control over the periphery. This was the case for Egypt (1952), Tunisia (1957), Iraq (1958), Yemen (1962), Syria (1963) and Libya (1969).[10]

These revolutions that led to the fall of monarchs in the 1950s and 1960s were the crystallization of deeply entrenched conflicts between the periphery and urban interests. The urban forces were the main actors in the exploitation and repression of forces of production delivered by the countryside. In these cases, class conflicts superseded with sectarian and religious conflicts. This was paralleled by massive rural–urban migration and the political rise of previously marginalized groups, such as those who would become the leading Ba'athists of Iraq and Syria ('Alawis, Druzes and Sunnis from rural, small-town roots).[11] In all these cases, incumbent leaders were unable to maintain existing patronage structures of the periphery. In need of manpower, armies were, for example, filled with those representing the peasants and upcoming middle classes, a dangerous situation, as these groups would use these institutions to stage military coups against monarchs.

The monarchies that survived the shockwave of revolutions of the 1950s (but nonetheless faced strong challenges to their rule) were better apt at maintaining the support of their periphery and avoid a direct clash of interest between rural–urban or Bedouin–urban forces. A contributing factor here was the relatively less urbanized nature of these societies as opposed to countries such as Egypt, Iraq and parts of Syria. Maybe also as a consequence of these lesser contradictions between urban and rural forces have the surviving monarchies been better apt at absorbing nationalist discontent and integrating it into their system. Jordan's monarch Hussayn Arabized the top command of the army and the Bedouin recruits allowed the latter to play a supportive role in favour of the monarch in contrast to the Egyptian and Iraqi cases. Meanwhile, rulers in Jordan, Morocco and the Gulf monarchies were better capable of absorbing nationalist forces into the political system and taking some distance from colonial powers. Morocco's King Muhammad V secured the country from French colonial encroachment and the *Makhzen* enjoyed fairly cooperative relations with the main independence movement party, *Al-Istiqlal*.[12]

Yet, in these cases again, the support of the periphery was crucial in upholding monarchical regimes and rulers displayed tactful skills to accommodate social change within peripheral groups, without losing their essential support structure for the regime. In Morocco, the Palace has always relied on the support of the periphery – via entrenched networks of rural notables – to exercise its power.[13] Also in modern times does the Palace depend largely on the support of rural areas via electoral gerrymandering strengthening the weight of the periphery as well as via the support or creation of parties representing the interests of the rural elites.[14] From their part, the oil-rich Gulf monarchies have also heavily relied on peripheral groups in consolidating their reign. Bedouins were historically allies of ruling families and counterweights against more urban forces and filled the ranks of the police and armed forces as loyal backers of monarchy.

The periphery in early postcolonial Arab republics

The postcolonial Arab states – surviving monarchies but also the modernist republics – hence all tried to maintain the support of the periphery as a main pillar of rule. In the populist republics, opposition between the countryside and urban forces became so strong and led to military coups of officers with a social background from rural or marginalized groups. Important is that the marginalization of the periphery was relative and took place in a period in which rural populations were facing major changes that relatively improved their situation and led to rising expectations (rising expectations are not uncommon factors conducive to social movements).[15]

The populist republics established in Egypt, Iraq, Algeria and Syria made the inclusion of the periphery and its social upgrading *the* central pillar of rule. This was often accompanied by policies that dethroned the landed aristocracy whose interests had been too closely allied to those of the monarchs and their colonial backers.[16] While large landlords lost much of their political power and large parts of their land because of nationalizing reforms, notabilities did not disappear but gradually shifted in level and regimes turned into military dictatorships. As demonstrated by Leonard Binder (1978) in the Egyptian case, a 'second stratum' of rural middle-class actors was a crucial supporter of the new regime: they do not rule but without their support the regime could not rule. Rich peasants and administrative local agents replaced the large landowners and became de facto new rural notables.[17] The inclusion of peasant and Bedouin strata was also a major pillar of legitimacy for Syria's and Iraq's Ba'ath leadership. Here too, while the agrarian and feudal elite families passed through difficult times during the most radical populist Ba'ath phases, the high level of education of their sons allowed this young generation to reinsert itself in the political system, to be a crucial resource for state-building.[18] Meanwhile, for the peasants, the reforms introduced by the Ba'ath created a more open social structure, in which peasants were socially upgraded and became dependent on the multiple structures of the Ba'ath state organizations rather than on individual landlords.[19] Establishment of peasant cooperatives and populist institutions contributed to the integration of the periphery and state.

The support of the periphery was also a strategy of regimes to counterbalance to urban politicized forces. In Syria, Hafez al-Assad resorted to a more flexible and pragmatic policy vis-à-vis the tribes and rural population to counterbalance emerging opposition from the Muslim Brotherhood (MB) in major urban centres. Despite the official rhetoric of 'no sectarianism' and 'no tribalism', the regime did not hesitate to resort to the tribes to suppress bloodily the uprising against the MB in Hama in 1982.[20] Tribes were also used to neutralize the Kurdish population in the northeast.[21]

Losing the support of the periphery: neoliberal Arab republics

Now since the 1990s with the neoliberal turn taken by the Arab republics to reduce their fiscal deficits, these regimes started to lose the crucial support of the periphery; resulting in the fragmentation of political patronage networks vis-à-vis rural and tribal populations in countries such as Syria, Egypt or Tunisia. This corresponds to broader shifts in the region, induced by forces of globalization impacting social structures and has been most disruptive in tribal and peasant communities uprooting a young generation and provoking competition over resources and leadership positions. This can be compared to what Eric Wolf described as a 'crisis in the exercise of power', arguing that capitalist intrusion led to major social dislocations in the countryside preceding peasant-led revolutions.[22] While globalization is not a new phenomenon to the region, the 1990s witnessed a new turn in which a change in macro-economic policies – characterized by a decline of direct state support to the economy – coupled with an even more disruptive factor: the communication and information revolution that reached the lives of the masses and particularly the Arab youth.

These two factors coincided with other structural developments in the Arab world, of which the most important are rapid population growth and the 'youth bulge'. Two-thirds of the Arab population are today under the age of thirty and are in search of jobs, identity and a place in retrograde political systems (average youth unemployment in the region is around 30 percent).[23] Population growth has been spectacular in the region and the highest in the world. Between 1990 and 2008 the population of the Arab world grew by 44 per cent, 108.7 million people.[24]

Meanwhile, life conditions in urban and rural areas deteriorated in this period until today as a consequence of a series of factors. Persistent droughts as well as neoliberal agrarian reforms contributed to the impoverishment and stagnation of local economies of tribal and rural communities. This was the case in countries as diverse as Syria, Egypt, Tunisia, Algeria, Iraq and Yemen. While protests in Egypt started in urban settings (as opposed to Syria and Tunisia) in Egypt too did rural economies disintegrate as a consequence of neoliberal agrarian reforms. The fragmentation of the clientelist networks of the ruling party – the NDP (National Democratic Party) – was manifested since the 1990s by the incapacity of rural notabilities to meet the demands of their clients who were demanding public sector jobs that these notables could not give them. These rising demands of rural populations were the consequence of aggravated social conditions in the countryside in Egypt over the past two decades. Entrenched rural elites were losing out against business elites in elections, who tended to win via direct and short-term vote buying, rather than the pre-existing more durable system of gift-giving of the older notabilities. Neoliberal reforms had a disruptive impact on pre-existing networks of patronage in the countryside on which the ruling party used to rely. The fragmentation of this network was revealed in the high level of rotation of parliamentary elites, as observed by Mary Vannetzel (2007).[25] In Tunisia, Algeria and Syria, similar deteriorations of living conditions in the periphery led to the fragmentation of regime patronage. In all cases, economic structural adjustment policies were coupled with growing rent seeking of the inner clique of ruling circles allied with businessmen and the disintegration of existing social and political hierarchies in the rural and tribal areas.[26] As we know today, these regimes witnessed popular uprisings in 2011.

It is not unsurprising that many of these uprisings started from the peripheries. In Syria, the revolution was started from the predominantly tribal area of *Dar'a*, organized by networks of tribesmen from the *Al-Zo'bi* and *Al-Masalmeh* tribes. The first protests were triggered as a response to the particularly disrespectful behaviour of the regime in the negotiation with tribal elders over the release of school children imprisoned for the writing of anti-regime slogans on the wall of their school. As a sign of respect for the regime representative, the tribal elders took off their headbands collectively and placed them on the table. The headband is a sign of manhood and chivalry and putting it off was thus the showing of respect in their request to liberate the children. However, the reaction of the regime representative was particularly rude: he threw the headbands in the rubbish bin and this triggered the first protests. Tribesmen responded collectively to the disgrace displayed towards these individual tribal elders – helped by the use of mass communication technology – in a logic of '*fiz'a*'; the taking up of arms in defence of the individual tribesmen whose honour (and thus the honour of the whole tribe) had been violated. This has also been considered a motor for the participation of other tribes in Homs, Hama and Deir Ezzor in the protests.[27] Because of the role of certain tribes in triggering the uprising, the regime was quick to resort to policies to strengthen the support of the tribes – a crucial pillar of support. On a crucial moment in the conflict, therefore, a Sunni Muslim of tribal background – Fehd Jassem al-Freij – was appointed as the Minister of Defence.[28] The latter and various other tribal leaders were co-opted to maintain the regime's authority in tribal areas. Already under Hafez al-Assad had the Ba'ath tried to fragment tribes internally, by sidelining traditional shaykhs in favour of newly appointed ones ('puppet chiefs') with close ties to the security services.[29] Initially, most tribal opposition originated from cities with high numbers of displaced tribesmen (Dar'a, Homs, Hama, Palmyra and Deir Ezzor).[30]

With the proclamation of the Islamic State (IS) and the Syrian city of Al-Raqqa as its capital (June 2014), the group actively sought to strengthen its alliance with Syrian tribes. This alliance was a marked shift from the tense relations between Syrian tribes and the MB, when the regime used to resort to the tribes to crackdown the latter. Videos of tribal heads pledging allegiance to the Islamic State (IS) in Al-Raqqa, in rural Aleppo and Deir Ezzor are indicative of the importance of tribal support for the IS which has today lost its territorial power. When reaching power, however, the group was quick in exploiting intra-tribal struggles by allying with young tribesmen who had built local prestige for their role in the fight against Al-Assad. The group had already almost a decade experience in the predominantly tribal Al-Anbar province of Iraq. These tribesmen were lured by oil deals and set up against elder tribesmen. This strategy allowed the IS to take swift control of towns in Deir Ezzor, relying on existing social infrastructure and exploiting generational tensions within tribes.[31]

In Tunisia where the 2011 uprisings started, the protests also began from the rural periphery. Here, neoliberal agrarian reforms stimulating export-oriented farming had importantly reduced the capacity of small farmers to make a living, raising unemployment among family members. This combined with food prices that skyrocketed and induced a food crisis in 2007–08 (as was the case in Egypt, Jordan and Morocco) and farmers' protest movements (land occupation, contestation of farmers' unions, refusal to pay for irrigation water), countering the images of Tunisia as a good student of the World Bank and IMF.[32] The opening of countries to world market competition strengthened regional disparities, as local production (such as textile) was not ready to compete with the world market. Globalization thus resulted in a growing gap between centre and periphery; spatial polarization that tends to be strongest in developing countries.[33] The self-immolation of the street vendor – *Muhammad Bouazizi* – in the Tunisian countryside in December 2010 was symptomatic of this social frustration stemming from the impoverished countryside. Higher food prices were most strongly felt in rural areas that are known to be the poorest in the region (40 per cent of the MENA's population is rural and 70 per cent earn less than 1.25 USD a day).

More recently, the 2019 revolution in Sudan which led to the overthrow of Omar al-Bashir's reign also had a strong role for the periphery, in contrast to Sudan's earlier revolutions.[34] Decennia of marginalization and economic deterioration – especially since South Sudan's independence in 2011 with the loss of major oil resources – created untenable situations on the countryside and therefore price rises and scarcity in basic supplies which hit strongest the countryside. Protests started in the northeast River Nile State and soon spread throughout the country with villages and cities participating that in the past never witnessed protest. The revolution has been a call to change power dynamics and give justice to the countryside.

From this quick overview, one can already point to a certain constant in all cases: the loss of support from the periphery for authoritarians. This itself has been a consequence of the new forces of globalizations that penetrated the region, under the ideology of the Washington consensus and its ideals of neoliberalism that favoured capital over labour. In this regard, fiscal deficits were cut by strengthening the role of the private sector and the tuning of local production towards exports. In all cases, it strengthened rural poverty and contributed to the disintegration of existing local socio-political hierarchies and the concentration of economic resources in the hands of a few rent-seeking elites. Existing notabilities often could not meet the rising demands of their constituencies that were asking for public sector jobs they were unable to provide. Instead, vote buying as a short clientelist transaction replaced more durable bonds, with regimes manoeuvring to deal with a rapidly changing periphery. This coupled with rising generational divides in society that were most pronounced in regions governed by traditional hierarchies. In this conundrum, the young were enormously frustrated about their future in the system and in search of a more equal share in the nation's polity. Similar complex and interdependent developments have taken place in non-rentier monarchies such as Morocco, but these regimes have so far been apt at better maintaining the crucial support of the periphery for their authoritarian regimes.

The periphery as a driver of political change

While modern political parties and ideologies have originated and been led by urban-educated middle-class people throughout modern history, the centrality of the periphery as a driver of political change and its role in revolutions has been recognized in social science literature.[35] Barrington Moore has been one of the first to underscore the importance of peasants in modernization processes, considering the failure of peasant revolutions as one of the main drivers of modernization.[36] In the 1960s and 1970s – inspired by the Vietnamese revolution in which peasants played an important role – a series of studies were published that focused on the debate under what social circumstances peasants would play a crucial role in revolutions and what impeded this role. One can think here of Joel Migdal, James Scott, Eric Wolf and Jeffrey Paige who all delivered substantial contributions to the field.[37]

All these authors – who come to different conclusions as to what are the conditions under which peasant revolutions take place – depart from an 'agency-inspired' approach. In this regard, they focus on the agency or not of peasants in mobilizing collectively against incumbent regimes. Skocpol (1982) discussed these works and their interpretation of which peasants are most prone to revolutionary behaviour; the role of political and military organizations in such revolutions; the role of capitalist imperialism in these revolutions.[38] In her own landmark study of social revolutions in Russia, China and France, Skocpol argues that peasant revolts against landlords have been a necessary condition in all these revolutions whereas urban revolts were not always necessary.[39] History has taught us that social revolutions have taken place in agrarian countries where peasants were the major productive force. Social and political marginalization and exploitation at the hand of the ruling classes provided the necessary (but not sufficient) conditions for peasant grievances against landlords and rulers.[40]

The focus on peasant communities can be broadened by referring to the periphery rather than rural populations per se. In this approach, the periphery refers to all communities that are relatively marginalized vis-à-vis a political centre. The political centre represents in essence urban forces. Urban communities have historically been the drivers behind the creation of political parties and ideologies.[41] This is the consequence of a complex set of factors that are related to what we call processes of 'modernization' that accompany urbanization and industrialization.[42] Urban centres are the first to be exposed to forces of globalization and to foreign influences, such as ideas and markets. Also, they are the first and most exposed to the complexification of social relations and the disintegration of close-knit *traditional* social hierarchies. The web of economic and social relations in urban centres is naturally less resistant to change than more isolated peripheral communities that traditionally faced little interaction with outside forces. While educated urban forces have been the driving forces behind the propagation of (modern) political ideologies, the more marginalized urban communities are more susceptible to political patronage, essentially pre-ideological – a consequence of their material and social marginalization.

Peripheral communities can be conceptually distinguished from urban forces on some major and interrelated aspects. First of all, they are relatively (on a national level) most **resistant to change** and governed by strict communal hierarchies. Secondly, they are relatively most **in need of mediation** in order to get access to the services and resources of the political centre. This is due to their relative marginalization vis-à-vis other groups of society with closer access to the political centre. Both factors together allow for non-ideological transactions between the regime and these communities in which the role of intermediary elites is crucial. The social base in these communities endorses these patronage transactions and this consent is what allows authoritarian regimes to uphold their control over the periphery.

Monarchies versus republics and the periphery: path-dependent legacy

In the postcolonial era, two diverging paths of state-building emerged in the Arab world: the populist-nationalist republics and the conservative kin-ordered monarchies. Their different paths of state-building and pillars of legitimacy had implications for the role of the periphery in both types of regimes and its elites.

The postcolonial Arab republics have had (at least in their most radical phase) policies that were more aimed at social engineering vis-à-vis existing social structures, as compared to the Arab monarchies. In the monarchies (apart from Bahrain), state-building has been softer, more inclusive and less disruptive. While authoritarian, these regimes incorporated society's major groupings into the ruling elite 'asabiyya, in a logic described by Khaldun al-Naqeeb as political tribalism. It can be compared to an authoritarian regime that heavily relies on decentralized and indirect forms of governance to rule, mediated through intermediary elites; as was common in multi-ethnic empires. In the monarchies, urban classes were never dethroned, but incorporated into the regime's 'asabiyya and the periphery was thus dealt with in a way that encompassed less social engineering. This is an abstraction that does not do justice to internal differences within monarchies, but it corresponds to a generalizable phenomenon across cases.

This having said, the populist republics have always needed to deal with tribalism and to absorb tribal elements into their system. This was done by manipulating existing tribal hierarchies. The logics of modernist state-building policies contradicted the need to integrate traditional social structures into the state.[43] In the case of Ba'athist Iraq – for example – the twin logic of 'etatist tribalism' (modern bureaucracy and tribal loyalty) led to inherent conflicts and the fragmentation of these 'asabiyyas. This privileging of certain tribes and clans over others and the very thin base of the Tikriti leadership naturally led to clashes and competition. The detachment from a broad social base necessitated the regime to be extremely repressive to uphold its clan-based leadership.[44] In Syria too – especially under the radical phase of Ba'athism – tribes were politically marginalized and policies aimed at fragmenting tribal leadership. This was essentially done by sidelining traditional shaykhs in favour of appointed puppet chiefs. Tribal chiefs also lost much of their prestige, as many of their functions were gradually assumed by state agencies. The abolition of customary law (*urf*), coupled with land reforms, further reduced the prestige of the tribal chiefs, as happened to urban and landed elites in the early phases of Nasserism and Ba'athism.

In later phases of the republics, regimes became more opportunistic and reliant on local social structures to govern. This was notably a result of reduced state capacity, itself a consequence of fiscal crises and the need of the state to rely on local structures in governance. Since the 1980s, in countries such as Iraq and Syria, regimes reached out again to tribal leaders, realizing that they often had much social clout and were indispensable partners in governance. The families that produced tribal shaykhs had retained much of their prestige, as they were the first to get access to high education, converting their skills into new positions.[45] In many cases these tribal leaders were sources of local power who could act rather independently (and thus could switch quickly from political allegiances), as they were never formally integrated into the realm of the state in the early phases of state-building. In Iraq, during the Iran–Iraq War, the regime became more reliant on tribal shaykhs.[46] In Syria, the regimes of Hafez al-Assad and Bashar al-Assad reinforced relations with tribal elites, although impoverishment and exploitation of peasants debilitated the clientelist networks connecting the regime to the periphery. As stated earlier, this was a rather common phenomenon in the neoliberalizing Arab republics since the 1990s.

The **Arab monarchies** (apart from Bahrain) have pursued policies that were less disruptive and more in harmony with pre-existing social hierarchies. There was no phase of revolutions and anti-elite policies and both urban elites and the periphery were included into the regime's sphere of influence. Consequently, elites were not dethroned and instead incorporated into the regime's 'asabiyya, which allowed for a greater continuity in social structures in the periphery. This was the case for both the oil-rich monarchies in the Arabian Gulf and Morocco and Jordan. In the small kin-based Gulf monarchies, oil significantly strengthened the regime's capacity to distribute resources to elites and respective constituencies, making regime policies more inclusive and class distinctions less pronounced.

In the oil monarchies, merchant elites formed the core of pre-oil opposition forces. This was all part of a tribal authority system, dominating political power and relations of production. As such, only Najdi elites of pure Arab descent were allowed to engage in pearling and palm tree cultivation in pre-nationalist settings. Non-Arab merchants were excluded from these sectors on the basis of kinship, an aspect often overlooked in historical work on the Arabian Gulf. Instead, they were active in the food and craft industries, with handicrafts considered as particularly low ranked within the tribal value system. These local merchant elites shared kinship ties with the ruling shaykhs and constituted the main opposition groups in pre-national settings, as these core groups could challenge the central elite status. Politically, the tribal rulers had most to fear from their *in-group* and thus tended to live apart from these merchant elites with whom they shared kinship ties and who could challenge their central elite status. Until today, this authority system largely holds in many Gulf Cooperation Council (GCC) countries.

The merchant elites that historically dominated the main economic resources continued to do so after the discovery of oil, but this time in a more subservient capacity as the main clients of the state, being granted the exclusive privileges of the private sector; that was often accompanied with their withdrawal from open participation in politics. Politically, these regimes continued to rely on the support of non-core groups, whose elites were co-opted and 'encapsulated' by rentier regimes as state-dependent elites. As such, tribal leaders became crucial middlemen for constituencies; a situation which led to a verticalization of power in a social structure (the tribe) historically characterized by continuous competition between lineages and personalities. Tribal leaders were keen to uphold the image of being *the* leader, although in reality this was part of the leader's 'role playing' (itself favoured by privileged access to the state) rather than reflective of truly fixed leadership patterns within tribes.[47]

In the non-oil monarchies (Jordan and Morocco), pre-national elites have also witnessed a relatively important continuity in positions and standing. These regimes, that since the 1980s have witnessed reduced revenues and engaged in a series of neoliberal reforms, combined policies of absorbing social change with maintaining traditional elites. Electoral gerrymandering and a legacy of local elite continuity enabled these monarchies – despite their liberalizing reforms – to maintain peripheral support via local elites with social outreach and an embeddedness in communities. The family nature of the monarchies and the absence of a modern political ideology underpinning the ruling elite's legitimacy seem to have given these monarchies greater leeway of dealing with social change and maintaining the support of the periphery than the republics of hegemonic one-party regimes. This itself might be due to the more inclusive and non-ideological nature of the ruling elite, allowing these monarchs to be more apt than their republican peers at playing the role of apparently neutral arbiters over society and absorbing new elites within its broader networks.

Using rural notables as a political support structure in Morocco dates back to the days of the French Protectorate (1912–56), when the French actively promoted traditional intermediaries as mediators of French interests. The idea was that indigenous rural elites were perceived as more authentic by local populations and were less politicized than the urban bourgeoisie that presented the core challenge to the monarchy. This legacy of allying with rural notables was continued after independence, with the *Makhzen* relying on these intermediaries to counterbalance urban nationalist forces. Given the importance of the rural notability to the *Makhzen*, the latter supported them in blocking the modernizing agrarian reforms that the urban bourgeoisie was pushing for.[48] The dependant and illiterate nature of a large section of rural populations contributes to the success of material and non-ideological transactions of patronage.[49] Also, campaigning tactics and regime policies (i.e. electoral rules and districting) all favour personality-based politics rather than ideological platforms.[50]

Economic liberalization and growing rural to urban migration since the 1990s were paralleled with a continued reliance of the regime on rural patronage structures and did not critically decrease their utility for the *Makhzen*.[51] This can be seen from the policies of the regime in recent years and the continuous reliance on rural notabilities. A case in point was the creation of the Party of Authenticity and Modernity (PAM) in 2008 by Fouad al-Himma; a close advisor to King Muhammad and former deputy minister of Interior. The PAM heavily relied on attracting rural notables and strongmen with the largest social networks to fill its ranks, leading in 2009 to landslide gains in the elections. This was accompanied by the defection of many notables enlisted with other parties to the PAM they considered more attractive to strengthen their power.[52] With ultimate decision power vested in the person of the King and with a legacy of the state's alliance with rural notables, power is essentially exercised via networks of personal intermediaries linked to *zuʿama*, who themselves are part of the close trustees of the King.

In Jordan, too, the making of the Hashemite monarchy depended on the co-optation and integration of the periphery into the nascent state institutions. Here too, traditional elites were integrated rather than dethroned as part of early state- and nation-building strategies.[53] Until today, this legacy of co-opting East Bank tribes and ethnic and religious minorities resonates in the regime's survival strategies. Jordan's monarchy too seems to have dealt with neoliberalizing reforms, in a delegated, decentralized way; via local notabilities co-opted by the regime. Here again, the periphery played a crucial role in upholding the Hashemite's support structure. A series of electoral reforms over the past decade allowed the regime to strengthen the support of traditional elites rather than more politicized ones. In these cases, the regime proved particularly apt at co-opting the locally strongest players, favoured by the creation of sub-districts to allow for even more localized representatives.[54] New capitalists were more easily integrated in Jordan's system (as in Morocco) than in the cases of Egypt or Tunisia. In these cases, the rise of entrepreneurs in politics was accompanied with stronger competition between a new and an old elite and the fragmentation of traditional notabilities. The more ideologically neutral position of the monarchies allows them to play a role of arbiter over segmented elites, as these regimes' nature is predominantly tribal and hereditary. In the republics, elite competition often involved the ruling elite itself, tied to different generations of elites (young and old guards) and sharing a lesser degree of 'asabiyya, in the absence of the dynastic 'asabiyyas. Adding to this might is a higher propensity of elite continuity in the monarchies, a consequence of a legacy of state-building that preserved and upgraded traditional elites of the periphery. This having said, I contend that everywhere in the region, the forces of neoliberal globalization have come to fragment the periphery since the millennium, uprooting its younger population.

Conclusion

This chapter has pointed to the importance of the legacy of early state-building in understanding the crucial role played by the periphery and its elites in supporting authoritarian regimes in the MENA. It argued that two factors are essential in explaining the capacity of the regime to uphold the support of its periphery. The first is the internal cohesion of the ruling elite, the regime's 'asabiyya and capacity to act as one bloc and maintain a certain balance between competing regime elites. The second refers to the ties of the ruling elite to the periphery, mediated via local elites. When one of these two factors fragments, regimes lose the crucial support of the periphery and are at risk to disintegrate and succumb to revolutions.

The support of periphery is the condition sine qua non-Arab authoritarians cannot maintain their rule. This chapter pointed to the importance of regime-type and strategies of state-building in understanding the difference between Arab republics and monarchies when it comes to regime politics towards the periphery and its elites. While both the surviving monarchies and populist republics made the support of the periphery their key pillar of rule, the monarchies did so without much social engineering. There, local elites survived and played a crucial role in nascent administrations. In the republics, these elites were dethroned and regimes have tried to change local social realities by upgrading the masses.

The latest wave of globalization, characterized economically by neoliberalism and culturally by the communication revolution, has reached the peoples of the periphery and uprooted existing hierarchies. This has contributed to a fragmentation of political patronage networks with the rise of a young generation counterveiling the power of the state and its community elders. Globalization has reinforced the divide between centre and periphery and its impact has been strongest in the republics many of which faced popular uprisings in 2011 stemming from their countryside and tribal communities. The monarchies have not been shielded from this wind of change but have been relatively better capable of absorbing social change into their system.

This is the consequence both of a legacy of more embedded social elites who have been upgraded in state institutions since independence and of an institutional structure and authority system favouring political patronage and the support of the periphery. Rentier monarchies have had more resources at their disposal and combined with small populations have been better capable of relying on patronage structures to reach out to constituencies in the periphery. The non-rentier monarchies have also been relatively apt at integrating new business elites into their system as compared to the republics. Not relying on a dominant ideology but instead on a dynastic legacy, it seems easier for such regimes to integrate social change into their wider networks. Yet, when monarchies have not been able to uphold soft-authoritarianism, notably by co-opting local elites, they resorted to overt forms of repression, itself an indication of the fragmentation of 'asabiyya. This is also what happened in Kuwait over the past years where the incapacity of the regime to reach out to its restless periphery resulted in growing incarcerations and repression of public dissent.

Having discussed the core argument of this work, I will proceed with the empirics of the case study on Kuwait. It will demonstrate how the two factors of Khaldunian 'asabiyya underpinning the regime's resilience have been put to test in the post-liberation era.

Part One

Traditional politics and the pre-oil authority system of the Al-Sabah (1716–1938)

Introduction

With its air-conditioned malls, skyscrapers and high-speed roads leading to residential areas segregated by social status, the Emirate of Kuwait hardly resembles the city-state it was at the start of the twentieth century. The discovery of oil in the Burgan field in 1938, followed by other discoveries, rapidly transformed this tiny tribal shaykhdom of the Al-Sabah – once a haven for transnational merchants searching for better conditions for trade – into a modern oil-producing state with its citizens enjoying the highest standards of living in the world. In no less than a couple of decades, the shaykhdom subject to British colonial administration was transformed into a hyper-affluent welfare state and integrated into the global capitalist system.

Despite the magnitude and rapidity of change, induced by the transformation of the political economy in the Arabian Gulf, the *pre-oil* dynamics of social and political life laid the foundations of what would later develop into the complicated semi-democratic *Sonderweg* of this rentier state. The reasons why and how the Al-Sabah of the 'Utub clan of the 'Aneza turned from a tribal shaykhdom into a ruling dynasty have been sufficiently covered.[1] Rather than recounting this history, this chapter analyses the nature of the authority system of the Al-Sabah in its relation to the traditional social forces living both within (*hadar*) and outside (*badu*) the walls of the old city. Emphasis is placed upon the impact of socio-economic transformations and colonial rule in changing this authority system since the mid-nineteenth century until the discovery of oil. It hereby focuses on how the traditional social forces adapted to these changes in the authority system, both vis-á-vis each other and vis-á-vis the Al-Sabah. System here refers to the continuous interaction between a structure and its environment.[2]

With traditional social forces, I refer to three distinct status groups or socio-
political categories that form the basis of Kuwait's social structure: *hadar* (urban
dwellers), Shi'a and *badu* (tribesmen). Until today, these concepts are lively present
in Kuwait's society and in popular parlance. They represent 'invisible walls', with
borders between citizens being deepened as a consequence of state policies, through
the segmented access to oil rents and state services, but also through divide-and-rule
regime strategies. In terms of political socialization and matrimonial strategies, these
groups represent the country's main voting blocs that can further be split into smaller
ascriptive sub-communities.

This chapter aims to grasp the nature of 'traditional politics' in pre-oil Kuwait,
in terms of the components structuring the old political community and the ruling
bargain. Understanding the idiosyncrasies of contemporary politics and citizen
identities in Kuwait necessitates a deeper analysis of the founding bricks of this atypical
political community in the Arabian Gulf. Literature on hybrid societies deals with
understanding the reasons behind the persistence of premodern forms of politics in
societies integrated into the globalized world, such as the resilience or reinvention of
traditional identities and authority structures that do not coalesce into cross-cutting
status-association along occupational lines. Oil monarchies have a particularly deep
historical memory. With regimes not having experienced revolutions and with
political legitimacy based upon the preservation of the old communal order in a
semi-corporatist way, oil revenues allowed to perpetuate or reinvent old alliances and
identities in a path-dependent process over time.[3]

In the following, I will focus on those dimensions of Kuwait's political history that
have been obliterated in both Western and Arabic sources or have only received attention
in passing. My focus is on the role played by non-core elites in Kuwait's pre-oil politics;
referring hereby to those elites that were not part of the Sunni merchant aristocracy,
but who nonetheless played an important role in politics. As will be demonstrated,
their status as outsiders to the merchant–Al-Sabah nexus made them crucial allies
to the rulers; as they could not challenge the central elite status. The high degree of
stratification within the group of merchants as well as within the broader population of
the town has often been overlooked in studies on Kuwait. Yet, this segmentation along
identity and occupational lines has played a key role in consolidating an authoritarian
shaykhdom, first in 1896 by Mubarak al-Sabah, and later with the discovery of oil.
No work exists which systematically traces these pre-oil elite alliances that I argue are
crucial for understanding contemporary politics in Kuwait.

Kuwait's classic socio-political categories: *hadar*, Shi'a and *badu*

The *hadar* trace their origins back to pre-oil Kuwait and refer to those who settled
in Kuwait before the discovery of oil (i.e. prior to 1938). Although many of the Shi'a
families settled in Kuwait in the pre-oil era, the Shi'a are referred to as a separate
category. In pre-oil Kuwait, the *hadar* were approximately 60 per cent of the population,
the rest largely composed of Shi'a. An elite of Najdi merchants participated in the
initial power-sharing with the Al-Sabah and were the advocates of parliamentarianism

to secure their interests, mostly embracing pan-Arabism. Today they have largely devoted themselves to their privileged commercial life, dependent on the state's rents. Apart from this Arab merchant aristocracy, the *hadar* Sunna are composed of a mix of diasporas from Iran, Iraq and Central Arabia, reflecting the *melting pot* nature of Kuwait's social fabric. The *hadar* from the Sunni parts of Iran (the Balushs) were largely a lower class group of workers and constituted a different sub-community that lived together with the Shi'a *'Ajam* in the Al-Sharq neighbourhood. One can think of the Al-Kandari or the Al-Balushi, whose toilsome jobs – such as those of water carrier – were shunned by the tribal aristocracy.

The Al-Naqib and the Rifa'i were among the families who came from the north, as well as the Sa'dun. The latter trace their origin back to an elite lineage of the Muntafiq tribe many of whose tribesmen converted to Shi'ism.[4] Among the various diasporas of Kuwait, micro-localism reigns, with place of origin figuring prominently as an identity marker; either directly in a family's name (i.e. Al-Balush) or by denoting groups of families according to their place of origin (i.e. Basrawis).[5] Another important subgroup here are the Qina'at (or Jena'at in Kuwaiti dialect). They form a clan of Sunni families who migrated from northern parts of Iraq to Kuwait in the nineteenth century, but claim descent from the Suhul tribe from an area in Najd. In Kuwait, the group presents one of the largest elite family groups (apart from the Sunni merchant aristocracy and the Shi'a merchants) and rose to prominence following the adoption by the Al-Sabah of the orphan Yusuf Bin Issa.[6] The person of Yusuf Bin Issa would have allowed the group – that until today tends to marry exclusively from within the family – to make inroads in commerce, as nouveaux riches. As they share with the Shi'a merchants a position of non-core elites, the Qina'at tend to be the most anti-Shi'a Kuwaitis, competing with the latter for the Al-Sabah's favour in commerce and access to management positions in the oil industry.

A related cleavage within the group of *hadar* is the distinction between *asli* and *bayseri;* between families that can trace back their roots to pure Arab descent and families that do not have such a pure Arab family tree, having mixed with non-pure or non-Arab lineages. Although a sensitive topic for the politically liberal-minded *hadar* Kuwaitis, these identity markers continue to have deep political, marital and economic implications. The aristocracy of merchant families tends to marry within each other's subgroup of pure Arab notable families. Until today, micro-localism and tribalism play important roles in social, economic and political affairs.

The *Shi'a*, although mostly *hadar*, socialize in distinct community-based institutions and also represent a mosaic of diasporas from Iraq, Iran, Saudi Arabia and Bahrain. The Shi'a have been key allies of the Al-Sabah family in its confrontation with different opposition forces throughout Kuwait's modern history, with only the tense interlude of the Iran–Iraq War marking an exception to this. Three main categories can be differentiated here: the *'Ajam* (from Iran), the *Hasawiyyin* (from Al-Hasa) and the *Baharna* (from Bahrain). The Shi'a from Iraq represent only a minority of families, such as the Al-Kadhemi (from Al-Kadhemiyya). The majority are the 'Ajam, who represent around 70 per cent of the Kuwaiti Shi'a that today form between 25 and 35 per cent of Kuwait's citizens (in the absence of a population census). An elite of 'Ajam merchants traditionally dominated this diaspora; families that enjoyed historically close relations to the Al-Sabah, like the Qina'at, as they could not challenge the central elite status. By the end of the twentieth century, migration from Iran was diversified with the arrival of poor farmers severely hit by the Pahlavi regime's administrative reforms. Most of them came from the region of *Tarakma* in southern Iran and are generally referred to as Tarakmas. In Kuwait, their diasporic identity was reinforced by the fact that they would constitute a subclass of workers, employed in the shipping industry and to a lesser extent in handicrafts. In general, the crafts were the domain of the Shi'a in Kuwait, shunned by the tribal aristocracy (and tribesmen in general) as activities of particularly low social status, contrary to maritime commerce, considered as necessitating tribal virtues of courage, wisdom, manhood and leadership.

As to the Shi'a from *Al-Hasa* (around 15 per cent), most of them came to the Emirate in the nineteenth century after the various Saudi conquests sweeping the Eastern Province. These *Hasawiyyin* have developed a particularly strong group identity in Kuwait coupled to their common belonging to a minority branch within Twelver Shi'ism: *shaykhism* that follows the teachings of Ahmad al-Ahsa'i (1753–1826).[7] The group identity of the Kuwaiti shaykhis has also been strengthened by the fact that an important line of the shaykhi *maraja'* itself settled in Kuwait by the end of the 1950s: the *Mirza al-Ihqaqi* family.[8] This strong group identity has led to the development of specific communal relations and distinct processes of socialization. As far as the Baharna Shi'a are concerned (around 5 per cent), they also combine ethnic membership with belonging to a specific current in Twelver Shi'ism as they are descendants of the *'Gharbi* tribe in Western Arabia and belong to the *Akhbari* school of thought.[9] Most of the *Baharna* came to the Emirate during the eighteenth century fleeing political instability after the settlement of the 'Al-Khalifa in Bahrain.

Finally, there are the *badu* who were later incorporated into the citizenry, representing today around 60 per cent of Kuwait's citizens. They were naturalized between 1965 and 1981 to form a loyal support base for the Al-Sabah in the face of *hadar* opposition, but are no longer a loyal constituency. Among the tribesmen that were present in Kuwait before the advent of oil, only the 'Awazem and the Rashaida along with some members of the *Bani Khaled* were the tribes that are considered original (*asli*) in Kuwait, as most of its members were living in the close vicinities of the town, already since the arrival of the Bani 'Utub. The 'Awazem and Rashaida are two landless tribes, serf tribes of respectively the Mutran and the 'Ajman.[10] Most of them were semi-nomadic (*arib dar*) and settled in Kuwait during the dry season, in which they took part in pearl-fishing and diving activities, and followed the rains in search of grazing or cultivable land. While they were part of the original inhabitants of Kuwait and enjoy more social prestige than the naturalized tribes, members of the 'Awazem and Rashaida are referred to as tribesmen in popular parlance and socialize in different networks than the Sunni *hadar*. This is a consequence of their lower social status in pre-oil Kuwait and lower tribal ranks. By the start of the twentieth century, up to 90 per cent of Kuwait's pearling fleet consisted of Bedouin divers and sailors.[11] Another reason contributing to their historically stringent relation with the Sunni merchant aristocracy is the role played by these tribesmen in supporting the Al-Sabah militarily at various occasions, exemplified by their role in Mubarak al-Sabah's killing of his siblings to usurp the throne (1896) and by the role of tribal recruits in the crackdown of the 1938 movement.

Between 1965 and 1981 the tribal population was expanded in a political move of the Al-Sabah, naturalizing en masse thousands of southern tribes, who they trusted and whose shaykhs were in Saudi Arabia; most of them were from the 'Ajman, the Mutran and the 'Aneza noble tribes. Life conditions in Kuwait were better than in neighbouring Saudi Arabia and Iraq which is why these tribesmen came to Kuwait for work, particularly in the nascent oil industry in *Ahmadi* where they came to work as watchmen of installations, guards of pipelines, etcetera.[12] While in the 1960s the door of naturalization was shut for a lot of northern tribesmen who later would constitute the majority of the stateless (*Bidun*), trusted tribes from Saudi Arabia were naturalized by thousands and were granted first-class citizenship. The precise number of these naturalizations remains unknown, but estimates converge on between 160,000 and 400,000 naturalized individuals, mostly from Saudi Arabia.[13] What is known is that the northern tribes from Iraq were excluded from these naturalization policies although they represented a clear majority of the armed forces back then.[14] The Iraqi threat and a hostile parliament were behind the Al-Sabah's main motives here to naturalize the more trusted southern tribes, while shutting the door of naturalizations to the northern tribes. Until today this dichotomy between northern and southern tribes plays a role in Kuwait's rulers' perception vis-à-vis the *Bidun* and ruler's reluctance to solve the issue. Many Kuwaitis across different social strata (apart from a few activists) remain wary of the *Bidun*'s claim to citizenship for similar reasons, adding to the obvious fear for competition with the group for access to the state's largesse. The dimension of trust played a strong role in these political naturalizations and ruler's personal ties with tribes and sometimes direct kinship ties were determinant here. It is well known among Kuwaitis that the powerful Minister of Interior - Jaber al-'Ali – naturalized many members of the 'Ajman who were living in Kuwait in 1967. Himself the son of an 'Ajman mother and with ambitions to become Crown Prince, these naturalizations enhanced his support base.[15]

These naturalizations of southern tribesmen infuriated the nationalist and mercantile *hadar* opposition, but also the Shi'a who had strengthened their political role in parliament as a consequence of the political awakening of its youth in the 1970s. Adding fuel to the fire, the government changed the electoral district system to give more weight to the periphery where the naturalized tribesmen were living. The ten districts were changed to twenty-five, making it easier for the government to engage in vote-buying and co-optation practices. The naturalization of southern tribesmen shifted the demographic balance in favour of the *badu*. It also strengthened the *hadar–badu* cleavage, deepened by state policies that institutionalized these divisions, through differentiated access to the state's services and oil-derived rents.[16] This has contributed to the reinforcement of the *hadar–badu* distinction, which has become more pronounced than the sectarian division between Shi'a and Sunna. *Hadar* Sunni and Shi'a citizens tend to be closer in terms of political orientation and worldview than the *badu*, whom they tend to refer to as latecomers having contributed to the tribalization and Islamization of Kuwait's society and being merely interested in reaping the benefits of Kuwait's oil state. As such, my interlocutor of a prominent *Nadji* merchant family told me: 'I am closer to the Shi'a than the Bedouins. I can talk to the Shi'a, I can trust them. The Bedouins have a tribal mentality. They do not think about questions related to the state. The Shi'a are very reasonable.'[17] Displaying similar perceptions, a Shi'a interlocutor told me: 'You need to look at their history. In the desert, they were looking for water, dried up the lands and then left. So they did not create anything. They do not want to develop Kuwait's society.'[18] While the *hadar* nationalists view the naturalizations as a regime strategy against them, the Shi'a argue in a similar vein, considering it a government's response to the high number of Shi'a in the 1975 parliament and the politicization of Shi'a identity in the 1970s regionally.

Deconstructing the dominant Sunni
hadar narrative

Introduction

As Tetreault demonstrates, Kuwait's politics and society are not reducible to one narrative, but instead composed of a myriad of contending narratives, emblematic of the contested nature of citizenship and the foundation myth of the political community. The often-cited works on Kuwait's history by Abdel Aziz al-Rashid, Yusuf al-Qina'i and Saif al-Shamlan were written by Sunni elite, most of whom were staunch supporters of parliamentarianism. These works tend to focus on the history of the *hadar* merchants in their relation to the Al-Sabah, underlining the power-sharing principles and the material power of Kuwaiti notables vis-a-vis the Al-Sabah. The Al-Sabah being the poorest of the important families of the Bani 'Utub would accept the job, because the opportunity costs for them were very low. The history of the Shi'a and the role played by the desert in the *high politics* of premodern Kuwait tend to be downplayed in these accounts. As a consequence of the gradual emancipation of the *non-core* groups of Kuwait's political compact – Shi'a and tribes – there has, however, been a steady rise of new history works on Kuwait that aim to reinsert these groups' role in Kuwait's foundation myths. One can think of work of Shi'a historians that emphasize the Shi'a's role in the Battle of *Jahra* (1920) or the work on lineage (*nasab*) and tribes flooding the shells of Kuwait's few bookshops that underline the role of the tribes in major battles and the good relations enjoyed with the Al-Sabah.

The rise of the Al-Sabah and the ruler–merchant nexus

The rise of the Al-Sabah was the consequence of an agreement between the most influential families of the Bani Utub in 1716, who decided to choose the Al-Sabah to supervise government affairs, whilst profits would be divided equally between three Utub families (Al-Sabah, 'Al-Khalifa and Al-Jalahimi).[19] Various sources converge as to the authority of the Al-Sabah over a tribal hinterland in explaining the choice for this in principle mediocre family.[20] They recall the fact that the Al-Sabah had the strongest connections to a tribal hinterland and the caravan route to Damascus. At a time at which tribal raids were still matters of direct concern to local shaykhs, the

Al-Sabah's authority over the tribes might have been a factor explaining the choice for this family, as it possessed the strategic leverage power towards foreign powers. The matrimonial linkages with important tribes as well as the 'zakat' (tribute) paid to the Al-Sabah by tribes active in caravan trade demonstrate the esteem of the Al-Sabah among the tribes.[21] Given their authority over the tribes, the Al-Sabah would have been preferred in deliberations with the Ottomans. This perspective is also recounted in a local founding myth, stating that after reaching Kuwait, the Bani Utub held a council and elected a representative to go to Basra and explain their peaceful intent to the Ottomans. The Al-Sabah would have been chosen because of their authority over the neighbouring tribes, at a time at which the Bani Khalid power declined.[22]

These works all portray the Al-Sabah as primus inter pares who only stood out for their political role, diplomatically and administratively, owing to their authority over a strategically important hinterland. Hence, the prime authority of the Al-Sabah rests upon their *political* skills, and not on their wealth or other attributes. It is important here to pause a moment to describe the families present at the Bani Utub Council that decided to choose the Al-Sabah for governing the town.

Few information exists as to the precise composition of members of the Council. Literature generally refers to an oligarchy, although not specifying who was part of it.[23] According to Lorimer's account of British records on the region, the Bani Utub did not constitute more than 10–15 per cent of the subsequently settled population. According to these accounts, by 1820 only a few hundred out of an armed population of 5000 to 7000 men were Utub by race.[24] Among the earliest tribal sections of the Bani Utub to settle in Kuwait were the Al-Jalahima, Al-Sabah, 'Al-Khalifa and Al-Mawda, fleeing droughts in Najd.[25] Three among these families, the most important, entered into an alliance in which they divided tasks and profits among them to strengthen their hold as rulers of the town. After consultation by a Bani Utub Council, the Al-Sabah emerged as the most capable of governing the city, leaving the realm of commerce and maritime affairs respectively to the 'Al-Khalifa and the Al-Jalahimi clans. By then the Bani Utub, albeit a minority, already turned into the ruling class of the town controlling the main factors of production (fishing, pearling and commerce).[26]

Given the minority status of the Bani Utub and their peaceful settlement in town, other influential members from outside the Bani Utub participated in this consultative agreement choosing the Al-Sabah as rulers. Following the death of Sabah I (1756–62) – chosen by the notables on account of his tribal qualities – the determining role of the merchants in choosing the ruler becomes apparent. After his death, a struggle broke out between the Al-Sabah and the 'Al-Khalifa over political power in the town. It was the already-powerful merchant oligarchy's support for Abdallah al-Sabah (5th son of Sabah I) which was decisive in appointing him as second ruler of the town (1762–1812). Following this event, the 'Al-Khalifa went off to Zubara (Qatar) and settled later in Bahrain (1783), where they invaded a territory populated by a dominantly Arab Shi'a population, which explains the fundamentally different nature of ruler–ruled relations in Bahrain.[27] Whilst in Kuwait, tribes and traders from diverse horizons came together in a flourishing port, the 'Al-Khalifa conquered Bahrain, imposing themselves *manu militari*.[28] Not much later, the Jalahimi left to Zubara, thus leaving the Al-Sabah in undisputed control over Kuwait. Despite their earlier dispute, relations with the 'Al-Khalifa remained cordial, with Bani Utub families of Qatar, Bahrain and Kuwait forming a larger war and trade alliance. By the end of the eighteenth century, power was well established in the hands of the Al-Sabah.

It was since the second half of the eighteenth century that the Sunni Najdi merchants rose in economic and thus political power. Also, over time the group of Najdi merchants was widened in Kuwait, with subsequent immigration waves (1676, 1748, 1767 and 1775) adding to the initial core of eight *asli* families: the Al-Ghanim, Al-Nusf, Al-Saqr, Al-Hamad, Al-Mudhaf, Al-Khali and Al-Marzuq.[29] Najdi origin, Sunni creed and pure tribal blood would have been the criteria of admission to this 'asabiyya.

The rise in power of the merchants as the town's most affluent capitalists was the consequence of a combination of factors. In the context of a changing political economy and expansion of the port's activities, the 'desert' gradually lost in importance in favor of the 'sea'. Hence, the traditional role of the Al-Sabah as patrons over a tribal hinterland became obsolete, as the strategic importance of tribal politics weakened and the economy became more oriented towards the sea. Moreover, the rise of Wahhabi power in Central Arabia gradually weakened the Al-Sabah's authority over the tribes, while relations with the Ottomans strengthened by the start of the nineteenth century.[30]

The flourishing of Kuwait's port, increasing mercantile activity, was itself a consequence of two main developments. First, the Persian occupation of Basra (1775), leading to the transfer by the British of the dispatch of their Gulf to Aleppo mail and the transfer of caravan trade to Kuwait. This transformed the town into a major entrepot for the export of merchandise from the British East India Company.[31] Furthermore, throughout the *eighteenth* century Kuwait witnessed an influx from merchants from Najd and Al-Hasa contributing to the strength of the local merchant class. These merchants fled tribal wars and Wahhabi expansionism in search for more stable grounds for their commerce and living.[32] Also, the unrest accompanying the occupation of Bahrain by the 'Al-Khalifa (1783) led affluent merchants to settle in Kuwait, bringing with them their wealth.

These factors all contributed to the predominance of merchants over Kuwait's economy and the waning importance of tribal relations in the political economy. The *real power* in the community came to lie in this class of pearl merchants (*tawawish*) and dhow owners (*nukhoda*), on whom the Al-Sabah were financially dependent. The group cohesion of this financial class was reinforced by their pure Najdi descent, socialization in the Al-Qibla neighbourhood and adherence to the Hanbali *madhab*.

With the increase in merchants' wealth and contribution to the rulers' treasury, they achieved a stronger say in governance.[33] Some merchants became so powerful that they had a stronger impact on decision-making than family members of the Al-Sabah. A notable example is the case of Yusuf al-Ibrahim, a wealthy Basrawi merchant who became one of the main advisers of Shaykh Muhammad al-Sabah (1892–6). Al-Ibrahim – himself from a Najdi lineage higher than the Al-Sabah – married the daughters of the rulers. Al-Ibrahim's influence in decision-making is described by Khaz'al, who describes the latter's influence in decision-making by Muhammad, 'who would not listen to advice by other members of the Al-Sabah, unless Yusuf al-Ibrahim gave his approval'. This enraged other members of the Al-Sabah and particularly Mubarak al-Sabah, who would later stage a coup against his half-brother.[34] Hence, power-sharing gradually extended to wealthy circles outside the initial Bani Utub, with merchants capable on account of their wealth to have a considerable weight in governance.

Their control over the productive sectors of Kuwait's economy (pearling, commerce and fishing) as a class with a political identity implied the transposition of tribal stratification patterns to a sedentarized community. Najdis, Zubairis or Basrawis, having arrived in Kuwait at different times and from different temporary places of settlement, all shared a strong pride in their noble, tribal descent. Nobility means essentially the traceability of the purity of their blood and origin through the presence of family trees proving their noble '*nasab*' (lineage). Owning camels, noble tribes differentiated themselves as camel pastoralists from the non-noble tribes, who grazed on the territory of the noble tribes, paying in return the protection tax (*khawa*: brotherhood). The merger of blood purity with class activity was transposed to the settled community, where these pure Najdis shunned activities regarded of lower social rank, notably the handicrafts, considered as particularly low.[35] Maritime commerce was regarded as high-ranked, necessitating tribal virtues of courage, wisdom, manhood and leadership; it allowed them to make sufficient profit to stay on top of the hierarchy in the settled community. Although as tribesmen little feeling of solidarity bounded these groups (tribal feuds were common), the diasporic experience in Kuwait sharing a common identity and kinship led to the crystallization of a class 'in itself' that would defend its interests as a powerful lobby once threatened.

These merchants, whose wealth was embedded in movable property and who had learned to sail, could voice their discontent through 'exit' when important interests were at stake. From their control of trade and imports and payment of customs, they were the moneylenders of the Al-Sabah and their departure would leave the shaykhdom without steady income to sustain its political power and to provide income to the town's residents. This threat of secession was exemplified by the strategy of a group of merchants against Mubarak al-Sabah's increasing fiscal demands for his desert campaigns. Some of the pearl merchants, such as Hilal al-Mutrani, left for Bahrain in protest and Mubarak, needing their financial support, was obliged to send a delegation to Bahrain to convince them of coming back.

Hence, although accounts vary on the exact context in which the Al-Sabah rose to political power by the start of the eighteenth century, they converge as to the primary mediating role of the latter and the limits to their rights to rule, constrained by the community of notables.[36] Disconnected from the tribal *dirah* ever since, the Bani Utub had appropriated a tribal identity of their own and had, during this economic diversification, 'attached to them other economic groups in a client-tribal relationship, notably the Sunna Najdi merchants'.[37] Until today, these families pride themselves on account of their wealth, referring to the fact that they were the lenders for the Al-Sabah and that the latter were 'so poor that they even ate in our house'.[38]

As Crystal argues, politics was structured around the ruler–merchant nexus, with merchants being the prime opposition force to the authoritarian inclinations of the Al-Sabah, because these families were at the origins of the choice for the Al-Sabah as rulers, being as *tujjar* (merchants) too busy with commerce to take care of the daily administration of the city-state.[39] Being part of an inclusive 'asabiyya and sharing a group identity based upon class interests, they were able to lobby for a quasi-exclusive entitlement to the spoils of the private sector. The loss of political independence was compensated by receiving the biggest share in the oil cake, agreeing on the principle that the merchants defend until today: 'governance for the Al-Sabah and commerce for the people' *(Al-hukm lil al-shuyukh wa al-tijara lil sha'ab)*.

Republican equality for those with equal status: Sunni Najdi families

In the old days of power-sharing in the city-state, governance recalled the working of the Athenian democracy or – as Salame (1992) argues – the Venetian republic. The republican spirit of Kuwait was remarked by foreign travellers who tend to describe Kuwait as a peaceful community and the Al-Sabah as rulers entertaining good relations with their subjects and with tribal affairs being generally well-managed, at a time the Ottomans had a difficult time in pacifying a rebellious *hinterland*, tormented by intra-tribal strive and expansionist and proselyte ambitions of the Al-Saud.[40] Unity and solidarity were reinforced by the 'exact uniformity of costume among all ranks and ages and the fact of there being no natives of any other country resident', as observed by J.H. Stocqueler, a visitor in 1731.[41] Other travellers who had travelled to other Gulf ports remarked the absence of armed forces and the rare infliction of punishments, suggesting that the dynasty of the Al-Sabah governed in a rather consensual way and that there was 'little need of an army'.[42]

Before the seizure of power by Mubarak al-Sabah, indeed, republican values of the classic polis characterized relations between the Al-Sabah and their subjects.[43] As in the case of polis, equality was only 'for those with equal status', the adult men of noble descent being integrated into the power-sharing 'asabiyya with the Al-Sabah, owing to their kinship ties to the federation of Bani Utub founding families or to their wealth derived from maritime and inland trade, mostly Najdis and Basrawis. Persian merchants or Shi'a merchants (from Arab or Persian descent) were excluded from this arrangement on the basis of ethnicity and confession, although some were equally fortunate in wealth. Stratification along identity lines, moreover, often coincided with differences in occupational specializations, structured over time by the coherence of emigrant communities, socialized in networks of neighbourhood (*firij*) proximity, religious networks and economic sub-communities.

In sum, the early political community in Kuwait's pre-Mubarak era was structured around values of kinship, early settlement in the Emirate (concomitantly with the Al-Sabah) and wealth. When making a tentative hierarchy of values determining access to the power-sharing 'asabiyya, the following classification seems the most pertinent: (1) kinship ties to the Bani Utub federation of founding families, (2) Noble (*sharif*) Sunni tribal descent from Najd, (3) date of settlement in the Emirate and (4) wealth. The closer related to the Bani Utub founding fathers of the Emirate, the higher one's entitlement to republicanism, in its ideal values of liberty, self-government and active citizenship.

The divided nature of Kuwait's merchant class: different diasporas

While sources tend to converge on the role played by a Sunni Najdi aristocracy on top of the city-state's hierarchy, there is far less information about the exact nature of power-sharing in old Kuwait and the families that were entitled to it. Rather than being a static and homogenous group, the merchants of Kuwait are highly stratified along lines of descent, lineage and sect. As with the general social fabric of Kuwait, the merchants are regrouped along different diasporas.

Merchants keep their place of origin as a central referent of their identity. Until today, many of these families cultivate strong ties to the region their forefathers left, reflected in marriage choices, charitable activities in their places of origin – like the construction of mosques – and participation in wider family networks. Yet, these transnational ties seem stronger today for the tribes and the Shi'a families than for the Sunni *hadar* families, for whom *nasab* and *madhab* seem to prevail over place of origin. This might be due to the fact that in the case of the Shi'a, although *hadar*, madhab and place of origin often coincide. In the case of the tribes, recently naturalized, transnational linkages are most salient in structuring communities' sense of belonging.

I argue that diaspora identity is more important than tribal hierarchies per se, reflective of the profoundly transnational foundations of the Emirate. Members of the noble tribes like the 'Ajman, Dawasir or Mutran that came to Kuwait engaged in a diverse set of activities. Some settled down in town; others were a semi-nomadic category, a class in between the *hadar* and the *badu* – the *'arib dar* – who engaged in activities such as pearl fishing in the dry season.[44] Yet very few of them were merchants. Non-noble tribes, such as the Rashaida and the 'Awazem, occupied a subordinate position in the Emirate, though they are considered as original inhabitants of Kuwait. By allying with rulers as the Al-Saud and the Al-Sabah, these tribesmen could liberate themselves from their serfdom to the Mutran and 'Ajman respectively and were dispensed from paying the tribal levy *'khawa'* to their lords. Their non-noble status excluded them from intermarriages with the Al-Sabah however.

Consequently, it seems that while pure Arab blood[45] and Sunni identity are a necessary condition for access to the highest merchant *'asabiyya*, it is not a sufficient condition. Entrepreneurial acumen, connections with fellow tribesmen and diaspora communities and privileged access to the Al-Sabah seem to have been determinant here. This also explains the non-static nature of the Sunni aristocracy that has been neglected in existing studies. Jill Crystal analyses the impact of oil on merchant–ruler relations and demonstrates how the merchants' initial independence was compromised as a consequence of oil.[46] In her work, the merchant class is analysed as a relatively homogenous bloc, whereas the cleavages within the group of merchants give us important indications about the nature of politics in pre-oil Kuwait; elite linkages that have been perpetuated in a path-dependent process with the growth of state resources. Many of the merchants that are today considered as old money actually came to Kuwait at the start of the twentieth century. They recount stories of their grandfathers having walked barefoot out of poor Najdi villages in the twentieth century seeking their fortunes in the city-state. Founders of the Al-Hamad, Al-Khorafi, Al-Shaya, Al-Sa'd and the Abdulrazzaks who today are considered among the top elite gained their wealth relatively late.[47] These families share pure Najdi origin. Similar nouveaux riches stories are recounted by Shi'a merchants, such as the Al-Kadhemi or Qabazard families, who also gained their wealth relatively late and at a period of general economic decline, during the Interbellum.[48]

For these reasons, it seems important to further dig into the different layers of the heterogeneous group of Kuwaiti merchants. This gives us insights into pre-oil elite linkages that would reverberate in the contemporary era. Some general observations can be made here that will be elaborated on in the following pages.

* First, there is the nucleus of early-settled Najdi merchant families (some of whom shared kinship ties with the Utub clan) who formed the core of the power-sharing agreement with the Al-Sabah. This agreement in general consisted of a delegation of tasks, with merchants – too busy with commercial affairs – leaving the domain of governance to the Al-Sabah. The decision to choose the Al-Sabah to supervise governance was itself a consequence of a tribal agreement between the most influential families of the Bani Utub in 1716. The latter's authority over a tribal hinterland played in their favour, at a time in which tribal politics were the high politics of the region (Beaugrand: 2010:91). By then, the Bani Utub, albeit a minority, had turned into the ruling class of the town controlling its main factors of production (fishing, pearling and commerce).[49]

*The nucleus of merchant families that would constitute the core of early oppositional politics were all of pure Arab blood, being either Najdis, Zubairis or Basrawis, referring to their place of origin. The Zubairis and Basrawis while having come from Iraq shared common descent from Najd and also follow the Hanbali madhab. The composition of the twelve-member advisory council of 1921 reflects this, with the Al-Saqqar, Al-Qina'i, Al-Humaydi, Al-Rushaid, Al-Naqeeb, Al-Ghanim and Al-Khudayr, Al-Badr, Al-Ghanim, Al-Khaled all fitting this classification.[50]

*Consequently, tribal values were transplanted to the socio-economic realm, not different from Bahrain or other neighbouring emirates where one can observe similar logics. Tribally organized sections of society have maintained control of the major economic resources: pearls, dates and nowadays oil.[51] They shunned the crafts and food industries that tended to be dominated by non-Arab merchants. Within the tribal value system, the handicrafts (an activity in which the Shi'a were largely engaged in Kuwait) were considered as low-ranking. Maritime commerce was regarded as high-ranking.

*Iranian merchants, often from Shi'a creed were not part of this merchant 'asabiyya and were excluded from it at crucial power-sharing moments, such as the majlis events of 1938. They lived in the same part of old Kuwait as the Al-Sabah, Al-Sharq, as a token of their proximity to the rulers. As rulers had more to fear from their in-group that could challenge their central elite status, rulers' alliances with Persian merchants were also commonplace in Dubai and to a lesser extent in Oman.

*The power distribution between the Al-Sabah and the merchant aristocracy was subject to a series of changes, as a consequence of socio-economic transformations and colonial rule. By the end of the eighteenth century, merchants gained a stronger role in the town's affairs – due to their rising wealth – while desert politics gradually waned in importance. The rise of the Wahhabi power moreover weakened the Al-Sabah's authority over desert tribes, while relations with the Ottomans strengthened by the start of the nineteenth century. In this period, the authority system of the Al-Sabah weakened gradually in favour of the merchants, some of whom became powerful advisors to the rulers. It is only with the advent of Mubarak al-Sabah (1896) that desert politics was revived, through the latter's engagement in various battles, provoking the resentment of the merchants who had to finance these wars.

*Relatedly, British encroachments in the region since the nineteenth century were received in different ways by different merchant groups. While the Shi'a merchants entertained positive relations with the British, the Sunni merchants did not have similar relations. Several factors explain this difference. First of all, the Sunni merchants had stronger ties with the Sunni Ottoman Empire, which was often engaged in wars with the Persian Empire. Also, as autonomous capitalist forces, these merchants had been the driving factors in forging political ties between Ottoman Iraq and Kuwait. British encroachment hurt their interests from the mid-nineteenth century on, as British goods flooded local markets and dislocated the regional carrying trade with desert hinterlands. The Shi'a merchants had good relations with the British and were the ones who lobbied for the signature of a protection agreement in 1899 through their relations to the Political Resident in Bushehr.

*In a context of great-power rivalry and frequent intra-family feuds, Mubarak's usurpation of the throne was accompanied with a strategy of alliance-building. Externally, British protection strengthened his autonomy vis-à-vis the merchants. Internally, he allied with non-core elites, Shi'a and tribal elites. This dimension of alliance-building with non-core elites has been overlooked in literature on Kuwait, but is crucial as it would lay the basis for contemporary regime relations with these two status groups.

The Shi'a and the tribes' contending narratives of participation

Prominent Shi'a merchants of long standing in the Emirate, living in Al-Sharq together with the Al-Sabah, criticize accounts that place them in a subordinate position within the stratification of pre-oil Kuwait. They refer to their wealth and proximity to the Al-Sabah historically, living next to the rulers in the Al-Sharq neighbourhood, as signs of their political influence and consider the accounts focusing on the Sunni merchant elite as politicized, either by the Sunnis, or as 'Western bias stemming from a sectarian reading of Arab politics'.[52] Shi'a argue, for example, that the Shi'a families from Persia, like the Ma'rafi and the Behbahani, were almost equally affluent, engaged in regional commerce as well as in crafts trading, and in close proximity with the rulers in Al-Sharq (contrary to the Sunni aristocracy that lived in Al-Qibla). These merchants contributed to the treasury and were close to the rulers, so how couldn't they have had a say in power-sharing is the general argument. Moreover, they argue that proximity with the Al-Sabah was reinforced by the fact that the Persian families of Al-Sharq, mostly active in crafts, stayed throughout the year in Kuwait, contrary to the Sunni aristocracy of Al-Qibla, whose members spent most time abroad in pearl-diving and commercial travels. In this perspective, the Sunni families were too often abroad to maintain strong ties to the rulers and a good perspective on issues of daily governance. Finally, report these Shi'a families, the Al-Sabah would send Shi'a representatives to consult with British authorities, because they were the ones who stayed in the town throughout the year (apart from a minority of Shi'a merchants who possessed dhows and travelled).

The dominant Sunni narrative on Kuwait's history has also been criticized, more recently, by the tribesmen, some of whose members were part of the original community (*asli*), present in the Emirate before the Battle of Jahra (1920): the founding myth. These tribesmen focus on their role in major battles supporting Kuwait's and Gulf rulers and in recent years bookshops have been flooded with books on tribes, written by tribesmen, in a narration blending tribalism with love for the nation. The Rashaida, the 'Awazem and some members of the Bani Khaled were indeed present in Kuwait at the time of the arrival of the Bani Utub. As mentioned, the Rashaida and the 'Awazem are two landless tribes, serf tribes of respectively the Mutran and the 'Ajman. In the part of her PhD thesis looking at tribalism, Beaugrand notes that most of them were semi-nomadic (*arib dar*)[53] who settled in Kuwait during the dry season, during which they took part in pearl-fishing and diving activities and followed the rains in search of grazing or cultivable land. "The 'Awazem were known for catching fish on the southern coast of Kuwait's town, as far as present-day Salmiyya and Hawali", and on the eve of the Second World War they were mostly sedentary. "The Rashaida occupied the plain called the Dabdaba, around 150 km west of the city, where they grazed, hunted and collected truffles."[54] In the context of the current animosity between the *hadar* and *badu* that mostly reflects anti-immigration feelings, it is difficult to imagine today that this dichotomy does not do justice to the historical interactions that existed between both groups, socially, economically and politically, and that fostered, according to Madawi al-Rasheed, cultural continuity rather than dichotomy.[55] Especially in Kuwait, the land- and sea-based economies were intrinsically linked and the presence of the *arib dar* as a middle category between pure nomads and settled population strengthened the continuity between both. For example, by the start of the twentieth century, up to 90 per cent of Kuwait's pearling fleet consisted of Bedouin divers and sailors.[56]

Also, although not part of the consultative agreement with the Al-Sabah from which they were excluded, these tribes played an important role in Kuwait's high politics, as demonstrated by Beaugrand (2010). Although not being the money lenders as the merchants, the tribes were of strategic importance, through their transnational connections, as their alliances or defections were essential to rulers' power. Therefore, the collectivity of the tribe, although geographically distanced from the town, was of crucial importance to the rulers and therefore the relation with tribal chieftains. As Beaugrand (2010) and Al-Rasheed (1991) rightly note, tribal politics were the high politics of the pre-oil era and raids were part of the process of military and political centralization. The merchant oligarchy, although being the financial force of the Emirate, was excluded from the political deals between ruling shaykhs and tribal heads.[57] This was the exclusive prerogative of the latter. Neither the British, nor the Ottomans or the local Sunni aristocracy could engage directly with tribes in such deals. In this regard, the tribes helped consolidate the territorial powerbase of the rulers and were an essential defence and policing force, explaining their later integration into the nascent police and army forces.[58] These institutions emerged out of a private system of the forces of coercion, relying upon private retinues of the shaykhs who were solely recruited among the tribesmen. These '*fidawiyyin*' - ready to sacrifice themselves at any time for their master - had to follow and protect their shaykh and obeyed his commands.[59] From this subservient role as guardians of the rulers stems the bias and deep-seated animosity of the old families towards the tribes, considering them as uneducated, a politicized and blindly obedient, at a time in which the merchant class already had a cohesive political identity, influenced by Arab nationalism. Later on this would be reinforced when rulers as Mubarak al-Sabah and, afterward, Shaykh Ahmad Bin Jabir would resort to the tribes (as well as the Shi'a) to affirm their role, by breaking the consultative agreement at the cost of the merchant aristocracy. This biased perception of the role of the tribes in Kuwait's history is expressed in the memoirs of Saif al-Shamlan, himself member of the Najdi elite: 'The people of the desert – let the truth be said – have had only a slender positive impact on the life of Kuwait. The raids and troubles that have affected Kuwait and Kuwaitis have come from the desert.'[60]

The aforementioned already gives us a glimpse of the complex and contested nature of the narrative of power-sharing and political stratification in pre-oil Kuwait, in terms of the rulers' relation to the main three traditional groups: the *hadar* Sunna, the Shi'a and the tribes. As this chapter demonstrated, the Al-Sabah dynasty relied on its non-core groups to consolidate its reign; supported by growing direct British interests in Kuwait since the end of the nineteenth century. The Shi'a nor the *badu* could challenge the central elite status, as they were outside the inner core of Najdi elites who historically participated in power-sharing with the Al-Sabah. It was this 'asabiyya that presented the strongest threat to the Al-Sabah that therefore resorted to clients and friends from outside this group to maintain dynasty. This confirms largely Ibn Khaldun's reading on the nature of political authority in Arabian dynasties. It is in this pre-oil period that the foundations were laid for contemporary regime–society relations in Kuwait, where historical memory has proved particularly deep.

Communal segregation and stratification in pre-oil Kuwait: *hadar*, Shi'a and the early-settled tribes

Introduction

Having discussed the main aspects of Kuwait's pre-oil political history and the contending narratives on the role of non-core elites, this section will switch the focus from narrative to history itself and analyses the role of the three status groups in Kuwait's political compact. The emphasis is on the nature of politics in pre-oil Kuwait, which was in essence the politics of notables, with urban elites acting as crucial intermediaries between the Al-Sabah and broader constituencies. As in other premodern Gulf societies, governance was an affair of networks of urban and tribal intermediaries.

The mosaic of diasporas that settled in Kuwait since the early *eighteenth* century had led to distinct processes of *communitization*, with communities socializing in different neighbourhoods and networks. This was in essence a *plural society*, in which different sections of the community lived side by side, but separately, and in which even in the economic sphere there was a division of labour along racial lines. In this society, the market place was the common denominator. It corresponded to a situation of indirect rule, resembling the Ottoman Empire, with rulers seldom trying to homogenize the population.

Understanding the segregation of communities in Kuwait's pre-oil urban geography gives us a better idea of the political dynamics that shaped social stratification and the nature of the relations between these groups and their leaders with the Al-Sabah. Until the advent of Mubarak al-Sabah, governance was in essence a laissez-faire policy. Yet, the coup d'etat in 1896 changed this equilibrium. Having lost the support of the powerful Najdi merchants, Mubarak created 'politics' by influencing the distribution of power and resources and thus relations between sub-communities. He consolidated the dynastic rule of the Al-Sabah and broke with the latter's initial role as benevolent overseers of affairs in the market place.

Traditional politics in Arabia: the politics of notables

Social forces in Central Arabia have been shaped by the interplay of two dominant themes of its environment: the desert and the sea. The juxtaposition of arid deserts, sea coasts and fertile oases or river valleys led to three main, distinct lifestyles: nomadic, maritime and agricultural. In Kuwait, the extreme shortage of water had impeded the development of agriculture and consequently the desert and the sea formed the two natural resources around which social forces were shaped in the traditional division of labour. Contrary to the alleged dichotomy between nomadic and urban forces, so present in Kuwait's popular discourse today, historically the forces of the desert and the sea intermingled in the market place and in the traditional productive sectors: pearling, fishing and commerce. No port can exist without its hinterland and the control of the desert tribes over trade routes, through their transnational connections and caravan trade, led to a mutual dependence. Tribes were both the consumers and the carriers of the merchants' products and their lucrative arms trade to the desert interior. Moreover, many of the tribes present in Kuwait were semi-nomadic, engaging in pearl-diving in the pearling season and in the winter in herding, fighting or semi-agricultural activities.

Notwithstanding this mutual interaction with the desert, the town emerged as the centre of productive forces on which its habitants depended.[1] The division of labour was very hierarchized with those dominating maritime and pearling commerce at the top of social stratification. These were the pearl merchants and the sea captains.

Being among the first settlers, these wealthy families became leaders of neighbourhood units (*firij*) in which migrants from similar backgrounds tended to settle, based upon common places of origin and ethnic or religious identities. Because of their economic wealth, these families provided the necessary services in their firij, such as sanitary services, the building of schools and the organization of religion (i.e. construction of mosques). For this reason, certain neighbourhoods carried the name of the leading family or clusters of families, such as the Al-Hasawi, the Al-Balush, the Al-Mutran, the Al-Qina'at, Al-Nusf and Al-Fadala, representing streets of sea captain families from both sects.[2] Due to their role in community affairs – in neighbourhoods, but also as job providers in pearling and commerce – and their independent wealth, these families were typical political notables in the pre-oil constellation. As such, they played a critical political role as intermediaries between the Al-Sabah and the communities in which they had social power. This social power was the consequence of both their *access to the centre*, due to their wealth and status and their *independent* social power within communities, making them crucial interlocutors for the political centre. These communities were grouped together along sect and place of origin, but constituted heterogeneous socio-economic categories, such as fishers, pearl divers and in the case of the Shi'a, craftsmen.

The concept of political notable – developed by Hourani – has rarely been applied to the study of Arabian Gulf societies.[3] The kinship nature of these societies has often been analysed from the perspective of anthropological paradigms, although the case of Kuwait provides an example par excellence of the politics of notables. All other Arabian Gulf societies to a stronger or lesser degree – depending on the centralized authority of the rulers – were governed through networks of intermediaries. As urban notables (such as merchants and religious leaders) and rural elites (such as village leaders and tribal shaykhs), these local elites played a crucial mediating role for ruling families. They contributed with taxes, public services and military assistance to their rulers and could offer their communities employment, protection and representation vis-à-vis the rulers.

Kuwait's merchant elite in perspective: local elites in the pre-oil Gulf

Literature on local elites and social stratification in the pre-oil Arabian Gulf is scarce. Yet it is important to understand the commonalities as well as particularities of the power of Kuwait's local elites in comparison to other Gulf states. This will give us a better apprehension of what explains the political Sonderweg of modern Kuwait. As the literature is limited on the topic, my conclusions are tentative.

While everywhere in the pre-oil Gulf local urban and tribal elites represented autonomous power centres that could challenge ruling shaykhs and offer checks and balances to their power, there were considerable differences in the nature of ruler–elite relations. In the smaller shaykhdoms of the Gulf, merchant elites were the most powerful actors. Bahrain, Dubai and Kuwait were all mercantile states. In these states, the powerful merchants shared kinship ties with rulers and were able on account of both wealth and kinship to play a role in power-sharing. This was exemplified in the early twentieth century in the opposition movements that erupted in these three shaykhdoms, led by merchants demanding parliamentarianism to protect their bourgeois interests, inspired by Arabism and anti-colonialism. In 1938, this culminated in three rather similar protest movements in Bahrain, Dubai and Kuwait, in which merchants allied with dissident shaykhs against the ruler and his British supporters.[4] Thus, bourgeois activism by a merchant elite was not unique to Kuwait. Nonetheless, Kuwait developed into a more open political community than the more authoritarian path of other Gulf shaykhdoms.

Having said this, the relative power of the merchant class in Kuwait vis-à-vis the ruler seems to have been strongest of all shaykhdoms. The merchant class in Bahrain and Dubai contained a large number of foreigners (mostly Indians and Persians), who were not nationals, but resided often temporarily in the shaykhdoms and paid taxes to local rulers. Moreover, these non-Arab merchants lived close to the ruling shaykhs, who, at times, allied with them to counterbalance opposition from the Arab merchants who could challenge the central elite status. In both Bahrain and Dubai, merchant nationalists opposed the privileges of non-Arab merchants in a context of nationalism and the discovery of oil that strengthened the stakes in the competition between rulers and merchants. In Oman too were there many foreigners among the merchants, while in Qatar the weak trade sector impeded the existence of a strong local class. In Kuwait, the merchant class was the most cohesive and enjoyed a rather privileged position.[5] This also explains why in Kuwait, unlike Bahrain or Dubai, there were no Indian merchants (*Banians*) at a time when Bombay was the commercial regional centre and the rupee the main currency in the Gulf.[6]

The presence of foreign merchants or non-Arab ones allowed rulers to extend their support base outside the circle of powerful Arab merchants who could challenge the rulers' prerogatives. In Kuwait, the ruler allied with the native '*Ajam* merchants of Shi'a creed. In Dubai, the ruler lived close to the Persian merchants, who specialized in foodstuff and textile trade, with pearling being the prerogative of the Arab aristocracy. In Bahrain, too, Indians were powerful and even 'Ajam merchants were considered as siding with the regime and early oppositional grievances were directed, among others, against the privileges of non-Arabs (mostly Indians) in the nascent oil industry. The Kuwaiti historian, Ahmad Bin Barjas, says the following about it:

The power of Kuwait's merchant class was the consequence of the flexibility of the Al-Sabah and their indulgence towards the merchants and their provision of appropriate circumstances for their commercial activities. As such, the Kuwaiti ruler created a company to serve the merchants in India, Ceylon (Sri Lanka) and Pakistan and these privileges were only for the merchants, not for the people. The situation of merchants in the Emirates and Bahrain differs from this in a major aspect. The majority of merchants here were not citizens and only lived in these areas and the rulers demanded from them relatively high taxes, different from merchants in Kuwait who were first-class citizens.[7]

In this regard, the merchants in Kuwait would have profited from a relatively favourable trading climate enabled by the Al-Sabah. These merchants were in essence transnational actors with branches of their businesses in Bombay, Karachi and Calcutta, where they had second homes, integrated into the local trade networks and were fluent in Hindi. One can think of Arab families such as the Saqr, Hamad, Ibrahim, Qina'i, Marzuq and Ghanim who flourished in India and controlled trade between Kuwait and India.

Only the powerful Arab merchants sharing kinship ties to rulers were sometimes capable of exempting themselves from paying taxes to rulers and could check the latter's power. In Bahrain, the tribal Sunni elite that engaged in pearling and owned palm-tree estates were particularly powerful and the 'Al-Khalifa were dependent on them to preserve their authority system. 'Al-Khalifa's governance resembled a feudal estate system with land being conquered by the 'Al-Khalifa, in alliance with Najdi tribes. As these tribes (e.g. *Al-Dawasir*, *Budayya* and *Zallaq*) had extended power in Central Arabia and Qatar and until the discovery of oil, the 'Al-Khalifa married into them to consolidate political alliances.

The extent of these tribes' leverage vis-à-vis the 'Al-Khalifa becomes clear in the following examples. The powerful Al-Dawasir tribe was capable of exempting itself from paying taxes to the 'Al-Khalifa and its leaders recognized the incumbent ruler (Issa 'al-Khalifa) in name only.[8] In 1923, heads of the Al-Dawasir opposed the British deposition of the ruler and the tax reforms that would place Shi'a and Sunna on an equal footing, curtailing their privileges. As a consequence of this, the entire tribe left for Saudi Arabia, backed by Ibn Saud. The ruler, fearing the loss of such a powerful ally, asked for their return. The tribe had demanded a set of conditions for its return to Bahrain (e.g. government compensation for the rents collected from their property in their absence and the restoration of their property that had been confiscated upon British request); conditions that the British opposed as it would show the ruler's weakness. Yet, the 'Al-Khalifa, realizing the importance of the goodwill of these powerful Sunni actors – the Al-Dawasir and the Al-Saud – decided to support all demands and allow the tribe to come back.[9] This example reveals the dependence of the 'Al-Khalifa on these local elites to preserve their rule before the discovery of oil. Different from the Kuwaiti case, however, was the fact that ties between the 'Al-Khalifa and the local tribes naturally strengthened as a consequence of the bigger sectarian split in society that overlapped with class divides. In this conundrum, the original Shi'a population, the *Baharna*, faced exploitation as palm cultivators and pearl divers at the hands of their Sunni lords and the 'Al-Khalifa. In Qatar too many of the tribal merchant families were exempt from taxation and the Al-Thani shaykh received only a modest yearly income.[10]

Consequently, while Kuwait's merchant class seems to have been stronger and more coherent than merchants in the pearling shaykhdoms, the independent power of merchants vis-à-vis rulers was not a unique feature of Kuwait. Everywhere in the Gulf did local power centres exist that could challenge the ruler's authority. Especially the inland tribes in Oman and Saudi Arabia acted as powerful opposition to rulers' centralizing tendencies.[11] As tribes, their autonomous power over constituencies was far greater than the merchants', whose wealth was the main basis of their power and who spent long months at sea, thus limiting their direct role in community affairs.

The merchants' power was thus derived from their wealth and kinship ties to rulers. Their power over constituencies was large, but was mostly a coercive power. They provided employment to communities and embryonic public services, but class relations were particularly repressive here, as the system of pearling was based upon pervasive indebtedness of divers towards the merchants and boat owners. While the native divers were free in theory (enslaved Africans accounted for a large number of the pearl divers), this system of quasi-perpetual indebtedness made divers face exploitation at the hands of the merchants. This system was designed to ensure the divers' loyal service year after year. Divers were often paid in rice and other staples and, being illiterate, fell prey to deliberate attempts at abuse, as they could not read the debt diaries in which their debts were recorded.[12] In its repressive nature, it was not very different from the indebtedness and repression faced by Baharna pearl cultivators at the hands of their Sunni lords.

Given the repressive nature of pre-oil class relations between merchants and their labourers, it is not surprising that merchants were quick at losing their power when the masses were politicized. Class distinctions tended to be too pronounced for the merchants to gain a strong popular following at the time of nationalist agitation and merchant clubs remained essentially elitist gatherings.[13] In the case of the Shi'a, class distinctions were blurred by a collective identity, and in both Bahrain and Kuwait Shi'a merchants had stronger social power in communities than the Sunni merchants. Also, as there were fewer Shi'a among the pearl merchants of Kuwait, the community was more cohesively engaged in activities in the old town, notably in the crafts and food industries.

In sum, this short section has demonstrated that the autonomous power of Kuwait's merchants vis-à-vis the ruler was not a unique feature and existed everywhere in the Gulf. In Kuwait, Bahrain and Dubai, merchants were the main elites who could contest the central elite's status, explaining why opposition emanated from this group. It also explains why rulers sided with elites and groups that could not challenge their status, as we have seen in the case of Persian and Indian merchants. What was unique to Kuwait was the cohesive identity of its merchant class, larger in number and sharing a Sunni Najdi identity. For this reason, foreigners were absent among its merchants and there was a sharp division of labour between the Al-Sabah and the economic elite (the first not entering into commercial affairs).

Having discussed the general structure of ruler–merchant relations in pre-oil Gulf shaykhdoms and the place of Kuwait within this overall picture, the next section will focus on the concrete role of urban and tribal elites in pre-oil Kuwait. The emphasis here is on spatial segregation of communities and the role played by elites in neighbourhood units (*firij*). As we will see, the particular segregation of diaspora communities in space was indicative of relations between the Al-Sabah and the three status groups and of social stratification in the old town. To my knowledge, this is material that has not been covered in existing literature. As Gulf monarchies have not witnessed radical social transformations induced by revolutions, most traditional social elites have never lost their full social standing in the post-independence era. Also, pre-oil identities and stratification patterns have been perpetuated by the state as a consequence of oil.

Governance of old Kuwait: intermediation and representation in a plural society

In plural societies people mix but do not combine. Each group holds by its own religion, its own culture and language, its own ideals and ways. As individuals, they meet, but only in the market place, in buying and selling. This is a plural society, with different sections of the community living side by side, but separately, within the same political unit. Even in the economic sphere, there is a division of labor along racial lines.[14]

This characterization fits Kuwait's pre-oil society well. Kuwait was in essence a plural society, where migrants settled together on the basis of their ethnic, religious and kinship affiliations. The different communities socialized in distinct neighbourhoods and networks. In this society, there is no holistic common, but a stratified coexistence between different groups, with the marketplace being the common denominator. As in a plural society, there is no real integration between the different communities and a division of labour stratified along communal lines. Although no full integration happened, the different communities in Kuwait were in continuous interaction with each other in the marketplace. Related to this concept of pluralism is the notion of pluralism as it existed in the Ottoman Empire, where rulers seldom tried to homogenize the population, with a coexistence of autonomous agglomerates and their interaction in the marketplace.[15] In Kuwait, as demonstrated, the role of the Al-Sabah before the seizure of power by Mubarak al-Sabah was essentially limited to policing the city-state, supervising early juridical mechanisms and maintaining peace between the populace.[16]

The old neighbourhoods of Kuwait city: Al-Sharq, Al-Qibla and Al-Murqab

Old urban Kuwait, Kuwait within the confines of the wall (*sur*) that was constructed after the Battle of Jahra, was in essence a small town that served as an entrepot for regional commerce and trade. The city was divided in four official neighbourhoods, each sub-divided in neighbourhood blocs (*firij*), often named after prominent notables of the neighbourhood. These four main neighbourhoods were Al-Qibla, Al-Sharq, Al-Murqab and Al-Wasat, and the smaller neighbourhoods were the Al-'Awazem and the Al-Rashaida, named after the two tribes living within the vicinities of the town.[17] Of these neighbourhoods, Al-Qibla and Al-Sharq were the biggest in size, hosting the houses of members of the mercantile elite, Sunna and Shi'a.

Al-Qibla (called 'Al-Jibla') was the most western part of the City, surrounding the seaside. Living next to the seaside was a sign of distinction, as this is the part where the most prominent merchant families lived, close to their boats and their work. It is also in this neighbourhood where most of the members of the Sunni Najdi merchant aristocracy lived: Najdis, Basrawis and Zubairis. Among the farij of Al-Qibla, from the western part until the eastern part, one finds Farij Bin Uthman (named after the Uthman family), Farij al-Saqqar (named after the Al-Saqqar family), Farij al-Baddar (named after the Al-Baddar family), Farij al-Saud (named after Shaykh Saud al-Sabah) and Farij Ghoneim (named after the Ghoneim family).

Al-Qibla was named Al-Qibla, diminutive of 'Qabila' (tribe), because of the fact that most of its members were descendants from families who migrated from western desert regions to Kuwait since the early eighteenth century from Najd and from other desert regions. This area hosted members of the merchant aristocracy and some families who would become prominent in the literature and academic field, such as the Al-Naqeeb, the Al-Badr, and Shaykh al-Khalaf. One of the most influential merchants of the neighbourhood was Hamad Saqqar al-Ghanim, a dhow captain with strong regional trade networks in Iraq, Yemen and India. Another influential family then were the Ghoneim, who were the trustees for the Al-Sabah. The Ahmadi School was located in Al-Qibla, the first school built in Kuwait by the merchant elite.

On the eastern side, there is the Al-Sharq neighbourhood, which hosted the Al-Sabah, as well as a number of prominent merchant families. This was an ethnically and religiously mixed neighbourhood, where Shi'a families, mostly from Persian origin, and a number of Sunni families lived. The latter were the ones who had emigrated with the Al-Sabah at the early *eighteenth* century from Southern Najd, to Qatar and later to Kuwait. Mostly from the Bani Utub, these families also prided themselves in sharing kinship links with the Al-Sabah. It is from this nucleus of families, from where the early power-sharing agreement started. One can think of the Al-Nusf (from the Al-Jalahima), the Al-Rumi as well as the house of Saqqar al-Ghanim.

The rest of Al-Sharq was mostly composed of Persian families ('Ajam) from both Sunni and Shi'a sects. The most prominent of the Shi'a merchant families, such as the Ma'rafi, Behbahani, Abl, lived in close proximity to the estates of the Al-Sabah. The old husayniyya of the Ma'rafi family – still present in Al-Sharq which has now been transformed into a commercial area – was at a walking distance of the Bayan castle of the Al-Sabah. This itself was a sign of the political proximity of the Shi'a families towards the ruling family.

This spatial proximity of the ruling family to a non-core elite was not specific to Kuwait. It was commonplace for Gulf rulers to live apart from the merchant elites (with whom they often shared kinship ties) while siding with forces that could not challenge their tribal elite status, such as the non-Arab merchants.[18] In Dubai, for example, the Al-Maktoum lived on the south side of the creek, together with the Persian merchants, whereas most of the Bani Yas merchants lived in Deira on the north side. And in Oman and Dubai, the merchant class was composed of a large section of non-Arabs – Indians and Persians – who were close to the rulers, often causing the resentment of the Arab pearl merchants, especially at moments when their commerce declined.

Next to Shi'a families from Persian origin, a minority of Arab Shi'a from Bahrain and Al-Hasa also settled in Al-Sharq. The Baharna came later than other Shi'a elite families. The latter, the Hasawi families, such as Al-Arbasch, Al-Sayegh and Al-Qattan, developed a particularly strong group identity, based upon their common belonging to a minority branch within Twelver Shi'ism: shaykhism, following the teachings of Ahmad al-Ihsa'i (1753–1826).

Apart from an elite of merchant families, the majority of the Persian families was however composed of manual workers. The 'Ajam were active in professions that demanded physical strength, for which they were known, and engaged in activities such as water carriers, '*kandari*', as well as in the crafts, as shop holders, cloth makers and ironsmiths; activities that were considered lower-ranked by the *hadar* aristocracy. The 'Ajam constituted the pinnacle of such laborious occupations.[19] As such, former parliamentarian Dr Jowhar recalls: 'The Shi'a controlled the main professions (hirf) and industries. Their names are often derived from their profession, the tailor (khiyat), the baker (khubaz), the fisher (siyadh), the ship maker (qallaf), the goldsmith (sayegh) etc. You could say that the Shi'a were the very nail of the economy.'[20] A similar narrative is presented by Dr. Al-Khalidi: 'The 'Ajam stayed in Al-Sharq throughout the year, because of their professions in crafts. For this reason, they were more settled in the town than the Sunni families in Qibla who were often at sea and, consequently, they were closer to the ruler.'[21]

Next to the Shi'a Persian families, there were a number of Sunni Persian families living in Sharq, who emigrated to Kuwait in different migration waves from the early nineteenth century onwards. These migrations were influenced by harsh climatic conditions, with severe droughts forcing hundreds of families from the coastal regions of Iran to migrate to the Arabian shore. Later on, the stringent reforms imposed by the Pahlavi dynasty (1926) – land reforms, military services – led to a migration of Iranians from rural background to Arabia.[22]

The Sunni Persian families, such as the Al-Awadi, Al-Khanji, Al-Kandari, Al-Balushi and Al-Tabtaba'i, came from different parts of Iran, with their names often referring to their place of origin. It is important to note that until the early twentieth century, the main division in Kuwait's plural community was structured along ethnic and not sectarian lines, namely between the Arab and Persian communities. In the context of the rise of Arab nationalism emanating from Iraq, this cleavage would become more pronounced, as members of the Sunni merchant elite were heavily influenced by Arab nationalism and its obsession with Iranian expansionism. This diaspora lived together with the Shi'a families and had a clear, distinct identity from the Arab Sunni families. These families spoke Persian, until today are bilingual, and shared common cultural identities with their Shi'a neighbours.

Consequently, Al-Sharq was a mixed neighbourhood, hosting the ruling family, its castles, as well as a number of Bani Utub families, a majority of Sunni and Shi'a families from Iran, as well as a minority of Jewish families, who had migrated from Iraq. The neighbourhood also hosted the residence of the British political agent, as well as three of Kuwait's most influential Sunni pearl merchants whose power was expressed through their temporary migration from Kuwait protesting against Mubarak al-Sabah's tax increases. These were Hilal al-Mutrani, Shamlan bin Ali al-Saif and Ibrahim al-Mudhaf.[23]

Sometimes there is a third neighbourhood mentioned between Al-Sharq and Al-Qibla: Al-Wasat, composed of solely some streets. However, Al-Wasat is considered to have been part of Al-Sharq: it is the neighbourhood where the castle of the Al-Sabah, the old Souq, the customs district (Jumrak), the steam boats district, the Literature Association (AL-Nadi Al-Adabi), Safat market, the Mubarakiya School (Kuwait's first school, named after Mubarak al-Sabah and funded by the merchant families), as well as the houses of prominent families, such as the Ma'rafi and the house of Shaykh Yusuf Ben Eissa al-Qina'i, the house of the Al-Adsani, Shahin al-Ghanim (Al-Zayid) were to be found. Yusuf Ben Eissa al-Qina'i became the first head of Mubarakiya School.[24]

The Qina'at families are a clan of Sunni families who migrated from northern parts of Iraq by the start of the nineteenth century and developed a strong group identity in Kuwait as members of a merchant aristocracy. Although from northern Iraq, they claim descent from the Suhul tribe from the Al-Washm area in Najd, historically known for its salt deposits.[25] However, given their fair complexion and European appearance, they have probably mixed during their residence in Iraq with Iraqi women. At present there are more members of the Qina'at living in Kuwait than in Saudi Arabia, their place of origin, and some are said to have emigrated with the Bani Utub to Kuwait. They constitute one of the largest elite family groups in Kuwait (next to the Sunni merchant aristocracy, the Shi'a merchant families and the Al-Sabah) – around 10,000 members at present – and until today tend to marry exclusively from within the family. The Qina'at families (like the Al-Sultan, Al-Saleh, Al-Issa, Al-Badr, Al-Mutawa') have risen to prominence in Kuwait, following the adoption by the Al-Sabah of the orphan, Yusuf Bin Issa, who was later appointed in the Legislative Council and defended the Emir against the opposition from the Sunni merchant aristocracy. The latter on its part considers the Qina'at as nouveaux riches who would have used the closeness of Yusuf Bin Issa to make inroads in commerce and finance. Although both were used as loyal counterforces against opposition emerging from the Sunni aristocracy, the Qina'at are considered as one of the most anti-Shi'a groups, because it competes (as a lower-ranked elite clan) with the Shi'a for the obtaining of favours from the Al-Sabah. However, it has never been capable of challenging the Sunni and Shi'a merchant groups.[26]

Then there was also Al-Murqab, the neighbourhood situated south of Al-Sharq and Al-Qibla, further from the seaside. It derives its name – monitor – from the fact that the ground was higher in this area and the tribal guards (*fidawiyyin*) of the Al-Sabah were stationed here in order to overlook the in- and outflow of people from outside the wall and to watch over possible dangers or attacks from outside forces.[27] Murqab, after the construction of the Wall, also hosted the houses and farij of a number of prominent families, such as farij Bin Humud al-Shay'a (from Najd), farij al-Hamad and farij Masil. Some of these families arrived relatively late to Kuwait, by the start of the twentieth century, such as the Al-Shay'a. Close to the Farij of the Al-Shay'a family was the house of the Al-Wazzan (Sunni branch).[28] It seemed to have been a neighbourhood without a strong identity, mostly inhabited by families after the construction of the wall, when it was considered safe.

The 'Awazem and Rashaida areas of old Kuwait

As already mentioned, the 'Awazem and the Rashaida were the two tribes considered as original (*asli*) in Kuwait, as most of their members were living in the close vicinities of the town (referring to the area protected by the 1920 wall). They lived in the peripheral settlements where semi-nomadic tribes lived, such as Salmiyya, Hawalli, Fintas, Fahahil and the oasis of Al-Jahra: areas that were mostly occupied by these two tribes, but also in lesser numbers by other *'arib dar*, such as the Dabbus in Fahahil.[29] Because they interacted with the hadar in the marketplace selling their products they were more familiar to them than to the Bedouin caravan carriers around the *sahat al-sufa* (the caravan station in *Al-Murqab*). These *'arib dar* were granted first-class citizenship on the basis of their historical presence in the vicinities of the old town.[30]

As for the 'Awazem, they used to live on 'Ajman land, being the serf tribe of the 'Ajman and, as such, landless and non-noble. The Rashaida were a sheep-herding serf tribe of the Mutran and non-noble. Semi-nomadic, during the winter months they followed the rains to allow their flocks to graze on cultivable lands and traded the products of their agriculture with urban Kuwaitis for supplies. During the rainless summer months when grazing was quickly exhausted, they took part in fishing and pearl-diving activities just like many urban Kuwaitis.[31]

The 'Awazem have a long presence in Kuwait, some of them probably as long as the Al-Sabah. They were known for their semi-nomadic activities in Kuwait, such as catching fish in then far southern coasts around Salmiyya and Hawali. On the eve of the Second World War, most of them were sedentary.[32] "This also explains why the Al-Sabah gave them land, the price of which skyrocketed with the later expansion of urbanization."[33] Their early semi-settlement in and around the old city explains why various streets and neighbourhoods were named after members of the Al-'Awazem.[34] An example is the *Al-'Awazem street* in Salmiyya, referring to the fact that the 'Awazem were the first to settle in Salmiyya during the dry season where they were active in fishing, or the *Musa'ad al-Azmi street* in Salmiyya, named after shaykh *Musa'ad al-Azmi*, the first Kuwaiti doctor in Kuwait. Other examples are the *farij al-'Awazem*, located in the north of Al-Murqab and stretching as far as the old souq of Kuwait (*suq al-tujar*). And *Hawali*, the name given to what is today mostly a crowded district with technology shops was named after one of the first residents of the place, a certain Hawali (from the a Al-'Awazem), who planted vegetables in the area. Also, it is said that the Al-'Awazem were the ones who lived in the area where the first oil well was discovered, namely in *Jaydan*, close to Ahmadi in the south. Jaydan contained numerous water wells and it was here near a tree that oil was first discovered by the Kuwait Oil Company (around 1937).[35] Another well-known camping ground of the Al-'Awazem was Wafrah, south of Kuwait, known for its numerous deep wells. They also engaged in grazing and herding activities during other seasons and their areas stretched from the far south to the northwest, from Jahra until the Batin plain, where they grazed together with the Dhafir on Iraqi lands and in the neutral zone between Kuwait and Iraq.[36]

While present in large numbers in the vicinities of Kuwait, branches of the 'Awazem were also concentrated in the eastern part of Saudi Arabia; around Al-Nu'ayriya, in the vicinities of lands of the 'Ajman, Mutran, Bani Khalid and Bani Hajir.[37] Being part of the 'high politics' of the time, tribes were used in the expansionary power strategies of local rulers in Arabia, through the usual 'carrot-and-stick policies', aimed at fragmenting and co-opting tribes. Given the autonomous local power of the tribes in the pre-oil era, the latter could also, themselves, play upon rivalries between ruling families and regional forces, for their own benefit; with alliance-making between tribes and rulers being the consequence of a rather dynamic power-play.

It is in this context that the 'Awazem have been both a strategic asset in regional power strategies and a source of tension, at times, between the Al-Saud and the Al-Sabah. Although historically considered a tribe of Kuwait with a long-dated allegiance to the Al-Sabah, the tribe that also had a presence in Arabia served at occasions as a loyal force to the Al-Saud against the radicalization of the *Ikhwan*. The latter were trained by the Al-Saud as tribal recruits fighting non-Wahhabi infidels in a campaign of territorial maximization. Yet, zealots in search of further territorial expansion turned themselves against their Wahhabi master, who feared an open conflict with the British in the case of conquests of areas under British protection. A series of wars started in 1927, led by the Mutran and 'Ajman, resulting in raids into parts of Transjordan, Mandatory Iraq and Kuwait.

By freeing the 'Awazem from their serfdom to the 'Ajman, thus dispensed from paying the '*khawa*' to their old 'Ajman lords, the 'Awazem supported the Al-Saud *manu militari* in battles against the Ikhwan. It was hence difficult for Faisal al-Duwish – reputed Ikhwan leader who attacked Kuwait – to win the Al-'Awazem to his side. The 'Awazem fought along Al-Saud and suffered a tremendous defeat against the Ikhwan at the Battle of Injair (1929), upon which its leaders who were still in Saudi Arabia moved to the north and asked for protection from the Kuwaiti shaykh and were granted so. The Saudi co-optation of the 'Awazem and the Al-Saud's decision to tax the tribe in 1917 were considered as hostile moves by Shaykh Salim, who responded by attracting the 'Ajman and Shammar living in Wahhabi land. These desert tribes moved en masse to Kuwait and developed strong relations with the Al-Sabah.[38] Eventually an agreement was reached and the 'Awazem renewed their old allegiance to the Al-Sabah. The question of the 'Ajman remained a burning one in relations between the Al-Sabah and the Al-Saud and was only settled in 1922 with the signature of the Protocol of 'Uqair, according to which Shaykh Ahmad al-Jabir would lose one-third of his territory to the Al-Saud, although it was only in 1966 that borders between Iraq, Saudi Arabia and Kuwait would definitely be fixed.[39]

Politically the Al-'Awazem were considered a loyal and apolitical force supporting the Al-Sabah. They fought wars for the rulers and functioned as personal guardians (*fidawiyyin*), notably under Mubarak al-Sabah's reign. The latter had close ties to the desert tribes and relied upon them in his power ambitions, within the family and towards his subjects. Until the present day, as seen by the online blogs of the tribe, the Al-'Awazem take pride in their participation in battles for the Al-Sabah.[40]

Today, the 'Awazem are the biggest tribe in Kuwait, constituting around 142,000 persons and around 32,325 registered voters, making them the strongest tribal voting bloc in Kuwait.[41] They live mostly in the areas of the fifth electoral district (where they account for around 20 per cent of the voters) and, to a lesser extent, the first district.[42] The fifth district, the 'wild south' of Kuwait's political districts, given the omnipresence of tribal politics (as the fourth) is the area south of Kuwait city, where historically the semi-nomadic tribes lived, such as Fahahil, Al-Ahmadi,

Fintas, Mahbula and Al-Riqqa. The first district – which today comprises the area of the old town *intra-muros* – has the highest number of Shi'a voters, although the Al-'Awazem, concentrated in the area around Salmiyya, also have a substantial voting weight here.[43]

Together with the Al-'Awazem, the Rashaida formed the core of tribes present in the vicinities of Kuwait, before the Battle of Jahra. The Rashaida, a sheep rearing tribe, were traditionally grazing on the land of the Mutran. Being non-sharif and a serf tribe of the Mutran, the Rashaida could only marry from non-sharif tribes. The Rashaida were semi-nomadic and in the winter, they occupied the area stretching from *Safwan* in the north of Kuwait until far southern Saudi territory, such as *Tawal al-Mutran*, *Jariya Sifli, Jariya Iliya* and *Wabrah*.[44] Already in the early days of the Al-Sabah, the Rashaida were considered to be nominally under the latter's control.[45]

Unlike the 'Awazem who displayed overt animosity towards their masters, the 'Ajman, the Rashaida entertained good relations with the Mutran and prided themselves of their Mutran connection. During the Ikhwan rebellion, half of the Rashaida threw in their lot with the Mutran, fighting along their side around Najd, although they returned back to their old allegiance to Kuwait after the fighting. The proximity of the Al-Rashaida to the Al-Sabah was reflected in the fact that the Rashaida were among the prime recruits of the loyal guards of the Al-Sabah. The Rashaida, along with a few recruits from the 'Ajman, are said to have been among the *fidawiyyin* helping Mubarak in the killing of his half-brothers.[46] And during the *Majlis* events of 1938, the Rashaida were recruited as prime military supporters of Shaykh Ahmad al-Jabir against the opposition from merchants and Arab nationalists.

The transnational ties of these tribes can serve as powerful vehicles for organized groups, such as Islamist movements. Modern means of communication (such as the internet) have moreover facilitated interactions between distant tribesmen, forging transnational ties that can serve domestic political purposes. The Rashaida have branches in Kuwait, Libya, Morocco and Sudan and traditionally four of its main lineages (*fukuhd*) were present in the old town as well as its paramount chief, Abdallah bin Mutlaq al-Musailam.[47] Kuwait is thus a strong point of reference for the tribesmen. A salient example here is the creation of the Abbas League (*Rabita Abbas*) in 2010, referring to the Abbas tribe, considered the founding tribe of the Rashaida.[48] The creation of the League was prompted by a rise in tensions between the Rashaida in Sudan and the Sudanese government, after the latter's confiscation of 400 vehicles the Rashaida had received from the Kuwaiti government in thanks for their political support for Kuwait during the Iraqi invasion. Kinship ties with prominent Rashaida figures and MPs in Kuwait, such as Mubarak al-Duwaila, led the latter to organize a collective initiative and mediate in the conflict between the Al-Rashaida and the Sudanese government, leading to a brokerage of a peace deal in 2010.[49] The main brokers were the Kuwaiti presidents of the Abbas League, Mubarak al-Duwaila and Faiz al-Boghaili. Following a conflict between the presidents, Al-Boghaili left the group and Al-Duwaila remained. The attempt to unify the Al-Rashaida under one regional umbrella – led by influential MB leader Al-Duwaila – might also serve the interest of the MB, to rally the Rashaida of neighbouring Sudan around the Egyptians MB. During

Muhammad Morsi's short-lived reign, Mubarak al-Duwaila announced in the media that Morsi descended from the Al-Rashaida, reinforcing the hypothesis of attempts to create tribal support for the MB on a regional level and the likelihood that the Abbas League served broader purposes than purely socio-cultural ones.[50]

Today, the Rashaida are mostly concentrated in the fourth constituency, where they together with the Mutran tend to dominate the political scene, although it is also considered the fiefdom of northern tribes, such as the 'Aneza, Shammar and Dhafir. In the fourth constituency, the Rashaida represent – after the Al-Mutran – the second strongest bloc, with around 13,000 voters out of a total of 103,280 voters in 2014 (approximately 12.6 per cent of the voters). More than 75 per cent of the Rashaida are concentrated in Al-Farwaniyya district and smaller numbers in the districts of Al-Umariyya and Al-Jahra, Andalus, Sulaibikhat and Julib al-Shuyukh.[51] Historically, those of the Rashaida who were living *intra muros* had a farij in Al-Murqab: farij al-Rashaida. Al-Murqab also hosted the farjan of other tribes and tribesmen, like the farij al-Mutran, the Al-'Awazem and the Hasawiyya, referring to the Arab Shi'a families from Al-Ihsa, the eastern province of Saudi Arabia.[52] Rashaida families such as Al-Duwaila, Al-Qulub and Al-Baydan used to live here and later moved en masse to Al-Farwaniyya, where most of the Rashaida live today.

A short note on the desert tribes

It makes sense to pause here briefly and look at the role played by the outlying desert tribes in the politics of Kuwait's rulers. These tribes, such as the 'Ajman and Mutran, did not live in the area of Kuwait and only some of their members had settled in the old town. Others engaged in agricultural activities along the palm trees of the oases. Jahra was known to have been the summer quarters of the 'Ajman.[53] Yet, these tribes and their leaders lived in the desert and did not interact with the urban population of Kuwait in a similarly close way as did the 'Awazem and the Rashaida. The 'Ajman lived in the area of Al-Hasa while the Mutran lived in a larger area stretching from Al-Qasim in the heartland of Saudi Arabia to Kuwait's southern borders.[54] The tribes were engaged in tribal wars against each other and, while allying separately with Kuwait's rulers, never did so together.

Officially the 'Ajman and Mutran were not present in pre-oil Kuwait and were only naturalized en masse as Saudi tribes between 1965 and 1981. Most of them were trusted and noble tribes, whose leaders were still in Saudi Arabia, as was the case for the 'Ajman, the Mutran and the Aneza. As life conditions in Kuwait were better than that in neighbouring countries in the 1950s, these tribesmen came to Kuwait to make a living, especially in the nascent oil industry in Ahmadi.[55] They came to live in the outskirts of Kuwait, close to the other badu; the fourth and fifth electoral districts, outside the wall (sur) of the old city that so prominently figures in Kuwait's citizenship myth. The 'Ajman are largely concentrated in the fifth constituency, together with the 'Awazem. The Mutran can be found in the fourth constituency, which is also the stronghold of the northern tribes – 'Aneza, Shammar and Dhafir – as well as of the Rashaida.[56]

Changes in the authority system: Mubarak al-Sabah, colonialism and alliances with *non-core* elites

Introduction

Until the usurpation of power by Mubarak al-Sabah in 1896, the role of the Al-Sabah shaykh was one of primus inter pares. This consisted in policing the city-state and maintaining peace among its population, while the real responsibility and power lay in the hands of the merchants who entrusted the Al-Sabah with issues of daily governance, operating largely a 'laissez-faire' policy overseeing the interaction of different diaspora communities in the market place. This was typical of plural societies.

The consociational form of governance that was so typical of Kuwait – due to its powerful merchant class – was broken with the usurpation of power by Mubarak al-Sabah. The latter broke the implicit power-sharing arrangement with the Najdi aristocracy by killing his half-brothers. To consolidate his power, new allies were sought, both regionally and domestically. Consequently, Mubarak created 'politics' by influencing the distribution of power and resources and thus relations between sub-communities in the old city. It is under Mubarak's reign that the foundations were laid into what was to become a Sunni mercantile opposition. It is also since Mubarak's reign that succession rules were set, with the development of the implicit succession custom of rotating power between the lines of two of his seven sons: Jabir and Salim. Later this would be further institutionalized as an outcome of the 1938 rebellion that created power-sharing mechanisms within the Al-Sabah and dynastic rule.

This chapter will focus on the reign of Mubarak al-Sabah, as it consolidated the authority system of the Al-Sabah prior to the discovery of oil. Under his reign, alliances were struck with non-core elites. These alliances laid the basis of new ruler–ruled relations and would be perpetuated over time favoured by the presence of oil. The period of Mubarak's reign has been overlooked in existing literature on Kuwait as a crucial period for understanding the crystallization of merchant opposition as well as the alliances with both the Shi'a and the Bedouins. This search for new allies can only be understood as part of the great power rivalry in the nineteenth century and British encroachment in the Gulf, which altered existing power dynamics and consolidated the power of allied ruling shaykhs at the cost of the local elites as autonomous capitalist forces.

Mubarak al-Sabah: Amir al-Badia

Mubarak al-Sabah (r. 1896–1915) is considered as the founder of modern Kuwait. It is since his reign that succession rules were set and later codified in the 1962 Constitution. After his death, the succession custom developed to rotate power between the lines of two of his seven sons: Jabir and Salim. Although not codified in the Constitution – which stipulates that power falls in the hands of the descendants of Mubarak – this custom was more or less respected until the death of Emir Jabir al-Ahmad in 2006. It is ever since that the Al-Jabir branch has dominated high executive positions, opening up a Pandora's Box for in-palace competition between competing branches and a new generation of princes.

Mubarak al-Sabah is a controversial figure. Europeans and Turks sometimes described him as 'an immensely sly fox', a local ruler par excellence who was able to use great power competition to his benefit. Many different interpretations exist as to the context in which Mubarak rose to power, the reasons behind his coup d'état and the nature of his reign. Social science work on Kuwait generally refers to Mubarak's reign as marking the end of the republican spirit of Kuwait, as Mubarak broke the power-sharing agreement over succession.[1] Contemporary historians tend to focus on the international context preceding Mubarak's rise to power and converge in their account of Mubarak being a pragmatic Arabian leader – as there were many – who exploited great power rivalry and the decay of the Ottoman Empire to his advantage.[2] Then there are also the accounts of local scholars who were present in Kuwait during or short after Mubarak's reign, such as the Kuwaiti historian Al-Rushaid (born in 1887) – who was a court historian for the Al-Sabah – and Shaykh Yusuf al-Qina'i (born in 1879). There is also a major volume of Kuwait's political history, written by Hussayn Khalaf Khaz'al, son of Shaykh Khaz'al of Muhammara, who gives a more positive image of Mubarak, given his father's proximity to the Kuwaiti ruler, but whose work is limited by the absence of a critical evaluation of his sources and a pro-Mubarak bias. While I will not recount these different interpretations here, I will try to shed new light on what I consider the fundamental rationale behind Mubarak's coup and the nature of his reign, which itself will shed light on the development of regime–society relations in Kuwait's post-oil political compact.

Regional context of Mubarak's rise: great power rivalry and small Arab leaders

Mubarak's rise to power was inextricably linked to the regional dynamic of British–Ottoman rivalry. Britain had been the dominant foreign power in the southern Gulf since the early seventeenth century. At first, British interest in the lower Gulf lay in the search of export markets for British goods as a consequence of growing commercial activities in India. A main aspect of its Trucial System was also to reduce piracy of British ships entering the Gulf and weapon smuggling activities (organized mostly from Kuwait). It was a rather low-cost system, in which Arab rulers would maintain order and regulate maritime affairs in return for British protection.[3] This was a very distanced one, as there was no British military presence on the Arab side of the Gulf.

By the end of the nineteenth century, British treaties included every major shaykh south of Kuwait, with the British Political Resident Office stationed in Bushehr, on the Persian shore of the Gulf. From here, the British organized relations with the entire Gulf region. Local rulers also signed Exclusive Agreements with the British. Bahrain and the Trucial states were the first to do so (1890 and 1892 respectively) and Kuwait followed in 1896.[4] The British had also developed a close cooperation with tribal leaders in southwest Iran, the most important of whom was the Arab Shi'a Shaykh, Khaz'al of Muhammara, a close friend and ally of Mubarak al-Sabah.

Khaz'al was an Arab Shi'a, belonging to the powerful Bani Ka'ab tribe which originated from the area which is present-day Kuwait. His ascendency in 1897 strikingly resembled the case of Mubarak al-Sabah, happening around the same time. Like Mubarak, Khaz'al seized power by killing his brother Maz'al by ordering his guards to kill him in 1897, upon which he proclaimed himself leader of the tribe as well as of the whole province. Like Mubarak, Khaz'al claimed that his brother had tried to concentrate power in his hands, by excluding him and his brother Muhammad from their father's estates and money.[5] Although there is no firm proof to claim British involvement in the crime, it is likely that the British had supported him as a crony to further their strategic interests in southwest Iran and counterbalance Russian influence. Two years before Maz'al's assassination, Khaz'al had told the British consul in Muhammara that he would 'assist British trade, would he ever be in a position to do so'.[6] Both Mubarak and Khaz'al feared technological developments that might endanger their position: the Ottoman–German railway plans for Mubarak and the Dutch–Persian plans to canalize the Karun river which was a tributary of the Shatt al-'Arab for Khaz'al. More importantly, like Mubarak, Khaz'al shared a similar predicament of the need to flirt and ally with foreign powers in order to avoid absorption by a great Islamic power, the Ottomans for Mubarak and the Persian Qajar dynasty for Khaz'al. Khaz'al, however, was much richer than Mubarak and owned large parcels of land in Iraq on the bank of the Shatt al-Arab as well as most of the land in Khuzestan and, consequently, had strong a network of contacts on the Arab side of the Gulf.[7] Khaz'al had the support of various Arab chiefs who considered him as a pillar to uproot the Persian Empire from the inside. Yet, while Mubarak was able to successfully lobby for a written protection agreement with the British, Khaz'al never succeeded – maybe due to his distrust of the British – which would eventually lead his province to lose its autonomy and be integrated in the Persian sphere of influence. Kuwait was spared from a similar destiny, although it would later in history feel the direct threat of absorption by Qasim's and later Saddam's Iraq, basing its claim upon the position of Kuwait as a *kaza* of Basra.

Khaz'al had many Arab allies in neighbouring Ottoman lands who used his territory as a base of operations as it was outside the Ottoman authority, allowing these leaders, hostile to Ottoman encroachment, to send secret telegrams from Muhammara. Frequent visits were made to Muhammara by these local Arab shaykhs, of whom Mubarak was one. These policies of alliance-building allowed Khaz'al to acquire support in case of conflict with the Shah. In the 1890s, Mubarak al-Sabah, Khaz'al and Sayyid Talab al-Naqeeb of Basra allied and joined the Arab calls to reform Ottoman power over its provinces and reached out to the British, fearing increased Ottoman power.[8] It is important to understand that the main fracture line in politics by then was between Persians and Arabs, and Shaykh Khaz'al – although being Shi'a – was part of the Arab local leaders searching for greater independence from the Ottomans, which drove them into the British sphere of influence. Arab local leaders used Khaz'al not only as a means to escape Ottoman oversight over their communications by going to Muhammara, but also as an Arab leverage towards the Persian Empire.

It is in this broader context that we can understand Mubarak's rapprochement with desert tribes as well as with the Shi'a; as part of his internal alliance-building, Shi'a merchants who had close relations to Khaz'al and Muhammara, where they owned date plantations, were instrumental in reinforcing relations between the two shaykhs. Also, the latter were crucial in signing the British protection agreement in 1899. As for the desert tribes, regional power dynamics explain Mubarak's alliance-building with the 'Ajman and the Mutran, supported by the British. In the following, I will take a closer look at Mubarak's reign and his alliance-building with the non-core elites.

Muhammad al-Sabah (r. 1892–6): usurpation of the family's budget and the alienation of the desert

Family coups were not uncommon in the Arabian Gulf for centuries. Mubarak's fratricide was thus less dramatic than is sometimes portrayed in historical accounts. Some have interpreted it as a revenge of Mubarak for being sent away by his brother, Muhammed, to the desert with the perilous task of policing the tribes. This is the account favoured by Dickson – political resident in Kuwait between 1929 and 1935 – who implies that managing tribal politics was considered to be of less political value. It should be noted that Dickson, despite his fine knowledge of Kuwaiti politics, was close to the successors of Mubarak and his account is influenced by a pro-Mubarak stance.

More local sources tend to focus on other factors which would have caused Mubarak's anger towards his brothers, Muhammed and Jarrah. One important factor seems to relate to a family dispute about the use of the family's resources. While the reign of Mubarak al-Sabah has been described as autocratic, these accounts underline attempts by Mubarak's brother Muhammad al-Sabah to concentrate the family's resources into his hands and the small clique of people around him: his sons, his brother Jarrah and Yusuf al-Ibrahim. The latter was a transnational Kuwaiti Najdi merchant who belonged to a wealthy family of tribal descent (higher than the Al-Sabah) with considerable business interests in Bombay.[9] Al-Ibrahim owned numerous estates on the lower Shatt al-Arab, as did the Al-Sabah, and was also known for his role in illicit arms trade in Arabia.[10] Intermarriage between Muhammed, Jarrah and the Ibrahim family reinforced the clannish nature of the three and demonstrated Al-Ibrahim's proximity to the rulers. Both Muhammed and Jarrah married wives from the Al-Ibrahim family.[11] Muhammed had deposited the Al-Sabah's family fortune in a bank in Bombay in his name and those of his sons exclusively. This provoked great concern from some members of the family and especially from those who felt they were already marginalized in their share of the family's wealth. This was the case of Mubarak, who was in desperate need of funds to finance the costly 'tribal portfolio' which he managed. Kuwaiti-born historian Al-Rushaid refers to various incidents in which Mubarak was desperately in need of funds and his brothers and Yusuf were unwilling to pay him. It is to be noted that Al-Rushaid gives a positive image of Mubarak, who he considers to be the man who placed Kuwait on the map. Yet, the French consul and the British Basra Diary's accounts also confirm that money was the crux of the dispute, giving credibility to Al-Rushaid's narrative. Al-Rushaid describes in detail the conflict between Mubarak and his brothers over money issues. Although he confirms Mubarak's taste for adventure, wars and power, he considers the exclusion and marginalization of Mubarak by his brothers and Yusuf al-Ibrahim as the main reason behind the fratricide. Relying upon the personal account of Sayyid Khalaf Pasha al-Naqeeb – one of the largest landowners in Iraq close to Mubarak – he describes the refusal of Mubarak's brothers to respond positively to his request of having an equal share in the family's wealth for his tribal portfolio. Mubarak, in need of funds, consequently resorted to some notables who demanded Muhammed to pay. However, Yusuf al-Ibrahim – having acquired a considerable role in political affairs – refused and another delegation was sent to Muhammed, who ordered this time to convene a meeting in Yusuf al-Ibrahim's house.[12] This time, Muhammed vouchsafed an account for Mubarak attributing his share of the date groves in Basra, but Mubarak was not satisfied and wanted Muhammed's oath on the offer. Muhammed only agreed upon this if Mubarak would sign a paper unconditionally accepting what Muhammed would offer, which Mubarak refused. Al-Rushaid then describes how Jarrah, adding insult to injury, convinced the Kuwaiti public not to lend money to Mubarak because he was broke.

Hence, more than a reaction to being relegated to tribal affairs, Mubarak's seizure of power seems to be a reaction to his personal financial difficulties and his exclusion from receiving an equal share of the family's resources. It represents a classical problem of dynastic monarchies which need to balance between different branches in order to maintain consensus within the family and thus guarantee dynastic rule.

Apart from this personal financial issue, Mubarak's fratricide also relates to a broader political phenomenon which was the marginalization of the desert under Muhammad's rule. Muhammad seems to have alienated the tribes and tribal interests by focusing too strongly on the sea forces and engaging too little in tribal politics, which were known to be costly and Muhammad might have preferred less costly policies in order to save money to bribe the Turks if necessary.[13] This marginalization of the desert was also the consequence of the flourishing pearl trade economy that developed in Kuwait by the end of the nineteenth century, expanding the wealth of Kuwait's largely merchant class.[14] Jaqueline Ismail notes the rise of the Sunni Najdi aristocracy since the second half of the eighteenth century as a consequence of the expansion of Kuwait's ports activities, following the Ottoman occupation of Basra (1775) and the transfer of caravan trade to Kuwait, but also following the influx of merchants to Kuwait from Najd and Al-Hasa fleeing Wahhabi expansionism.[15]

Whilst merchants gained a stronger grip on the town's affairs due to their rising wealth, the role of the desert was waning in high politics. The rise of Wahhabi power in Central Arabia gradually weakened the Al-Sabah's authority over distant desert tribes, while relations with the Ottomans strengthened at the start of the nineteenth century.[16] Also, the Al-Sabah's traditional role as policers of a tribal hinterland and the caravan routes from Najd, Hasa and Basra was hampered as a consequence of the Wahhabi conquests disrupting caravan trade throughout the second half of the eighteenth century. Moreover, Muhammed al-Sabah was said to have alienated the tribes.[17]

Under Muhammed's reign, some merchants became so powerful that they had a stronger impact on decision-making by the ruler than other members of the Al-Sabah, who felt marginalized. A notable example is the aforementioned case of Yusuf al-Ibrahim, the wealthy Basrawi merchant, who became one of the main advisers of Shaykh Muhammad al-Sabah (r. 1892–6) and, although not sharing kinship ties with the Al-Sabah, married the daughters of the rulers. Hence, power-sharing gradually extended to wealthy circles of merchants from outside the initial Bani Utub federation, with merchants capable on account of their wealth, Sunnism and pure Arab descent of exerting considerable weight in governance.

Mubarak al-Sabah's alliance-building with desert tribes

Mubarak al-Sabah's deep ties to the desert stemmed from his role in conducting wars against external aggressors under the reign of his brother. Under Muhammed's short reign, Mubarak led several campaigns against local tribal raiders as well as for the Ottomans against foreign rulers. The 1890s were one of the most critical decades in Kuwait's history. This was the heyday of imperial expansionism with great powers avidly searching for 'vacant' territories. By the 1890s Ottoman pressure on Kuwait had increased, a reaction to British attempts to encroach on Ottoman territory. Kuwait's rulers who had until then been de facto independent without any taxes or custom duties – despite Kuwait's official status as a district of Basra province – started to fear Ottoman domination. By that time, the Ottoman Empire, now the 'Sick Man of Europe', was disintegrating. It had suffered great losses in the Balkans and feared British encroachment in the Arabian Gulf. Consequently, Ottoman Sultan Abdul Hamid II (r. 1876–1909) tried to reinforce his grip on a region over which the Ottomans already had weak power, especially in the restless Basra province, to which Kuwait belonged.

In this context of renewed Ottoman interest in the Arabian Gulf, various expeditions were undertaken. In 1871, rivalries within the Al-Saud and a disrupted caravan trade triggered an expedition to Al-Hasa supporting Emir Abdallah al-Saud against his brother. Following the conquest, the Ottomans created a provincial administration for Al-Hasa, with headquarters in Hofuf and district centres in Qatif and Mubarraz. Not much later, the ruler of Qatar, Shaykh Qasim al-Thani, who had earlier accepted the title of 'kaymakam', now decided to resign from this position, feeling threatened by the Ottoman presence. This prompted an Ottoman military expedition in 1894. The conflict was ended with Kuwaiti intermediation. Also, weak control over a restless Basra province had led to the appointment of a new Wali of Basra, Hamdi Pasha. As a naval officer, Pasha was thought to be a good candidate in the context of British–Ottoman rivalry over control of the Ottoman coasts of the Gulf.

It is in this context that Mubarak al-Sabah participated with tribal regiments in Ottoman expeditions, such as the ones in Al-Hasa and Qatar as well as during the troubles in Qatif (1878) and southern Iraq (1897). Although Kuwait played a peripheral part in intertribal disputes recurring in Najd and southern Iraq – *except in providing arms* – Kuwait suffered from disturbances and had to defend itself against threats from the Bani Rashid and factions of the Muntafiq, Thafir, Mutran and Bani Hajir.[18] Through his participation in these wars, Mubarak had built an extensive network of tribal contacts, which would make him a valuable resource for the British. The refuge of the Al-Saud in Kuwait, following the capture of Riyadh by the Al-Rashid (1887) had given further uplift to Mubarak's power within the tribes. With the Al-Rashid in power and the Al-Saud in exile, many of the tribes between Riyadh and Kuwait shifted their allegiance to Mubarak.[19] The defeat suffered in the Battle of Sarif (1902) against the Al-Rashid further motivated his alliance-forming with desert tribes. The Rashaida, 'Awazem, 'Ajman were among the main tribal recruits in these operations.

In the context of growing British interest in the region and the port-city of Kuwait, Mubarak became a lynchpin in the latter's attempt to fragment the power of the Emir of Ha'il (House of Al-Rashid).[20] British interest in Kuwait was also the consequence of increasing incidents of piracy, organized from Kuwait.[21] On various occasions, the British had approached Muhammad al-Sabah on the issue and proposed collaboration, but the latter had refused their proposals, supported by Yusuf al-Ibrahim.[22] When the British became aware of the dispute between Mubarak and his brother, they saw a chance and approached Mubarak and proposed cooperation.

In this context, the British would have advised Mubarak to widen his support base by reaching out to desert tribes that by then were still in friendly relations with the Al-Rashid, although not subject to them: the Mutran and the 'Ajman.[23] In later years, overt enmity broke out between these tribes (themselves engaged in feuds with each other) and Ibn Rashid, upon which the 'Ajman leader, Rakan Bin Huthlayn, settled in Kuwait and asked Mubarak for British protection. Also, fearing the power of the Ibn Rashid, Bin Huthlayn, would have advised Mubarak to kill his half-brothers to safeguard his rule.[24] This followed a particularly tense battle in 1892 in which Ibn Rashid, who had earlier sworn his vengeance against the 'Ajman, attacked in a place close to Kuwait's borders, allegedly saying to the 'Ajman leader 'See, I am capable of coming to you'.[25]

In order to consolidate these alliances, Mubarak married the women of these tribes. As such, he married two daughters of 'Ajman chiefs Falah Bin Rakan Bin Huthlayn (Lulu'a Muhammad al-Thaqib) and Daydan Bin Huthlayn. This already happened in the 1880s, years before the signature of the protection agreement with the British. Mubarak also married Hazi Bint Duwaish, daughter of Fahad al-Askah, shaykh of the Al-Mutran, as a clear sign of his open alliance with the Al-Mutran and opposition to the Al-Rashid, with whom the Mutran were perpetually at feud.[26] The motive for marrying a daughter of the shaykh of the Mutran was also probably to reconcile the perpetually feuding Mutran and the 'Ajman, to whom he was already related.[27] After Mubarak's death (1915), Al-Sabah rulers continued to marry women from the 'Ajman and Mutran tribes. Intermarriage with the Mutran occurred again under Shaykh Jabir al-Ahmad (r. 1977–2006), who is said to have married various Mutran women. These early intermarriages with the 'Ajman and Mutran have also had some impact on the process of the future naturalizations of tribesmen since the mid-1960s. Intermarriages with the Rashaida and the 'Awazem were excluded however because of their non-noble tribal status.

Mubarak's coup d'état and the crucial role played by tribal allies

The killing of Mubarak's half-brothers in 1896 has been subject of many different stories and interpretations, with contradictory information about who fired the shots.

Notwithstanding the difficulty of coming to a firm conclusion about the event, within Kuwaiti tribal circles there is a consensus about the role of certain tribesmen from the Rashaida and 'Ajman in helping Mubarak to kill his half-brothers.[28] These alliance-building strategies of Mubarak should be placed in the *double logic* of regional rivalry intersecting with internal ambitions of a ruler. Regionally, Mubarak was the lynchpin for the British in their attempts to fragment the power of Ha'il.[29] Domestically, these regional tribal alliances allowed Mubarak to strengthen his legitimacy outside the circles of the Najdi urban elite.

Strategic alliances with desert tribes were a means to confront the challenge of his enemy, the Al-Rashid Emirate in Ha'il. It was from the Rashaida and 'Ajman that Mubarak drew the followers to help him in killing his half-brothers. According to local historian Ahmad Bin Barjas, the 'Ajman chief, Rakan Bin Huthlayn, would have been the one advising Mubarak al-Sabah to kill his half-brothers and usurp power.[30] While the 'Ajman leader allegedly incited Mubarak, the support of the Rashaida, the original tribe of Kuwait of non-noble texture, was crucial. The latter were part of the personal guards of the Al-Sabah, exclusively recruited from the Bedouins. Among these retainers there were also personal slaves, identified by their dark skin. Their role literally consisted in "sacrificing themselves for their master", hired on the basis of their personal acquaintance with a shaykh and completely accountable for the latter's safety. "They did not have a specific task to perform, but had to obey their master's orders and follow him wherever he went".[31] These fidawiyya played a role too in policing the nearby desert and later the petroleum wells, often complementing the private patrols offered by oil companies. The gatekeepers policing the city wall (1920) constructed as a consequence of the Ikhwan threat were taken from the Emir's private retinue. Until the late 1960s, the fidawiyya would still exist in Kuwait and various Al-Sabah shaykhs were known for commanding groups of Bedouins who were entirely under their control. Beaugrand (2010) refers to the fidawiyya as the precursor of Kuwait's modern army. Until 1945, these armed Bedouins lived in tents, in designated areas, and later received a small salary in return for which they demonstrated impeccable loyalty to their shaykh-patron.[32] Today, the term *fidawi* is a rather negative term in the collective memory of the tribesmen, associated to a form of blind obedience to the ruler. This also explains why one of the first politicized tribesmen – Mubarak al-Duwaila of the Muslim Brotherhood – used the term '*mada ahd al-fidawiyya*' (no more fidawiyya) in 1989 in his lectures calling for the political emancipation of *badu* citizens.

While tribal elites such as the 'Ajman leader were crucial in the coup d'état, the role of the tribal retinue was part and parcel of their role as blindly obedient guards, executing the orders of their shaykh-patron. An interesting account here is given by Mubarak al-Duwaila, himself from the Rashaida:

> Some important events are to be told about the Rashaida. An important one was the seizing of power by Mubarak the Great. It is known that a number of important Rashaida people have participated in the killing of his brother. It is told that when Shaykh Mubarak asked one of the Rashaida to kill Muhammad and Jarrah, one of the Rashaida men would have told the shaykh: I am sorry, shaykh Mubarak I hold the door for you (to avoid people coming in), but you are going to kill your brother. I will not kill him, because if I would do that, they will kill me in the future.[33]

The crucial role of tribesmen in Mubarak's coup and the alliances struck under his reign with desert tribes have not been covered in existing literature. One should not forget that important parts of the region's history continue to be transmitted through an oral tradition and traditional Western historical scholarship has not readily adapted itself to this reality, with the risk of wrong interpretations of historical events.

The killing – a sensitive political event – is referred to briefly by local sources without elaborating on the details of the act and who was present. Al-Rushaid and Khaz'al give some details about the aftermath. Khaz'al gives a description of the event and places Mubarak's act in the context of the humiliation suffered from his brothers who had refused to grant him his part of their father's inheritance. He continues:

> In the early morning of 17 March 1896, Mubarak al-Sabah, accompanied by his sons, Salim and Jabir and three of their servants and guardians, headed to the house of the two shaykhs. It was night and silent outside … Shaykh Mubarak went to the room of his brother Muhammad and asked his son Jabir and a couple of guardians to go the palace of Shaykh Jarrah, while commanding his son Salim and the rest of the men to hold guard and prevent anyone from entering the courtyard and the doors of the house.

Khaz'al then describes Mubarak's entering of Muhammed's room, who was awakened from his sleep and killed by the shots fired by Mubarak. According to Khaz'al, the noise of the shot fired at Muhammad was the signal for the first son of Mubarak, Jabir, to kill his father's oldest brother, Jarrah, with the help of the guardians who accompanied Mubarak.[34]

Mubarak's coup was mostly contested by the clique directly concerned: Youssef al-Ibrahim and Muhammad and Jarrah's sons, who fled to Iraq searching for Ottoman support.[35] The gathering of notables would have accepted the act as a fait accompli and swore allegiance to Mubarak, who pledged his commitment to justice, reform and consultation. It is at this occasion that Mubarak would have told his sons Jabir and Salim that they would be his two preferred sons in succession affairs, upon which they also pledged full obedience to their father.[36] The search for Ottoman help by the deposed brothers reduced the internal support for Mubarak's opponents in Kuwait, as Mubarak's rule was considered a lesser evil than direct Ottoman rule.[37]

The signing of the British protection agreement (1899) and the role of Shi'a merchants

Although scarce information exists about relations between the Shi'a and Mubarak al-Sabah, the evidence from historical sources indicates that a group of Shi'a notables played an important role in forging relations between Mubarak al-Sabah and the ruler of Muhammara, Shaykh Khaz'al. While relations between Kuwait and Muhammara dated back to the 1840s, when Shaykh Sabah had sent military assistance there, relations intensified since the 1890s, under the influence of a group of 'Ajam merchants who had close relations to Khaz'al and Muhammara, where they owned date plantations.[38]

Moreover, Shi'a sources and interlocutors tend to refer to the role played by these notables in proposing to Shaykh Mubarak to sign a protection agreement with the British. As such, local historians Khaz'al and Abdelmohsin Jamal refer to some Shi'a merchants who were among the close advisors to Mubarak who advised the latter to search for British protection, in the context of dangers emanating from Yusuf al-Ibrahim and the sons of the murdered shaykhs who resided in Basra asking help from the Ottomans against Mubarak. According to these sources, a Shi'a merchant who was part of a wider group of merchants close to Mubarak, Ali Hussayn Abd Al, was the person counselled Mubarak to seek protection from the British to ensure the stability of the country.[39] Hussayn Abd Al, a wealthy merchant, had close relations with the British Political Resident in Bushehr as well with Shaykh Khaz'al, who would have proposed to Mubarak to convince the British authorities of the need for a protection agreement. Given his close ties to the other side of the Gulf, Abd Al was sent by Mubarak to Bushehr to meet the British resident there, who later on went to Kuwait and signed the protection agreement with Mubarak.

Another factor explaining the proximity of the Shi'a to Mubarak finds its origin in the role played by Shaykh Khaz'al, the Arab Shi'a leader of Muhammara, himself. Shaykh Khaz'al's fraternal ties to Mubarak – who granted him land in Dasman to build his castle – played in favour of the Shi'a. He played an important role in community affairs and as a sign of respect to him, the Shi'a named the first ever built husayniyya[40] in Kuwait after him: Khaz'aliyya (1918). Khaz'al had himself designated the personal secretary of Shaykh Mubarak, Molla Salih, an Iranian who would be instrumental in turning the 'Ajam into a powerful pro-Mubarak constituency. The latter basically represented the government of Kuwait for more than forty years as the Emir's personal secretary. The 'Mulla' system of administration was common at that time for (semi-) independent shaykhdoms, placing their trust in one person, often a foreigner, for the delegation of daily governance issues.[41] Molla Salih was much appreciated by the Iranian Shi'a, but despised by the Sunni merchant elite for his role in contributing to the breaking down of the consultative agreement under Mubarak's reign.[42] Molla Salih would also serve under the reign of Mubarak's successors and later his son, Abdallah. This lasted until the reign of Jabir al-Ahmad, who relied less on family members than on his private secretaries, Molla Salih and Izzat Beg Ja'afar. The latter was a Palestinian. During the majlis events in 1938 under Shaykh Ahmad al-Jabir, the Sunni elite demanded Salih's dismissal, threatening to stone him if he did not abdicate.[43]

Mubarak al-Sabah also reached out to the Shi'a merchants, for strategic reasons. Growing threats emanating from the Al-Rashid Empire and the terrible defeat of Mubarak against the latter in the Battle of Sarif (1901) increased his needs for resources to finance his expeditions. By that time, regional weapons trade was flourishing, with Kuwait as its centre.[44] Arms trade was exclusively in the hands of Shi'a merchants of Iranian descent, 'Ajam. This trade made a substantial contribution to Mubarak's income, which explains the proximity to the Shi'a merchants. Weapons arrived in Kuwait via Muscat, which was the hub through which arms from Europe penetrated the region. These merchants had close ties to the French and Belgian representatives in Oman, which allowed them to export arms to Kuwait, as French firms were prominent importers of British arms. The British basically turned a blind eye to this weapons trade, as long as it reached the government of India's local allies; such as Mubarak and the leader of Arab Khuzestan, Shaykh Khaz'al. The most prominent weapon traders were the merchants Najaf Bin Ghalib and Muhamed Rafi' Ma'rafi, who were the main contributors to Mubarak's treasury through their role in weapon smuggling and continued to be so until the early decades of the twentieth century.[45]

In sum, under Mubarak's reign, the Shi'a were thus a pro-shaykh constituency, profiting from his protection and their direct link to Molla Salih, chief secretary of Mubarak. Moreover, the Shi'a merchants provided the main source of income to Mubarak to finance his 'affairs of state'. Following Mubarak's death, the Shi'a would not always feel protected and at those moments resorted to the British, fearing the anti-Iranian sentiments arising from the Sunni Najdi elite.

The crystallization of alliances with non-core elites: the 1938 *Majlis* movement

Introduction

British encroachment on the region enabled local tribal shaykhs to consolidate their reign, often by violently sidelining their family members. Growing British influence also led to socio-economic changes that curtailed the autonomous power of the productive forces in the region: the Sunni Arab pearl merchants. Not only was their role in power-sharing strongly reduced as a consequence of ruling shaykhs' alliances with the British, but also were they at various occasions hurt by new economic developments. The development of the steam engine (1862) hurt them, as the sail boats, the *dhows*, could not compete with the steam boats that carried British goods flooding local markets, dislocating the regional carrying trade with a tribal hinterland as export markets for merchants' goods. The collapse of the pearling industry in 1929 brought a final blow to these merchants and it was only the discovery of oil that saved them from their economic downfall. Their socio-economic and tribal noble status made them receive the biggest share of the oil cake, being bought off as a class.

These changes coincided with the penetration of ideas of nationalism and ethnic identity in the region since the nineteenth century. Arab nationalism emanating from Ottoman provinces in Iraq, the Levant and Egypt proved a successful ideology for the disenfranchised merchant elites to preserve their power, threatened by authoritarian rulers and their external allies. This was not different from the embracement of nationalism by urban notables in the Levant or Palestine in this period.

As a consequence of socio-economic changes intersecting with identity fault lines, Mubarak's reign coincided with growing splits acted upon politically within Kuwait's population. The Arab merchants embraced nationalism and excluded the 'Ajam merchants from their oppositional politics. The latter resorted to the British and the Al-Sabah as pillars of support. Similar tensions between Arab and non-Arab merchants occurred in other shaykhdoms, such as Dubai, intersecting with different material interests. Also, in a context of elite opposition, rulers resorted largely to Bedouin allies as loyal forces to crackdown on nationalist agitation in Kuwait, but also in Dubai. By then, the Bedouins were a rather loyal constituency, depoliticized and obedient to their shaykh-patron. This would last until the late 1980s, when the urbanized tribesmen, now settled as full-fledged citizens, would not be a reliable constituency anymore for the Al-Sabah.

In the following, I will focus on the consequences of alliance-building with non-core elites, started under Mubarak al-Sabah and culminating in 1938, when the authority of the Al-Sabah ruler was seriously challenged by merchant opposition and the first direct threat of Iraqi irredentism. The year 1938 marks a crucial moment in the historical memory of Kuwaitis and laid the basis for new relations between the Al-Sabah and Kuwait's main status groups. This section will be confined to demonstrate how 1938 provided a crucial moment in the consolidation of the authority system of the Al-Sabah through patronage and divide-and-rule logics that would be perpetuated with the discovery of oil and only be challenged from the late 1990s as a consequence of politicization among the *badu* and a gradual blurring of existing socio-political boundaries between *hadar,* the Shi'a and the *badu.*

The protection agreement divides Kuwait's merchants

An aspect that has not been covered in literature is how the rivalry between Britain and the Ottoman Empire divided Kuwait's people and its merchant elite.[1] Mubarak's coup and subsequent alliance with the British exacerbated tensions between the Arab and non-Arab merchants as well as between communities. While grievances were largely socio-economic, they intersected with identity fault lines. This was the consequence of a largely ethnic division of labour, the ruling shaykh's alliance-building outside the Arab merchant 'asabiyya and a regional context in which ideas of nationalism were penetrating the region. It was the logical result of a tribal authority system, in which the Al-Sabah strengthened their rule by relying upon the non-Arab merchants, the Kuwaiti 'Ajam Shi'a families.

In her by dependency theory-inspired analysis of social change in Kuwait, Jacqueline Ismail (1982) analyses the rise of Sunni mercantile opposition to the Al-Sabah and the British from the prism of economic grievances of a bourgeois elite. The aristocratic tribal identity of the Najdi elite, clustered together in Al-Qibla, was coupled with a coherent class identity. Being merchants engaged in regional trade and pearling, carrying trade from the east to Ottoman markets through Basra and Najd, these merchants were regionally oriented and had been a driving factor in forging political ties between Ottoman Iraq and Kuwait. As such, Ismail argues that they represented autonomous productive forces; a process of development which was reversed after the British protection agreement and Kuwait's integration into the British economic sphere of influence. The development of the steam engine (1862) hurt these merchants because British goods flooded local markets, dislocating the regional carrying trade with the hinterland in Najd and Basra and Syria. In the Interbellum period, these merchants' interests were further compromised with the interdiction by Ibn Saud of commerce with Najdi tribes in Kuwait (between 1923 and 1937), with trade turning away to the ports of Al-Hasa. The collapse of the pearling industry in 1929 – a consequence of the development of Japanese cultured pearls – presented a further blow to the merchants. Although the smallest merchants were hit most, the *asli* merchants were not spared and only around eleven families remained with substantial capital.[2]

Consequently, argues Ismail, British encroachment was mostly contested by the Sunni aristocracy because of their class interests, as capitalists which had been mostly affected by commercial developments since the end of the nineteenth century.[3] These interests were later promulgated in early representative institutions formed by this elite to protect their interests; interests that were mostly linked to the protection of their economic interests and the curtailing of the control of the Al-Sabah over the economy, and thus of the British hold on Kuwait.[4]

Arab nationalism was the ideology these merchants embraced, a natural fit to their Arab Sunni identity and a vehicle for mobilization to restore some of their lost power. The 'Ajam merchant elite was excluded from pre-parliamentary politics of Najdi merchants on account of their non-Arab ethnicity. Yet, this should be read in a broader context of material interests coinciding with identity. Regionally, everywhere, there was a division of labour along identity lines that has been neglected in existing studies on the merchant class in Kuwait.[5] Pearling was the exclusive prerogative of the Sunni Arab elite of pure Najdi descent and this was a common trait everywhere in the Gulf.[6] Persian merchants, non-nationals and long-settled nationals such as the 'Ajam in Kuwait all specialized in foodstuff and textile trade. In Kuwait, they were particularly known for trade in wood, dates and arms trade, which was quasi-exclusively the domain of the 'Ajam in Kuwait.

As such, there was a clearly distinct economic specialization, explaining why the Shi'a merchants were less hurt when the income from pearling declined. This was the consequence of their minority status unable to challenge the central elite. They had close relations to the British and were generally hostile to the Sunni Ottoman Empire.[7] This is similar to Dubai where Arab merchants of the Bani Yas tribe directed their anger against the Persian merchants in periods of economic decline, as the latter were unharmed by the collapse of pearling. And, as we have seen, ruling shaykhs also allied with these non-Arab elites to counterbalance the power of the core Arab aristocracy.[8] Throughout history, minorities have been used by regimes as a political support base and this was nothing specific to Kuwait.

This explains the profoundly different stance of the Shi'a merchants vis-à-vis the British and the Al-Sabah. In my interviews, the old Shi'a families (such as the Ma'rafi, Behbahani, Hayaat and Al-Wazzan) underlined their historical proximity to the Al-Sabah as well as their positive relations with the British, beneficial to their commerce. Already before the advent of Mubarak, they had close ties to the Al-Sabah: a consequence of their less threatening minority status.

Not different from the Sunni merchants, they consider themselves to be the true pillars of Kuwait's nationhood as the merchants enabled the old city to prosper and to develop into an independent political entity. However, whereas the old segments of the Sunni oligarchy tend to be rather critical of the Al-Sabah, the Shi'a merchants are in favour of the ruling family whom they consider the true protectors of Shi'a against hostile societal forces. The historically close relations to the Al-Sabah are also reflected in the urban geography of the old city, as the fiefdoms of the Emir were located in the middle of Al-Sharq, a predominantly Shi'a neighbourhood.

Furthermore, the pro-Al-Sabah stance of these merchants is generally blended into an overtly patriotic narrative in which Shi'ism and love for the nation are assimilated. One of our interviewees, belonging to the ancient Shi'a merchant Al-Wazzan family paraphrases it as follows: 'We can never give up Kuwait for anything in the world. Loving your country is like loving your Imam.'[9] During our interview, the Al-Wazzan brothers proudly presented me an article from Al-Qabas in which the role of the family in protecting Miriam al-Sabah against the Bani Ka'ab tribe during the Battle of *Al-Riqqa* is mentioned. The Kuwaiti Shi'a proudly refer to this battle as showing their nationalist inclinations, as it was a battle in which they fought along the ruler against a tribe of similar Shi'a creed, and in the case of the Al-Wazzan, even similar tribal descent.[10] According to the family, because of their role in protecting the Emir's wife during Kuwait's first sea-battle, they were granted the exclusive right to weigh products coming into Kuwait; a monopoly granted by the Emir himself. This shows that economic patronage vis-à-vis loyal elites preceded Mubarak al-Sabah.

Under Mubarak al-Sabah's rule, the proximity to the ruler was strengthened, with the Shi'a generally having a positive narrative about the British and refer to their encounters with the British as being advantageous for their commerce. The Shi'a families tend to refer to the openness of their great grandfathers to the British, with some having made their fortunes at the start of the twentieth century, a period of economic hardships for the general mercantile class of Kuwait. As such, these families presented a group of 'nouveaux riches' profiting from their proximity to the Al-Sabah and good ties to the British to advance economically. An example is the Qabazard family whose ancestors started as simple pearl divers but profited from the integration of Kuwait into the world capitalist system by trading with the British power. The patriarch of the family, Mohammed Qabazard, developed close relations with the British, thanks to which he was appointed as head of the port of Kuwait. In the Interbellum – a difficult period for merchants because of the closure of trade with Najd – he got his best opportunities. After the discovery of oil, the family became one of the biggest state contractors for the building of roads and houses in Kuwait.[11] The same is true for the Al-Kadhemi family, from *Al-Kadhimiyya* in Iraq that settled in Kuwait around 1921. During our interviews, the family underlined the success of their grandfather as a 'self-made man' who was able to gain his wealth during the Interbellum and became one of the richest merchants of the Muhammara port. After the discovery of petrol, the Al-Kadhemi family became the commercial agent of Mercedes.[12] Contrary to the Sunni oligarchy, these aforementioned merchants have gained their wealth during a period of relative economic decline and profited from the new economic configuration under British tutelage. We could hypothesize that these 'nouveaux riches' had profited from a deliberate policy of co-optation by the ruler in order to weaken the Sunni mercantile opposition.

The Shi'a were not the only ones who profited from a policy of economic patronage by the Al-Sabah in the pre-oil era. It was often through personal ties to local rulers that groups could make inroads in commerce, co-opted by their shaykh-patron. This is what happened as we have seen with the Qina'at, who through the person of Yusuf Bin Issa – adopted as an orphan by the Al-Sabah – got access to economic privileges as nouveaux riches. Sharing with the Shi'a a position of non-core elites, the latter are known to be ferociously anti-Shi'a, competing with them for the Al-Sabah's favour in commerce and access to management positions in the oil industry.

There were also new Sunni Najdi elites, who made their fortunes at the start of the twentieth century, although they are considered today as part of the old elite. This was the case of the Al-Khorafi, Al-Shaya, Al-Saʿd and Abdulrazzaks.[13] Although Najdi and Sunni, none of these families were part of the core of young politicized Najdis elites who opposed the Al-Sabah in pre-parliamentary councils of power-sharing.[14] There is little information on the context behind the rise of these families at the start of the twentieth century, but it is likely that these families have also profited from access to privileged *wasta* from Al-Sabah shaykhs as a counterweight to the opposition, as they rose in a context in which the independent power of merchants was waning.

The 1938 Council events: alliance-building with the Shi'a and tribes

The Sunni Najdi elite was a coherent ʿasabiyya, sharing class interests, pure tribal descent, adherence to the Hanbali *madhab* and socialization in Al-Qibla (apart from the few aristocratic families of Al-Sharq that had migrated together with the Al-Sabah to Kuwait). Many of them had their date plantations in Basra and were active in transnational regional trade with Basra and Najd, in which their own tribal affiliation helped in forging close commercial relations with a tribal hinterland.[15] Some of the merchants would later even use their connections to lobby for the naturalization of fellow tribesmen, in the aim of gaining supporters in parliament. This was the case of *hadar* Mutran elites, such as Yusuf al-Mughlid and Hilal al-Mutair (a former pearl merchant); a tribe known for its antithetical stance vis-à-vis political power.[16]

Politically, these families had strong ties with the Ottoman province of Basra and sided with the Ottoman Empire during periods of great power rivalry. While Shi'a families had date plantations in Basra too, the far larger group of Sunni merchants had more significant investments in date plantations in Iraq and sent their sons to Iraq for education.[17] Because of political ties to Iraq and often residing long periods in Basra or Baghdad (apart from Bombay and Karachi where they also resided for months) these merchants were heavily influenced by emergent nationalism and anti-British sentiments in Iraq. Iraq witnessed in the 1920s a series of mass protests that cross-cut sectarian divisions, with both Shi'a and Sunni Iraqis rejecting imperialism.[18] It was a major pan-Arab revolt, resonating with older pan-Arab ambitions in which Shaykh Khazʿal played a prominent role. Iranians were considered as potential fifth columns for Iran plotting to weaken the Arab nation with the rise of nationalist propaganda.[19] The largely Arab ethnicity of Shi'a in Iraq favoured this cross-sectarian mobilization in the name of nationalism; contrary to the predominantly Persian origins of Kuwait's Shi'a population.

These events in Iraq in the 1920s would have an important impact on local politics in Kuwait. Young members of the merchant elite had close ties to Basra and Baghdad, where they studied and had their date plantations. As a consequence of their socialization in Iraqi nationalist circles, they were the forbearers of nationalist opposition in Kuwait and established political parties such as the Youth Party and the National Bloc (*Al-Kutla Al-Wataniyya*); the latter being an outgrowth of the Arab Nationalist Youth movement in Iraq.

The young merchants had built up their frustration vis-à-vis the arrogant leadership of the Emirate since Mubarak, excluding any form of consultation with them. With the sudden death of Salim in 1921 and the consequent succession issue raised, the most influential of them formed a Consultative Council (*Al-majlis Al-istishari*). While its immediate objective was to forestall factionalism within the Al-Sabah, the creation of the Council was a means to restore the merchants' role in decision-making.[20] The new Emir, Ahmad al-Jabir had pledged to work with the Council, but the latter was dissolved within two months. Infighting among its members was one of the main reasons behind its dissolution. Nevertheless, activities continued, largely organized from Basra, where these elites got the support from King Ghazi (1933–9), a staunch defender of nationalism and anti-British monarch who threatened to annex Kuwait.

In the 1930s, activism continued against Ahmad al-Jabir, mostly in the form of a propaganda campaign organized from Basra. Writings on street walls in Kuwait calling for reforms directed against the ruler, activists chanted *Ahmad al-Jabir, send away your evil entourage or we will replace you ...* and *Rush on to the revolution*. A certain Muhammad al-Barrak – advisor to rebellious merchant Abdallah al-Saqqar and member of the Youth Party – was declared guilty of these writings and publicly flogged. Following the event, the merchants went armed to their places of business. The main grievances of the nationalists were the Al-Sabah's monopolization of resources for private use, economic malaise and poverty. Very little money was allocated to public administration and Al-Sabah family members complained about the tiny allowances received by Jabir al-Ahmad.[21] A lot of anger was directed against the personal secretary of the ruler, the Iranian Molla Salih, who as we have seen represented de facto the government and was an important patron for the Kuwaiti 'Ajam. The fact that he was an Iranian naturally added to the nationalists' fervour who threatened to stone Salih if he would not abdicate.[22]

The Arab revolts in Palestine (1936–9) provided a further impetus to nationalist fervour, with nationalists being aided by King Ghazi who organized a propaganda campaign against the Kuwaiti ruler from Iraq.[23] The rebellions soon took the form of a popular movement, with many citizens allegedly swearing to defend the nationalists with arms. Among the demands of the activists were a set of administrative reforms and a fairer budget for public affairs, the end of the monopolization of resources by the Emir, the reform of the Al-Sabah House to avoid succession crises, the cleaning up of the ruler's entourage (mainly his Iranian secretary Salih) and the closure of Kuwaiti borders for non-Arabs (mostly Iranian) and cooperation with Iraq to implement these reforms.[24] In 1938, a secret society was formed, the National Bloc (*Al-kutla Al-wataniyya*), petitioning the Emir to fulfil his pledge for power-sharing and create a Legislative Council.

The reliance of Ahmad al-Jabir on a clique of secretaries from outside the direct family also angered other Al-Sabah members whom according to British officers he 'neglected in favor of a few ignoble cronies'.[25] Abdallah al-Salim was the main opponent of Ahmad al-Jabir and was supported by his brothers. An ambitious young prince, he allied with the nationalists and was elected as head of the Legislative Council of 1938.[26] Elections for the Council, held in the Diwan of Al-Saqqar, were an affair for a select group of Sunni notables; out of 320 voters, fourteen candidates were chosen, only two of whom had served in the previous Consultative Council of 1921. As in 1921, they represented the Najdi Sunni elite and its young politicized members.[27]

The movement radicalized when its members pleaded for the direct annexation of Kuwait to Iraq, backed by King Ghazi who threatened to invade Kuwait. British Archives even refer to rumours of Abdallah al-Saqqar being offered the shaykhdom of Kuwait by Iraqi officials in 1939, following his lobbying in Iraqi political circles.[28] The movement was violently crushed down by Shaykh Ahmad al-Jabir and its members exiled, but King Ghazi continued spreading his public statements through broadcasts in Kuwait until his murder in 1939, likely killed by the British. The latter's fear for Iraqi irredentism was expressed in internal correspondences, emphasizing that Kuwait 'has received no advice from its Majesty's government for three months, but received almost daily advice from the Muntassarif of Basra.[29]

The Arab nationalist stance of its members isolated to the Shi'a elite from participating in the Council's elections. This is illustrated in the account of Habib Hayat, from the Al-Hayat merchant family: 'The Sunnis only invited two persons: my uncle (Mahmud Hayat) and Ahmad Ma'rafi. Ahmad Ma'rafi said OK. But Al-Ghanim told them "we only brought you here to listen, not to vote, because you are a minority". After this my uncle and Ma'rafi decided to organize a movement in husayniyya Khaz'aliyya, with Sayyid al-Qazwini.'[30] The exclusion of the Shi'a is further acknowledged by a member of the Sunni elite, Humud al-Nusf (owner of Al-Qabas):

> My uncle was one of them, but he was one of the conservatives. When they became too extreme, he withdrew. There was an important influence of Arab nationalism, the young people wanted to have Kuwait for Arabs only and get rid of the Iranians. It was a big mistake, you can't exclude other ethnicities. These others were a lot, and Kuwait was small.[31]

Also, the nationalists' anti-Iranian stance provoked fear among Kuwait's Shi'a, largely 'Ajam, who consequently resorted to the British for protection after their pleas for reforms addressed to the Council by the religious leader of the 'Ajam, Sayyid Mahdi al-Qazwini, were rejected, with the Council members insisting that Kuwait was an Arab country and that they wanted to keep it as such. Among these demands were the creation of a Ja'afari court and representation of Shi'a in the Legislative Council as well as in the nascent public administration.[32] Following the rejection of these demands, Al-Qazwini and Shi'a notables went to the British with a petition signed by more than 4,500 Kuwaiti Shi'a demanding British citizenship. These demands for British citizenship followed a tense interlude in which the Council members had asked for the departure of Molla Salih, the Emir's chief secretary since Mubarak. A patriarch of the Ma'rafi family recounted this episode:

> They were very nationalistic and told us that everyone not from the Arab world should leave the country. So the Shi'a supported the ruler, we would not accept other than the Al-Sabah, because they look to all in an equal way. At that time, my father went to the British Council and told him that they should protect Kuwait. He was only 28 years old. They asked him if he was the leader of the family. He said no, but I am the bravest one to come to you.

By then, the rough British estimations of the Shi'a in Kuwait counted around 18,000 out of 65,000 Kuwaitis, with 10,000 of them being 'Ajam.

British Archives indicate that among these 4,500 petitions were also some *Baharna* and *Hasawi* Shi'a, apart from the non-Arab Shi'a, the 'Ajam.[33] This means that the Council movement mobilized the Shi'a, likely for the first time, collectively on a confessional basis, transcending ethnic differences. Contributing to the Shi'a' fear was the departure of their patron, Molla Salih, upon the Council's request. This was different from Bahrain where in 1938 there was a coalescence of forces, with Shi'a labourers joining the protests organized by the Sunni elite, likely favoured by the Arab ethnicity of the Baharna and their demographic weight.[34]

Consequently, the radicalization of the nationalists pleading for Kuwait's annexation as well as the isolation of any non-Arab elements led to splits within its community, between the Shi'a and the Sunna and between two neighbourhoods: Al-Sharq and Al-Qibla. According to a local historian, 'The First World War and rivalry between Britain and the Turks separated the people of Kuwait in two parts: the people of Al-Sharq, who sided with Ahmad al-Jabir and the British and the people of Al-Qibla, who supported the Turks and later the nationalists.'[35] In Kuwait, 1938 marked a crucial moment in the Shi'a' collective memory, when they rallied behind the Al-Sabah in a context of perceived societal hostility. A similar situation would be reproduced in 2008, but this time, a context of hostile Sunni Islamist forces would lead to the Shi'a' backing of the Al-Sabah, as a minority.

While the Shi'a rallied behind the ruler, Ahmad al-Jabir relied on the Bedouin tribes to crack down on the protestors. As in the case of Dubai's reform movement in 1938, the Al-Sabah used the Bedouins as unpoliticized forces against the modernized urban forces. While rulers' alliance-building with the tribes was as old as the House of Al-Sabah, it is during the Council events that an open confrontation occurred with the *hadar*.[36] The overt reliance of the rulers on tribal recruits to crack down on early parliamentary activism naturally contributed to the general anti-tribal bias among the older generations of *hadar*. When the first council was dissolved in 1921, semi-nomadic tribesmen from southern parts of Kuwait answered Emir Jabir's call to take up arms and entered the city. Also the dissolution of the second council (December 1938 – March 1939) was accompanied with the use of force by *fidawiyyin* and their tribal allies.[37] Ahmad Bin Munais, a Kuwaiti resident of Basra, had addressed the rump council, declaring the Al-Sabah unfit to rule and advised its members to resist until the Iraqi army should arrive. Three Kuwaitis were shot and Bin Munais was brutally hanged in the public square: an episode marked in the memory of Arab nationalists as one of the worst displays of savagery by the rulers and their tribal allies. In her interview with icon of the Arab Nationalist movement, Ahmad al-Khatib, Claire Beaugrand (2010) quotes the latter referring to the role played by the Saudi King Abdulaziz – who upon British instructions–helped Ahmad al-Jabir during the event by ''sending 600 tribesmen, among whom 300 from the 'Ajman and 300 from the Mutran'' (the latter were turned down by the Emir for their role in attacking Kuwait during the battle of Jahra).[38]

While crushing Kuwait's parliamentary efforts, the 1938 events marked the start of the development of Kuwait's modern police and armed forces, relying upon tribal recruits. Article 2 of the inaugural law of the Legislative Council had called for the establishment of a law of Public Security.[39] It resulted in the creation of a Police Department and a Department for Public Security, replacing respectively the town guards and the fidawiyya. While the first focused on surveillance in the town, the Department of Public Security's jurisdiction lay in the control of public order outside the wall, including border control, visa issuance and the supervision of oil facilities and the oil town of Ahmadi.[40]

The year 1938 also led to the institutionalization of the principle of dynastic rule in Kuwait, as the dissident members of the Al-Sabah (Shaykh Abdallah al-Salim and his brothers) turned against the Council when it radicalized, realizing that its radicalization would mean the downfall of hereditary monarchy as such. The discovery of oil contributed to the balancing of stakes within the ruling elite, by appointing Al-Sabah princes in sovereign portfolios. Kuwait was the first Gulf shaykhdom to consolidate this system of dynastic monarchy; which Michael Herb considers one of the main reasons behind the resilience of traditional monarchy.[41] This system of dynastic rule has been put to a test however since 2003, with the increased incapacity of the Al-Sabah to present a united front in the face of public dissension from their population.[42]

In sum, 1938 marked an open confrontation between social forces in Kuwait and demonstrated the Al-Sabah's divide-and-rule strategies in terms of societal challenges, allying with non-core elites outside the Najdi ʿasabiyya. With Kuwait's independence (1961) and promulgation of a constitution (1962) – unprecedented regionally – allowing for a powerful parliament, the Al-Sabah would continue these regime strategies of alliance-building with groups outside the merchant ʿasabiyya. Things would change from the early 2000s on when previously loyal constituencies would turn against their shaykhs-patron. Yet, at crucial moments, the alliances of 1938 would be reactivated.

Part Two

Oil and the consolidation of a tribal authoritarian shaykhdom: ruler–ruled relations 1961–90

Introduction

Having discussed the nature of traditional politics in pre-oil Kuwait and the consolidation of the Al-Sabah authority structure, this part will focus on the development of Kuwait's rentier regime. The period covered here is from Kuwait's independence until the Iraqi invasion (1961–90), a tragic episode that fragilized the Al-Sabah and allowed for a renegotiation of ruler–ruled relations.

In this section, the emphasis is on how a tribal and informal authority system – mediated through notables and British support – evolved into what resembles a modern state while retaining premodern alliances and stratification patterns. The regime that opened up politically in an unprecedented way within the Gulf – while remaining authoritarian – did so by resorting to classical pre-oil strategies of rule. Old elites were incorporated into the state's administration, being granted high executive positions and a privileged share of oil wealth. Consequently and favoured by oil resources, state-building was less disruptive than that in those Arab countries that faced revolutions and were built upon anti-elite and anti-colonial legacies.

Despite the modern accoutrements of the political system with a powerful parliament, Kuwait's Al-Sabah regime continued to resort to intermediaries to reach out to the masses. At first these intermediaries were the same social elites that entertained privileged relations with the Al-Sabah in the pre-oil era: urban and tribal elites with a rather independent power base. With the emancipation of the masses benefitting from the resources of the welfare regime, new leaders from middle-class background started to replace the old elites. Often more capable of doing politics and representing their constituencies, these *political entrepreneurs* replaced the notables as intermediaries with the regime. Some of these elites rose as a consequence of direct state co-optation, to balance vis-à-vis other more threatening groups. In the 1970s and 1980s, Sunni Islamist groups and tribesmen profited from state support to become a loyal constituency against the secular, liberal and leftist opposition. Others were more independent and elected on an oppositional platform but often also succumbed to being entangled in princely patronage games.

While social change happened within each traditional socio-political category (*hadar*, Shi'a and *badu*; although for the latter this change started only since the late 1990s), regime policies of state-building contributed to a segmentation of social groups along their pre-oil fault lines. Divide-and-rule strategies and segmented access to the state's welfare contributed to reinforce cleavages between the three classical status groups. It is these divisions that allowed the regime to maintain its semi-democratic *Sonderweg*, enabling the Al-Sabah to play upon societal divisions, with parliament as a forum where such patronage games were being played out to avoid the creation of a cross-cutting parliamentary opposition. Until the Iraqi Invasion, the main opposition emanated from the *hadar* elite, with the Al-Sabah relying largely on Sunni Islamists and tribesmen to bolster their power.

This section will focus on how the Al-Sabah's power was exercised and contested until the Invasion. This will be done by analysing social change from the prism of the three traditional social categories, both in their relation towards the Al-Sabah as well as vis-à-vis each other. Specific attention will be paid to the role of those elites acting as intermediaries between these status groups and the political regime. As noted by Nazih Ayubi (2009), Arabian monarchies were effective in creating a sort of 'politics that consisted of a continuous need for intermediaries binding the individual and groups to the state.'[1]

Understanding the nature of power of these intermediaries and its evolution over time will offer crucial indications about state power in Kuwait. This will provide a framework for comparison to analyse the evolution of political clientelism in the post-Invasion era, which as we will see has become less effective and contributed to a fragmentation of the authority of the Al-Sabah.

External threat consolidates inter-elite power-sharing (*musharaka*)

Iraqi irredentism and Kuwait's adoption of a liberal constitution

The reasons behind Kuwait's political Sonderweg have been the object of numerous studies. Some attribute it to the power of the merchant elite in the pre-oil setting and the coherence of its 'asabiyya relative to merchant–ruler relations in other Gulf states, such as Qatar (Crystal: 1992). Others place emphasis on the democratic inclinations of Kuwait's ruler – Abdallah al-Salim – in pushing for a liberal constitution upon independence. Both visions are often idealized *a posteriori* by Kuwaitis to explain their country's regional 'exceptionalism'. Although all these explanations are part of the truth, the main reason behind Kuwait's Sonderweg seems less voluntary and is rather the consequence of an external factor of repeated Iraqi irredentist threats. This combined with its particular geographical setting and a divided society has favoured power-sharing and explains Kuwait's regionally unprecedented constitutionally enshrined parliamentarianism. As a small country located between powerful neighbours to which its domestic communities are tied via kinship/sect/ethnicity bonds, Kuwait has been particularly affected by regional influences and ideologies since its very beginning. These factors have allowed for a greater role of power-sharing with elite groups outside the ruling circle than in the case of its larger neighbours.

Yet, oil reduced the necessity of power-sharing and gave the rulers absolute control over resources, reducing the role of merchants as independent elites to those dependent on the Al-Sabah's goodwill to maintain their elite position. It is not unlikely Kuwait's rulers would have opted for a similar rather hegemonic path as its neighbours following independence, had it not been threatened in its existence at various times by Iraqi irredentist claims. It is this external factor that explains the survival of Kuwait's parliamentary life and liberal constitution, rather than its small size per se in the oil era.[2] While similar factors of a small state amidst powerful neighbours explain Bahrain's initial opting for a liberal constitution – in Kuwait's footsteps – the presence of a majority opposition of Shi'a citizens vis-à-vis a minority Sunni dynasty naturally led to a quick end of this power-sharing experience.[3]

As we have seen, the power of Kuwait's merchant class was the most cohesive in regional comparison, although in all the small shaykhdoms merchants were powerful elites challenging ruling shaykhs and demanding a share in governance. As an educated elite, it socialized in circles in Iraq and Egypt where nationalism flourished and had the time to devote itself to cultural and political activities, contrary to the impoverished masses too busy with earning their livelihood. This elite had opposed British imperialism, as it had contributed to its loss of independent power, with local rulers now relying upon foreign support. With the collapse of pearling in the 1930s and the discovery of oil, an open conflict between the merchant nationalists and local rulers broke out. This resulted in 1938 in *Majlis* movements in the shaykhdoms of Dubai, Kuwait and Bahrain. In these cases, merchants allied with dissident shaykhs against the ruler and his British backers.[4]

The intra-family competition within the ruling families was nothing new. What was new in the 1930s was the extent of the competition between merchants and rulers as well as within ruling families. This was the direct consequence of the discovery of oil. It naturally strengthened competition over access to oil revenues, with merchants demanding power-sharing to institutionalize checks-and-balances on the ruler's treasury and to use legislative mechanisms to ensure a role for themselves in receiving the spoils of the new economy.

Historically, intra-family and inter-elite disputes were often caused by the unequal distribution of resources within the elite and the monopolization of resources by rulers. Strenuous relations between the Al-Sabah and merchants since Mubarak's reign were caused by rulers' tendencies to consider the public budget as their personal one, explaining the rationale behind the merchants' call for an end to the monopolization of resources by the Al-Sabah. And intra-family disputes often derived from a feeling among Al-Sabah shaykhs of being relatively deprived of resources. Mubarak's resentment against his brothers stemmed from his lack of resources to govern the tribal portfolio.[5]

Ruling shaykhs responded to opposition in the pre-oil era with repression and in all cases the pre-parliamentary *majalis* were dissolved by rulers. The period between 1938 and the 1960s was characterized by a continuation of autocratic rule in these small shaykhdoms – Kuwait, Bahrain and Dubai – with differences as to their degree of settling intra-family disputes. To this effect, Kuwait was the first to consolidate a mechanism of balancing power within the Al-Sabah, as a consequence of the 1938 movement.[6]

Yet, when the movements flared up again in the 1950s as a consequence of Arab nationalism and revolutions in Egypt and Iraq, different paths were taken by the small Gulf shaykhdoms in terms of ruler–ruled relations. Kuwait and Bahrain – for different reasons – adopted rather liberal constitutions (in 1962 and 1973 respectively). In both cases, their small size amidst large neighbours was a propitious factor in this.[7] Yet, while Bahrain's constitutionalism was short-lived, Kuwait constitutional life remained intact, although it has faced numerous authoritarian setbacks. Qatar and the UAE also faced nationalist agitation, but this had largely faded away in the 1960s. As in other cases of the Gulf, the merchants were bought off as a class through exclusive import and construction licenses granting them monopolies in certain franchises (e.g. Mercedes, Rolex).[8] Dubai never opened up politically while leading the UAE as a vibrant entrepot economy. The illiberal constitution adopted by the UAE in 1996 (drafted in 1971) was a consequence of bargaining between ruling families, from which merchants were excluded.[9]

Kuwait's unique liberal political design in the Gulf was first and foremost the consequence of the threat of Iraqi irredentism. The process itself was supported by a liberal-minded ruler – Abdallah al-Salim – who was on good terms with the merchants and nationalists. Michael Herb (2015) has argued that this external factor is the most convincing in understanding Kuwait's different path of state-building in the region. I support this analysis, as the chronology of ruler–opposition relations since 1962 corroborates the crucial role played by the external context in understanding domestic policy choices. A threatening regional context explains the Al-Sabah's resorting to parliamentarianism as a means to absorb a part of popular discontent and strengthen its domestic legitimacy. This was the case in 1961 (preparing the adoption of a constitution), in 1981 (reinstatement of parliamentary life) and in 1990 with the subsequent concessionary stance of the regime vis-à-vis the opposition. Located on the periphery of powerful forces (Saudi Arabia, Iraq and Iran), Kuwait had been forced to focus on maintaining autonomy and the creation of a national identity, domestically and in terms of its foreign policy.

Iraqi irredentism has been a recurring threat since the fall of the Ottoman Empire, with Iraqi rulers making the contested claim that today's Kuwait used to be under Iraqi control as part of the *wilayat* of Basra. In 1938, the Iraqi threat was felt, when merchant nationalists, supported by King Ghazi pleaded for Kuwait's annexation to Iraq. On 25 June 1961 – less than a week after Kuwait's independence – Iraq's leader General Qasim threatened to annex Kuwait, with its troops reaching Kuwait's borders. This prompted Kuwait's ruler to start an intense international lobbying campaign to recognize Kuwait's sovereignty. The UNSC refusal for Kuwait's application for UN membership, due to a Soviet veto, led Kuwait to continue its diplomacy with Arab capitals that by then considered the shaykhdom as a rather retrograde monarchy.[10] However, successful lobbying of Kuwaiti delegations composed of merchants and nationalists allowed it to strengthen its legitimacy in the face of such an imminent threat. It is not accidental that the process of liberal constitution-building coincided with this larger project of gaining foreign Arab support for its nationhood.[11]

The crucial role of merchants in Kuwait's constitutional design

While merchants were granted a privileged position in the post-independence order in all the Gulf shaykhdoms, the merchants in Kuwait had a direct say in writing the liberal constitution adopted in 1962 that until today structures the semi-authoritarian/semi-democratic nature of the Emirate. In fact, power-sharing (*musharaka*: sharing) with the merchant elite was consolidated as a direct consequence of external threat. Had this threat not have occurred, the Al-Sabah would have likely opted for a more authoritarian turn, following the footsteps of its neighbours, empowered by oil resources to end power-sharing.

It is thus in the crucial first decade after Kuwait's independence that the Najdi merchants were able to guarantee and institutionalize for themselves a share in power, via their preponderant role in lobbying for Kuwait's independence and in drafting the constitution, but also a semi-institutionalization of their economic prerogatives as it would be the nucleus of the few Najdi families that would receive a lion's share in the wealth via the creation of a private sector, thus becoming the largest client of the Al-Sabah.[12] This nucleus of families would dominate until today membership of the Kuwaiti Chamber of Commerce (KCC) – their official arm – and profit most throughout the 1960s from the country's land acquisition program (LAP) as a quick means for economic patronage.

When parliament was created and the constitution promulgated, it was largely a means for the *hadar* elite to safeguard its power in a future political order. As argued by Samuel Huntington (1968), autonomous centres of traditional power are often the first to espouse liberalism in times of change, for non-liberal purposes. In the early years of parliamentary life, these families were still chosen on account of their inherited power (wealth/access to the Al-Sabah/inherited social status) to represent an electorate, typical of notables. In this period, only elites could devote themselves to politics, being wealthy and cultivated enough to present themselves for office in order to protect their elite status (Weber: 1946).[13] One should not forget that the electorate then was highly selective: the prerogative of a restricted group of *hadar* male citizens who could trace their origins back to before the Battle of Jahra (1920), as original (*asli*) citizens. This would change since the 1960s until the 1980s with the *extra-legal* naturalization of thousands of tribesmen granted full citizenship rights (including political rights) from the outset.[14] Consequently, these naturalizations had a direct impact on the political balance, by strengthening *badu* representation.

However, the *majlis al-umma* that in its early years represented an elite group of notables soon allowed for the empowerment of the masses, the 'other Kuwaitis', as a third group upgraded as state-dependent middle-class actors. It is likely the merchants did not anticipate, in the 1960s, that the very parliament they helped create would in the future become the most vocal mechanism to voice opposition against their elite interests; itself a consequence of the particular class conflict in rich rentiers that pits the masses (state employees) against the business elite. In this conundrum, the masses do not have an interest in the profitability of the private sector from which they do not receive jobs nor welfare and consequently vote for populist and anti-business agendas (Herb: 2009).[15]

As an educated elite that had demonstrated its political strength in 1938, merchants were elected as members of the Constitutional Assembly (CA) and appointed to the Constitutional Committee (CC), entrusted with discussing the draft constitution.[16] The CA was an elected body of twenty members, two chosen out of each of the ten constituencies that Kuwait had in 1962. Much to the British dislike, fearing Arab nationalism, an Egyptian advisor was given the lead to draft the constitution. Just before elections of the CA, a major disagreement developed over the number of electoral constituencies. The merchants favoured one constituency, while the Al-Sabah favoured twenty. The latter would give them the opportunity to ensure a stronger role for the peripheral Bedouin zones that were known for their loyalty to the Al-Sabah. In the end, a compromise was reached of ten constituencies, but the issue would flare up again in 2006, driven by reformist youth. The outcome of the CA elections gave a predominant role to merchants, who then dominated local politics and were favoured by the restrictive electorate of male *hadar asli* citizens.[17] The president of the CA was Abdellatif al-Ghanim, a powerful merchant, and Ahmad al-Khatib, icon of the nationalists was appointed its vice-president. This time, Shi'a notables were elected too, with Mansur al-Mezidi and Muhammad M'arafi elected in Al-Sharq, a predominantly Shi'a district.[18] On the whole, the CA was dominated by the merchant group.

The relative ease of the constitutional process was facilitated by the fact that the five-member CC – entrusted to study the draft constitution – was composed of four merchants, apart from one ruling family member, Shaykh S'ad, son of the ruler, Abdallah al-Salim.[19] Any action proposed by this committee would thus almost certainly be accepted by the CA. Also facilitating the process was the inclination of the ruler, Abdallah al-Salim, in favour of a liberal constitution. Under his reign, he was able to fence off the power of anti-constitution lobby within the House of the Al-Sabah. As such, ministers within the CA were not allowed by the ruler to vote on the constitution.[20]

Diverging views between the CA members and the Al-Sabah were resolved in a rather conciliatory way. Merchants pleaded for a majority to be sufficient to vote non-confidence in a minister, while Shaykh Sa'd and the Al-Sabah wanted two-thirds. And merchants wanted fifteen ministers, while Sa'd wanted twenty; an important issue as ministers were de jure members of parliament. As a token of his mediatory role, the Emir intervened and it was decided that sixteen ministers were chosen and the principle of cabinet resignation was accepted (defended by the merchants). In return, the merchants accepted the principle of choosing ministers from outside parliament and giving them the right to vote (except for a vote of no confidence).[21]

The resultant constitution, ratified on 12 November 1962, was unprecedented in the region.[22] It stipulates respect for political, civil and human rights, including freedom of expression and association and included important provisions for respecting the inviolability of private space in personal residences – *diwaniyyas* – that consequently became the loci par excellence for political activities.[23] It guaranteed significant welfare entitlements and conferred upon Kuwaitis a sense of national identity in a regional context of threat.[24]

It was a consequence of the determining role played by the merchant elite in bargaining for its share in power. Today, merchants have lost their social power and have come to see parliament as an obstacle to their interests, a venue for populism and for economically unsound policy-making.

Kuwait's semi-democratic design breeds crises

While being unprecedented in its liberal nature compared to other GCC constitutions, the parliamentary design in Kuwait is only semi-democratic and gives ultimate power to the person of the Emir: a consequence of the bargaining between merchants and the Al-Sabah, without much consideration for democracy per se. Because of this institutional structure, the system is *inherently* prone to crises and to executive–legislative deadlocks, explaining the numerous parliamentary dissolutions since its inception.[25] Parliament exercises some veto-power on the monarch through its capacity to question and grill ministers, to veto legislation and its ability to disapprove of an Emir's appointment.[26] However, the Emir is solely responsible for nominating the cabinet.[27] Also, the Emir is mentioned both as an authority in legislative and executive powers and has the final say in both instances, compromising popular sovereignty.[28] While parliament can overturn an Emir's veto to legislation it proposed with a two-thirds majority, the Emir has a major lever at his disposal here: he can dissolve parliament at will (as can the Constitutional Court), on the condition that elections are announced within sixty days. Also, the Emir can resort to the highly contested 'emergency decrees' *(Al-marasim Al-darura: art.71)* when parliament is not in session.[29] The problem here lies in the absence of a clear definition of what constitutes an emergency; rulers have tended to resort to these decrees in times of oppositional threats, as happened in 2012 following the ruler's dissolution of a vocal parliament.[30] There is, furthermore, no full separation of powers, and ministers (maximum 16) are ex-officio members of parliament in addition to the fifty elected members.[31]

Similar to 'competitive authoritarians', parliament has often served as a forum for the ruling elite to strengthen its authority over societal groups via co-optation and divide-and-rule strategies towards MPs. Two logics are at work here. On the one hand, there is the Al-Sabah family regime that strives to maintain its authoritarian grip by patronizing society's main groups in parliament and avoiding parliament to become too independent to overturn the Emir's decisions and appointments. On the other hand, parliament has been a means for contending royals to play out their feuds, strengthening divisions within the family that spill over to parliament.

One major goal of the regime is to avoid a majority of oppositional MPs. Therefore, it tries to create loyal allies in parliament via a plethora of policies, ranging from the privileged provision of state services (e.g. housing/jobs) to specific constituencies to the bribing of elites and the support of local personalities capable of reaching out to constituencies on the grassroots level who, once elected, will return their favours and display a pro-regime stance. The monopolization of resources by the Al-Sabah allows for segmented and personalized distribution of rents to constituencies. While this has reinforced dependency on the regime's *wasta* via the creation of situations of unequal access to the state's resources, it has also inadvertently resulted in a regime increasingly bogged down in a degree of citizen expectations it has created and voiced via populist claims of MPs over the state's resources.[32] For this reason, the austerity measures the government started implementing in 2016 in response to a budget shortfall caused by the global decline in oil prices could count upon a major backlash in parliament, with nearly half of the seats being won by opposition candidates campaigning on reversing austerity measures.[33]

Contending royals have resorted to parliament to play out their feuds, by co-opting MPs and societal groups. The reason for the interest of princes in parliament lies in constitutional provisions. Article 4 regulating succession matters *(qanun tawarith al-imara)* stipulates that the Emir's choice for a Crown Prince (CP) needs to be approved by an *absolute majority* of parliament. If a new CP fails to win parliament's approval, the Emir then submits the names of three eligible members of the family to parliament, which then selects one of them. This is why it is so important for ambitious princes to build loyal support structures in parliament.[34] Until today, this law explains the rationale behind patronage politics of royal contenders in Kuwait. In 2006, the force of parliament was for the first time demonstrated, when it decided to intervene in a difficult succession by deposing unanimously the first one in line of succession,

CP S'ad, considered too sick to rule and instead voting in favour of the then prime minister (PM) – Sabah al-Ahmad – who, only third in line of succession, had been very apt in forging ties with MPs in order to succeed in becoming Emir. This historical *impeachment* showed the force of article 4 and shocked neighbouring Gulf regimes.

The 2006 events should also be read in the context of the separation of the position of CP and PM since 2003 by late Emir Jaber al-Ahmad; a consequence of the weak health of CP S'ad. This has unleashed competition between the CP and PMs. Before, the PM was a CP and thus more secure in his position, whereas today the PM competes with the CP. His role as head of the Cabinet allows him to be more directly involved in parliamentary politics and in forging allies in parliament, as did the current Emir Sabah al-Ahmad rather successfully. While in the past powerful princes with ambitions for the position of CP did so from a variety of ministerial posts (Guidance, Interior), today it is the PM who has become the most important contender for the throne. The closer ties to parliamentary politics give him more leeway to influence MPs in the hope of a future loyal parliamentary majority voting in favour of him in approving the Emir's choice for a CP. In this regard, the PM position has become even more politicized than in the past and princely competition has taken a new and more overt turn. This trend can be observed since Sabah al-Ahmad became officially PM in 2003 (after having de facto acted as one since 2001), following the separation of the posts of CP and PM. Then, Sabah al-Ahmad competed with S'ad al-Abdallah and won the battle in 2006 when parliament deposed Emir S'ad.

Consequently, parliament has become an even stronger forum for princely politics whilst the regime has been less capable of acting with one voice and has been increasingly divisive in its dealing with parliamentary elites. Until 2006, parliament's role in succession was limited to a formal one of ratifying the Emir's decisions after consensus had been reached within the Family Council and it never resorted to its constitutional prerogatives in succession. One could say that since 2006 parliament has started to act like the maker of princes too (in addition to the other way around). In sum, three factors explain the more overt role of family politics in parliamentary life: (1) the separation of the position of CP and PM, which unleashed a politicization of the PM position; (2) the unprecedented role of parliament in deciding over a difficult succession; and (3) the breaking of the custom of rotating power between two family branches by Sabah al-Ahmad, who has concentrated all major executive posts (PM and CP) in the hands of the Al-Jabir.[35] The controversial premiership of Nasser al-Muhammad (2006–11) and his alleged role in corrupting parliamentary forces should be read in this context.

Finally, another indication for Kuwait's semi-democratic nature is the role played by the judiciary: a field where the Al-Sabah play a direct role.[36] Although the Constitution stipulates that the judges are independent (art. 3), they are appointed by the ruler himself (acting on the advice of the Supreme Judicial Council).[37] The Al-Sabah tightly control the composition of the highest court, the Constitutional Court (*Al-Mahkama Al-Dusturiyya*) that deals with constitutional matters. Given this compromised neutrality, the Al-Sabah have often threatened opposition in parliament with constitutional litigation, as MPs know well that in general the Constitutional Court supports the regime's interests.[38]

In fine, the executive – meaning the Al-Sabah – dominates all spheres of institutional power, facilitated through its pervasive networks of economic patronage as a consequence of its oil resources. These politics of patronage have only been exacerbated in recent years as a consequence of intra-family struggles that have led to the exploitation of the judiciary, the media and legislative powers by princes in their competition for power.[39]

Apart from Abdallah al-Salim's rule, the Al-Sabah have demonstrated a willingness to curtail parliament's power by dissolving it or proposing constitutional amendments and it was external threat that enabled the survival of Kuwait's parliamentary life.[40] Electoral and judicial gerrymandering have been rather frequent tools resorted to by the Al-Sabah. The redistricting of electoral constituencies allowed the Al-Sabah to change the demographic equilibrium in favour of its loyal supporters.

The *hadar* elite's power in early parliamentary life: 1962–76

Political tribalism

Oil has facilitated the emergence of a system of neo-patrimonial rule, in which the ruling family patronizes large sectors of society via economic patronage. The abundance of resources strengthened dynastic monarchies. It made it easier to balance interests between competing branches of the ruling family and to create what Herb (1999) calls dynasties. Within this system of neo-patrimonial rule, *power* is exercised via different venues. Informality and personalized patronage are at its core and ruler–elite relations are largely forged behind the scenes and behind formal institutions, such as parliament. This is reinforced by the fact that as a minority having lost its social standing in communities, the merchant elite does not have the power in parliament to voice its interests effectively and has different venues to exercise its power, i.e. high government positions, ownership of media, direct access to the Al-Sabah and membership of the KCC.

One can consider this system of informal rule as both pyramidal and circular, composed of *halaqat*: of different circles of elites, groups or clans.[1] The first group is the closest to the Emir and the ruling elite, while the second group is linked to the ruler via the first group, in a form of complex relations of interdependence. Some of these elites thus represent broader constituencies and allow the ruler to reach out to broader constituencies, often via economic patronage. Through these informal channels, the Al-Sabah can influence political life; by co-opting powerful social elites, representing different *corps* such as workers' unions, religious groups and tribes. Over time, as a consequence of social change, new elites can be added to this circle, leading to the juxtaposition of different elites representing similar or new constituencies. In cases, this can cause friction between new and old elites, with old elites denouncing the 'newcomers' as unauthentic, lacking family prestige and a glorious past, and considering them as solely interested in profiting from the Al-Sabah's patronage. What matters is that in all cases, informal ties to Al-Sabah shaykhs – sometimes via mediators – determine outreach to constituencies, in which individuals play a key role. The presence of large oil resources strengthens the Al-Sabah's capacity to engage in these different layers of patronage games, favoured by a monarchical regime that does not have a particular ideology underpinning its rule, allowing for a relative flexibility in domestic alliances.[2]

This system has been described by Kuwaiti sociologist Khaldun al-Naqeeb as *political tribalism* and would be characteristic of the tribal oil monarchies. In this conundrum, the regime deals with society via elite representatives of society's major groupings. These are both traditional status groups and more modern groups formed in the post-independence era such as professional bodies. As a part of the monarchies' strategies has consisted of upholding pre-oil identities, the system has reinforced the tendencies of traditional groups to reinvent themselves in the state on the basis of their primordial group attachment, leading to a process of *retribalization* or *repatrimonialization*.[3] In this regard, the traditional authority structure inherently weakens modern governance (mediated through law rather than persons), as argued by Al-Naqeeb. These group 'asabiyyas (i.e. tribal, merchant, Shi'a) reinvent themselves in the rentier monarchy to defend their collective interests and access to state patronage. The consequence is a hybrid state, in which modern elements of governance coexist with informal rule based upon personalized ties and traditional group attachments.

What matters here is that this system of informal rule underpins the mechanisms of power at the disposal of *hadar* elites in the political realm, despite their gradual retreat from the legislative arena. In the following section, the emphasis is on the evolution of power of the *hadar* elites since 1962 until 1990. Power should be considered in its broadest sense, meaning the capacity to influence decision-making, to influence actors within society (via access to the Al-Sabah, ownership of media and support of groups as well as social prestige) and preserve its elite interests.

Power relations within the Al-Sabah under Abdallah al-Salim

As observed by Al-Najjar (1984), Crystal (1990) and Herb (1999), Kuwait was the first Gulf shaykhdom to establish a family regime that balanced between different ruling factions.

The first mechanisms of power-sharing within the family were established in the aftermath of the 1938 *Majlis* events. A weak ruling family faced with eminent internal and external threat led the ruler – Ahmad al-Jabir – to expand power to other members of the family and notably the contending Al-Salim branch. Abdallah al-Salim and his brothers had contested Ahmad al-Jabir over the latter's monopolization of revenues and power and therefore had allied themselves with the nationalists, a classic issue of contention within ruling families in the Gulf. To strengthen the unity of the family in the face of threat, Ahmad al-Jabir had to placate Abdallah al-Salim and his partisans, leading to a division of responsibilities along both lines. Abdallah al-Salim came to handle the important portfolios of finance, customs, supplies and police.

The discovery of the first oil fields gave a further impetus to organize the family and extend power to a larger group of Al-Sabah shaykhs, as more princes wanted to have a stake in the new, skyrocketing family resources. Family allowances were increased, leading to a land grab among the princes who anticipated a rise in prices in view of future urban development projects. As a result of this land acquisition programme, ruling family members were able to enter the business community and invest in economic activities by establishing companies or by investing in the real estate market, different from the pre-oil era where the Al-Sabah had respected the merchants' monopolization of the economic sector.[4] Also, family members were given positions in pre-independence administration portfolios, with considerable power concentrated in the hands of a few overambitious princes. When Abdallah al-Salim took power in 1950, Abdallah al-Mubarak and Fahad al-Salim were among such princes. Abdallah al-Mubarak had been heading the security forces since the 1940s and owned large plots of land in the desert area. By the end of the 1950s he became so powerful that he openly dared to defy the ruler in his diwaniyya. Fahad al-Salim was the ruler's half-brother and headed the municipality and the health department. His ambitions to strengthen local clienteles had placed him in conflict with the British firms that received tenders to develop the health service.[5]

Both shaykhs were a thorn in the side of Abdallah al-Salim as their corruption had contributed to the diversion of funds for personal uses rather than development. Attempts had been made to reduce Abdallah al-Mubarak's power and he was finally ousted in 1961, following a conflict with the ruler.[6] With the natural death of Fahad al-Salim in 1959, Abdallah al-Salim had succeeded in consolidating in the early 1960s a family regime that functioned as a dynasty. In an unprecedented move, he appointed his brother – Sabah al-Salim – as heir apparent whose low profile allowed the ruler to strengthen the unity of the family. New bodies such as a Supreme Council (a proto-cabinet) were established whose membership consisted only of shaykhs. Abdallah al-Mubarak had been replaced by Abdallah al-Salim's son S'ad as head of Public Security and Fahad al-Salim's death allowed the ruler to appoint his own brother – Sabah al-Salim – to the position of head of the health department. To placate the Jabir's side, Jaber al-Ahmad was allocated the portfolios of finance and oil.[7] The violent crackdown on the Al-Malik branch by the ruler was unanimously accepted by Al-Sabah members and demonstrated the leadership of Abdallah al-Salim in balancing family affairs.[8]

Increasingly, the ruler had been delegating tasks and distributing fiefs to members of his family. This contrasted largely with the situation before 1938 when the ruler had ruled mostly by himself and relied upon external advisors from outside the family. The new regime created upon independence tried to balance power between the Al-Salim and Al-Jabir branches via land acquisition and the allocation of government portfolios to princes.[9] Also, Abdallah al-Salim had effectively built independence vis-à-vis the British by strengthening the unity of the family and offering concessions to powerful internal forces, the merchants and nationalists.[10]

Upon independence and the formation of a government, all appointed ministers were ruling family members (leaving only a few elected commoner ministers). Although there had been a gradual decline in ruling family ministers, the Al-Sabah continued to monopolize the most powerful ministries – Interior, Defence, Information and Foreign Affairs – and the post of Prime Minister.[11] Over time, the role of the family moreover expanded to other powerful sectors that were previously the exclusive domain of the merchants, notably media, the private sector and the field of sports. Under Abdallah al-Salim's reign, the principle of family rule was institutionalized and consolidated. This strengthened the role of the ruling family, but nonetheless intermarriages with the Najdi merchant elite and Bedouins continued to cement old and new alliances (especially in the context of the naturalizations of *badu* throughout the 1960s, 1970s and 1980s).

Abdallah al-Salim (r. 1950–65) and the merchant and nationalist elites

Abdallah al-Salim's reign was characterized by rather good relations with societal actors. He was popular among the merchants, a legacy of his participation in the 1938 parliament as a dissident shaykh along the nationalists. He was generally popular in Kuwaiti society for his promulgation of the constitution and the start of generous welfare and development programmes. During his rule, he was able to fend off the power of anti-constitutional elements in the ruling family. Things would change after his death.

Although having good relations with the opposition, Abdallah al-Salim's reign witnessed a tense period preceding independence in which he had to skilfully balance nationalists internally and the threat of Iraqi irredentism. In the absence of parliamentary life then, political activities were organized in the culture and sports clubs (*andia*) and in diwaniyyas of prominent activists. As was the case in Bahrain, these clubs remained largely elitist gatherings, as the masses were still too busy with earning their livelihood. Jamal Abdel Nasser's leadership was a major inspiration for these nationalists – led by Ahmad al-Khatib – whose activities concentrated on the National Culture Club (*Nadi al-Taqafa al-Qawmi*) that would become in 1962 the Independence Club (*Nadi al-Istiqlal*). Inspired by Nasserism, they had been rallying for modern governance and Kuwait's independence.[12]

The opposition in the 1950s that developed in the shadow of Nasserism was heavily influenced by the presence of Arab expatriates (notably Egyptians, Iraqis and Palestinians) who were working in Kuwait's nascent administration. Events in the region would resonate in Kuwait through these expatriates who were close to politicized Kuwaitis: the nationalists. Pro-Nasser speeches were heard in the Culture Club in 1956 during the Suez crisis and an anti-colonial stance was taken by its members. The popularity of Nasser in Kuwait concerned Abdallah al-Salim, who allegedly said to one of his friends, the merchant Yusuf al-Nusf, after the evening prayer seeing cars in the streets displaying photos of Jamal Abdel Nasser: 'Don't these people understand that Abdallah al-Salim is the ruler of Kuwait?'.[13]

Partly to reduce the threat of Arab expatriates, the Nationality Law in 1959 made a sharp differentiation between Kuwaitis and non-Kuwaitis, strengthening borders between the two groups and conferring a sense of unity and privilege upon Kuwaitis entitled to citizenship. Yet, 1959 also saw direct confrontation between the regime and the opposition. This happened when nationalists used the occasion of the first-year anniversary of the United Arab Republic to denounce reactionary regimes, including Kuwait.[14] Following the incident, the ruler resorted to Abdallah al-Mubarak (who had earlier been critical of the ruler's tolerance) to crush the movement, supported by the British and tribal regiments. This led to the arrest and exile of many nationalists. All political gatherings were banned and societies were closed down and media was censored until independence.

Despite these rather tense events, on the whole, the ruler's relation with the nationalists remained good. The latter's anger was namely directed against the person of Abdallah al-Mubarak, who was a generally unpopular shaykh, due to his corrupted lifestyle and extravagance that earlier already had been denounced by nationalists in pamphlets.[15] A factor possibly favourable to the ruler was the negative perception of other shaykhs towards Al-Mubarak, who was expelled in 1961.[16] This itself strengthened Abdallah al-Salim's capacity to control power in the family. Qasim's threat to annex Kuwait in 1961 further strengthened Abdallah al-Salim's popularity, as it prompted a quick response to open up for power-sharing as a means to safeguard Kuwait's sovereignty. Immediately after the threat, Abdallah al-Salim included the merchants in the process and composed a committee of merchants, while one Al-Sabah member (Jaber al-Ahmad) lobbied for independence among Arab capitals and promised the principles of participatory governance. The Iraqi threat united Kuwaitis behind the ruler, considered as a figure of unity in times of crisis. This was reflected in the popular reaction following the threat, with crowds marching towards the Emir's palace chanting '*Ya Bu Salim, 'atina silah* (*Son of Salim – give us arms*).'[17]

Another factor that added to relatively cordial ties of the merchant elite with the ruler was the personal bonds he had with them and with some prominent nationalists. Ahmad al-Khatib was the physician of Abdallah al-Salim and was a close friend to his son, Sa'd al-Abdallah. As a further sign of his proximity to ruling circles, he married the daughter of the son of Molla Salih – Abdallah al-Salih – the (Sunna) Iranian special advisor to the Al-Sabah since Mubarak's reign.[18]

Abdallah al-Salim did not have good relations with the British, who kept in mind his participation in nationalist agitation in 1938 and considered him an anti-British figure. His reign focused on oil and state-building. In this regard, he was rather concessional to the demands of the merchants. Their interests often conflicted with the British, who aimed to carve out for themselves the spoils of the oil economy. As such, Abdallah al-Salim obliged foreign firms to have local partners from the merchant elite. Also, the merchants were effective in cancelling a series of development tenders for British firms that threatened their economic position. Further, the creation of Kuwait's National Bank (*Al-Bank Al-Watani Al-Kuwaiti*) – established in 1952 – was a direct consequence of these merchant's lobbying, an initiative which the British resented fearing it would compete with the Imperial Bank of Iran's monopoly over banking in Kuwait, which did not expire until 1971.[19] Until today, the board of National Bank of Kuwait represents the nucleus of the Sunni Najdi elite.[20] As a further concession to the merchants, the KCC (*Al-Ghurfa Al-Tijara wa Al-Sina'a*) was created. Its membership continues to represent the interests of the old elite of merchants, dominated by the Sunni elite and with an average of two out of twenty-four seats allocated to the old Shi'a elite.

Another venue to represent the merchants' interests was the early parliaments. In 1963, shortly after the promulgation of the constitution, a fifty-member parliament was elected. While merchants had a smaller role in this parliament compared to the CA, they were still a rather powerful and unified group. Broadly speaking, the 1963 assembly represented five social categories: (1) the merchants (apart from some merchant nationalists), (2) professionals/rising middle classes, nationalists and those without a clear political line, (3) Al-Sabah members as ministers with de-facto membership of parliament, (4) the Shi'a who were for the first time represented, (5) a limited number of tribesmen for the first time represented.[21] Most of the members of the CA were re-elected as members of the 1963 parliament.

Between 1963 and 1965, relations between the Al-Sabah government and parliament were relatively smooth and differences were largely resolved via direct access to the ruler, who had close ties to elites in parliament. In those years, opposition did not really come from the nationalists, but more from those groups who opposed the nationalists; some of whom were supported by powerful anti-democratic Al-Sabah members. The proximity of the merchants and nationalists to the person of the ruler also explains why it was only after his death that a group of nationalists presented their resignation in protest of what they deemed to be anti-democratic legislation.[22]

Redistribution of oil-derived rents to the merchants

As demonstrated by Jill Crystal, the nucleus of Najdi families that participated in the *Majlis* events was compensated with preferential contracts and the spoils of the land acquisition programme as part of the country's state-building and development projects.[23] This was a general pattern in Gulf shaykhdoms, where the merchant elites maintained their position on top of social hierarchy. The board members of modern firms like Kuwait National Bank, Kuwait Airways and the Kuwait Oil Tankers Company were all members of the pre-oil elite. An example is the Al-Ghanim family – Najdi pearl merchants – who participated in the 1938 movement, fled to Iraq and later returned to Kuwait on a royal amnesty after which the family invested in the nascent oil industry as the top supply and labour contractor (*mukawil*) of the Kuwait Oil Company (KOC) – with almost 800 men under the family's supervision. Yusuf al-Ghanim, patriarch of the family, became the contractor for many foreign groups (e.g. General Motors, Philips TV, British Airways, Gulf Air), a privilege granted to him by the ruler himself. In the 1980s his group had become the fifth largest Arab merchant house. His trajectory was a common one for the Najdi elite that had participated in pre-oil politics.

Land acquisition was not only a way of balancing power within the Al-Sabah, it was also a prime mechanism of quick wealth distribution to the merchants, who were the second major beneficiaries of the programme.[24] The programme was initiated in 1951 and officially designed to encourage moving people from old areas to the new suburbs as part of a government urbanization programme. Strongly supported by the British initially (who saw in it a means to profit from lucrative development tenders), the programme was in essence a means to resolve intra-elite struggles and strike a deal with the merchants. As the merchants owned the best and largest parcels of land in the old city, they benefitted most from the programme. The state purchased this land at high prices and later resold it at low prices to the same merchants. This gave a boost to the real estate sector and speculation and allowed merchants to use the received money to invest in development projects.[25] An additional factor helpful to the merchants here was their privileged access to state bureaucrats and Al-Sabah shaykhs who were active in the development programmes and could give them information on future areas of state purchase. Using this for buying new lands that would be developed soon allowed them as well as some well-placed bureaucrats to make huge sums of money by selling these lands at inflated prices to the state.[26]

The establishment of the Chamber of Commerce (1955) was a further sign of the merchants' lobbying power and became the centrepiece of their interests. It replaced a smaller merchants' committee and served as the institutionalized voice of the group vis-à-vis the Al-Sabah. Whenever they were not content with an issue, it would be raised via the Chamber, which offered a far more effective channel of communication than parliament where they had to compete with other groups.

In the 1960s, merchants were also encouraged to participate in the nascent industrial sector. This was done by providing them with similar incentives as in the case of land acquisition. The government stimulated the merchants' investment in industrial joint stock companies by promising state support in case of losses and other preferential guarantees. This complemented the merchants' monopoly in trade and services, fields characterized by extreme economic nationalism in which expatriates were banned from any meaningful independent activities.[27] While legislation objectively distinguished between Kuwaiti firms and foreigners, government contracts and tenders *implicitly* differentiated between the old Najdi elite and other Kuwaitis; the first receiving a quasi-monopoly in these domains. Until recently, the Central Tenders Committee (*Lajna al-Munaqasat al-Markaziyya*) attributes the lion's share of lucrative tenders to members of this old elite; an issue of increased contention in parliament. Recently the law has changed and allowed for competition - but the question is how it will be applied. Many government contracts that were given to old domestic firms were pure transfers of rent in which these firms contributed neither capital nor management. It was only oil that constituted the domain exclusively in the hands of the Al-Sabah.

Other venues for the merchants were high executive positions in government (as ministers) and in ministries; posts they tended to combine with their commercial activities.[28] Until today, they dominate high executive positions in ministries, although since the late 1980s, the Najdi elite has receded in terms of occupying ministerial posts, coinciding with a rise in ministers' posts given to Islamists and tribal elites. The predominance of the *hadar* elites in high executive positions was a recurrent theme and thorn in the eye of many of my badu interlocutors.

Consequently, under Abdallah al-Salim's reign (1950–65), the merchants were placated by the government, being bought-off as a class, not different from the other Gulf shaykhdoms. The large welfare projects that for the first time created on a wide scale roads, schools, mosques and provided free health care and housing to Kuwaitis advanced the material position of the masses enough to reduce opposition towards the privileges of the merchants.

Sabah al-Salim (r. 1965–77) and the *hadar* elite

Upon Abdallah al-Salim's death, the faction in the ruling family that had supported a more hostile stance towards constitutional liberties strengthened its power. Although Abdallah was succeeded by his brother in 1965 – Sabah al-Salim[29] – the real power came to lie in the hands of the Al-Ahmad camp, represented by Jaber al-Ahmad (PM) and Sabah al-Ahmad (MFA). It would mark the start of the restoration of a more authoritarian style of rule.

Having lost their privileged Al-Sabah patron, the *hadar* elite raised its oppositional tone in parliament since 1965. Immediately after Abdallah al-Salim's death, the nationalist bloc resigned in protest of legislation they deemed anti-democratic.[30] This gave the government more leeway to crack down on political opposition, which became clear with the turn of events after 1965. With nationalists now out of parliament, the government of Jaber al-Ahmad stepped up the crackdown on expatriate Arab nationalists. It also dissolved the board of the Municipal Council (*Al-Majlis Al-Baladi*) that had served as a rather critical body vis-à-vis the land acquisition programme.[31]

The increasingly authoritarian stance of the Al-Sabah became clear in the results of the 1967 elections that were characterized by large-scale fraud. It was a parliament dominated by pro-government forces, with only four out of the previous thirty-seven opposition candidates re-elected. Merchants and nationalists that had allied to strengthen their forces in preparation of the 1967 election suffered a terrible defeat.[32] Ahmad al-Khatib lost to the conservative editor of *Al-Ra'i al-'Am*, Abdulaziz al-Musaid. Also, the candidates in the largely tribal district of Al-Ahmadi – dominated by the 'Ajman – all lost. They were known for their alliance with Jaber al-'Ali – the powerful Minister of Guidance – whose power ambitions made him ally with social forces and notably the 'Ajman that he had helped naturalize.[33]

The extent of electoral fraud was partly due to rising competition within the Al-Sabah between Jaber al-'Ali and Jaber al-Ahmad; although it is difficult to find precise information about the issue.[34] Jaber al-Ahmad had succeeded Sabah al-Salim as PM and CP in 1965. His political ascension was not smooth. He had lost the position of CP in 1962 to Sabah al-Salim, the brother of the then incumbent ruler. Jaber al-Ahmad had previously headed the finance and oil portfolios and was initially known as a young, progressive shaykh with good contacts with the nationalists.[35] In his memoirs, Ahmad al-Khatib refers to Jaber al-Ahmad as one of the most open-minded persons within the Al-Sabah who in his young years supported the nationalist cause. Responsible for oil, he was instrumental in bidding for stronger nationalist clauses in oil contracts with foreign companies. Also, he had close ties to young nationalists, was close to nationalists such as Al-Qatami in the writing of the constitution and was the shaykh who had accompanied this group in their lobbying for Kuwait's sovereignty among Arab capitals in 1961. The situation changed, argues Al-Khatib, when the ambitious prince, Jaber al-'Ali – one of the main rivals of Jaber al-Ahmad in the competition for the future position of CP – started to co-opt forces to attack the merchants and nationalists in parliament: groups that initially had good relations with Jaber al-Ahmad and the government.

This started in 1964, when a group of MPs fiercely opposed the presence of merchants in ministerial positions, referring to article 131 of the constitution. This article stipulated that ministers were not allowed to hold any other office or activities than their government position to avoid a conflict of interest. Opposing MPs criticized the presence of three merchant ministers in the government as a sign of the violation of article 131. However, the MPs who opposed the article could hardly be considered oppositional and many were government supporters without a clear political stance, mostly from middle-class background. Among them were tribal MPs instigated by Al-Sabah princes.[36] Their actions were by large directed against the Arab nationalists and their merchant allies. This resulted in eleven members of the nationalist group and their supporters walking out of parliament in protest, eight of whom would resign collectively. Confronted with the crisis, the Emir urged the PM Sabah al-Salim and his deputy – Jaber al-Ahmad – to constitute a new cabinet. The merchant ministers resigned as did the speaker of parliament that represented the merchants, Abdulaziz al-Saqqar, also chairman of the KCC.

There are many reasons explaining what is called the 'crisis of article 131'. Some have referred to it as the start of a middle-class opposition against the tacit bargain between the Al-Sabah and merchants, consisting in the idea that merchants should stay out of formal politics in exchange for economic privileges.[37] In line with this idea, groups excluded from this elite bargain would use parliament to voice their opposition to the merchant prerogatives. However, as it was the group of nationalist MPs that had been the key advocate of protecting public interests (i.e. its role in nationalizing the oil sector) and given the fact that the MPs opposing article 131 were known as loyalists, the argument of implicit co-optation by contending royals seems more plausible. In this regard, the powerful Jaber al-'Ali allied himself with these MPs against his rival Jaber al-Ahmad, the deputy PM and Minister of Finance. Jaber al-'Ali – nephew of Abdallah al-Salim – was ambitious and had served as Minister of Electricity and Water and later as Minister of Guidance and News. Under Abdallah al-Salim and until 1965, he was one of the powerful contenders to the position of CP in the case Abdallah al-Salim would die and Sabah al-Salim (then CP) would become Emir.[38] He competed with Jaber al-Ahmad, who was deputy PM and likely to succeed Sabah al-Salim. While Jaber al-'Ali lost the battle to become CP in 1965 when Al-Ahmad was appointed, the competition with Al-Ahmad continued and Jaber al-'Ali did not lose his aspiration to become CP one day, now competing with Sa'd al-Abdallah. This became apparent in his role in co-opting forces in the 1971–5 parliament.[39] The situation ended when Shaykh Sa'd al-Abdallah was appointed as CP in 1978, prompting Jaber al-'Ali to resign from the Cabinet and leave the country until his death. Since his early years of competition for the position of CP – since 1963 – Al-'Ali was instrumental in naturalizing, arming and bringing 'Ajman royalists to parliament.[40]

Jaber al-'Ali's support to the group of MPs that opposed article 131 – a group that tends to be classified as middle-class group as it lacked a coherent political vision[41] – threatened Jaber al-Ahmad, who in response allied with Shaykh Sa'd al-Abdallah; a pragmatic alliance as the two personalities did not go along well and Sa'd moreover belonged to the competing Al-Salim branch. Nonetheless, their alliance reportedly played a crucial role in the widespread electoral fraud of 1967; anticipating a landslide victory for opposition forces and the new Bedouin allies of Jaber al-'Ali, they supported opposing forces and bribed candidates.[42]

It is in this context of intra-family competition that one should read the context preceding the 1967 elections. The results were condemned by the nationalists and also the merchants, who – despite their new dependence on the state – joined the petition denouncing the rigging of elections, a move unexpected by the government.[43] Understanding the loss of crucial merchant support in state-building, now that they had collectively withdrawn, CP Jaber al-Ahmad issued a lengthy speech in advance of the 1971 elections deploring the fact that some important groups (among them the merchants) had withdrawn from nation-building and criticizing some MPs who would place personal benefits before the public ones. His speech further called upon the merchants to participate in the upcoming elections. The display of self-criticism by the ruler found a favourable hearing among the opposition forces but was criticized within the Al-Sabah.

The rise of new middle-class elites and the decline of the *hadar* elites

Fragmentation of the nationalist movement after the 1967 defeat

By the 1970s, a gradual change in political forces had occurred; a change that played in favour of the Al-Sabah and the ruler, Sabah al-Salim. The year 1967 was a double defeat for Kuwaiti nationalists. Not only were they excluded from parliament, but also suffered a trauma as a result of Nasser's loss of the Six-Day War. The catastrophic military defeat of Egypt, Syria and Jordan against Israel in 1967 split the ranks of the nationalists everywhere in the region. It led to a phase of self-questioning and introspection, as Arab voices unprecedentedly blamed themselves rather than colonialism for their defeat. This paved the way for the rise of Islamist currents and for more short-lived Marxist-Leninist streams, with many nationalist defecting to either of the two. Islamists tended to raise the idea that the defeat was punishment for the support of alien ideologies, a great deviance from Islamic faith.[1]

In Kuwait, the nationalists splintered in different political groups. A small section opted for a radical, Marxist way and was supported by students and members of the workers union. They were in favour of armed struggle and were close to the PLO and to the communist-backed insurgents in Dhofar, who staged a rebellion against the Sultanate of Muscat and Oman, which were supported by Britain and Iran.[2] In 1968 it led to the creation of the Revolutionary Youth Movement in Oman and the Arabian Gulf. A second group stayed totally faithful to Nasser. This was the group of Jasem al-Qatami, a merchant, who created the Nationalist Gathering (*Al-Tajamu'a Al-Watani*). Finally, there was the group of Ahmad al-Khatib that favoured a more leftist line, without being overtly Marxist: the Democratic Gathering (*Al-Tajamu'a Al-Dimoqrati*). Many of the young men of the first group would later join Ahmad al-Khatib and be among Kuwait's prominent leftist intellectuals. One can think of Ahmad al-Rabi'i, Ahmad al-Diyan and Abdellatif al-Daij.[3] For the merchants, while some supported Jasem al-Qatami, most of them distanced themselves from the Nasserist and socialist project which opposed their elite interests; a split that was observed everywhere in the region.

These divisions within the opposition camp were reflected in elections for the boards of cultural societies that were the main venue for political activities. The most important was the Independence Society, but other fiefs were the Teachers Society, the Graduates Society, the National Union of Kuwaiti Students, the Lawyers Society and the General Union of Kuwaiti Workers. Elections for the Independence Society were won by Al-Khatib's group, who also stayed in control of the weekly magazine *Al-Tali'a* (The Vanguard) that exists until today as their mouthpiece. Al-Qatami's group took control over the Teachers and Graduates Societies and still had a strong influence in the Ministry of Foreign Affairs, as he had been undersecretary for the MFA in 1961 and recruited many nationalists there.[4] The less influential Marxist groups gained control over the General Union of Kuwaiti Workers.

On the eve of the 1971 elections, these divisions were manifested in the splits among the groups about whether or not to participate. The merchants welcomed participation, while Al-Khatib's group was suspicious. Nonetheless, the latter decided to take part in the elections. Surprisingly, Al-Qatami's group that had good ties with the merchant community boycotted the elections. This further split the opposition, as now one group was outside parliament.

Economic patronage outside the established elite: Souq al-Manakh

Another factor playing in favour of the government was the rise in oil prices in the 1970s, as a consequence of the OAPEC's decision to raise prices in reaction to Western support to Israel in the Yom Kippur War in 1973.[5] The price hikes strengthened oil income and allowed the government to step up its rent redistribution to society and, importantly, to actors outside the established elite. Scores of shareholding companies were created and for the first time members of the middle class entered en masse into stock market speculation. In this context, the government tolerated the creation of the *Souq al-Manakh* bubble that provided opportunities to the small investor. This shadow stock market existed on the sidelines of the official market and dealt primarily with the trade in stocks of companies banned in the official market – lacking records and assets – that had Kuwaiti owners but were registered elsewhere in the Gulf. The bubble was caused not only by the fact that companies tended to exist on paper only, but also because of the widespread use of so-called forward dealings; post-dated checks with premiums of 25 to 500 per cent that were written in advance.[6] Speculation led to the exorbitant rise in prices of obligations.

The established merchant elite was not much involved and thus little hurt, as it traded on the official market that needed larger sums of investment and came out of the crisis stronger, because this elite played an important role in resolving the crisis negotiating settlements via the KCC and used the crisis to promote protectionist policies. However, elite groups like the Qina'at were prominently involved in the Al-Manakh market and lost considerably as one of their members – Jasem al-Mutawa'a – was the first to be unable to pay the value of a cashed check, sparking the crash. For this reason, many in the Sunni aristocracy tend to blame the crash on the unbridled greed of the Qina'at – their competitors in the private sector – and were eager for the stock market nouveaux riches to be 'nailed to the wall'.[7] The aftermath of the crisis allowed the government to strengthen its ties with the indebted and members of the Qina'at clan, as they benefitted from bail-out schemes by the government and thus government patronage.

Revivalist Sunni Islamism supported by the government

Al-Ikhwan Al-Muslimin (MB) and Jam'iyyat al-Islah

The government from the 1970s onwards also supported the rise of Sunni Islamist currents politically and economically. The first group to profit from this was the MB current in Kuwait, represented by its Society for Social Reform (*Jam'iyyat al-Islah al-Ijtima'i*).[8] The Kuwaiti Brotherhood emanated from the Guidance Society (*Jam'iyyat al-Irshad*) that was created by shaykhs and merchants – inspired by Islamic reformism.[9] Given the absence of a local religious class, they imported – under the patronage of *Al-Azhar* – several shaykhs to teach in public schools and preach in mosques, diffusing Islamic revivalist thought.[10] They had to deal with opposition from more radical established Islamic voices in society.

Many of the group's founders belonged to merchant and religious elite families outside the Najdi elite – second-tier elite groups close to the Al-Sabah – although it also counted a minority of young members belonging to the Najdi elite.[11] The Qina'at group in particular had a strong influence in the Ikhwan movement of Kuwait, as many of its founding members belonged to the Qina'at. Abdelaziz al-Mutawa'a was the founder of the movement and elected as the general supervisor of the Guidance Society. His brother Abdallah played an important role too, and the first office of the society was located in the house of their father, Ali Abdelwahhab al-Mutawa'a. Shaykh Yusuf al-Qina'i and Khaled al-Issa, leading members of the Guidance Society all were part of the Qina'at. Yusuf al-Qina'i was president of the society. Other influential members (such as Muhammad al-Adsani) were also from urban elite families known for their close ties to the Al-Sabah.[12]

As so often in Kuwait's history, transnational personal ties would be crucial in transmitting ideologies.[13] Abdelaziz Ali al-Mutawa' forged ties with the MB founder – Hassan al-Banna – during his studies in Cairo – and was also in close contact with founders of the Iraqi MB. Upon his return to Kuwait, he established the Guidance Society (1952), benefitting from the political opening enabled by the new ruler, Abdallah al-Salim, that saw the flourishing of clubs (*andia*). The name Ikhwan was shunned, as it revived memories of the Wahhabi zealots who had attacked Kuwait in 1921. Kuwait's Guidance Society was directly created as part of the Egyptian MB organization and its influence spread in Kuwaiti society via the arrival of expatriates (mainly from Egypt and Palestine) who came to Kuwait to work in nascent government bodies. By then, membership of the clubs that flourished in the 1950s was open to foreigners and allowed these expatriates to spread the MB's ideology in society.[14] Although the movement was established by Kuwaiti notables, foreigners had a major influence on the organization and Kuwait's Guidance Society was organizationally linked to its Egyptian mother organization.

However, until 1967, the society was rather small, a pious elite gathering and not very popular in society, as nationalism was still the reigning ideology of the time.[15] Combined with splits between more radical and moderate voices of its members, the Guidance Society fragmented and finally closed its doors in 1960, as it had lost many of its Kuwaiti members to the nationalist current.[16] While boards of other societies – dominated by the nationalists – were closed by government decree in 1959 following nationalist upheaval denouncing reactionary regimes (including Kuwait), the Guidance Society was the only one to be allowed to exist – a token of its loyal stance vis-á-vis the Al-Sabah – and it was internal fragmentation that led to its closure. It was in 1963 – in a context of renewed political opening following the Iraqi threat – that thirty members established the Society for Social Reform (*Jam'iyyat al-islah al-ijtima'i*) that became the official wing of the Kuwaiti Ikhwan, although it also had members who were Islamists but did not necessarily share the ideology of the Ikhwan. With the creation of a Salafi organization (*Ihya al-Turath*) in 1981, some of them would leave the organization and opt for Salafism.

The new organization resembled its predecessor in rhetoric and goals but would this time profit from a more favourable context to strengthen its social outreach. This was the consequence of the military defeat of Egypt, Syria and Jordan by Israel and the blow it presented to Arab nationalism as an ideology incapable of reviving Arab power in the face of what was considered imperialism by Israel and Western powers. Public opinion shifted considerably and the vacuum left by a fragmented nationalist movement was gradually filled by a growing role of religiosity in public life. While mosques had been rather empty in Kuwait in the early 1950s, now, a change occurred, with people displaying overt signs of religiosity.[17]

The consequent shift in public opinion was beneficial to the Kuwaiti MB who had been present for two decades and were able to build an organizational infrastructure.[18] In 1967, the creation of a 'secret organization' (*Al-tanzim Al-sirri*) complemented the Society for Social Reform; following in the footsteps of the Egyptian and Iraqi Brotherhood that were forced to engage in clandestine activities as a consequence of the repression they faced from secular nationalist authorities in their countries. It would only be after the Iraqi invasion that this clandestine group would gain an official representation in Kuwait as the Constitutional Islamic Movement (*Al-haraka Al-dusturiyya Al-islamiyya*).

This reorganization coincided with the rise of a new generation of activists that gradually supplanted an older *hadar* elite. The movement had been established by merchants under the leadership of Abdelaziz al-Wahab al-Mutawa'. By then, it was largely dominated by merchants, with a rather high number of members from the Qina'at grouping.[19] The new young guard, mostly from middle-class background, had profited from education abroad and, once returned home, opted for more revolutionary ideas for social change via Islam as all-encompassing reference. One can think of Ismail al-Shatti, Naser al-Sana'a, and Mubarak al-Duwaila, Yusuf al-'Atiqi, Tareq al-Suwaidan and Shaykh Jasim al-Yassin.[20] Their ideas clashed with the older generation – founders of Al-Irshad – who were mostly merchants and favoured a less politicized role, focusing on the Islamization of values that did not endanger their business interests; many of whom decide to leave the organization in protest.[21] Some of these older men occupied high posts in the administration, such as Muhammad al-Adsani who was ambassador of Kuwait and minister before occupying the post of speaker of parliament in 1981 or Abdel Rahman al-'Atiqi or Yusuf al-Rifa'i who all occupied ministerial posts for various years.[22] This general split was not only between members but also occurred within families between older and younger members.

In the 1960s, while maintaining its clandestine nature, an elaborate hierarchal structure was put in place, composed of both Kuwaiti and non-Kuwaiti Muslim Brothers.[23] It further relied on its magazine *Al-Mujtama'* (1965) to diffuse its influence in society, especially in the wider region.[24] Although until 1989 the group was led by two exiled Iraqis (Abdel-Wahab 'Aman and Muhammad Ahmad al-Rashid), since the 1970s a gradual process of *Kuwaitisation* was set in motion, as the young Kuwaitis gained a stronger role in the organization at the expense of Arab migrants. These changes also had their influence on the Society for Social Reform.[25] When Abdallah al-Mutawa' succeeded Yusuf al-Haji as its head in 1976, the role of the activist young men would become stronger.[26]

These changes in the political strategies of the Ikhwan in Kuwait coincided with growing government patronage of the group to counterbalance the secular elite, i.e. established merchants and nationalists. In the 1970s, the growing confrontation between the movement and the secular leftist groups was supported by the government. The transfer in 1970 of the headquarters of the Society for Social Reform from a humble building in the Um Sida area to a new location in Rawda on a big plot of land was partly funded by the government.[27] Also, the group was allowed more influence in organizing the *zakat* collection and was granted government land in the most expensive area of Kuwait – the industrial area of Shuweikh – to build Kuwait's first Islamic Bank, the Kuwait Financial House (*Beit al-Tamwil*), in 1977 that was dispensed from financial oversight by Kuwait's Central Bank and that would have a monopoly on Islamic finance until 2003.[28] Then, the group was allowed to collect money for charities with little government supervision, leading to the expansion of charitable committees and mosques linked to the movement. The group's members were also granted privileged positions in the Ministry of Education, leading to a growing role of Islam in educational curricula. While co-optation had been implicit in the 1960s, in 1976 an open alliance between the government and the Islamic movement occurred. The Ikhwan were the only one not to protest the dissolution of parliament in 1976, in exchange for which they received two ministers' posts. Yusuf al-Haji was appointed Minister of Religious Endowments (*Awqaf*) and Abdelrahman al-'Atiqi Minister of Finance.

In the 1970s, the activities of the Kuwaiti Ikhwan expanded via the Society for Social Reform and mosques, encompassing the fields of *da'wa*, culture, society and education. The office in Rawda would organize conferences, theatre plays and activities for the youth, a privileged target for the movement. Thematic events were organized – such as competitions to memorize the Qur'an, book fairs and *Haj* travels – that considerably strengthened the role of the movement in society. The success of study circles organized for the youth in mosques led to the opening of additional study centres and libraries in mosques diffusing Ikhwan thought.

Also, while initially concentrating its activities on *hadar* zones *intra muros*, in the 1970s the movement expanded its presence to the tribal regions that were ignored by its predecessor, Al-Irshad. Between 1975 and 1980, new branches were opened by Al-Islah in Al-Jahra, Umariyya and Farwaniyya, making the movement the first to have such a geographical outreach.[29] By then, the tribal zones were largely unaffected by organized Islam. The Ikhwan penetrated the Bedouin areas by allying with the sons of the most important tribes in the region, visiting their mosques and diffusing their ideas.[30] In a context of sweeping social change affecting the rapidly urbanized tribesmen, the ideology of Islamism presented a vehicle for social ascension for these young tribesmen and a new societal framework that matched the generally conservative tribal milieu.

The main activities of the Ikhwan were focused on young people, considered an important resource for social power. For this reason, universities and schools were *loci par excellence* for their activities. As Arab school teachers had been important carriers for nationalist thought in Kuwaiti society, they were also important carriers of Ikhwan thought and notably since the 1970s following the decline of secularism.[31] In 1971, the rising power of the Ikhwan among the youth was manifested during the debates over coeducation at Kuwait University and the presence of many young men supporting the society's stance opposing coeducation.[32] Young Ikhwan members such as Ahmad al-Da'ij, Issa Majid al-Shahin and Abdelrahman al-Sumayt were successful in gathering a large number of followers. In 1977, the movement won the board of the Union of Student's in Kuwait (*Al-Ittihad Al-Watani Li Talba al-Kuwayt*) that until then had been dominated by the leftists and nationalists. Also, intellectuals and preachers linked to the movement gained a strong popular appeal in society via their televised sermons, religious programmes and books. Some famous mosque orators were Shaykh Muhammad al-'Awadi, Shaykh Ahmad al-Qattan and 'Abdel Hamid al-Bilali.[33]

Throughout the 1970s and early 1980s, the influence of the Kuwaiti MB in society would only strengthen, as its members had succeeded in penetrating many of the clubs, labour unions and food cooperatives, appealing to large sections of society at the grassroots level.[34] The Islamic Revolution in Iran and the boost it gave to Islamism provided a further impetus to the group's strength. By the mid-1980s the government had further bolstered the Islamization of Kuwaiti society. The change was observable: while in the 1960s, Kuwaiti faculties were stuffed with students wearing Western-style garments, by the 1980s this had made place for more religious vestimentary habits – men growing beards and women wearing the black *'abaya* with *hijab* and for the very pious, with *niqab*.[35]

Empowered by their success, after the announcement of elections in 1981 after a four-year closure of parliament the Ikhwan decided for the first time to present their own candidates (apart from supporting many others) in a programme focused on the Islamization of laws. Electoral redistricting from ten to twenty-five constituencies further strengthened the power of pro-government forces, Islamists and tribes, who had shown an inclination in favour of the Islamist movement that was able to gain a foothold in the tribal areas since the 1970s. The results of the 1981 elections demonstrated the growing power of Islamists. While only two direct candidates of the Kuwaiti MB were elected, most of the others it had supported also succeeded in the elections. Parliament also for the first time saw a bloc of four oppositional Islamist MPs, led by the *Ikhwani* Issa al-Shahin. Adding to the success of the Islamists was their organization of primaries (*far'iyyat*) in urban areas to strengthen their power in the face of nationalist and Shi'a opposition.

While the bulk of Islamists remained supportive of government, the parliament of 1981–5 marked the rise of a more independent and vocal stance of Islamists. Throughout these years, they lobbied for the change of article 79 of the Constitution, making Islam *the* instead of a main source of legislation; a proposition that was never accepted by the government and Constitutional Court. Other proposals included a ban on Christmas celebration, alcohol importation and the imposition of the veil on women. While most of these proposals never gained the force of law, the growing assertiveness of Islamists was watched with mixed feelings by the government.

To avoid any group from establishing a dominant position in society, the Al-Sabah regime started policies to fragment the Islamist movement by continuing to court the tribes, as well as new groups that were competitors or outright enemies of the Kuwaiti Ikhwan. The government removed two Ikhwan ministers from the new cabinet.[36] Nationalists were again allowed more space in media. And importantly, the regime supported the rise of the Salafi movement as a counter-current to the Ikhwan.

The Salafi current (*Al-tayyar Al-salafi*)

Since the end of the 1970s, the government started to give more space to the Salafi current and support its growth in society in order to avoid the Ikhwan from becoming a too dominant force.

Although the first contacts with Salafism in Kuwait date back to the start of the twentieth century via tribal contacts with Wahhabi zealots on the border areas with Najd and via the interaction of Kuwaiti *'ulema* with the Najdi clerical body of the Al-Saud, the first activities of Salafism started in the mid-1960s. Again, migrants would play a crucial role in transmitting the ideology and the transnational movement. By then some Salafi *da'is* (preachers) settled in Kuwait – part of the expatriate working force – who, inspired by the work of literalist *Ibn Taymiyya* (1263–1328), aimed at transmitting their interpretation of what is 'pure Islam', which in Salafi creed promotes a literal understanding of Qur'an and the Sunna and leaves very little place for human reasoning (*'aql*) and opinion (*ra'i*).[37] Doing so, Salafis try to emulate the practices of the first three generations of Islam, of the righteous ancestors (*Al-salif Al-salih*): the companions (*sahaba*) of the prophet Muhammad and the first two generations of their followers. Because Salafis leave no place for philosophical reasoning and because of their strict interpretation of the oneness of worship (*tawhid al-'ibada*) – that leaves no place for intercession (*tawassul*) or aid (*istighata*) from saints – Salafism rejects practically all other Islamic currents.[38] Hostility towards the Shi'a, however, lies at the core of their ideology. In theory, Salafis consider them as a rejectionist sect (*rafidin*: rejecters) outside of Islam, although in practice some consider only their leadership as such and are milder vis-à-vis the Shi'a masses whom they consider to be deviant Muslims, according to the idea '*amat al-shi'a muslimin wa al-qada kufar*' (the Shi'a masses are Muslims and the leadership are unbelievers). Also, in some cases, pragmatic considerations can lead to cooperation with Shi'a actors.[39] However, in principle, a strict application of the Salafi doctrine leads to a hostile view of the Shi'a, because of their veneration of martyrs and saints via pilgrimage and the emulation of the *maraji'* whom they consider as delegates of the imams with access to the hidden (divine) message of the Qur'an and who therefore become a source of emulation: *maraji' al-taqlid*. Most Salafis would consider this as deviance or unbelief (*kufr*) as it would confer upon the *maraji'* the power of mediators to reach out to the divine message that, in their view, could lead to the worship of humans. This complements Salafis' general abhorrence of mysticism and philosophical reasoning that characterizes Shi'ism.[40] Apart from denouncing the Shi'a, the Salafis also openly targeted the two dominant Sunni Islamist currents in Kuwait they considered to be deviant versions of Islam: *Jama'at al-Tabligh* and the *Ikhwan al-Muslimin.*

Among the main Salafi *da'is* who settled in Kuwait were the Palestinian Abdallah al-Sabt, the Egyptian Abdulrahman Abdel Khaleq and the Saudi Umar al-Ashqar.[41] Especially Al-Sabt and Abdel Khaleq would play a defining role in the development of the Salafi current in Kuwait. Abdallah al-Sabt was a Palestinian junior clerk in Kuwait, autodidact in his religious learning, avid reader of Ibn Taymiyya and Al-Albani. Upon his initiative, a study circle was formed with young Kuwaitis in the *Ahmad Bin Hanbal* mosque in the area of Fayha. Without any clear direction, they decided to establish a movement, called '*Al-da'wa al-salafiyya*' (the Salafi predicament). Around the same time, an Egyptian preacher came to Kuwait from Saudi Arabia where he had graduated from the Islamic University of Medina but was forced to leave due to conflicts with authorities about his criticism of certain public procedures he deemed contrary to Islam. While not intending to stay long in Kuwait – heading for Syria – some influential Islamic figures of Al-Islah, among whom, Abdelrazzaq al-Mutawa', convinced him to stay. Soon he developed his study circle, in a mosque in the same neighbourhood as Al-Sabt, the *Abdel Jalil* mosque. Initially, he attracted Kuwaiti Ikhwan. This was not surprising, as he shared the organizational background of the Ikhwan. Moreover, until the creation of a proper society for Salafism in 1981, Kuwait's Islamist landscape was dominated by the Ikhwan, who headed Al-Islah Society and Islamists with other tendencies tended to join Al-Islah.

Things would change in 1974, when Abdel Khaleq would overtly choose Salafism. This followed a conflict with Kuwaiti Ikhwan members after a lecture Abdel Khaleq gave on Sufism, in which he fiercely denounced Sufis for being unbelievers (*kuffar*); a criticism that was not shared by leading Ikhwan figures who denounced him for his intransigence. The incident would mark the start of the ideological positioning of Salafism as a distinct movement from the Ikhwan. Salafi members of Al-Islah decided to leave the organization and joined Abdel Khaleq who would become the symbol of Salafism in Kuwait. Via his books and weekly columns in *Al-Watan*, he was able to reach a growing number of Salafis and provided the intellectual basis for the Salafi current in Kuwait. While his activist (*haraki*) stance distinguished him from mainstream Salafism, he then still benefitted from government support, as Salafism *as a whole* was considered a useful support for the Al-Sabah regime in the face of considerable external and internal pressure in the 1980s. Moreover, the differences between his activist stance and the purist strand did not lead to overt splits then and would be overshadowed by a context in which Salafism enjoyed growing popularity and government support. Splits would occur overtly in the aftermath of the Invasion, leading to the ouster of Abdel Khaleq from the direction of *Ihya' al-Turath* in favour of the purists, Abdallah al-Sabt and his followers.[42] This was largely the consequence of a switch of government support to the purist Salafis after the Invasion, as Abdel Khaleq had personally sympathized with Saddam Hussayn prior to the Invasion (for the latter's anti-Shi'a stance) and his *haraki* stance made him a potential danger for the monarchy, as its system of hereditary rule and governance that did not fully comply with *shari'a* and alliance with the West made it prey to criticism from *harakis*. Most of the *harakis* namely adopted Sayyid Qutb's concept of the sovereignty of God (*hakimiyya*) that says that governance should be completely based upon *shari'a* and that the ruler's legitimacy relies on a free oath of allegiance (*bay'a*) by the community of believers that has the right to criticize the ruler.

With the politicization of Sunni Islamism, one can understand why there have been ambiguous relations between Sunni Islamist movements and the Al-Sabah regime, continuing until present day. On the one hand, these Islamist forces represent a considerable social and political resource and a source of religious legitimacy for the Al-Sabah (who although not claiming direct religious legitimacy nonetheless heavily rely on religious symbols and Islamic tradition to 'authenticate' and legitimize their rule). On the other hand, they represent a potential threat to hereditary rule, given the insistence on *bay'a* and full *shari'a* compliance. Since the end of the 1980s, this politicized strand has been empowered in Kuwait which consequently poses a potential threat to the regime. For this reason, the latter has switched its support to the purist stance of Salafism after the Invasion.

Until the Invasion, however, the splits within Salafism in Kuwait were not yet exploited by the Al-Sabah and both Abdel Khaleq and the purists were allowed to strengthen their influence in society. His books and columns soon spread in Kuwait and since the mid-1970s, he had a weekly column on Friday in *Al-Watan* daily in which he exposed his *haraki* thought. In these columns, he argued that politics and human development are more important than religious practice per se.[43] He further provided arguments to legitimize the entrance into politics of Salafis; a controversial topic, as purist Salafism rejected politics as an arena of competition inherently prone to strife (*fitna*) and preached full obedience to the ruler, even if the latter has reached power by force, because the institution of governance was considered indispensable.[44] This was the stance of the Wahhabi state *'ulema* as well as of Abdallah al-Sabt. Abdel Khaleq argued that this purist stance would lead to weak rule serving Western interest and had played into the hands of the enemies who destroyed the Caliphate. Political parties, he argued, allowed for *da'wa* and the imposition of righteousness by commanding right and forbidding wrong (*amr bil ma'ruf wa nahy 'an al-munkar*).

While potentially threatening, Abdel Khaleq was allowed to diffuse his ideas and became rather popular within the Salafism stream in Kuwait. His blatant targeting of other currents – Sunna and Shi'a – then played out in favour of the Al-Sabah regime and it weakened potentially threatening forces. His politicized version of Salafism allowed him to target these groups better than the purists focused on religious practice and da'wa.

In the aftermath of the Iranian Revolution, revolutionary fervour reached various groups: the Shi'a, the leftist elite as well as the Ikhwan al-Muslimin and other more radical Sunni groups. The direct consequence of the Islamic Revolution was the crystallization of a social movement in Kuwait, led by Shi'a cleric Abbas al-Mohri, who became Khomeini's delegate and organized pro-Khomeini events in the Sha'ban mosque that drew a large gathering, among them Kuwaiti leftists and their leader, Ahmad al-Khatib. This obviously alarmed the Al-Sabah and led to the exile of Al-Mohri and his family from Kuwait. The Iran–Iraq War further alarmed Kuwait's

Al-Sabah as it enhanced sectarianism in society and led to fears among a ruling family whose perception – ever since Qasim's threat – was that any coerced minority could weaken Kuwait's fragile political community and absorb it into the sphere of influence of external powers. Kuwait fell prey to the regional war, with a series of attacks orchestrated by the Lebanese Hezbollah against Kuwaiti targets throughout the 1980s, in retaliation of Kuwait's support for Iraq.[45] During this period, the Shi'a were subject to extensive government discrimination as their Shi'ism made them potential allies to Iran, resulting in a series of arrests, detentions and general discrimination in public life. This would intensify in the second half of the 1980s, following a series of bombings in Kuwait, mostly orchestrated by foreign Shi'a, but which also saw the involvement of a minority of Kuwaiti Shi'a.[46]

Revolutionary fervour also emanated from Saudi Arabia in 1979, where Salafi zealots under the lead of Juhayman al-'Utaybi occupied the Grand Mosque in Mecca and decided that the reign of the Al-Saud was illegitimate because the latter did not have Qurayshi origins. The fact that a number of Kuwaiti citizens were among Al-'Utaybi's men alarmed the regime.[47] Also, the example of a successful Islamic revolution inspired Sunni Islamists and strengthened their politicization as the Iranian example gave hope that their project of Islamists coming to power could be implemented. In the case of the Ikhwan in Kuwait, articles were published on the importance of political participation as a means to change society although they rejected the idea of an Islamic state in the absence of fertile conditions for its establishment in Kuwait.

As a consequence of this tense regional context that spurred religious fervour among various groups in Kuwait, the co-optation of the Salafis was a logical regime strategy. The Salafis directed their attacks against all of these groups and therefore strengthened divisions in society that worked to the benefit of the Al-Sabah. The Shi'a revolution in Iran was rejected by both the purist and the *haraki* streams in Kuwait, with both of them being still supportive of the Al-Sabah back then. Finally, in a context of the Iran–Iraq War in which Kuwait supported its former enemy Iraq, the regime needed a form of religious legitimacy which the Salafis could provide. The Saudi regime perused similar strategies of co-opting particular apolitical Salafi groups.[48]

The leftists were the target of the Salafis for their role in supporting Abbas al-Mohri's movement, apart from the Salafis general abhorrence of their secular political stance. In this regard, a prominent Salafi figure – Ahmad al-Baqer – wrote an article in *Al-Anba* newspaper in 1985, entitled 'The left and the right' in which he vehemently criticized the leftists for their support to Al-Mohri and the revolution.[49] It is noteworthy that *Al-Anba* was a newspaper that was owned by pro-government merchants and that had earlier as well played a role in criticizing the opposition.

The Shi'a were a natural target for the Salafis and were targeted in public space for their Shi'ism which made them potential allies with Khomeini's regime. While in 1938, Arab nationalism was their main enemy, this time it was extremist Sunnism. They tend to refer to the interlude of the 1980s as one of the most difficult ones in their political history. Moreover, they tend to link the rise of Salafism with the naturalization of tribes and see it as a regime strategy to weaken their influence in the aftermath of 1975 when they were able to have ten MPs in parliament.[50] Leftist opposition also considers the rise of Sunni Islamism as a regime strategy against their power.

Finally, the rise of the Salafis and Abdel Khaleq stirred competition with the two other main Sunna groups: *Jama'at al-Tabligh* and the *Ikhwan al-Muslimin*. In his columns in *Al-Watan*, Abdel Khaleq took a clear stance against Juhayman al-Utaybi's movement, denouncing violence and calling it a provocation to internal strife (*fitna*). Competition with the Ikhwan was most overt, as the *Jama'at al-Tabligh* had already lost many of its largely tribal Kuwaiti members in the 1970s to the Salafis and Ikhwan.[51]

This competition started by the end of the 1970s, parallel to the rise of Abdel Khaleq and his politicized Salafism, following his conflict with the Ikhwan in 1974. Doctrinal differences with the Ikhwan became more overt. These differences centred around diverging interpretations about who was part of the people of tradition and community (*ahl al-sunna wa al-jama'a*), about the attributes of God (*asma' wa sifat*) as well as on the Shi'a. For the Salafis, the *mu'tazilites* and the *ash'aris* are considered as apostates, while they are considered as part of the *ahl al-sunna* by the Ikhwan. The Shi'a and Sufis are considered as deviant sects by Salafis, but the Ikhwan still consider them Muslims. These differences soon reached the realm of power politics. While in 1977, the two movements still cooperated in elections for the powerful student unions against the leftists, since 1980 overt competition broke out. The Salafis now presented themselves on a separate list for the student and teacher unions, where they competed with the Ikhwan.[52] Competition also took place in the elections for the supermarket cooperatives that have been springboards for political careers.[53]

In 1981, the Salafis were granted their own organization after lobbying efforts. The Society for the Revival of Islamic Heritage (*Jama'iyyat Ihya al-Turath*) was established. This gave Salafis an official wing, with which it could compete with the Ikhwan. *Ihya' al-Turath* was funded by the government as well as by private funding from merchants of the Salafi movement. Among its most prominent ones were those belonging to the Qina'at group, such as Khaled al-Sultan and Tareq al-Issa. These rich Kuwaitis were the ones who had provided the Salafi *da'is* such as Abdel Khaleq with the initial social capital to spread their ideas via mosques and their diwaniyyas. While *Ihya' al-Turath* was created for charitable purposes, it served since its beginnings multiple purposes and gave an organizational framework for the Salafis to enter into politics.[54] In 1981, for the first time – unprecedented regionally – Salafis entered into politics by presenting themselves for elections. Two candidates were elected – Khaled al-Sultan and Jasem al-'Awn. While both MPs campaigned for the change of article 2 of the Constitution (making Islam *the* source of law), they displayed a clearly loyal stance to the Al-Sabah by guaranteeing publicly that Salafism did not contradict with hereditary rule.[55] Finally, in 1983, another token of government support, the Shari'a Faculty was created at Kuwait University that would become the fief of Salafism and produce many of its elites.

Consequently, the government had played upon emerging differences within the Sunni Islamist movement to avoid a too strong domination of the Ikhwan. Although the Ikhwan were still a loyal force, the context of the 1980s and the growing influence of Sunni Islamism made the regime resort to its typical divide-and-rule strategies, courting the competitors or enemies of its enemies.

The social foundations of Sunni Islamism in Kuwait (1960s–90)

Political naturalizations of tribesmen

The support for the Sunni Islamist current since the 1960s coincided with the political naturalization of thousands of southern tribesmen by the Al-Sabah regime. The topic is surrounded with opaqueness, as it happened outside the context of the law and is highly political being referred to with bias by many *hadar* who feel they are losing power in a society that today is composed of a majority of *badu* citizens.

To start with, it is important to note that these naturalizations either happened outside the context of the Nationality Law of 1959 or sometimes happened with a hint of law, but always with law being used arbitrarily for political purposes. In case the naturalizations happened outside the context of the 1959 Law, they were passed by decree from the Minister of Interior. Most of the badu were reportedly naturalized in this way, in exchange for joining the army (particularly after Abdel Karim Qasim's threat to annex Kuwait). In the case when some hint of legality was given, they were naturalized under article 5 of the Law that quotes 'exceptional or special services' as allowing for naturalization. However, the definition as to what constitutes exceptional services is highly flexible and gives extreme discretionary power to the Al-Sabah.[56] In all cases, the stringent stipulations in the Nationality Law of 1959 have not been applied in the case of the naturalizations of the southern tribesmen. Nationality is considered a sovereign matter by the Al-Sabah with no court referral possible, meaning that the government has used the law rather arbitrarily.

These political naturalizations that mostly happened in Kuwait in the period between 1958 and 1988 find a striking resemblance to the political naturalizations of Sunna in Bahrain. Since the coming to power of the new King – Hamad Bin Issa (1999) – mass naturalizations have been ongoing of Sunni Muslims, mainly from Bedouin tribes from Saudi Arabia, Syria, Yemen, Jordan and Baluchistan.[57] Here too, the naturalizations are a strategy of the regime to strengthen its loyal support in the face of a majority population of Shi'a citizens who have been in conflict with the 'Al-Khalifa regime since its inception. In Bahrain, too, these political naturalizations are left to the total discretionary power of the King and are often passed under a similar article quoting exceptional services for 'extraordinary' citizenship.[58] As was historically the case in Kuwait, also in Bahrain do the naturalized tribesmen serve essentially in the police, army and security forces. In the face of societal opposition, the least threatening option is to rely on 'foreign' elements to staff police and military forces, as a periphery to rely on.[59] In Kuwait, as we have seen, both the largely 'Ajam Shi'a and the Bedouins have since Mubarak al-Sabah's reign been used as reliable forces to counterbalance the *hadar* Najdi opposition.

In the case of Kuwait, many Western sources refer to 1967 as the crucial year for these naturalizations, paralleling the large-scale fraud committed by Jaber al-Ahmad's government in these elections. However, the reality is more complex and nuanced. Naturalizations started far earlier and were not as rational or intended by the regime as is often described.[60] In fact, different actors were crucial in naturalizing specific tribesmen and for different reasons.

Although no clear begin and end dates exist, most of the political naturalizations took place between 1958 and 1988. In 1958 – the year of the first official population statistics – not more than 22 per cent of the population of Kuwait was composed of desert tribes; as a separate category from the *'arib dar* and the tribes that had been settled in Kuwait since long before (Rashaida and 'Awazem and individuals from other tribes). Around fifty years later, this would increase to around 53 per cent and today the tribesmen constitute around 60 per cent of Kuwait's citizens.[61] While the average yearly population growth in Kuwait is around 2.44 per cent, in the period between 1958 and 2005, the yearly population growth was 17 per cent average. Different estimates exist as to the number of naturalized people in the period between 1965 and 1988, but most converge around a number of approximately 220,000 naturalized in this period.[62] Different opinions exist about the end dates of the naturalizations too. Some refer to 1981 and others to 1988, but there is consensus that after the Invasion the process of mass naturalizations ended.[63]

The Bedouins that were naturalized in this period were mostly southern tribes, as distinct from the northern tribes. In popular parlance in Kuwait, the northern tribes refer to the tribes that are largely present north of Kuwait, in Iraq, while the southern have a concentrated presence to the south of Kuwait, in Saudi Arabia. Among the northern tribes, one finds the *Dhafir,* the *'Aneza* and the *Shammar* (the latter two are tribal confederations). Important southern tribes are the *'Ajman,* the *Dawasir* and the *Mutran.* The distinction plays such an important role in Kuwait because the northern tribes from Iraq were excluded from the naturalization policies, although they represented a clear majority in the armed forces back then. Apart from the domestic political considerations, the Iraqi threat in the early 1960s prompted the government to shut the door of naturalizations to northern tribes, while allowing for the naturalization of more trusted, southern tribes whose leadership was mostly in Saudi Arabia then. As a result, some of these tribes have two nationalities, an issue which has recently provoked great debates in Kuwaiti media, instigated by anti-tribal MPs and media figures, such as Mohammed al-Juwaihal. Relatedly, the northern tribes were exposed to the conversion to Shi'ism in the nineteenth century and one finds both Shi'a and Sunna among the northern tribes.[64] Many of the northern tribes present in Kuwait were to become part of the stateless category (*Bidun*) and until today their Iraqi affiliation plays a role in the ruler's reluctance to solve the issue. Many Kuwaitis remain for similar reasons wary of the *Bidun*'s claim to citizenship, having biased views as to the latter's role during the Invasion; apart from the obvious fear in a rentier state of competition with more citizens for access to the state's largesse.

Various reasons explain these naturalizations, used by different actors for different reasons. One of the less cited reasons of the early naturalizations was the fragile context of Kuwait's lobbying for independence which necessitated a growth of its very small population. As such, the British informed the ruler of Kuwait – Abdallah al-Salim – during his visit to Great Britain in 1958 that Kuwait had a structural lack of a national population to form the core for a modern state.[65] This is what allegedly prompted the ruler to introduce the second Nationality Law in 1959, which aimed in specific to naturalize people in order to strengthen Kuwait in the face of powerful, threatening neighbours. The first wave of naturalizations of tribesmen thus occurred already in

1959 before Kuwait's independence. Bedouin human resources were used in this process of international legitimacy building, as they constituted the bulk of the police, security and army forces.[66]

Another factor relates to the personal power ambitions of Al-Sabah princes. A main example here is the case of the powerful Minister of Interior – Jaber al-'Ali – who was instrumental in naturalizing en masse the members of the 'Ajman tribe residing in Kuwait. Himself born to an 'Ajman mother, Al-'Ali was a fierce competitor to Jaber al-Ahmad. Competition started as early as 1963 when Jaber al-Ahmad was appointed deputy PM under Abdallah al-Salim's reign. Jaber al-'Ali therefore tried to forge alliances with political and social actors, ranging from the 'Ajman tribesmen to middle-class groups and later even the nationalists. In 1964, Al-'Ali was successful in being chosen deputy PM himself against his rival, but upon Abdallah al-Salim's death (1965), he lost the battle and Jaber al-Ahmad became CP. Competition did not end here. Al-'Ali was staunchly ambitious and aimed at becoming CP even after Al-Ahmad's turn; leading him to continue his politics of alliance-building. However, when in 1978 S'ad al-Abdallah was chosen as CP, Al-Ahmad gave up, resigned from Cabinet and left the country. During this whole period between the early 1960s until the late 1970s, Al-'Ali was instrumental in naturalizing, arming and electing 'Ajman royalists to parliament.[67] Today, the 'Ajman are one of the four prominent tribes in Kuwait; representing a little less than 30,000 of Kuwait's voters and more than one-third of the total members of the 'Ajman live in Kuwait; the others are in Saudi Arabia.[68]

The 'Ajman were not the only ones to be naturalized. Among the main tribes naturalized one finds also the Mutran, the Duwaisir, the 'Uteibi as well as members from the tribes historically present in old Kuwait: the Rashaida and the 'Awazem. A common aspect here was that the tribes were trusted by the Al-Sabah patrons who naturalized them.

Abdallah al-Mubarak was another ambitious Al-Sabah member who was instrumental in naturalizing tribesmen. The fact that he was considered a staunch Arab nationalist and active in the early clubs created in Kuwait did not hinder him from being very close to the tribesmen.[69] He had been heading the security forces since the 1940s and via his position patronized a lot of tribesmen. His power went so far that the whole of the Rashaida were said to be personally loyal to him, although his influence and prestige were also felt among other southern tribes.[70] He was a powerful contender to the throne to succeed Ahmad al-Jabir (1922–50) and tried to seize power in 1950, but Abdallah al-Salim (1950–65) was enthroned. His power ambitions continued and by the end of the 1950s he was so powerful that he openly denounced the ruler in his diwaniyya. Until his removal from office in 1961, he was moreover the Vice-Emir (*Na'ib al-Hakim*) under Abdallah al-Salim and a powerful figure, as he was the last son of Mubarak al-Sabah and also in charge of the security of the city of Kuwait after the death of his uncle, Ali 'al-Khalifa. According to my interviews, the naturalizations of Rashaida by Abdallah al-Mubarak occurred as early as 1959 and continued until 1961 when he left the country.[71] His aspirations to the throne made him need the support of powerful societal actors, even before the institution of parliamentary life.

Many of the Mutran were also naturalized in this period: a tribe that was historically known for its defiance of political authority and was the leading force in the Ikhwan rebellion that started in 1927 when the Mutran and 'Ajman took the lead in rebelling against the Al-Saud, as their Wahhabi zeal was not stilled and they wanted to expand their Wahhabi conquests, which clashed with the interests of the Al-Saud and the British. In 1921 – still under Saudi patronage – the Ikhwan movement had clashed with the Al-Sabah in the Battle of Jahra, when the Al-Sabah had resorted to the British and help from the northern Shammar tribe to defend itself. While the conflict with the Saudi regime over the Najdi borders was over in 1922 with the creation of a neutral zone (Protocol of 'Uqair) and the drawing of borders – with Kuwait losing one third of its territory to the Al-Saud – the area remained tense due to the territorial ambitions of the Ikhwan.

The naturalization of the Mutran was largely an affair of powerful *asli* Mutran merchants in Kuwait who wanted to strengthen their support in parliament and naturalized most of the tribes in this period. As the topic is rather sensitive, a lot of details of their howabouts are undisclosed.

As merchants were then the link between the Al-Sabah and wider populations, they were the ones who were asked by the nascent government to register citizens as part of the Nationality Law that differentiated between different categories of Kuwaitis. In specific, it differentiated between the original (*asli*) citizens, referring to those who were in Kuwait before 1920 and presumably fought in the Battle of Jahra. These were citizens *bi'tasis* (original) who were granted citizenship *madat ula* (art. 1); having the right to vote as well as access to all benefits of the welfare state. Others who came after 1920 could be granted citizenship as naturalized (*mutajannissin*) Kuwaitis, on the condition (art. 4) they were proficient in Arabic and prove their lawful residence in Kuwait for eight years (for Arabs) or fifteen years (for non-Arabs). These naturalized Kuwaitis would enjoy socio-economic rights but were only to receive political rights after a 'probation' period. This period initially was ten years, but later became twenty years (1966 Law) to be amended in 1986 to become thirty years and in 1995 was again reduced to twenty years.[72] In the 'legal' context, when the government registered its population, it resorted to merchant notables to ask if they could confirm if they knew persons or could come up with lists of persons, as merchants were the ones with social power due to their economic role and role in neighbourhood affairs. Merchants were the ones who signed most of the citizen declarations, as well as tribal heads present in Kuwait.[73] Some of these merchants exploited the absence of the Al-Sabah's oversight over the population back then to add far larger groups of people to these lists than those who were in reality residing in the old town. This is what reportedly happened in the case of the Mutran, where powerful merchants with strong ties to the nomadic members of the tribe naturalized their kinship fellows for political purposes. According to my interlocutors, mainly Hilal al-Mutairi and Yusuf al-Mughlid al-Mutairi were the ones who naturalized the Mutran in Kuwait, to strengthen their support in parliament. Hilal was in the pre-parliamentary *majalis* and Yusuf was MP in each parliament until 1992. Hilal al-Mutairi was known in Kuwait as the one who mediated between the Al-Sabah and Faisal al-Duwaish (Ikhwan leader) and enabled the latter's refuge in Kuwait only nine years after his attack in Al-Jahra.[74] While the Mutran were only present in terms of individuals in pre-oil Kuwait, the naturalization led them to become the second largest tribe in Kuwait (by registered voters), after the 'Awazem, with around 27,130 voters and a concentration in the fourth constituency, which is also the fief of northern tribes ('Aneza, Shammar and Dhafir) as well as the Rashaida.

The naturalizations supported by Jaber al-'Ali happened in a similarly inchoate process of population registering. While he himself *extra-legally* naturalized thousands of the 'Ajman, he also encouraged the naturalization of other tribesmen that often had a hint of legality. For that purpose he reportedly gave lists to MPs allowing each MP to come up with fifty names to be naturalized to build alliances. When he became Minister of Interior he changed the status of these naturalized from second to first citizenship (*madat ula*), allowing them to have direct voting rights.

This overview already gives important indications about the how and why of the naturalizations that run counter to the idea that portrays the naturalizations as a rather unified strategy by the Al-Sabah regime to counterbalance the liberal and nationalist opposition. Some of my badu interviewees expressed the idea that Jaber al-Ahmad as well as S'ad al-Abdallah were opposed to the naturalizations, as these policies worked mainly in the interest of their rival, Jaber al-'Ali whose clients in parliament were known for their stance in supporting interpellations against Al-Ahmad's government (1965–77).

However it seems more plausible to assume that the naturalizations were supported both by the regime (PM and the Emir) acting in the interest of the regime and by individual shaykhs acting in their personal interests of power politics. In the 1980s, the role of the regime became more prominent in naturalizing the tribesmen. This was the consequence of the tense regional context of the Shi'a revolution in Iran, the Iran–Iraq War (1980–8) and the regime's concerns about the empowerment of potentially disruptive groups that could challenge its power (Shi'a groups, but also Sunni Islamists and the nationalists). For this reason, it was desperately in need of loyal forces, explaining the intensification of the process of naturalization in this period under Al-Ahmad's and later (since 1977) S'ad al-Abdallah's governments.[75] This was also reflected in intermarriages between the Al-Sabah and the naturalized tribes. Jaber al-Ahmad, for example, married eleven times and in most cases with Mutran women to consolidate the alliances.[76] These policies coincided with the strengthening of the Sunni Islamist current, to counterbalance the *hadar* leftist elite.[77] In 1981 the number of tribal MPs reached twenty-six and ever since tribal MPs have constituted an average of twenty-five MPs in each parliament, while in 1963 this number was only eighteen.[78] The redistricting by the government in 1979 from ten to twenty-five constituencies further strengthened the tribal vote.

From this short overview of the naturalizations that occurred in the period between 1959 and 1988 one can conclude that the process was far from organized and unified and highly dependent on relations of trust between the Al-Sabah, individual shaykhs and tribesmen. Some of these tribesmen were loyal to a certain Al-Sabah patron (in the case of the 'Ajman and Jaber al-'Ali) rather than the government, while in other cases they were loyal to powerful societal figures (in the case of the Mutran) and also to the regime as a whole (in the case of those tribesmen naturalized in the 1980s). For the *hadar* elite and the Shi'a, they considered these political naturalizations as a regime strategy which was directly intended at fragmenting their ranks.

Transformation of tribal loyalties in the nation state

The naturalized tribesmen would alter the political and social balance in Kuwait. Until the Invasion, they would largely be loyal to the Al-Sabah regime. Yet, in order to understand the socio-political changes within tribal populations in Kuwait that were only to be felt in the post-Invasion context, it is important to discuss how tribalism changed in terms of its sociological structure once integrated into Kuwait's state. As we will see, initial tribal hierarchies and identities experienced important changes as a consequence of integration of entire tribes (or the bulk of a tribe) into the nation state. Also, in the period of the 1970s until the Invasion, the Islamist movement implanted itself in tribal areas and was a vehicle for socio-political ascension for tribesmen in search of new identity markers in a period of quick and drastic changes of lifestyle. It would sow the seeds of an alliance between Sunni Islamism and tribal forces that strengthened in the post-Invasion era. While the following analysis is short, it will provide the building blocks for the last part of this book that talks about the political rise of a tribal opposition in Kuwait.

The analysis of tribal solidarities in politics has been the subject of much social science literature on the MENA.[79] This literature has suffered from a tendency to generalize tribal complexities in simple patterns in an *ahistorical* approach and a general bias vis-à-vis the nomadic phenomenon considered as 'traditional' with hierarchical leadership structures implying a form of blind obedience to the tribal shaykh and an aversion to change.[80] This bias is often expressed by *hadar* elites who criticize tribesmen for being blindly obedient to their shaykh. Yet, this literature does not do justice to the complexities of tribalism in the Arab world and obliterates one important aspect of it, which has contrasted it from tribalism in contexts such as Inner Asia, namely the relatively egalitarian nature of Arabian tribalism. This itself has had important repercussions for social structure and political processes, through specific matrimonial strategies, raids and alliance-building patterns.

In the pre-state nomadic system, tribal authority was an honorific title subject to checks by others and only rarely enjoyed full consensus. The tribal leader 'emerged' and his position depended on a continuous process of the construction of authority by showing his mediation and redistribution skills, poetic abilities and importantly a good reputation within and, importantly, beyond the tribe. In some way, the shaykh is regarded as the ideal 'everyday man', a primus inter pares, although a little more equal than the others. The tribesmen do not obey him but cooperate with him.[81] While tribal authority is inherited (via birth to extended families of lineages that produce leaders to the tribe), there are no strict rules to succession. The shaykh can be succeeded by his brother or patrilineal cousins, depending on their leadership qualities. Moreover, as the tribe itself rarely came together and lineages were the political and economic units in the pre-national era, a situation of competition and anarchy characterized tribalism, between lineages and between powerful personalities within lineages (often agnatic rivals), comparable to competition within the Al-Sabah family between ambitious princes. In this absence of clear hierarchies and succession rules, a situation of competition between personalities naturally results, each trying to build up their own support structure.[82] Importantly, regimes can also rely on this internal tendency for competition to fragment and co-opt tribal constituencies; a strategy the Al-Sabah have tended to use. This was, for example, the case more recently with the 'Awazem tribe, whose leader – Shaykh Falah Ben Jama'a – had supported the opposition movement that erupted under Nasser al-Muhammad's government. He was the only tribal chieftain to be oppositional, as opposed to the co-opted leaders of other major southern tribes. In reaction, the Emir resorted to a series of divide-and-rule and co-optation strategies. As part of this, he invited the older brother of Ben Jama'a, Habib Ben Jama'a, from Saudi Arabia to visit the Emir in his palace; a move that was a direct threat and embarrassment to Ben Jama'a, as it warned him that he could be easily replaced by his brother as he did not have roots in Kuwait, but in Saudi Arabia.[83]

Today, in the context of social change uprooting a young generation of tribesmen in the region, this competition becomes all the more apparent. Modern means of communication have allowed personality cult-inspired behaviour to flourish. Interestingly, one can see that today young tribesmen portray themselves as *shaykh-likes* on Twitter, through a set of symbolic means; featuring the 'self' prominently, sometimes in plurifold, in traditional tribal *dishdasha*,[84] while displaying symbols of status, notably by depicting their proximity to the Emir and shaykhs; blending features of the tribe with symbols of attachment to the nation displayed in an overtly patriotic manner. Not unusual, those who present themselves as the staunchest patriots are often those who have been historically excluded from the national community or considered as its second-class citizens: Shi'a and the badu.

Consequently, Arabian tribalism is traditionally devoid of a pyramidal structure with a clear leadership and stratified hierarchies.[85] Moreover, it distinguishes itself by a very particular marriage pattern, namely of close paternal kin, meaning that a young man should marry the father's brother's daughter; 'parallel cousins' in contrast to the 'cross-cousins' as was prevalent with tribes in Inner Asia. As one can imagine, the first leads to a structure of fragmentation, through the creation of small nuclei within the agnatic group, while in the second case of cross-cousin marriage, a process of integration follows.[86] In the first case the marriage creates nuclei that are still part of one's initial patrilineal descent group. In the second case exogamy out of the descent group is the result.

The aforementioned model has also been described as the **segmentary lineage model**, developed by the anthropologist Sahlins, referring to a model which lacks permanent leadership and is characterized by complementary opposition between agnatic rivals,[87] leading to a situation as 'I against my brothers, my brothers and I against my patrilineal cousins, my patrilineal cousins and I against the world'.[88] This remark is important and confirms the historical experience of the pivotal role of the 'lineage' (*fikihd;* referred to as *Al-jama'a* by its members) as the basic economic and political organization of Arabian tribes.[89] The lineage was responsible for the protection of wells and pastures, the collection of *khuwwa* (status tax), the decision on family disputes, practice of vengeance (*tha'r*) and the declaration of war and peace.[90] Lineages are composed of several extended families (sing. *hamola*) – themselves part of clans of which the tribe is composed – that each had their own leader (*shaykh*) and economic strategies. The scattering of tribes into lineages was the logical consequence of the natural conditions in the desert with a scarcity of resources, leading to political and economic separation within the larger tribe. The tribe itself was much more a social imaginary of common descent and a source of honour and status than reflecting a concrete political or economic organization. And only in very rare cases did the tribe come together collectively in a major battle (*manakha*); in most cases the tribal identity was decentralized and replete with feuds between competing lineages.[91]

This competition between lineages has led authors such as Ibn Khaldun and the Iraqi sociologist Ali al-Wardi to believe that the tribe is inherently prone to internal strife and feuds; it is one of the reasons Ibn Khaldun gives the lifecycle of Arabian dynasties to last for only four generations.[92] Indeed, tribal wars were often wars between tribal lineages and even the Shi'a–Sunni split can be traced back to a feud between two lineages of the Al-Quraysh tribe. As such, the great wars between the Al-Shammar and Al-Mutair tribe were in reality wars between the lineages of both tribes and many tribes emerged from what were initially lineage confederations. Also, this lineage competition explains why the Mutran in Kuwait split over the question of whether or not to support the grilling of PM Nasser al-Mohammad in 2010, with one branch of the tribe having business interests linked to the government opposing the grilling while another one supported the grilling.[93]

However, with the integration of the tribe in the national context and its 'encapsulation' by the rentier regime, these tribal hierarchies have changed in important regards. First of all, the tribe has become a political and economic unit rather than the lineages, although the lineages continue to play a role in politics. Kuwait might be different here from more authoritarian contexts such as Saudi Arabia where tribes lost their collective coherence as a result of state dominance. In some regards, Kuwait's electoral system might have empowered them as political collectives. This was rather unique as in the past the tribe rarely came together. Another important change is the role of the tribal shaykh. While initially his position was acquired through personal capabilities, the latter's role has become fixed in the context of the nation state and has shifted to a relatively independent social role to a role of being co-opted by the regime, with the shaykh transformed into the main 'middle man' for his tribal constituencies in getting access to the state's services. A main aspect of the rule of the Al-Sabah has been to rely on intermediary elites to reach out to broader constituencies, despite the development of the country into a modern state system with legal and institutional provisions and bodies that present official mechanisms of interaction between the state and society. In fact, reliance on loyal intermediary elites 'encapsulated' by the rentier regime allowed it to manage social change in a top-down fashion; logics of clientelism that have increasingly witnessed their limits in the post-Invasion context. This reliance on intermediary elites was particularly the case in the regime's dealing with its periphery – the Shi'a and the tribesmen – although more recently the youth has become a new social group to be dealt with separately via intermediary elites and bodies.

The naturalized tribesmen often worked in Kuwait in the 1940s and 1950s in its nascent oil industry and industrial sectors and were also employed in large numbers its police and security sectors. Before, many of them had worked in the collapsed pearl industry in summertime. Abandoning their nomadic lifestyle, they came to settle in large numbers in search for new employment opportunities from the 1940s onwards. Initially, they came to settle in shanty towns close to the oil companies and when the state started its urbanization projects in the 1960s, these shantytowns were demolished and the tribesmen were allocated housing projects for 'limited-income households'.[94] Some of them were also explicitly brought in by the regime from Saudi Arabia as part of the political naturalizations.[95] They came to live in the outer areas, whereas the *hadar* were allocated the inner areas, in analogy to the old hierarchy of the town and its wall.

Unlike the *hadar* areas, the Bedouin cities lacked quality state services and commercial and educational services. This social marginalization coincided with political integration (reinforced with the electoral redistricting in 1979) and contributed to the development of the 'tribes' as a distinct political category in Kuwait.[96]

In the new context, the tribal leader was integrated in the territorial state and became the person par excellence for the Al-Sabah to reach out to the tribe. These Emirs also became or were already Kuwaitis, such as the Emir of the Rashaida (*Mufrij al-Musailem*) of the Al-'Awazem (*Ben Jama'a*) the Emir of the 'Ajman (*Bin Huthlayn*) and the Emir of the Al-Mutran (*Faysal al-Duwaish*).[97] Until the Invasion, these tribal shaykhs still had an important influence over the tribesmen. As in the pre-independence context, the tribal shaykhs were the persons with whom the regime dealt to reach out the tribesmen. It was via the shaykh that tribesmen were recruited for participation in battles and were employed in the police and army in the 1940s and 1950s.[98] However, this time the tribal leader has become more of a co-opted figure than an independent source of power: an intermediary to lobby for the interests of his fellow tribesmen vis-à-vis the government. His role as service provider gave him extra authority – apart from his hereditary claim to a leading lineage – but this authority and hierarchy remained subject to competition by agnatic rivals and by personalities from competing lineages.[99] Tribal primaries allow in this regard to reactivate tribal leadership and more often than not tribal leaders lose in these primaries that are a new mechanism for the tribes in the context of the nation state. Since the 1990s, tribal shaykhs have lost a lot of their influence over tribesmen and in intermediation with the regime, a consequence of the rise of a young generation of oppositional MPs.

What also changed following the integration of tribesmen into the state was the strengthening of the tribe as a social and political unit. In the past, the smaller units – the lineages – were the main economic and political units. In this regard, the Al-Sabah regime and its resources have enabled tribesmen to reinvent the tribe as a political unit to strengthen their lobbying capacity vis-à-vis the Al-Sabah. This has been further strengthened in the context of the communication revolution since the 1990s that has allowed for the strengthening of the tribe on a *transnational* level. The tribal shaykh has become the intermediary par excellence for the regime in dealing with tribesmen as a broker for state services. Also, since 1975, tribal primaries (*far'iyyat*) have been organized to pre-select the most popular candidates who are capable of gaining most of the tribal votes in legislative elections, a natural selection mechanism.[100] Here comes by that tribesmen have been regrouped in terms of housing policies and have collectively faced social marginalization (since the 1940s the badu had been drawn towards the city, but state housing policies pushed them back to the desert).[101] Under the old twenty-five district system, each district moreover represented approximately a tribe, strengthening both tribal cohesion and the regime's capacity to dominate the tribes. This has strengthened tribal solidarities both within the tribe and between tribes in their interaction with the state and the *hadar*. Strong tribes tend to win in districts where they dominate demographically. Also, tribes often compete against each other in tribal districts on the basis of their tribal affiliation. And within the tribe, the candidates who are from a lineage that has a good reputation and is demographically strong tend to win elections.[102] In addition, tribal councils (*majalis qabaliyya*) have been created to discuss tribal affairs, a body that did not exist in the history of the tribes and comes close to providing a political platform for the tribe.[103] Tribal hierarchies and solidarities thus play a role in electoral politics although over the past two decades changes have been ongoing in these hierarchies and solidarities.

While tribalism continues to be a structuring factor (although reconfigured and reinvented) in Kuwaiti politics among the *badu*, the *hadar* do also attach important value to tribal descent and Arab blood. As we have seen, historically only Sunni Najdi status allowed merchants to be part of the elite of pearl merchants. This 'asabiyya has been perpetuated in the modern state whose regime continues to function according to tribal authority structures. It is the small group of Sunni Najdi merchants that until today dominates the economic sphere, with kinship loyalties reproduced in the KCC as well as in the boards of banks and companies. As such, Kuwait's Central Bank is known to be the fief of the Sunni Najdi merchants, while the Ahli Bank is mostly Shi'a as is the International Bank of Kuwait and the Gulf Bank is historically dominated by the Qina'at group. Also, categories as *aseel* vs. *bayseri* noble vs. non-noble), *Ijmi* vs. *Najdi* (Persian vs. Najdi Arab) and *Ahl al-Sharq* vs. *Ahl al-Qibla* continue to be identity markers among *hadar* in Kuwait with deep political, matrimonial and economic implications.[104] Yet, in the case of the *hadar* the importance of these kinship ties relates to smaller groups of persons (as solidarity relates to tribal *hadar* status combined with high socio-economic standing) rather than to a collectivity of a tribe or a lineage. Consequently, the *wasta* networks are smaller and focused on a minority elite group.

Social foundations of the Sunni Islamist movement: 1960s–90

Family ties are an important resource for acquiring social and thus political standing in Kuwait. This situation continues until today, favoured by a small, divided population and the absence of political parties strengthening personalized politics within movements and the competition between personalities rather than ideas.[105] Inherited family prestige has been a crucial resource for political elites and members from the same families have often driven political change, with young members demarcating themselves from their elders with more activist and revolutionary political positions. In this regard, family groupings tend to produce the political elites. This is the case for all three status groups (Sunni *hadar*/Shi'a/tribes), although in the case of the tribes not only the family unit, but also the lineage and the larger tribe itself have provided an important political resource, strengthened by state policies that have reinvented and upgraded the tribe.

In the case of the Sunni Islamist movement, its leadership was largely drawn from *hadar* elite families; merchants and shaykhs. Apart from these elite families, its early membership consisted of middle- and lower-class *hadar*, among whom Persian Sunni families (such as Al-'Awadi and Al-Kandari) and early-settled tribesmen (such as the Rashaida).[106] In the 1970s and 1980s membership extended to the tribal zones that became important resources for the group's political success. The Ikhwan were the first to reach out to the tribal zones by creating branches in outer areas. They did so by infiltrating the largest tribes and associating with the sons of important members of powerful lineages (e.g. Ahmad al-Dabus, Hamid Falih). They gained popularity among young tribal members uprooted by sudden urbanization and in search for a new ideology matching their aspirations and worldview. The absence of competitors strengthened the success of the Ikhwan. Other political groups confined their activities to the urban areas and Wahhabism was then a rather limited phenomenon of an old generation.[107] The resources of the Ikhwan and its modern Islamism attracted young tribesmen, some of whom had previously been part of the *Jama'at al-Tabligh*.[108] Despite Salafism's natural links to southern tribes, the movement spread later to the tribal areas and was initially concentrated in *hadar* areas, such as Kayfan.[109] This would change in the post-Invasion period, when Salafism became a strong phenomenon among tribesmen.

A main family group that has produced elites for the Ikhwan and Salafi currents is the Qina'at. As we have seen earlier, the Qina'at relate to their patriarch – Shaykh Yusuf al-Qina'i – who was the first mufti of Kuwait and orphaned by the Al-Sabah. He was a member of the 1921 and 1938 councils and his proximity to the Al-Sabah allowed members of the kin group to make inroads in politics and business. Being a Sunni clan that has likely lost its purity of blood when mixed with Iraqi women the Qina'at were not part of the Sunni Najdi aristocracy.[110] The latter moreover considered them then as 'newcomers' with a less independent status, relying on the Al-Sabah to advance materially. In this regard, it invested in other venues to strengthen its influence in society and politics. As we have seen, the Qina'at had profited from government support in the 1970s and 1980s in business and dominated the Gulf bank as a group. Another major venue would be the Islamist movement. The shaykh status of its patriarch gave them religious capital to invest in Islamism.

Yusuf al-Qina'i and Abdelaziz al-Mutawa' (also Qina'i) were the founders of Al-Islah. Political change can sometimes come from members of the same family. One can think here of the Mutawa'. Abdelaziz al-Mutawa' – founding member of Al-Islah – was considered as an elite member and his moderate stance provoked criticism from young men in the 1960s. However, when Abdallah al-Mutawa' became head of Al-Islah (1976), he would represent a young generation with a more politicized stance than the elder members of his family.[111] Also, prominent members of the Salafi current were drawn from the Qina'at group. One can think here of Khaled al-Sultan or Tareq al-Issa. As we have seen, it was Abdelrazzaq al-Mutawa' who convinced Salafi *da'is* to stay in Kuwait and expand their call. Other prominent Salafis represent the Persian Sunni community, such as Ahmad Baqer and Walid al-Tabtaba'i: a group that historically occupied a secondary status among the *hadar* for their Iranian origin.

Another example of the reconversion of family capital is the case of Abbas al-Munawar. From the early-settled Rashaida, he was a prominent figure of the Ikhwan in the 1970s and 1980s. Al-Munawar is the uncle of Mubarak al-Duwaila (by marriage to his aunt), who himself has been a businessmen and leading figure within the Ikhwan since the 1980s until today. Finally, Abbas al-Munawar is the uncle of Osama al-Munawar, a lawyer and close to the Salafi current, who was a member of the deposed 2012 parliament. In analogy to his uncle's diwaniyya movement in 1989 to reinstate parliamentary life, Osama al-Munawar organized a movement in his diwaniyya in 2012 to protest the dissolution of the 2012 parliament.

Another example of such a family grouping are the persons related to Shaykh Sayyid Yusuf al-Rifa'i, from the prominent Al-Rifa'i family and former MP and minister and founding member of Kuwait's early MB. Yusuf al-Rifa'i was among the founding members of Al-Islah, a shaykh himself and is the grandfather of Osama al-Shahin, one of the founders of the political wing created after Liberation, *hadas* (*Islamic Constitutional Movement*). Issa al-Shahin – also one of *hadas*'s founders – is Osama's father and the brother of Sulayman Majid al-Shahin (Secretary of State for Foreign Affairs in 1999) and Ibrahim Majid al-Shahin (Secretary of State for Municipal Affairs in 1991). The family thus produced many political elites.

Another example outside the Islamist spectrum is the case of the icon of the opposition movement, Musallam al-Barrak. He inherited a part of his popularity from his father – Muhammad al-Barrak – a popular MP in the 1960s who was instrumental in naturalizing many members of the Mutran. Also, Al-Barrak's sister was one of the wives of late Emir Jaber al-Ahmad (1977–2007) who married many tribal women to consolidate alliances.

While Sunni Islamism spread to the outer areas since the late 1970s, its leadership was drawn from *hadar* elite families. This continues until the present day, although there has been a rise of badu in the committees and boards of the Ikhwan and Salafi groups since the millennium: a change that corresponds to the empowerment of the badu in the political realm since the Invasion.

In sum, this part on the social foundations of Sunni Islamism has demonstrated that Sunni Islamism was carried by Sunni *hadar* elites who tended to be second-stratum elites, outside the Najdi 'asabiyya that had participated in early oppositional politics. Apart from the elite, its members were from middle-class *hadar* families, such as Persian Sunni families or others who in the pre-oil community were part of the commoners. Since the mid-1970s, Sunni Islamism spread to the tribal areas, where the Ikhwan were the first to set foot and establish local branches. While tribesmen would become the main supporters of Sunni Islamism in the post-Invasion period, in the period until 1990 only a few tribal Islamist figures would rise whose political stance distinguished itself from the bulk of tribal MPs, who were still loyal to the government and were elected on a purely tribal ticket. As latecomers to the nation state, they were profiting from access to the Al-Sabah that used them as a loyal constituency, therefore many tribal MPs presented themselves as 'service deputies', providing services (i.e. jobs, medical service, housing) to their electorate. Social marginalization vis-à-vis the *hadar* was then not acted upon politically, a consequence of the loyal stance of the bulk of the *badu* electorate. In this conundrum, the Al-Sabah regime could still reach out to the *badu* via elite representatives, either the tribal chieftains or the new MPs acting largely as service deputies. Only a minority of tribal MPs would rise as more independent voices and those were MPs that had been 'Ajman MPs patronized by rebellious Prince Jaber al-'Ali and a few Islamist MPs of the Ikhwan. Mubarak al-Duwaila (Rashaida) was the most prominent and the first tribal MP to participate in an interpellation (1985).[112] *On the whole* tribal and Sunni Islamist forces backed the Al-Sabah regime, reflected in their participation in National Council (1990), a proto-parliament of appointed members that basically served to endorse government decisions following the dissolution of parliament by the Emir.

Things would only change with the coming to age of a new generation of tribesmen born in the 1970s and 1980s, had full access to the welfare state and are highly educated. Their rise in society since the end of the 1990s would change the political attitude of young tribesmen; a shift that was also found among *hadar* youth, but was more disruptive in terms of politics in the case of the tribes where traditional hierarchies had dominated relations with the Al-Sabah regime.

8

Socio-political change within Kuwait's Shi'a population

*This chapter is a modified version of a chapter that was originally published under the title 'The Politics of Shi'i Merchants in Kuwait (Rivka Azoulay) in the edited volume *Business Politics in the Middle East* (eds. S. Hertog, G. Luciani and M. Valeri, London: Hurst, 2013).

Introduction

Historically both the Shi'a and tribesmen were used as *non-core* groups by the Al-Sabah to strengthen their authority in the face of *hadar* opposition and particularly the Najdi elite. The minority status of the Shi'a and tribal hierarchies allowed the regime to deal with elite representatives via political patronage. Yet, these policies only proved themselves successful with the consent of the social base, the constituencies supporting these regime-dependent patrons. In effect, patron–client relations are always ones of mutual obligations, never of coercion, with both actors benefitting from the alliance. The gerontocracy of the Al-Sabah contributes to the perpetuation of traditional regime strategies to deal with society, as the Al-Sabah ruling elite that is in power gained its political experience in the 1950s and 1960s. Yet, since the Invasion, a younger generation within the Al-Sabah has started to push for change and asserted its role within the Family.

In its dealing with the *hadar* the regime relied upon currents and ideologies as opposed to the more traditional form of patronage via semi-traditional elites that it used to reach its *non-core* groups. The Sunni merchant elite had lost its community power since the very inception of the modern state and was too independent to allow for such a role playing.[1] When the Al-Sabah realized – since the millennium – facing a restless society that they had no effective *hadar* intermediaries, they tried to reach out to businessmen from outside the Najdi elite (mainly Jasem al-Khorafi), but without much success.

The period of study here transcends the Invasion as this will allow me to demonstrate the phenomenon of regime–Shi'a relations in its complexity and nuance. Despite the tense interlude in the 1980s as a consequence of the Iran–Iraq War, the minority status of the Shi'a has allowed the regime on occasions to revive its classic patronage strategies of intermediation via co-opted elites. This was the case in 2009 under the governments of powerful PM Nasser al-Muhammad. In 2009, the perception of a hostile society made the Shi'a rally around the Al-Sabah (as they had done in 1938).[2] Yet, the Bahraini uprising in 2011 and its violent crackdown by a Saudi-led GCC Peninsula Shield Force would illustrate the limits of personal co-optation and sectarian-based policies.

The social base is essential for understanding the position of political elites vis-à-vis the Al-Sabah: an overlooked assumption in rentier state theory that tends to consider the masses – as public sector workers – co-opted by the regime. The social base here refers to the constituencies that support the elites acting as their political patrons. It is the social base and the electorate that can make or break a political figure and MP, depending on the qualities they search for in this 'representative' voicing their demands.

Since the 1970s, a process of political modernization reached Kuwait's Shi'a, via the arrival to Kuwait of Shi'a Islamists from Iraq, in a similar logic as the implantation of Sunni Islamists in Kuwait. They revolutionized Shi'a politics via the conscientization of younger generation. The merchant notables lost their seats in parliament and much of their community power was lost as a consequence of the rise of a new elite of *political entrepreneurs*, who would devote themselves full-time to politics, defend a political programme or ideology (political Shi'ism) and enjoy more popularity than the notables.[3] It changed the conundrum of regime–Shi'a relations that had so far been mediated via the merchant notables and focused on community demands (i.e. mosques, religious schools), but would not ask for the emancipation of the Shi'a on the national level. The new Shi'a elite turned against this co-optive relationship, itself the consequence of political emancipation of Shi'a masses discontent with their position in the political compact.

Yet despite the official retreat of Shi'a merchants from community politics in 1976, they continued to play a role behind the scenes and could be reactivated by the regime in times of need. As such, they could be asked to mediate or present themselves as occasional mediators or brokers for Shi'a constituencies. Here comes by that Shi'a merchants were historically supportive of the Al-Sabah: an alliance that started with Mubarak's reign and crystallized in 1938 during the *Majlis* events. This makes it easier for the Al-Sabah to reach out to them in times of trouble. Adding to the importance of the social base is the minority status of the Shi'a, which strengthens group cohesion, contrary to the case of the *hadar*, where the merchants have become too detached from the reality on the ground. In Bahrain too – and different from the Sunni merchants – the Shi'a did have social power in *Baharna* villages: ties they had forged via their role as teachers, government clerks and gift givers.[4] Class distinctions in both Kuwait and Bahrain have been blurred by a collective identity constructed either through a long history of sectarian oppression (Bahrain) or through a minority status reinforced via a shared historical memory (Kuwait).

Different diasporas and merchants as political notables

As in the case of Kuwait's general social fabric, the Shi'a in Kuwait are composed of different diasporas, from Arab and Iranian ethnicity. Before the politicization of Shi'ism in the 1970s, the Kuwaiti Shi'a were a rather fragmented community, divided into different ethnic subgroups that all socialized in different neighbourhood and community networks (distinct processes of *Vergemeinschaftung*).[5] Albeit this ethnic diversity also concerns the Sunni *hadar,* ethnicity often coincides in the Shi'a case with religious belonging. The group formation effect was strengthened by the double membership both to an ethnic group and to a distinct religious affiliation within Shi'ism.

We can differentiate three main categories: the *'Ajam* (from Iran), the *Hasawiyyin* (sing. from Al-Hasa) and the *Baharna* (from Bahrain). The majority of the Kuwaiti Shi'a (around 70 per cent) is of Iranian descent and emigrated to the Emirate from the end of the eighteenth century on in a migration pattern that continued until the twentieth century. The earliest migration flows consisted mostly of Iranian merchants from the Western provinces who escaped the harsh fiscal measures of the Qajar regime. Some of the wealthiest families, like the Ma'rafi and the Behbahani, arrived in this period. By the beginning of the twentieth century, Iranian migration was diversified in its social composition with the emigration to Kuwait of poor farmers who were severely hit by the administrative reforms of the new Pahlavi regime (1926).[6] Most of them came from *Tarakma* in southern Iran and are generally referred to by Kuwaiti Shi'a as *Tarakmas.* Their particularly strong group identity was reinforced by the fact that, once in Kuwait, they would constitute a subclass of workers, employed in the shipping industry and to a lesser extent in handicraft.

As to the Shi'a from Al-Hasa (around 15 per cent), most of them came to the Emirate in the nineteenth century after the various Saudi conquests sweeping the Eastern Province. These *Hasawiyyin* have developed a particularly strong group identity in Kuwait linked to their common belonging to a minority branch within Twelver Shi'ism; *shaykhism* that follows the teachings of Ahmad al-Ahsa'i (1753–1826).[7] The group identity of the Kuwaiti shaykhis has also been strengthened by the fact that an important line of the shaykhi maraja' itself settled in Kuwait by the end of the 1950s: the *Mirza Allhqaqi* family.[8] This strong group identity has led to the development of specific communal relations and distinct processes of socialization. As far as the Baharna Shi'a are concerned (around 5 per cent), they also combine ethnic membership with belonging to a specific current in Twelver Shi'ism as they are descendants of the *'Gharbi* tribe in Western Arabia and belong to the *Akhbari* school of thought.[9] Most of the *Baharna* came to the Emirate during the eighteenth century fleeing political instability after the settlement of the 'Al-Khalifa in Bahrain.

Within this heterogeneous group of Shi'a, socialized in distinct community institutions, merchants were the central pillars of community life and intermediaries between the masses and the Al-Sabah clan. Their position as political notables was the consequence of both their social power within respective communities and their privileged access to the ruler. Within the ethno-religious community, social prestige was mainly the consequence of charitable giving in the religious field. Since there was no indigenous Shi'a clerical class in Kuwait (as there were hardly any clerics among the Shi'a who came to settle in Kuwait), merchants were the central actors in religious life and, as such, enjoyed strong social prestige.[10] They played a central role in popular religion, financed the mosques and negotiated with the *mujtaheds* in Najaf or Qom to identify clerics ready to come to Kuwait to act as religious leaders. Because of their social capital within their constituencies and their status as affluent merchants, these families were central interlocutors between the Al-Sabah and the Shi'a minority. As paraphrased by one of our interviewees:

> The merchants were the link between the common Shi'a and the ruling family. In order to reach the people, they would go through the merchants. Even in finding out where people were coming from. This became very helpful in organizing nationality. This minister would ask the merchants if they knew the person. So if you go back to the old files of each Kuwaiti, you will find the signature of my father (Mohammed Qabazard), of Mohammed Rafi Ma'rafi, etc.[11]

Moreover, after the coup of Mubarak the Great (1896), these Shi'a merchants were co-opted to counterbalance nascent mercantile opposition. Being a national minority without any kinship ties to the regime, the Shi'a were less problematic allies, as they could not contest the central elite's status.

Political Shi'ism, middle-class political entrepreneurs and the decline of notables

It was in the 1970s that the foundations were laid of the contemporary political and religious Shi'a field in Kuwait. As demonstrated by Louër (2008), the politicization of the *marja'iyya*[12] in Iraq since the 1960s reached Kuwait through the arrival of several leading activists of the Al-Da'wa movement.[13] Following Ba'athist repression of Al-Da'wa, its activists were chased out of the country and went into exile in Kuwait, where they arrived through the networks of the marja'iyya of Najaf, as *'ulema* for local mosques. Facing a Kuwaiti state that had no policy of granting refuge to political exiles, this dual positioning of the activists (being activists and *'ulema*) allowed them to establish themselves in Kuwait. They were integrated into existing community institutions, where their aggressive, politicized style of speech galvanized a young generation. These 'young men' (*shabab*) – referring to their young age and willingness to break away from traditional patterns of politics – called upon the Shi'a mass to emancipate itself in the name of political Islam and break away from the patronage of the notables.

At the same time, another movement spread in Kuwait's society, this time through the settlement in Kuwait of the marja' himself: Mohammed al-Shirazi. Like the Al-Da'wa activists, Mohammed al-Shirazi (1926–2001) sought refuge in Kuwait following Ba'athist repression of the Shi'a clerical establishment. His installation in Kuwait in 1971 was rendered possible because of his good connections with some prominent Shi'a merchant families, whom he had known from their pilgrimage to Karbala, not different from the implantation of the Sunni Islamist movement in Kuwait. As a self-proclaimed mujtahed, Al-Shirazi, scion of a prestigious clerical family of Karbala, challenged the marja'iyya of Najaf as a source of religious authority.[14] It is within this context of competition that one should place the birth of the *Shiraziyyin*, following the marginalization of Karbala as a learning centre and its rivalry with Najaf.

The competition between the two movements, Shiraziyyin and Al-Da'wa, representing two different maraja' was transposed to Kuwait's local political scene, as it combined with cleavages that started to develop within the Shi'a community between the old generation of merchants and the young counter-elite of political Islamists. Whereas the merchants generally disapproved of the politicization of Shi'a identity, for the bulk of the Shi'a the Islamist discourse of Al-Da'wa meant a religious awakening and an assertion of their Shi'a identity. These young Shi'a – socialized in the networks of Al-Da'wa – adopted the emancipation of the Shi'a on a national level as their primary goal.[15] Contrary to the old notables, they considered politics as a primary vocation to which they were devoted full-time. Their emergence in the political field marked the transition from the politics of notables to the politics of a group of political professionals who radically transformed the political field through the creation of political Shi'a movements. As a consequence, mass politics was introduced, which gradually led to the demise of the power of the merchant notables as they lost their social power in community affairs to a new elite of middle-class Islamist politicians.

In this process towards horizontal political integration of the community, an interesting mixture between the traditional way of doing politics by the notables and the new strategies of the political entrepreneurs could be observed. In order to acquire social power, the young men appropriated the old local traditions prevalent in society – centred on traditional 'asabiyyat[16] – and appropriated traditional structures of socialization. A first objective of the young men was the takeover of the *Jama'iyyat al-Thaqafa al-Ijtima'iyya*[17]; a Social Society for Culture established by the merchant notables that essentially served as a means to unify the different Shi'a fractions under one umbrella in order to exercise effective influence over their electorate. The institution was mainly engaged in promoting what its members considered the Shi'a culture (*thaqafat al-Shi'a*) in the sense of an ethnic, inherited identity. The young men, criticizing what they considered to be narrow-minded political interests of the notables, succeeded in 1972 in winning the elections for the board of the Social Society for Culture and transformed it into a front for the Al-Da'wa movement. However, since the young men were still dependent on the social capital of the notables to reach the Shi'a masses, they decided to join forces with the notables for the elections of 1975 by supporting candidates from the notability. Profiting from the new electoral law, they succeeded in having ten Shi'a deputies in parliament, which also enabled them to negotiate the appointment of the first Shi'a minister, Abdelmutalib al-Kadhemi, who became Minister of Oil.

The dissolution of the parliament by the Emir in 1976 – in reaction to the vocal opposition of the Arab nationalists and the liberals – brought an abrupt end to the cooperation between the notables and the young men. Whereas the young men fiercely criticized the dissolution and organized themselves to oppose the government's decisions, the notables refrained from any criticism. For these merchants, for whom government procurement had become a major source of their business profits after the oil boom,[18] personal interests of maintaining close ties to the government prevailed over ideological conviction. Following the abstention of the notables, the young men circulated a petition in which they denied the deputies any right to represent the Shi'a community.[19] This episode marked a turning point in the political history of the Shi'a in Kuwait, as a new generation of Shi'a Islamist deputies – displaying an oppositionist discourse – would come to dominate the representation of the Shi'a community in parliament, a situation that lasted until 2008.

The advent of the Islamic Revolution in Iran only exacerbated the rift between the merchants and the masses. It triggered great enthusiasm among the majority of Shi'a from middle-class background and would be the start of the emergence of a pro-Iranian political current in Kuwait, as an off-spring from the Al-Da'wa movement; the Hezbollah line or Imam line (*Khatt al-Imam*), referring to its support of the *wilayat al-faqih* of Ayatollah Khomeini and present-day Ayatollah Khamenei. In the 1990s, with the re-establishment of Kuwaiti political life, the group was transformed into a formal political movement: the Islamic National Alliance (*Al-Tahaluf Al-Islami Al-Watani*), referred to as *Al-Tahaluf* throughout this text. Only a minority of former Al-Da'wa activists would stay faithful to the initial Al-Da'wa line and follow the marja'iyya of Mohammed Hussayn Fadlallah, the spiritual mentor of the Lebanese Hezbollah. In 2005, this rump movement would be transformed into *Al-Mithaq* (The Pact), in which the merchant Abdelwahhab al-Wazzan was to play a leading role.[20] Consequently, the initial factionalism between the Shiraziyyin and Al-Da'wa was gradually substituted by a new division between pro- and anti-Iranian currents. In Kuwait, the first was represented by the popular Al-Tahaluf movement, whilst the latter would refer to the Shiraziyyin.

The Shi'a merchant families were generally sceptical about the Iranian Revolution, as they used to have very close relations to the regime of the Shah, which was related to their commercial interests in Iran. According to Jasem Qabazard:

> We were very shocked by this, my father used to have a very good relation with the old regime, with its ambassadors. For you want to boast about your roots. But when they started to blend politics with religion, we weren't happy. Before the Revolution, being Shi'a in Kuwait was only a religious issue. The older generation never talked in terms of Shi'a-Sunna because that would have been the downfall of our country.[21]

Moreover, the Islamist project was in profound contradiction with the nationalist inclination of the merchants, who considered themselves the pillars of Kuwait's nationhood. Yet, for the Shi'a masses, notably those of Iranian origin, the revolution gave them an important sense of pride in a society where they constituted a minority and had for a long time been dependent on merchants as patrons.

Despite the advent of mass politics, the Shi'a merchants were still favoured by the government in its communication with the mass. Although they had ceased to be the 'faces' (*wujaha*) of their constituencies, they continued to act as intermediaries and **behind-the-scenes bargainers.** When the cleric Abbas al-Mohri, who was the imam for the *Tarakma* community and the representative of Ayatollah Khomeini, together with his sons started to organize political meetings that gained a wide audience including the Arab nationalists, the patriarchs of the Ma'rafi family intervened to ease the tensions: 'He exceeded the red line in criticizing the government. So I went with my two cousins to Sayyid al-Mohri and said to him "What your son is doing, to show that you are powerful, isn't a good thing.""[22] However, since the contestation of the Al-Mohris was of a political nature, they did not accept the bargaining attempt, resulting in their expulsion from Kuwait.

The Iran–Iraq War would only further aggravate sectarian tensions in Kuwait's society as the country became the theatre of violent terrorist attacks. The gravest attacks took place in the midst of the 1980s with the hijacking of a Kuwaiti airplane on its way to Karachi and five months later the assassination attempt on the Emir Jabir al-Ahmad. Their perpetrators, members of *Islamic Jihad* – a splinter group of Al-Da'wa – wanted to pressure the government into releasing some of their members from prison who were held responsible for the 1983 attacks on the French and the American embassies in Kuwait.[23] Imad Mughniyeh was considered the brain behind these attacks. In this extremely tense period for Kuwait, Shi'a citizens suffered from social discrimination because their Shi'ism made them suspect as potential allies of the Islamic Republic. This feeling of a hostile society would reappear in 2008 with the Mughniyeh affair that tore open the old sores within the Shi'a community.

In this context of increased societal tensions, the government resorted to parliament as an instrument for moulding societal forces according to its needs of the moment. It is the rentier nature of the state in Kuwait that explained the relative ease with which the government switches its political alliances by courting the enemies of whatever opposition group it fears most. This explains the election results of 1985 where the government, in an attempt to weaken the influence of Shi'a Islamists, encouraged its old enemies, the Arab nationalists, by allowing them more political space in the public arena.[24] Redistricting hurt the Shi'a in particular, whose representation fell from ten to three seats, two of which were occupied by pro-government Shi'a deputies belonging to the merchant elite.[25] However, exacerbating regional tensions led to the dissolution of parliament in 1986. It was also in this period that Kuwait Shi'a *citizens* were for the first time involved in political violence against the state.[26]

In sum, the official split that took place between the merchants and the Shi'a mass in 1976 was symptomatic of their deep underlying social and political divergence. The ideology of political Shi'ism was discarded by the merchant elite. For them it endangered not only their relations with the rulers but also their privileged position with the Shi'a community. By the end of the 1980s they had lost most of their social power within their constituencies. For the government, the tense interlude of the 1980s raised the awareness that it needed more effective interlocutors with the Shi'a mass in order to maintain control over this minority.

Recompositions of power of the old merchant elite

Although the Shi'a merchants share a class identity as an old elite, these class interests are not translated into coordinated political action. Instead, *vertical relations* to the state, personified in the sovereign, determine the merchants' political action and undermine the crystallization of class-based politics. This explains the competition between the old Shi'a families and what they consider to be *newcomers*; those merchants from middle-class background who gained their wealth during the 1980s and 1990s. It also explains the generational decline of the old merchant families, who have ceased to be part of the top elite stratum around the Al-Sabah family and the esprit de corps that incorporates the country's major social groupings, such as affluent merchants and the *shuyukh* from important clans and tribes.[27] We could argue that it is the rentier context that impedes cohesive class formation, because entrepreneurial classes become dependent on the state's discretion for access to the rent circuit.[28]

When analysing the current position of the old Shi'a merchant families, we can rather quickly conclude they have become marginalized in politics relative to new Shi'a actors. However, the end of the politics of notables has not been accompanied by the fading of the traditional modes of politics, since the political entrepreneurs of the 1980s have to a certain extent taken up the role of notables. The latter is reinforced by the fact that MPs in Kuwait generally function as de facto personal intermediaries between their voters and the government, whom they represent and for whom they facilitate numerous services, ranging from acquiring government permissions to providing them with government jobs. Hence, and notwithstanding their legislative power in Kuwait's parliament, MPs tend to act as intermediaries (*wusata*) and brokers for state resources.[29]

The political movements they represent are *parties of cadres* rather than broad-based parties of masses, reinforced by the fact that political parties are still illegal in Kuwait.[30] The legitimacy of these deputies generally depends on their personal social capital to mobilize resources. In this regard, the electorate is not actively engaged in the political process of the party and its elite. An example is the popular pro-Iranian al-Tahaluf movement that does not divulge its executive structure and where a very small group of deputies has successively been elected to parliament without any formal role in the movement.[31] Moreover, like other members of the new middle class that came to the political scene in the 1980s, the Shi'a political entrepreneurs have re-appropriated local social traditions to acquire political visibility. An example is the creation of personal *diwaniyyas* that play until today a pivotal role in politics, notably during elections. This was a general trend in Kuwait since the 1980s with the rise of the middle class and the investment of new middle-class elites in political capital, with the diwaniyya being and remaining an indispensable asset for those with political ambitions.[32] The constitutionally enshrined protected status of the diwaniyya makes it one of the sole semi-private/semi-public spaces that offer an independent locus for political debates in the absence of political parties.

Finally, although these political entrepreneurs often represent political movements, their electoral success in many cases derives from traditional solidarities. One example is the fact that each Shi'a sub-community tends to favour deputies from its own group of belonging notwithstanding their political differences.[33] It is in this logic that one should understand the long-lasting political visibility of those deputies belonging to the *Tarakma*,[34] as the bulk of their electorate is constituted of the *Tarakma* Shi'a who represent the demographic majority of the 'Ajam and have come to play a more pronounced role in the electoral process with the advent of mass politics. Another primordial factor explaining the deputies' electoral success is the fact that the *sayyids* are particularly successful in parliament.[35]

One of the reasons for the merchant's political decline is their low-profile stance in the Shi'a political field, which has been dominated since the 1980s by the pro-Khomeini movement Al-Tahaluf. Yet, albeit the old merchants do not play an overt role in politics, it becomes clear from our interviews that they do support some of the Shi'a Islamist movements, namely those which display a nationalist political discourse, such as *Tajammu'a al-Adala Wa-Salam* (*Assembly for Justice and Peace*) and *Al-Mithaq* (*The Pact*). A Shi'a political movement that particularly counts on the moral and financial support of the old merchant families in Kuwait is *Al-Adala Wa-Salam*, the political branch of the Shiraziyyin movement. Already upon his arrival to Kuwait, the marja' Mohammed al-Shirazi succeeded in developing very close ties with the Shi'a merchants, through whom he was also introduced to the royal family.

It is this historical legacy that explains the current merchants' support for *Al-Adala Wa-Salam*. The movement's narrative is centred on *religious* rather than political emancipation of the Shi'a in Kuwait, on Islamic unity, rejects Khomeini's *wilayat al-faqih* principle and profoundly supports the ruling house.[36] The considerable financial resources of the Shiraziyyin stem from the support of the affluent old Shi'a merchant families for whom its nationalist bent does not only correspond with their political convictions as an old elite historically loyal to the Al-Sabah, but has also become their only access to public politics as merchants in the rentier-state context, as they have lost their own notable status. The movement has transcended ethnic affiliations, since the shaykhi-hasawi community – whose members are particularly affluent in Kuwait – seems to be particularly committed to the Shiraziyyin. This has been so especially after the death of the late Mirza al-Ihqaqi that led to a split within this community, as some do not recognize his son as their marja' and instead switched to the marja' of Sayyid al-Shirazi.[37] This support from Kuwaiti shaykhis for the Shiraziyyin is due to the fact that, during his stay in Kuwait, Mohammed al-Shirazi had explicitly developed close ties to the *Al-Ihqaqi* marja', forming like the Shiraziyyin a minority branch within Shi'ism.

Hence, it is the merchants' support which explains the prominence of the Shiraziyyin movement in the religious field. The Shiraziyyin have the largest number of mosques in Kuwait and numerous charitable institutions in and outside Kuwait.[38] This stands in stark contrast to the politically strong Al-Tahaluf movement, which is only marginally represented in the religious Shi'a field in Kuwait. Moreover, the Shiraziyyin are known to have heavily invested in modern means of communication. It was the first to create an explicitly Shi'a satellite channel emanating from a marja', *Al-Anwar* (2003).[39] However, despite their strong visibility in the religious field, the Shiraziyyin are marginalized in the political field where they could not compete with Al-Tahaluf, the movement supported by the Shi'a masses.

Revival of merchant elites in a strategy of co-optation

This section will focus on developments in regime–Shi'a relations in the post-Invasion period and particularly under the governments of former PM Nasser al-Muhammad (2006–12). Under his premiership, an overt alliance was struck with Shi'a elites in parliament and in the business sector. In effect, the regime relied on its classic regime strategy of resorting to merchants as informal mediators and brokers with its minority. However, this time, the merchants would be new ones, who had gained wealth late and profited from direct government patronage to make inroads in business, without prior social capital. The event that enabled the regime's outreach to the Shi'a was the commemoration organized by a group of Al-Tahaluf members for the assassination of Imad Mughniyya, one of the leading figures of Lebanese Hezbollah. The act provoked widespread indignation in Kuwaiti society, as Mughniyya was thought to be the mastermind behind the terrorist attacks of the 1980s, including an assassination attempt on the life of the Emir. This revived sectarianism, with accusations in the media from radical Sunni Islamists; a period perceived as particularly tense by the Shi'a, which my interlocutors compared to their plight in the 1980s.

It is in this context that new Shi'a merchants close to the Emir and PM were able to broker a deal between Al-Tahaluf and the regime; merchants that had also become very active in community affairs via their investment in media, support for political factions and charities. One of the most prominent would be the Iranian-born Mahmud Haider, who for a time would become one of the most mediatized businessmen in Kuwait and whose rise was contested by the majority of *badu* and Sunni Islamists, as well as by the Saudi leadership that stepped up its pressures on Nasser al-Muhammad's government to change its perceived pro-Iranian stance.

Yet, in 2011, the witnessing of overt repression of Bahraini co-religionists emboldened Kuwaiti Shi'ites – even those elites recently co-opted – to use their power in media and parliament to defend the cause of Bahraini Shi'ites, acting independently and transgressing the limits of their alliance with the Al-Sabah. This was facilitated by the resignation of Shaykh Nasser himself (November 2011) following mass demonstrations. The Shi'ites, having lost their patron in government, had more leeway to voice independent political demands and were empowered by their high representation in the 2012 and 2013 parliaments that had witnessed an opposition boycott.[40]

Competitive authoritarians:
parliamentary life (1961–90)

Introduction

Contrary to the idea of a more democratically inclined ruling family in comparison to other Gulf monarchs, the experience of parliamentary life shows that the Al-Sabah have been more often than not willing to curtail parliament's powers or disband it all together. Yet, the particular sensitivity of Kuwait's constituencies to regional influences has ever since Qasim's threat convinced the regime that any coerced minority could weaken Kuwait's fragile nationhood and absorb it into the sphere of influence of neighbouring powers. At moments of a threatening regional context, the regime thus resorted to parliament as an instrument to absorb restless forces into politics and avoid an escalation of political opposition to its regime, avoiding that political claims would transform themselves into a questioning of the political entity that had consolidated its authority with the help of a tutelary power and against the wishes of its larger neighbours. In 1961 – following Qasim's threat – this led to the promulgation of a regionally unprecedented liberal constitution and the institutionalization of power-sharing (*musharaka*). In 1981, parliament was reopened after a four-year period of parliamentary void. Again, a threatening regional context prompted the Al-Sabah to call for elections. When in 1985 parliamentary groups showed a growing proclivity to cooperate with former foes on common issues *against* the government, parliament was suspended without a call for new elections. It would be the invasion of Saddam Hussayn's troops in August 1990 that quasi-obliged the Al-Sabah to reinstate parliament and open the political arena to those groups that had formed a proto-government as crucial leaders of the resistance while the rulers were in exile in Saudi Arabia.

The survival of Kuwait's semi-democracy is thus a rather involuntary consequence of the fragility of a small, divided political community surrounded by powerful neighbours. Meanwhile, these same divisions are favourable to the survival of the Al-Sabah regime. Playing upon divisions in society allows the monarch to present himself as a neutral figure, arbitrating between different and sometimes antagonistic social forces. While small is pluralistic, these divisions have in the case of Kuwait strengthened its family rule and semi-authoritarian regime. If one group in society dominated vis-à-vis others demographically, then Kuwait's open parliamentary life would have likely ended early, as was the case for Bahrain

(1975). Therefore, cross-cutting political opposition presents a real threat to the regime and has become more common since the millennium with the rise of middle class-inspired opposition.

Kuwait's experience resembles that of hybrid regimes in which elections have not seriously challenged the authoritarian nature of regimes, but instead served as an instrument to strengthen these regimes as part of *managed reform*. In these cases, the electoral arena is the place where the regime can renew its ties with parliamentary elites and try to co-opt them to avoid constituencies from becoming too independent vis-à-vis the political regime. This is a common strategy of 'competitive authoritarians'.[1] Of course, these strategies do only work in the interest of the regime if parliamentary elites do not transgress the red line of criticizing the Al-Sabah, by making political demands that do not question the regime's status quo or by overtly presenting a pro-regime stance as 'service deputies' who do not present any political programme but are merely brokers for state services. In times of sweeping and potentially threatening social change, authoritarians would naturally be in need of co-opted parliamentarians with outreach to wider constituencies. In the cases of the 'neo-liberalizing' Arab republics in the 1990s, the 2011 revolutions have taught that the integration of new (business) elites into the political realm was rather unsuccessful and symptomatic of the fragmentation of clientelist networks of these postcolonial regimes.

1967–76 parliamentary life

This first phase of parliamentary life was characterized by a gradual process of political modernization among the Sunni *hadar* and Shi'a, a consequence of their social ascension as part of a new state-dependent middle class. Until 1976, the main threat for the Al-Sabah regime came from the leftist and nationalist elite, although since the 1975 elections the Shi'a strengthened their representation in parliament, a consequence of growing politicization of this co-opted minority.

Empowered via parliament, these members, who were part of Kuwait's urban community, gradually released themselves from the patronage of merchant notables. Consequently, this period saw the rise of new middle-class actors in politics who invested in the social and cultural spheres. As such, new *diwaniyyas* were created by middle-class Kuwaitis as *loci* to build up relation capital in a community in which face-to-face contacts are a necessary resource to succeed in politics. The diwaniyyas (as well as parliament) moreover constituted a purely Kuwaiti phenomenon and allowed Kuwaiti elites to demarcate themselves from the large groups of expatriates that then still dominated the state's administration and were the carriers of political ideologies. Defending in some cases an articulated political ideology, all political elites were required to rely on personalized networks of family, neighbourhood and trust to build social capital. Icon of the nationalists Ahmad al-Khatib considers this as one of the main ails for his movement where personality politics often impeded the coherence of acting with one voice as well as the capacity of reaching out to other political groups.[2]

In the period between 1967 and 1976 several main factors structured relations between the Al-Sabah regime and parliamentary elites. First of all, the main perception of threat by the regime came from the Arab nationalists and merchants; to which it responded by divide-and-rule and economic co-optation strategies. A second factor that impacted parliamentary life throughout this period was the ambition of Jaber al-'Ali to become CP one day who therefore co-opted various parliamentary and societal forces between 1963 and 1978. The nationlist threat was the main challenge for the regime and therefore the latter tried to curb the power of expatriate forces in society because of their role in spreading nationlist thought. More stringent nationality laws were issued and temporary bans on culture clubs to create stricter walls between nationals and expatriates and reduce the latter's influence in domestic politics.

Now, parliament itself is not a sufficient factor for getting a complete picture of the regime's perception of threat and its patronage policies. In addition to parliament, the Cabinet is a place for the co-optation of elites and broader social forces as are other bodies such as entire ministries (sometimes staffed by a group: i.e. Awqaf and Islamic Affairs by Sunni Islamists), university faculties and private sector groups that are rather divided along solidarity networks of kin- or status groups – dynamics perpetuated by segmented clientelism by the Al-Sabah. Although the Al-Sabah dominate sensitive ministerial posts (PM, Defence, Interior, Foreign Affairs), the Cabinet has witnessed a gradual growth of posts awarded to members outside the Al-Sabah clan. Until the late 1980s, civilian posts were mostly filled by members of the Najdi elite: a handful of families. Yet, in 1975, the Shi'a were able to lobby for the first Shi'a minister, appointed to the sensitive post of oil. It is noteworthy that this post would in the future often be occupied by a Shi'a (1975, 1976, 1992, 2012 and 2013) and by regime-co-opted elites (Ikhwan, Salafis, tribes) – apart from ruling family members – but never by a member from the Najdi elite. In this regard, one can argue that the exteriority of the Shi'a to the ruling 'asabiyya makes them a less serious threat to the Al-Sabah.[3] A similar situation occurs with the Minister of Information, a sensitive post most often occupied by an Al-Sabah and in some cases by civilians; from loyal elites (tribes [Shammar, 'Awazem, 'Ajman], Shi'a [2003], Ikhwan [2003]) but none from the Najdi elite. The Najdi elite saw a decline in its representation in governmental offices since the late 1980s, coinciding with a rise in government posts attributed to Sunni Islamists and tribal elites.

In the period between 1971 and 1975, patronage politics entangled MPs and even some nationalist MPs, who supported Jaber al-'Ali in the 1971–5 parliament against his rivals, PM Jaber al-Ahmad and S'ad al-Abdallah (Defence/Interior). Oil had been the leading issue of this parliament and following the price hikes of 1973 spurred a wave of national fervour to guarantee the use of oil wealth for the Kuwaiti public rather than foreign companies. In this period the government nationalized its full control of oil, transforming Kuwait into an international oil player in its own right. Yet, as the ruler was the sole owner of oil, signing agreements with oil companies was done on a personal title: a situation which displeased the merchants who therefore tried to create their own fiefs, but that also remained dependent on regime-derived rents (e.g. Kuwaiti National Bank, the Company for Oil Transports, insurance companies). Formally the merchants represented by Abdelaziz al-Saqqer's group (KCC) had been outside this parliament, as their group had boycotted the 1971 elections (together with Jasem al-Qatami's group), criticizing government corruption and the naturalizations of Bedouins.

In the context of growing antagonism with the Islamists following 1967, these conflicts were transplanted to parliament, intersecting causes defended by the nationalists (i.e. nationalization of oil) and exploited by an ambitious prince.[4] In this regard, a series of interpellations were filed against Al-Ahmad's government in 1973 and 1974 that were according to Al-Khatib a direct result of members of his group's alliance with Al-'Ali.[5] These interpellations were directed against ministers who moreover were part of the Ikhwan. In December 1973 this led to an interpellation against the Minister of Oil and Finance, Abdelrahman al-'Atiqi, known for his proximity to Al-Ahmad. Only two months later, in February 1974, members of Al-Khatib's group presented an interpellation against Khaled al-Adsani, Minister of Commerce and Industry. Not much later, another interpellation was filed against Abdelrahman al-'Atiqi by Abdallah al-Nibari. Opposition in parliament was not only constituted of Ahmad al-Khatib's group, but was supported by certain tribal MPs known for their ties to Jaber al-'Ali. Among them were most of the 'Ajman MPs in the 1971 parliament as well as Yusuf al-Mukhled and Ghanam al-Jamhur from the Mutran and Naser al-'Asimi from the 'Utban.[6]

The majority of parliament was still composed of co-opted elites: tribesmen, Shi'a and loyal independents of middle-class background. Some Islamists were also elected. These were independents chosen by the Ikhwan on the basis of their local power after the publication of lists of candidates. The strongest ones were chosen, approached and then ties were established, followed by a campaign in which the Ikhwan publicly announced their support for these persons in advance of elections. Once chosen, as a sign of gratitude, these MPs would continue to support issues of concern to the Ikhwan. And the spread of the Ikhwan in Kuwait's society – supported by regime patronage – made individual MPs eager to show their inclination to support their agenda in the hope to be the lucky ones to receive their support in forthcoming elections. In 1971, the Ikhwan supported in this way Sayyid Yusuf al-Rifa'i – who won in the first district – and Abbas al-Munawar (Rashaida) in the fourth district.

The 1971 elections further saw around twenty-two MPs who won on a tribal ticket, as representatives of their tribes. Some of them were oppositional to the government, but this only concerned the minority of certain 'Ajman allied to Jaber al-'Ali. The bulk of tribal MPs largely functioned as 'service deputies' in a context in which the recently settled Bedouins faced social marginalization and a strong lack of access to the state's *wasta* networks.

A new parliament was formed in 1975 that also had a majority of loyal forces and witnessed the engineered rise of the tribal vote. In 1975, the regime moved large numbers of *badu* voters into city constituencies in the hopes of unseating some of the leftists, at a time in which it was still possible to transfer voters from one constituency to the other.[7] Another difference of the 1975 elections was the rise of the Shi'a vote, a consequence of the emergence of new Shi'a Islamist leaders who – in their attempt to maximize the Shi'a vote – cooperated with Shi'a merchant notables whose social capital was still an essential resource. As a result, ten Shi'a deputies were elected. It also led to the successful appointment of the first Shi'a minister, of oil. Then, the Shi'a were still displaying a supportive stance. Finally, the 1975 elections also saw the rise of other primordial groups, a consequence of the flexibility in transferring voters from one constituency to the other. In this regard, ethnic minorities such as the *Kanadrah* and *Awadiyah* (Sunni Persians) as well as the *Salab* (non-noble tribe) rose in elections on the family grouping ticket.[8]

In less than a year after its inception, parliament was dissolved (1976). The reasons behind the ruler's decision to shut down parliament were many – as notes Crystal – and linked to both domestic and international concerns. A main factor seems to have been the international context and the fear of a spillover of the Lebanese civil war to local expatriate Lebanese and Palestinian communities that would entangle nationalists and leftists who socialized with these expatriate communities in the clubs and who had been advocates of the Palestinian cause.[9] A subsequent factor was pressure from Saudi Arabia to shut down the parliament and follow in the footsteps of the 'Al-Khalifa, who had closed their assembly just one year earlier. Saudi pressures to curtail Kuwait's parliamentary activism have been a recurrent theme and the Al-Sabah have displayed a sensitivity to their neighbours' concerns.[10] Domestically, while the majority was loyal in parliament, oppositional MPs were capable of raising critical issues, such as state corruption and the conflict over the role of the judiciary.

The latter was particularly critical and likely prompted the Emir's decision. Parliament had attempted to promulgate a law granting the Supreme Council of the Courts the authority to review the constitutionality of government administrative orders. The law was vetoed by the Emir, but parliament attempted to push through a second vote in the new session by simple majority as it was not able to gain the two-thirds needed to override the Emir's veto to the proposal. Likely fearing an undesirable precedent, the Emir dissolved the body.[11] Not much later culture clubs were shut down and media was censured while the government dismantled boards of teachers and student unions and replaced them with appointed members. Al-Khatib's Independence Club, which had been a main platform for nationalist opposition, was banned.

The boldness of the regime was a consequence of a favourable context. The oil boom had allowed the regime to expand its distributional politics profiting a 'Third Estate', middle-class Kuwaitis. Less than a month after the dissolution, the Emir, CP and PM ordered the municipality to increase its acquisition of land and particularly in the peripheral areas; Jahra and Failaka, to focus on the neglected areas in a period in which the regime bolstered its support for the Bedouins via mass naturalizations.[12] Apart from politicized MPs and members of unions, the dissolution of 1976 was little contested by Kuwaitis at large and some even applauded it, placated by the oil boom and the involvement of a significant segment of the population in the stock market that enriched them.

1976–90: former allies becoming restless, the threat of *cross-cutting* alliances

In subsequent years of parliamentary void (1976–81), the Al-Sabah dealt with society via loyal elites. The context of booming rentierism for the first time resulted in a state-dependent middle class. Also, the new groups with which the Al-Sabah had allied were still rather unconcerned with values of parliamentarianism: the southern tribesmen and Sunni Islamist groups. In 1976, the alliance with the Islamists was cemented, when the Kuwaiti *Ikhwan* were the only group that did not protest the dissolution of parliament. They would be rewarded in 1981 with the appointment of one of theirs as minister of *Awqaf* (Religious Endowments). The empowerment of Islamists coincided with a context in which Islamism was supported as part of an American strategy mediated via its ally – the Al-Saud – to assert its control in the region against the Soviets, relying from their part on local nationalist and leftist currents. This situation would change following American deployment of forces on 'holy' land during the Gulf War (1990–1), prompting an Islamist counter reaction.[13]

In 1981, the Al-Sabah decided to reopen parliamentary life. As in 1961, the regional context was the factor explaining the new ruler's decision. The Lebanese civil war (1975–90) was feared by Kuwaiti authorities for its possible spillover to Palestinian expatriates and local communities.[14] In 1979, the double threat of religious fervour that resulted in a Shi'a revolution in Iran and in the occupation of the Grand Mosque in Mecca by Sunni religious alerted the Al-Sabah. The start of the Iran–Iraq War (1980–8) further alarmed Kuwait's elite as it spurred sectarianism in its divided society. In this context of regional politics trickling down to domestic communities, the best of the worse options was to call for elections.

To strengthen its power, the government announced that it would extend the number of districts from ten to twenty-five, in order to empower the Bedouin populations as loyal supporters of the Al-Sabah. By then, the Islamist movement had greatly strengthened its social outreach. Empowered by their success, Ikhwan and Salafi groups decided to present for the first time their own candidates in elections to support a programme to Islamize laws. The result of the elections of 1981 confirmed the government's success of co-optation. The majority of the 1981–5 parliament was constituted of pro-government forces, mostly Islamists and tribesmen. As for the nationalist elite, they did not succeed in having even one candidate elected, a consequence of the new electoral districting as well as a regional context strengthening Islamism and sectarianism.[15] The Shi'a also witnessed a drop in successful candidates, from a record of ten in 1975 to only four, also the consequence of electoral gerrymandering.[16]

While the bulk of Islamists remained supportive of the government, a more independent stance was observed among younger members of Kuwait's Ikhwan. Issa al-Shahin led a bloc of four Islamist oppositional MPs in 1981.[17] In reaction to this strengthened independence of certain Islamists, the regime favoured the rise of the Salafi trend to fragment Sunni Islamism. The Salafis proved a useful countercurrent to more radical jihadi groups, as well as the leftist and Shi'a.[18]

The call for elections in 1985 saw a return of independent forces to parliament with the election of many nationalists who had been able to reorganize themselves after a decade of absence from parliamentary life. Also, with a government increasingly anxious of Islamist activism, the latter had courted the Islamists' enemies: the progressives.[19] Cooperation between secular, liberal and nationalist forces as a front of civil (*madani*) groups had further strengthened their electoral weight.[20] Apart from thirteen MPs linked to this current, the 1985 parliament saw a rise in a new generation of Ikhwani forces, more independent from the older guard. One can think here of Mubarak al-Duwaila, Hamud al-Rumi and Abdallah al-Nafisi, replacing older members (such as Issa al-Shahin and Khalid al-Issa).[21] It also saw rising competition between the Ikhwan and Salafi currents, resembling competition in the 1960s and 1970s between nationalists and communists.[22] In total, the Sunni Islamists had six candidates in parliament and did not fare as well as they had hoped. Finally, it marked a growing trend of the rise of tribal forces who reached twenty-seven members in parliament; more than half of the total seats.[23] It also saw the emergence of the first tribal Islamists, who rather than running on a tribal ticket ran as part of an Islamist movement. This was the case of the Ikhwan's alliance with members of the Rashaida; resulting in 1985 in two of their members elected to parliament: Mubarak al-Duwaila and Muhammad Jifidan.[24]

The presence of both nationalists and a number of independent Islamists made the 1985 parliament a particularly vocal one. It coincided with a tense period both locally and regionally. Locally, the aftermath of the Souq al-Manakh crisis (1982) had raised anger among middle-class Kuwaitis who felt the government had a large share of responsibility in the crisis. Also, in these years Kuwait was the theatre of a series of bombings by Hezbollah militias that raised questions about the quality of the security apparatus.

These issues concerned the general public and thus allowed for *cross-cutting* action between MPs representing different ideological stances. Liberals and Islamists cooperated in launching interpellations against ministers and transgressed a red line by directing interpellations to Al-Sabah members; a new phenomenon that would continue in subsequent decades. As such, tribal Ikhwan MP Mubarak al-Duwaila joined the leftists in presenting a successful interpellation against the Minister of Justice, Shaykh Salman Da'ij al-Sabah accused of being involved in diverting funds destined to help the small investors that had lost their money during the 1982 crisis. He was forced to resign. A couple of months later, interpellations were filed against the Minister of Oil (Ali 'al-Khalifa al-Sabah), the Minister of Finance (Jasem al-Khorafi), the Minister of Transportation (Issa al-Mezidi) and the Minister of Education (Dr Husan Ibrahim). Also Al-Sabah members, Ali 'al-Khalifa (Minister of Oil) and Naïf al-Sabah (Minister of Interior) were accused of their incapacity to properly protect the oil installations against the bombings that hit the country's installations in 1986.[25] This coincided with rising tensions between the Al-Salim and Al-Ahmad al-Jabir branches and some of the interpellations were supported by opponents of Sa'd al-Abdallah (PM).[26]

This rise in interpellations against Al-Sabah shaykhs had alarmed the ministers who resigned collectively on 1st of July. It was an unprecedented act in the Gulf; displaying the power of a parliament vis-à-vis the royal house and its representatives. This rather embarrassing show of force prompted the Emir two days later to dissolve parliament all together without calling for new elections.[27] By then, tribesmen on the whole sided with the dynasty, apart from those very few MPs wearing the double head of the Ikhwan. This would be markedly different from the tribal stance in 2012 following the dissolution of parliament.

Unlike 1976, the dissolution this time led to the start of a social movement that was initially *cross-cutting* and organized via the *diwaniyya* networks, constitutionally protected space. Every Monday, thirty-two activist MPs (under the lead of Ahmad al-Sa'dun, speaker of parliament) gathered in their diwaniyyas to call for the restoration of parliament. It was a diverse group of young, educated activists, consisting of Shi'a, tribal, Islamist and progressive men united around a common cause.[28] By the end of

1988 the movement strengthened its mobilization tactics, reaching out to members with strong popularity within local communities from all walks of life. This enlarged 'group of 45' would be entrusted with diffusing the message of the deposed MPs in their communities, ranging from professional circles (student and trade unions) to neighbourhood and family units.

Following repeated refusals by the Emir, via his Emiri Diwan, to receive petitions of activists, the latter stepped up their action and created in 1989 the Constitutional Movement, which laid the basis for an organizational infrastructure throughout the country, including the peripheral tribal zones.[29] Merchants of the KCC group, previously hesitant to support the movement, now did and presented a petition to the Emir pleading for the restitution of constitutional life.[30] Every Monday the leaders of the movement organized meetings that were open-doors for citizens in the area and from then on, the movement was referred to as *Al-diwawin Al-ithnayn* (the Monday diwaniyyas).[31] Initially focused on the inner city, the movement extended its meetings to the diwaniyyas of former MPs in the tribal areas.[32] Although tribes remained a pro-government constituency, it was for the first time in 1989 that some of its activist elites started to plead for an end to the far-reaching loyalty of tribesmen to the Al-Sabah (such as Mubarak al-Duwaila).[33]

Repression and co-optation to maintain the periphery's crucial support

The Monday diwaniyyas were not only a thorn in the sight of the Al-Sabah, but also of neighbouring autocrats, particularly the Al-Saud that pressured Kuwait's rulers to repress any gatherings, marches or demands for democracy, as it would do any time popular activism mounted in Kuwait.[34] It is noteworthy that most violence to repress the movement was used in the tribal areas when the movement reached the peripheral zones. This is rather logical, as the regime considered the tribes as its loyal base and hence an essential support structure.

As a means out of the impasse, the Emir issued a speech in which he sharply denounced the gatherings while calling for dialogue. In response, activists wrote a statement to the Emir in announcing the cancellation of gatherings in exchange for dialogue. Yet, to their surprise, the statement never passed censorship. The CP – Sa'd al-Abdallah – then opened dialogue with different sections of society, Islamists, merchants and with the leaders of the Monday movement. In 1990, the government announced the creation of a National Council (*Al-Majlis Al-Watani*) to replace parliament. Being a purely consultative body with fifty of its seventy-five members appointed by the Emir, the opposition decided to boycott its elections, supported by the president of the KCC Abdel Aziz al-Saqqer.

Yet, it was here that the Islamists and the tribesmen *on the whole* displayed their support to the Al-Sabah, with some of its activist leaders breaking away from the opposition movement. Islamists had been courted by the CP earlier, as he decided to meet with them as a group, to weaken cross-cutting action of the activists. Not much later, the Islamists issued a telegram to the Emir in which they, although in implicit wording, recognized the legitimacy of the National Council, while expressing their hopes that it would be a transitional arrangement before the full restoration of constitutional life. As a consequence of this stance, some activist members who had previously participated in the Monday movement left the opposition.[35]

The tribal zones largely ignored calls by the opposition to boycott elections for the National Council. The violent reaction of government forces against the Monday gathering in the diwaniyya of deposed tribal MP Ahmad al-Shari'an in Al-Jahra had cautioned tribesmen against putting their bets on the opposition, as the Al-Sabah had shown their intention to crack down violently on any form of dissent emanating from the tribal region. The use of batons, teargas and beating of protestors, including deposed MPs, were a clear warning to the *badu* not to pass a red line in relations with the government (a similar display of force would happen in 2008 in the diwaniyya of *Jum'an al-Harbash*, but with different consequences this time it would not still tribal opposition). The regime did not dare to display similar force vis-à-vis the Monday meetings in the *hadar* areas, as it had to accommodate, at least to a certain extent, its discontent in order to not violate the elite bargain underlying its authority structure; a dual contract with a privileged *hadar* elite. Here comes by that as latecomers to the welfare regime, tribesmen had much to lose from bad relations with the Al-Sabah that had only so recently upgraded them as a group.

With Sunni Islamists and tribesmen now supporting the Al-Sabah, the National Council only consisted of pro-government members – notables and service deputies – while being boycotted by the Sunni merchant aristocracy (represented by the KCC), the leftist and nationalists and a small fringe of Islamist leaders (i.e. Mubarak al-Duwaila, Ahmad al-Baqer and Abdallah al-Nafisi). For the Shi'a, the Council represented a return of their merchant elites, who had displayed their continued loyalty to the government even during the tense events following the 1979 revolution and the Iran–Iraq War.[36] It was in this context that on 2 August 1990 Saddam Hussayn troops invaded Kuwait: a traumatic experience, which rallied Kuwaitis behind the ruler and behind one cause – resistance against the occupant.

Conclusion

Between 1963 and 1990, Kuwait's political life has seen a number of changing alliances between the Al-Sabah and domestic groups. Until the 1980s and despite changing coalitions, the main opposition came from the leftist and liberal *hadar* elite, represented by leaders such as Ahmad al-Khatib, Jasem al-Qatami, Ahmad al-Sa'dun and Abdelaziz al-Saqqar. The Sunni Islamist current – while strengthening its independence – still remained rather supportive of the government, as was manifested in the aftermath of the two unconstitutional dissolutions of parliament in 1976 and 1985. With Islamists and tribal constituencies largely behind the ruler, the status quo upon which Kuwait's modern political order was built was not challenged: an elite bargain between Sunni merchants and the Al-Sabah, in which the masses are upgraded as a state-dependent middle class, but do not challenge the *exclusive* prerogatives of the political and economic elite.

Part Three

New forces of globalization and the rise of the tribal periphery in Kuwait (1990–2014)

Introduction

Two main socio-political dynamics of change have been unfolding in Kuwait since Liberation and have led to the erosion of the old status-quo based upon an elite bargain between the Al-Sabah and an 'asabiyya of Najdi merchants. The first trend that was set in motion since the mid-1990s is the rise of a younger generation of *badu* citizens in search of new modes of politics and better access to state resources, breaking away from previous modes of the regime's dealing with its tribal constituency. The second trend is the rise of elite rivalry since 2006, upon the death of Emir Jabir, which has taken a new turn, breaking with succession custom and resulting in power struggles between second-generation princes spilling over to parliament and public life.

The political opposition of *badu* citizens finds resonance among a broader group of middle-class Kuwaitis who despite social divisions converge in their opposition to corruption and more recently to austerity measures. Since 2016, the government has started to implement austerity in response to a budget shortfall caused by a global decline in oil prices. These measures are part of the 'New Kuwait' development plan aimed to radically shift Kuwait's economy from its oil-dependency and transform it into a regional and financial hub by 2035. The much-needed restructuring of Kuwait's economy has strong political costs and finds critical backlash among its citizens who for decades have become accustomed to a generous welfare regime. Austerity measures threaten their entitlements and as public sector workers, the masses do not have a direct interest in strengthening the private sector, although in the future they will have to take private sector jobs as the extremely high ratio of public sector workers in bloated bureaucracies are financially unsustainable for the government. In this transition process, a new social contract is in the making that threatens the elite-bargain on which the House Al-Sabah was established. The political emancipation of the tribesmen has started to fragment the regime's ties to its periphery, thereby undermining its authority.

These trends have been unfolding in a rapidly changing regional context of heightened sectarianism and political upheaval since 2003, following the fall of Saddam Hussayn's regime and intensified with the political storm of the Arab uprisings (2011) that reverberated throughout the Gulf monarchies and ushered in a phase of regional competition between Qatar and Saudi Arabia aiming at strengthening their power in a regional power play. Kuwaiti princes and societal actors tapped into burning regional issues and networks (i.e. Arab revolts, Syria crisis, Qatar–Saudi rivalry, Iran–Saudi rivalry) to enhance their power position.

Both phenomena – the loss of support from its periphery and struggles within the Al-Sabah family – reduced the regime's capacity to maintain social control via its traditional political patronage networks. The latter relied upon ensuring the support of *non-core* groups – Shi'a and the *badu* – via their elite representatives acting as intermediaries and brokers between the Al-Sabah and constituencies. This system of political patronage upon which Kuwait's political order was built is crumbling today. The old tripartite societal categories (*hadar*, Shi'a and *badu*) have become blurred and new forms of *cross-cutting* politics are in the making, with an opposition employing rhetoric focused on a state of law, accountability and pleading for transparency in the government's dealing with society. This as well as the need to restructure the economy towards a post-oil future threatens the foundations of the regime's authority system, based upon the co-optation of the periphery via elite representatives as personal channels for regime patronage.

In reaction to the fragmentation of its bonds towards the periphery, the regime has resorted to more repressive methods to deal with societal opposition. The rise of the tribal Islamist opposition that gained strength since Iraq's invasion of Kuwait has led the regime to step up the repression of public activism since 2012 (resulting in incarcerations and juridical measures to restrict [virtual] public space). Repression is in essence the manifestation of the failure of co-optation methods to deal with societal challenges and follows the footsteps of powerful neighbours and notably the Kingdom of Saudi Arabia which reasserted its regional role as protector of Arab Sunni monarchies.

The birth of a tribal opposition

Introduction

Since the Liberation from Saddam Hussayn's seven-month occupation, regime–society relations in Kuwait witnessed a series of changes. Until Saddam's Invasion, the main opposition stemmed from the leftist and liberal *hadar* elite. While a younger generation of MB Islamists started to display a more independent stance vis-à-vis the Al-Sabah following the dissolution of parliament in 1986, the regime was capable of maintaining the overall support of Sunni Islamists and tribesmen. The violence used by the regime against the Monday gatherings in the tribal areas in 1989 *then* proved to be an effective deterrent for tribesmen against participating in oppositional activities. Yet, when the regime took an increasingly strong stance against tribal primaries after 2008 the tribal base proved less concessionary and mandated its representatives to voice opposition to the regime. In 2012, the dissolution of a parliament dominated by a tribal–Islamist opposition spurred a vocal reaction. This time, tribesmen constituted the bulk of the forces that boycotted the 1 December 2012 elections, opposing a change in election law that meant to break the power of the tribal–Islamist alliance. This volte face in regime–tribal relations will be discussed as it is crucial for understanding socio-political change in Kuwait since the millennium.

Fragmenting tribal hierarchies and new leadership patterns

The fragmentation of traditional tribal hierarchies and the loss of political power of tribal chieftains (*shuyukh al-qaba'il*) since the 1990s are the consequences of a series of processes. One of these is temporal and generational and marked by the arrival of a first generation of highly educated tribesmen (born in the 1960s and 1970s) who have risen up against old hierarchies, customs and the 'blind obedience' of their fathers. Initially a small elite of tribal political entrepreneurs who wanted to change existing political transactions, their attitude has been supported by a young tribal social base. This can be compared to similar processes of social change among the *hadar* and Shi'a constituencies – respectively in the 1960s and 1970s – leading to the demise of notables and the rise of political entrepreneurs as young men. What differs in the case of the tribal population is its demographic weight and relative position vis-à-vis the *hadar*, together with the more traditional nature of its group codes and hierarchies. Combined with acculturation in a globalized world of communication technology, this process of social change has had disruptive and disintegrative consequences in terms of traditional hierarchies. And the consequences of this process have dramatically been felt in Kuwait, as tribes constitute today around 60 per cent of the citizen population. Empowered with regionally unprecedented legislative prerogatives, it has had important implications for Kuwait's parliamentary life. While being empowered in parliament, the *badu* continue to be marginalized in the private sector and the much-needed reform and opening of the private sector to competition will imply the breaking of the oligarchic power of the Najdi elite, therefore compromising the old elite bargain.

Since the 2000s, a younger generation born in the 1970s and 1980s rose to prominence and it is this generation which has been the main driver behind new forms of tribal politics and regime–tribal relations. These young tribesmen are in a situation of 'in-between', in search of a new identity, which is different from their parents' as well as from the *hadar*'s (both of which they cannot adhere to). Semi-illiterate and badly integrated parents, recently naturalized, produced highly literate children who cannot accept anymore the traditional modes of dealing with the regime and the unquestioned loyalty of their parents to the monarchy. The uprootedness vis-à-vis their own past and their parents is inextricably linked to an uprootedness vis-à-vis the regime. This has resulted in privileging new and more independent leaders to represent their interests. A case in point is Musallam al-Barrak (*Mutran*) – branded the conscience of the Nation (*dhamir al-umma*) – who has been the uncontested leader of the tribal youth although increased government repression and his exile to Turkey in 2018 to avoid serving a prison sentence have decreased his direct influence in society. Salafism has also been an identity 'par excellence' to empower the uprooted tribal youth. Salafism is perceived as authentic, as it is inherent to the Arabian Peninsula and as the tribes have historically been considered the carriers of Salafism.

This transformation of Kuwaiti tribalism and leadership has been accompanied by a process of reinventing tradition, in which tribalism is used as a source and symbolic frame for political purposes. Globalization and its impact on communication networks has played a crucial role, as it strengthened transnational connections as a resource for social networks that transcend national borders. The repercussions of this process have been felt everywhere in the region and it is this process of social change within tribal populations that is perhaps among the most important carriers of change in the region's political make-up for the decades to come.

The 1992 elections were the first to show change in tribal leadership patterns. It was the first-time tribal *shuyukh* who had presented themselves as candidates lost in elections. Emirs of the Rashaida, the 'Awazem, the Mutran all lost against a new generation of younger, activist leaders who had often played an important role in organizing the civil resistance against the Iraqis during the Invasion. They all represented a generation which had benefitted from good education and recently graduated from universities, often abroad. Some of them had been among the participants in the Monday Diwaniyya movement (*Al-Diwawin Al-Ithnayn*) that in 1989 reached the tribal areas and received a particularly violent reaction from government forces that heavy-handedly cracked down on these rallies in peripheral areas so crucial for the regime. Abbas al-Munawar

(*Rashaida*), Mubarak al-Duwaila (*Rashaida*) and Ahmad al-Shari'an (*Dhafir*) were among the prominent tribal leaders who joined the Constitutional Movement of 1989 pleading for the restoration of parliamentary life. They represented a new leadership style, with a new discourse, markedly different from the tribal chieftains who often lacked these skills and were elected on the basis of their inherited status, coupled with their role as *the* crucial service-providers for constituencies since their integration into the nation state. Tribal leaders were the ones via whom the naturalizations took place and who informed ruling *shaykhs* about constituencies. They were also the ones who since long time gathered and recruited the manpower for wars and later for the army and police forces. And their diwaniyyas became the crucial loci for fellow-tribesmen to get access to *wasta* to get a government job, driving licenses and other state-related services.

Many of these new tribal political entrepreneurs had been socialized in the Islamist movements, a main vehicle of social ascension for tribesmen. Such was the case of Mubarak al-Duwaila – member of the *Ikhwan al-Muslimin* – who somehow epitomized the first generation of this new tribal leadership and its willingness to break with previous hierarchies. His lecture, given in 1989 in the diwaniyya of his uncle Abbas al-Munawar, was symbolic in this regard. Entitled '*Mada Ahd al-Fidawiyya*' (The period of the fidawiyya has gone/no more fidawiyya), he pleaded for an end to the blind obedience of tribesmen to their tribal shaykh and the regime and to stand up for their rights as full citizens.[1] As we know, historically the tribes constituted the bulk of the *fidawiyyin* – the loyal guards of Al-Sabah *shaykhs* who sacrificed their lives to serve their masters.

These changes cannot but be placed in the context of the aftermath of the Invasion.[2] The Invasion left the Al-Sabah fragilized and traumatized and with no other option but to offer concessions to those civil forces that had organized the resistance and de-facto governance during the Occupation. While the Al-Sabah were quick to flee to neighbouring Saudi Arabia, around a third of Kuwaitis stayed in the country and organized an extensive network of inter-aid via the popular committees (*Al-lajan Al-sha'biyya*), the supermarket chains (*Al-jami'yyat Al-ta'waniyya*), mosques and diwaniyya networks to deliver food to the besieged Kuwaitis. Many of these popular committees were active in areas with a high number of Salafis, such as *Kaifan*, *Al-Faiha'*, *Al-Qadisiyya* and the tribal area of *Al-Jahra*. While the elite of the Ikhwan al-Muslimin had largely been abroad during the Occupation, many Salafi leaders (Jasim al-'Awn, Ahmad Baqir and Khalid al-Issa) stayed in Kuwait, which strengthened the appeal of Salafism after Liberation.[3]

Both the Ikhwan and the Salafi movement were active on the ground and in tribal areas with so-called solidarity committees (*lajan al-takaful al-ijtima'i*) or popular committees (*lajan sha'biyya*) – as the Salafi ones were called – that provided food and other daily necessities to Kuwaitis under occupation. Islamists had developed strong networks in this regard through their role in the boards of the supermarket chains and in other activities on the ground (mosques/neighbourhoods). Also, as many tribesmen escaped to Saudi Arabia during the occupation (they often shared family ties with Saudis), they socialized in different Saudi Salafi networks and got involved in Salafi debates and schisms. Upon their return to Kuwait, their religiosity was strengthened and many opened *zakat* committees and charities.

As tribesmen – and the general public – felt a sense of disappointment vis-à-vis the Al-Sabah's handling of the crisis, coupled with their socialization in Salafi networks, the tribal social base voted for changing leadership in the 1992 elections. For the first time, Islamists who ran on a non-tribal ticket saw themselves elected in parliament. One can think of Jumu'an al-'Azemi ('Awazem/Ikhwan al-Muslimin), Mubarak al-Duwaila (Rashaida/Ikhwan al-Muslimin), Ahmad al-Shar'ian (Dhafir/Popular Action Bloc) and Khaled al-'Awda ('Ajman/Salafi).[4] Their participation in civil work during the occupation and more distinguished and professional speeches enabled them to win against more traditional leaders, the tribal chieftains, many of whom presented themselves in 1992 under the banner of 'National Council Deputies' (referring to their role in the National Council; the rubberstamp parliament that was erected in 1990 by the government and lacked real legislative and supervisory powers). These National Council deputies who presented themselves in 1992 – all Bedouins – were dealt a great blow as only eight out of the twenty-four members were able to regain their seats; a token of the resentment of the Bedouin electorate vis-à-vis the political regime during the Occupation.[5]

These – then still modest – changes within the voting patterns of the tribal electorate fitted in the larger context of the 1992 parliament that saw the unprecedented number of thirty-three opposition MPs and can only be compared in terms of strength to the parliament that was elected in 2012 in the aftermath of the popular movement against the PM and the larger context of Arab revolts. These elections witnessed for the first time the formation of political blocs (six oppositional blocs) that were tolerated by the regime, which moreover allowed for the first time to have six ministerial posts assigned to members of these oppositional political blocs. Islamists were the real winners of these elections and the only forces that had considerable local power as a consequence of their ground-level presence in neighbourhoods. The elections marked a new turn in relations between the regime and the Islamist movements, as three Islamist ministers were appointed in a move that reflected the growing popularity of Islamism in Kuwaiti society, two of whom were tribesmen.[6] Jumu'an al-'Azemi became Minister of Awqaf, Abdallah al-Hajeri became Minister of Commerce and Jasem al-'Awn became Minister of the crucial 'wasta' ministry, the Ministry of Social Affairs.

These Islamists would have a lasting impact on Islamizing Kuwaiti society and its laws. In the new parliament, a petition was sent to the Emir by thirty-nine MPs who announced their willingness to Islamize the laws. Between 1993 and 1994 a strong movement developed in this regard. A main issue was the change in the wording of article 2 of the Constitution, making Islam *the* rather than a principal source of law, a proposition which has always been blocked by the Emir as this could potentially threaten the Al-Sabah's hereditary family rule. Earlier (December 1991) the regime had allowed the Ikhwan al-Muslimin to create a high consultative committee to realize the application of the *shari'a*. The focus on the Islamization of laws led to strong debates with non-religious forces in parliament, who were subsequently the target of *takfiri* campaigns of the Islamists. Another thorn in the side of the Islamists was gender mixing at educational institutions and in 1996 – after years of efforts – a coalition of Islamist MPs succeeded in passing a law on gender separation that was extended to private universities and schools in 2000.[7]

The Islamization of society was accompanied by a growing role of neighbouring Saudi Arabia in Kuwaiti affairs and in those of the wider Gulf region. Saudi Arabia had been the refuge of the Al-Sabah during the occupation and many Kuwaitis had left to Saudi Arabia where they socialized in Salafi networks. As a consequence of the Gulf War, Saudi Arabia emerged as a main reference for local Kuwaiti Salafis. For many Kuwaiti Salafis, the official body of 'ulema ('ulema al-sulta') – represented then by Grand Mufti Shaykh Abdelaziz Ibn Baz (1912–99)[8] – was their reference in their actions and visions on social, religious and political issues. They represented the *purist* strand in Salafism, which is characterized by its unconditional obedience to the ruler as long as the latter is not an open apostate. In Kuwait, they became known as the Islamic Popular Gathering (*Al-Tajamu'a Al-Islami Al-Sha'bi*): the political wing of the Foundation for the Revival of Islamic Heritage (*Ihya al-Turath*).

Yet, the politicization of a minority of Kuwaiti Salafis around the person of Shaykh Abdel Khaleq during the Occupation became a nuisance to the Kuwaiti authorities. He had sympathized personally with Saddam Hussayn and his stance was challenging the regime, as these *haraki* Salafis strongly denounced the presence of and assistance from foreign forces during the Liberation. For this reason, Abdel Khaleq was ousted from *Ihya al-Turath* in 1997 in favour of the purist camp led by Abdallah al-Sabt and his followers. The *harakis* developed their thinking since the Invasion, influenced by the Saudi Sahwa movement.

The most important of the younger generation of Kuwaiti *harakis* is probably Hakim al-Mutairi, who became the de-facto leader of the youth wing within *Ihya al-Turath* that remained loyal to Abdel Khaleq. The profile of Hakim al-Mutairi fits in a more common pattern of young tribesmen who socialized in Saudi Salafi circles during the Occupation and who, after the Liberation, strengthened their activist Salafi thinking. As many Kuwaiti tribesmen, Hakim al-Mutairi studied an Islamic curriculum in Saudi Arabia at the Umm al-Qura University of Mecca, where he got involved in the emerging debates between activist and purist Salafists and got to know Muhammad Surur Zain al-'Abadin, a leading member within the Saudi Sahwa, who heavily inspired Al-Mutairi's thinking. Because of his charismatic personality, Al-Mutairi was soon able to gather around him a group of Kuwaitis who had also escaped to Saudi Arabia and who socialized in Al-Mutairi's network in Al-Qasim, where he was residing. Together with Kuwaiti Shaykh Hamid Ali and Abdelrazzaq al-Shayiji, they became the core of the *haraki* youth wing of the Salafi movement and founded a political movement, the Salafi Movement (*Al-Haraka Al-Salafiyya*).[9] Yet disagreements between the leadership led to the creation in 2005 of the *Hizb al-Umma* (Umma Party) by Hakim al-Mutairi: a movement which explicitly aims to be a political party without *da'wa* and charitable activities and claims to be the first political party in the Gulf. It aims the creation of an Islamic State and the removal of foreign troops and does not refer to Kuwait nor to democracy or constitution in its founding principles. The Salafi movement continued as the Salafi Scientific Movement (*Al-Haraka Al-Salafiyya Al-'Ilmiyya*) – with Hamid Ali as its SG – that has become the main Kuwaiti *haraki* Salafi movement. While forming an important network and hub of transnational *haraki* Salafism, the movement has never been able to become as influential as the purists and usually only has one member in parliament (a position often filled by Dr Walid al-Tabtaba'i). Yet, since the millennium, the activist Salafis have gained in popularity within tribal constituencies, whereas the purists have a stronger foothold in the *hadar* areas; indicative of the general changes in tribal–regime relations in recent years.[10]

Since the Invasion, the purist strand of Salafism has become more influential in politics and society and has an approximate number of eleven MPs in Parliament (compared to the average number of 6 MPs for *Hadas* – the political wing of the Ikhwan). Both movements have relied heavily on tribal support to gain political strength as tribal constituencies have tended to vote in favour of social conservativism, an agenda propagated by Islamists. For this reason, the liberal movement has been unsuccessful in implanting itself in tribal regions, despite efforts to do so. Between 1999 and 2006, for example, the Salafi Islamists Hussayn al-Dayhani (Mutran), Mukhlid al-'Azemi ('Awazem) and Khaled al-'Adwani ('Ajman) controlled the constituencies of Jleb al-Shuyukh, Al-Salmiyya and Al-Ahmadi. In the same period, *Hadas* was successful in controlling Al-Jahra al-Qadima, Al-Jahra al-Jadida and Al-Sulaybihat by presenting tribal Islamists: Dr Muhammad al-Busayri ('Ajman), Khudair 'Aqla and Jumu'an al-Harbasch ('Anezi).[11]

While relying on tribal solidarities, the rise of the Islamist movement in tribal constituencies also changed existing tribal hierarchies. As we saw, the person of the tribal chieftain lost in favour of a new generation of educated, politicized tribesmen with a generally Islamist orientation. Some of the Islamists pass through tribal primaries, while others have been able to win outside the primaries, although their criticism vis-à-vis the primaries tends to be mild as they themselves rely on tribal support.[12] And those who overtly defy the primaries and tribalism have found it difficult to gain durable political power. One can think here of S'ad Ben Tifla ('Ajman) or Jamal al-Nasafi (*Rashaida*). The latter – a career diplomat – told me:

> Because of my values, I haven't been able to be elected and tried it three times. I am against the tribal elections and against the tribe itself. Musallam al-Barrak gained first through the primary elections and latter was able to become a direct leader within his tribe and therefore could bypass the primaries. Yet, what he is saying is not against the tribal values.[13]

Another example of the continued strength of tribal hierarchies despite leadership changes is the importance of lineages (*fukhud*) in understanding the electoral success of tribesmen. In case a candidate comes from a small lineage or tribe in a certain electoral district, it is very unlikely that he will be elected. The large tribes organize the primaries and they are the ones that dominate the elections and competition in the fourth and fifth districts. This is illustrated by one of my interlocutors – Muhammad al-Oteibi. Al-Oteibi is a young man whose career represents the path of social ascension taken by many tribesmen since the Invasion. About the role of tribal hierarchies, he says:

> It still plays a role, in marriage patterns and even in the choice of MPs. For example, if I want to present myself in elections and the number of my fikhd (lineage) or tribe is small in the electoral district, then I have no chances to win. They can only

break through these logics if the leader of a (small) fikhd has good relations with the royal family.[14]

As Al-Oteibi's tribe ('Utban) has a weak presence in the electoral district, he has never opted to present himself for elections. The dominance of stronger tribes was also revealed by another interviewee, a prominent member within the Ikhwan's Social Reform Society in Kuwait. Himself a young tribesman, he gives me examples of some 'breakthroughs' where Ikhwan candidates were able to win, although they were not themselves member of a large tribe. In these cases, alliances with smaller tribes proved crucial to overcome the domination of the bigger tribes, as Islamism per se was not enough to construct local power.

> An example is the case of Muhammad al-Oleimi, from the Mutran. He presented himself in a district (Sabahiyya area) where the Mutran are a minority and where the 'Awazem have since long ago dominated the area and its politics. Because of his Islamic affiliation and his capacity to build alliances with smaller tribes by creating a popular gathering (gathering a group of smaller tribes), he succeeded in transcending the power of the 'Awazem. Another example is the case of Dr. Muhammad al-Busairi, from the 'Ajman. There were other tribes dominating the district, such as the 'Anezi, but through his alliance with smaller tribes and membership of Al-Islah, he was able to unite these smaller groups and win elections.[15]

The rise of the tribal Islamist phenomenon occurred in a period in which the general political capacities of the tribesmen strengthened, resulting in a higher degree of professionalization in the field of politics. Tribal primaries have been an effective instrument in thinning out the number of tribal candidates, preventing the fragmentation of votes and thus strengthening a coordinated tribal vote. Although proscribed in 1998 with the application of a law prohibiting primaries, these pre-elections have been tolerated by the Kuwaiti regime for a long time.[16] It was only in 2008 that the regime took a confrontational stance vis-à-vis the primaries, leading to violent situations, as the regime feared the increased oppositional stance of the tribal electorate. In the 2003, 2006 and 2008 elections, the tribesmen organized primaries on a wide scale which boosted their share of seats in Parliament.[17] Tribesmen moreover used increasingly sophisticated techniques to conduct primaries in a way making it difficult for the Ministry of Interior to detect them. For example, the technique of 'random samples' was employed requesting samples of voters to come to a certain place in small groups and at different times; masking primaries by giving different reasons for these meetings (i.e. to celebrate university graduation).[18] Also a token of the growing professionalization is the transferral of technical know-how developed via education and positions in government to the body of the tribe. In this regard, administrative logics are employed in an attempt to strengthen the tribe as a political unit. An example in this regard is the creation of so-called tribal councils (*majalis al-qabila*) that are new inventions to strengthen the organizational capacities of the tribe, used during primaries.[19] Primaries have also been organized at the university level – a rather recent phenomenon – in preparation of the elections for the boards of students at Kuwait University via tribal committees (*lajan al-qabail*) of the large tribes to preselect candidates, as the control of student boards is a major springboard for a political career in Kuwait.[20]

Until 2006, the trend of social change within tribal constituencies that was set in motion with the Invasion did not present a considerable challenge to the regime. While the seeds were sown for a growing assertive stance of the tribal electorate, the regime still tolerated and implicitly relied upon tribalism and its tribal constituencies as a pillar of support. Even after the Invasion, the practice of primaries was tolerated by the regime, as the tribesmen that were pre-elected in these primaries tended to have a rather pro-regime stance as MPs. Many of my interlocutors have pointed to the role played by the government in strengthening tribalism and recreating it in the context of the state. As we have seen, these policies initially allowed the regime to act and 'communicate' with its tribal constituencies in a primordial corporatist way, dealing with tribal solidarities collectively and via the person of a tribal mediator (initially the tribal chieftain and later new MPs).[21] Also, the Islamist trend – though strengthening its independence and professionalizing its methods – was still largely a force that supported the regime, as its main focus was the Islamization of society; issues that made it stand at odds with liberal currents and the Shi'a, but that did not threaten the Al-Sabah monarchy.

Social change and the rise of politically minded young tribesmen

The aforementioned process of social change gave rise to a new generation of young, educated and politicized tribesmen. Despite different political orientations and educational backgrounds, they all experienced huge changes in lifestyle and worldview as compared to the generation of their parents. It is this change within the tribal youth that explains a large deal of the political and social struggles in Kuwait today and in the future to come. In the following, I will sketch some trajectories of young tribesmen I interviewed that I deem exemplary of this trend.

An example in case is Muhammad al-'Oteibi, born in 1983. From a modest background, he was born and raised in the Fardus area of the Al-Farwaniyya district (fourth electoral district), south of Al-Andalus, where Musallam al-Barrak has his electoral fief. In this district, the Mutran and Rashaida tribes dominate the seats for parliament; with each tribe having approximately five seats in parliament. Al-'Oteibi himself is from the 'Otban, a small tribe originally from the area of Najd that was known for its cooperative stance vis-à-vis the Ikhwan Wahhabi zealots. Al-'Oteibi's father was an officer at the Ministry of Interior (as many tribesmen) and his brothers, as well as himself, were able to climb the social ladder through education. As many Kuwaiti tribesmen, he studied in Jordan (others who opt for a religious career study in Saudi Arabia) and took a BA and MA in Law. For different reasons, tribesmen seem to study more in Islamic countries than in the West; some have attributed to this to the availability of tribal *wasta*, while others have said that tribesmen themselves favour to study in an environment closer to home and the home culture.[22]

Al-'Oteibi recently opened a law firm in Al-Riqa'i, in the outside area of Al-Farwaniyya, where he was raised. His office, rather small, decorated in a kitsch style, is clearly distinct from the *hadar* firms that tend to be located more at the centre of the city in better buildings and more expensive locations. Al-'Oteibi comes across as an ambitious young man, who clearly tries to create a reputation of a successful tribal youth leader. Al-'Oteibi attributes his pro-regime stance to the long-time pro-regime inclination of his tribe, the 'Otban, although in reality his tribe is split between pro- and anti-regime sympathizers and one of its members, Faisal al-Muslim, is part of the opposition. Al-'Oteibi however opted for the pro-government path as did his family members. Al-'Oteibi is member of the Kuwaiti Society for Human Rights (*Jam'iyyat Huquq al-Insan*), a position he obtained via board elections. It is important to note that the Society had been dominated by *hadar* elites since its inception and the victory of tribesmen in the board elections, among whom Al-'Oteibi, was a breakthrough.

Muhammad al-Boghaili is another example of such an ambitious, well-educated tribesman who also opted for the pro-regime path and is a friend of Al-'Oteibi. He is the son of the famous *Khaliji sha'ir* (poet) Muhammad al-Boghaili, who occasionally receives in his diwaniyya prominent members of the Al-Saud family. Nonetheless, the family's house is rather modest, located in the area of Al-Rehab that hosts a large tribal population of the Mutran and Rashaida tribes, to which Al-Boghaili belongs. Al-Boghaili is also in his early thirties and has been ambitious and productive. He is a writer and poet from the Al-Rashaida tribe: known for its historical longevity in Kuwait, but in the capacity of guardians of the Al-Sabah. Al-Boghaili worked as a journalist and has written various fiction books, often on topics related to love and ambitions of a young tribal student, but is also the author of the book *Al-Qabila wa Al-Sulta,* a published version of his MA in Political Science at Kuwait University. He recently obtained his PhD in Political Philosophy in Jordan, with the 'Dr' title adding to his social standing. He has been particularly active in student life and was the official representative of the Bloc of the National Youth (*Kutla al-Shabab al-Watani*). While he was active within the tribal youth movement that raised its oppositional tone since 2007, he is presently a political researcher at the Diwan of the PM, a job he has occupied since 2007. His rise to this position is part of a broader initiative of the regime to co-opt the youth and particularly the tribal youth in recent years. Since 2012 notably, many projects were initiated to provide new channels to communicate with the youth. One can think of projects such as the 'National Plan for the Youth' (*Mashru'a al-watani li al-shabab*) or 'Kuwait Listens' (*Al-Kuwayt tasma'a*) that were initiated by the Emiri Diwan.[23] 'Kuwait Listens' resulted in the creation of a Ministry of State for Youth Affairs (MoSYA) in 2013 after a lobbying campaign which started in 2006 in a context of rising youth discontent. In 2015 the Youth Public Authority was created that established the Youth Council (*Majlis al-Shababi*) invested with implementing a strategic vision for the youth as part of Kuwait's development plans. These are platforms to strengthen the role of the youth in decision-making, but in a top-down way in a logic of managed reforms. Yet, the individuals appointed to the boards of these platforms tend to be already rather loyal youth, as the oppositional figures refuse such co-optation strategies. This all fits in a larger strategy of GCC regimes vis-à-vis their restless youth population since 2011;

activities that have often been coordinated by GCC regimes and in which Saudi Arabia has played a leading role.[24]

Competition between personalities is particularly strong among the young generation of tribesmen in Kuwait and in part inherent to the decentralized and egalitarian nature of Arabian tribalism. Integration into the nation state created a certain verticalized structure, in which the tribal chieftain plays the role of leader. In reality, however, his position is never uncontested, but always prone to competition from within members of his family. While personality politics permeates Kuwait's political culture that lacks political parties, Bedouin communities tend to be particularly active in personality cult-driven behaviour that involves men of all ages and social background. This personality cult behaviour is coupled with other strategies to strengthen the solidarity and authority of the tribe or lineage, by relying on modern tools of communication.

This differs in some respects from the young *hadar* Kuwaitis who, different from the young tribesmen, have actually failed to produce new leaders. Since the millennium, there has been a void in *hadar* leadership, as the old popular symbols (Ahmad al-Khatib, Abdallah al-Nibari) represent a current that does no more correspond to the worldview of *hadari* Kuwaitis.[25] One could say that the *hadar* youth is less embedded in its local community, more attuned to the globalized culture and living in a certain state of anomy in which it feels disconnected from local politics and therefore finds refuge in its rather comfortable life of consumerism and travels; a life style that also disrupts family bonds (*hadar* communities have a particularly high number of divorces).

Coupled with access to higher education and the drive to succeed as latecomers to the nation, this has important social consequences, as follows from the account of Ahmad Bin Barjas, a historian on Arabian tribalism:

> Social change is enormous because of education. You can see that tribesmen dominate the hadar in terms of university graduates. Also, if you go to the Diwan of Civil Service, you'll see that out of 100 Bedouins you'll only find one hadar guy. So within 10 years, the hadar will disappear here. Their children either fail in education or go for a long study or life abroad to the US and other places. They come back after a long period, when the positions in government are already allocated to others. If you go to a hadar family with let's say 6 people, you can see that they are often not together. The mother is an employee, the father is travelling, the children are travelling ... They do not have the same family ties. The Bedouin families are living in Kuwait, studying in Kuwait and this threatens the hadar. They fear they will be marginalized in society and therefore have become more loyal to the government, as they fear the tribes.[26]

This example points to the strong social embeddedness of tribesmen, allowing young tribesmen to more effectively build their personality and authority among constituencies. One could dedicate a whole study to the analysis of Twitter profiles of this young generation of tribesmen. For those tribesmen that have continued their support of the Al-Sabah regime, their profiles blend patriotism with images featuring the 'self' prominently, sometimes in plurifold, in traditional *dishdasha*, while displaying symbols of status, notably proximity to the person of the Emir (mimicking the tribal shaykh). In these depictions, tribalism combines with strong nationalism.

Apart from these young tribesmen opting for the regime path, there are many more that have become part of the broader opposition movement that culminated in 2012 with the ouster of the PM Nasser al-Muhammad. One such lead figures of the tribal opposition is Tariq Al-Mutairi. A blogger, he became known for his blog 'altariq2009. com', in which he voiced his criticism of Arab regimes and the Kuwaiti government of PM Nasser al-Muhammad (2006–12). Already in 2009, Al-Mutairi coined the term '*irhal*' (leave), an expression he directed at the person of the PM and which – according to Al-Mutairi – would have later been taken up by youth bloggers on Facebook in Tunisia and Egypt in 2011. As many tribal youngsters, Al-Tariq socialized in the Islamist movement and gradually took a more oppositional and activist stance. As such, he was member of the Ikhwan movement (*Hadas*) between 1995 and 2010, when he resigned from *Hadas* to join the *Hizb al-Umma*; created by Dr Hakim Al-Mutairi as the first Salafi political party within the Gulf that aims the creation of an Islamic State and has an oppositional stance vis-à-vis GCC regimes.

Yet, disagreements led to his secession, after which he founded the Civil Democratic Movement (*Al-Harakat Al-Madaniyya Al-Dimoqratiyya*), known as *Hadam*. Hadam represents the young generation of youth, particularly active on social media and that cannot identify itself with existing political groups. Its main objective is to create a new parliamentary system, change the electoral law and have an elected PM and government (*hukuma muntakhaba*). As a consequence, Hadam aimed to create a rational and pragmatic movement and to avoid ideology, trying to appeal to *hadari* youth as well. The movement grew as part of youth mobilizing from 2005 on to plead for a five-district electoral system (*nabiha 5* campaign; we want 5 campaign) and that later developed into a movement against Shaykh Nasser al-Muhammad in 2009. Tariq, having developed star status on Twitter – with almost 53,000 followers – had enough followers to create such a movement. While aiming to be an inclusive group, Hadam has attracted mostly tribal youth – socially conservative, but politically liberal – and has lost in recent years some of its *hadar* members with a more liberal outlook. Aiming to be independent, some societal voices have mentioned an alleged role of ambitious princes such as Shaykh Ahmad al-Fahd and neighbouring Qatar in supporting members of the movement, which led to schisms within hadam and the defection of some of its members.[27]

Another example of a prominent, opposition tribal leader is Dr Obeid Al-Wasmi (1971). A Constitutional Law professor at Kuwait University from the Mutran tribe, Al-Wasmi gained notoriety for his eloquent speeches and for an incident in December 2010 in which he became victim of public beating by security forces. Following the incident, he became extremely famous on Twitter with over 920,000 followers, including many from across the GCC.

The incident occurred during a gathering in the diwaniyya of MP Jumu'an al-Harbasch, following the discovery of corruption scandals allegedly originating from PM Nasser al-Mohammed. The gathering attended by many tribal activists was heavy-handedly repressed by security forces. Photos and videos circulated soon on social media showing the beating of Al-Wasmi, whose popularity rose and who was elected in the 2012 oppositional parliament. With a PhD from an American University and a prestigious position at Kuwait University, Al-Wasmi represents a new generation of highly educated tribesmen that plead for a better inclusion into the nation's fabric and defend a discourse that focuses on social justice and the indiscriminate application of laws to citizens; often targeting the privileges of the *hadar* merchant elites. This having said, these new leaders rely on tribal allegiances to gain power.[28] One could say that as latecomers to the nation, these tribesmen present themselves as staunch defenders of constitutionalism, mimicking the old role played by the *hadar* elites. In recent years, the loud voice of these tribal MPs has come to attract middle-class *hadar* citizens, criticizing corruption and austerity measures aimed at reducing the costs of the welfare regime and at shifting the economy away from oil-dependency.

These short examples are exemplary of a larger trend of a tribal social base that is largely young, much better educated than their parents and that refuses to accept the docile stance of the previous generation of tribesmen in dealing with the regime. At present, tribesmen dominate the university colleges and particularly the faculties of law and medical school and have come to challenge the *hadar* as an educated elite, while continuing to be marginalized in terms of access to the spoils of the private sector. From all registered Kuwaiti companies, the percentage of owners that are tribesmen is only 4.4 per cent. In 2010, the tribesmen only received 19 per cent of the tenders, while the rest was allocated to *hadar*.[29] Social ascension through education, combined with a feeling of distress (*nakma*) and discrimination by the state has led to a sentiment of relative deprivation among this tribal social base. This is well described by Khaled al-Fadhala; former head of Kuwait's National Democratic Alliance; a *hadar* liberal who was one of the leaders of Kuwait's youth movement against the PM and has been one of the few who cooperated strongly with tribal youth. He says:

> At university, Law School, Medical School, the hadar Sunna families have become marginalized and the tribes are overrepresented. It is normal to see a lot of Mutairi, Rashaidi etc. as doctors, whereas tribes used to serve the regime in the police and army. Lawyers, doctors, they are now practically all from the tribes. I have a friend, a Mutairi, whose uncle was the first to study engineering in the US. There is a true decline in the hadar as a class and force in politics. Not only are the Bedouins the highest percentage, they also feel they have something to prove, their loyalty to the country, their capacities, etc.[30]

This change in the political culture of tribesmen went along with a growing tribal participation in political activism and notably in the broader 'Orange' movement that started in 2005 to plead for the reduction of electoral districts from twenty-five to five (*nabiha 5* campaign), inspired by the Orange Revolution in the Ukraine. For the first time, social media were used on a large scale to mobilize people, departing from previous modes of mobilization that relied mostly on family reputation and money to build social networks. While this movement was initially led by a liberal-minded *hadar* youth, the resurge in youth activism since 2007 was dominated by the tribal youth, allied with Islamist forces. The youth movement in Kuwait emerged in response to growing government ineffectiveness, as a consequence of corruption and unsound policy-making – themselves results of intra-elite competition and the regime's social contract that places the commercial elite on top of social stratification. It represents the frustration of a young generation that cannot find its place in an archaic political system, both politically and socio-economically. Politically, it resists the regime's traditional modes of governance, relying on clientelism and traditional hierarchies. Socio-economically, the youth has an increasingly hard time with housing shortages for young couples and an increasingly expensive life in a society flooded with consumerism but that has started to implement painful austerity measures to shift the economy away from oil-dependency.

It is these changes within the young tribal social base that impacted the stance of the tribal and Islamist MPs representing them and who made a volte face in the period between 2007 and 2011. Many of those in the oppositional bloc (*Kutlat al-Mu'arada*) in the 2009 parliament were actually previously rather loyal to the regime and had profited from its support.[31] What united them was their stance against corruption (in reaction to the discovery of corruption scandals in 2009 allegedly at the hands of the PM), a position they had to defend in order to maintain the support of their largely tribal social base. In this regard, regime-instigated elites are only effective as long as their function is endorsed by the social base they represent.[32] It is also the social base that decides to go or not to go to the streets. The 'Dignity of the Nation' (*Karamat al-Watan*) marches that were organized by the opposition – under the lead of Musallam al-Barrak – since October 2012 against the change in election law to one-vote-a-person were only successful in the tribal districts, while similar demonstrations in *hadar* areas witnessed opposition from residents.

Relatedly, the liberal groups cannot anymore mobilize a large group of people, even when they are part of the opposition force, as it is the young tribal base that constitutes the crucial support of the latter. Instructive in this regard are the remarks of a prominent Kuwaiti lawyer and activist on the social base of the liberals:

> They cannot mobilize the streets anymore. An example, today (19 November 2012), there was a gathering at Will Square (Sahat al-Irada), organized by liberal groups. A decision has been made by the Majority Bloc and the Islamic groups (including the tribes) to join them and participate in the gathering. It was thanks to the presence of those groups that the gathering was crowded and a success. The merchants and liberals are too small in number now. Two weeks ago, approximately, the same group of liberals called for a gathering on the Al-Sahafa Street. However, participation was very low and not more than around 150 people. If the Majority Bloc or Islamists call for demonstrations, more than a thousand people will participate. That is the difference.[33]

In a similar vein, *Hadas*'s loss of candidates in the 2009 Parliament was the consequence of the movement's stance against the popular pleas to drop consumer debts on households (*isqat al-qurud*), an issue defended by tribal MPs in parliament. *Hadas*'s position against the wishes of its largely tribal social base explains why it lost so many votes in the outside districts of Kuwait in 2009.[34] Social change among young tribesmen – that went along with increased political awareness (*wa'i*) – thus impacted the stance of MPs in Parliament, some making a volte face from regime loyalists to defenders of the opposition's cause which converged around its fight against high-level corruption in which former PM Nasser al-Muhammad was accused to be involved.

The reinvention of tribalism and its encounter with globalization

In their quest for integration into Kuwait's nationhood, the search for authenticity has been a crucial strategy of tribal social networks that went along with the reinvention of tribalism and of a common heritage. Salafism – itself a modern phenomenon – has provided tribesmen this perceived identity of authenticity and therefore continues to attract this young generation of uprooted tribesmen. I consider globalization as the main factor to understand socio-political change in Kuwait as well as the sweeping changes that have marked the MENA region since the millennium, culminating in the Arab revolts (2011) and their aftermath that saw the rise of jihadi groups capturing territories, of civil wars and cases of blatant state failure. Ironically enough, postmodernism has been accompanied by the resurge of tribalism and its reinvention. Today, it is from these peripheral populations (rural and tribal) – long governed by minimal clientelist arrangements of regimes – that change is coming.

One major consequence of the communication revolution and the internet has been the strengthening of transnational initiatives by members of tribes. Examples are the websites and blogs developed by tribes glorifying the tribe, its lineages and families, poetry and role in historical battles.[35] On these sites, one finds information about the tribe, but also about gatherings and forums (*multaqiyyat*) and comments on political affairs via interactive blogs. Also, TV channels have been created that explicitly deal with Bedouin life (*Al-hayat Al-badawa*) that show poetry contests or falcon races and are diffused within the GCC region. The internet has strengthened these networks among members of the same tribe and in recent years, there has been a surge in meetings of tribesmen from different countries. Examples are fora of the Bani Qahtan, the Mutran and the 'Awazem.

Within Kuwait, the political rise of the tribes has also been reflected in the surge of publications and books produced by tribes to reinsert themselves in Kuwait's national narrative. The few bookshops of Kuwait are flooded with books dealing with *nasab* (lineage) and glorifying the history of tribesmen in Kuwait and the region. This should be read in the light of the process of political emancipation among this group of latecomers to the nation who counter the dominant *hadar* narrative of Kuwait's founding myth.

In recent years, political movements and leaders have also reinvented tribalism in order to gain political clout and in some cases historical memory plays a role in the political stance of tribesmen. Although all tribes are split between pro- and anti-regime elements, the Mutran and 'Ajman tribes have produced a large group of oppositional MPs since the millennium. These tribes inherited a culture of being historically opposed to leaders and of distrusting political leadership (*Al-sulta*). They were the leading tribes in the Ikhwan battles that started in 1927 and led to violent confrontations with the Al-Saud, the British and their local trustees. Because of their historical support for activist Salafism, the *haraki* Salafi movement fares well among these tribes. Also, the Mutran that today are the prime oppositional tribe in Kuwait do not really follow their shaykh, even historically. According to Ben Barjas, historian of Arabian tribalism: 'The Mutran have this trait ... they do not really follow their shaykh or any form of leadership. They do not really follow their Emir, even in the case of Faisal al-Duwaish in the past. They were then following the class of the Mutran, they believed in Al-Duwaish's ideas, but they did not follow him'.[36]

Apart from this, one can see instances in which political leaders rely upon historical tribal battles to gain political influence. An example was the attempt by Faisal Al-Duwaish – shaykh of the Mutran – during elections to capture the votes of the Rashaida tribe too of the electoral district. He did so by referring to the wars fought by the Rashaida and Mutran tribes together against other tribes.[37] This strategy worked then, but does not work today anymore, as Al-Duwaish has lost his standing among tribesmen for his proximity to the regime. Musallam al-Barrak – the uncontested opposition leader from the Mutran – has also used tribal symbols and rhetoric. In this regard, the sentencing of Musallam al-Barrak (who was later to be released on bail) in April 2013 provoked mass demonstrations of the Mutran, who allegedly called upon their Saudi brothers to join their ranks in a tribal call (*tanga*) for disobedience. In his speech, Al-Barrak said that the security forces had transgressed the sanctity of his house and violated the dignity of his families' wives and children, a particularly powerful message that mobilized tribesmen.

In some cases, the invocation of historical memory on social media can provoke inter-tribal tensions. An example were the declarations from a Mutran member on Twitter in December 2012, who had bragged about the Mutran's role in vanquishing the Emirate of Ibn Rashid (Shammar). This was considered as an insult against the Shammar, whose members reacted online saying that these remarks were not so different from Al-Juwaihal who defamed the tribes in general. As a result, a hashtag soon went viral, quoting the name of the Mutran member saying he defamed the Al-Shammar (*#al-Jid'i ... yas'a li-qabilat Shammar*). Virulent discussions followed on Twitter and a Shammar blogger replied 'I am sorry, Musallam al-Barrak cites the verses of the late and honorable Emir of Najd, while this guy recalled historical events to vulgarize the capacities of the Shammar'. Other Mutran tried to appease tensions, saying the individual did not speak in their name, while the blogger himself justified what he considered the glorification of his tribe in a context in which the *fulul al-nizam* (old regime elements referring to Nasser al-Muhammad) attacks his tribe.[38] This example shows the extent to which tribal imaginary is recreated on social media and blended into contemporary issues of contention.

As we have seen, Islamist movements have also heavily relied upon tribal allegiances to gain power in the outside areas of Kuwait. Sometimes, this influence transcends national borders. An example is the case of the Abbas League (*Rabita Abbas*), created in 2010, referring to the Abbas tribe: the founding tribe of Rashaida. The creation of the League was prompted by a rise in tensions between the Rashaida in Sudan and the Sudanese government. The Rashaida have branches in Kuwait, Libya, Morocco and Sudan. Yet, Kuwait has been a main reference, as historically its main lineages were present in the old town together with its paramount chief, Al-Musailam. This explains the importance of Kuwait in fostering ties between tribesmen on the transnational level. Groups with an international outreach – such as the Ikhwan – have profited from these ties. The main brokers in the conflict in Sudan were two Kuwaiti members of the Abbas League – Mubarak al-Duwaila and Faiz al-Boghaili.[39] Following a conflict between the presidents, only Al-Duwaila remained. The attempt to unify the Al-Rashaida under one umbrella led by an influential Ikhwan figure – Al-Duwaila – likely served the interests of the Ikhwan in a broader strategy; rallying the Rashaida of neighbouring Sudan around the Egyptian Ikhwan in case of a secession of the eastern part of Sudan. During Mohammed Morsi's short-lived reign, Mubarak al-Duwaila announced that Morsi descended from the Al-Rashaida, reinforcing the hypothesis of attempts to create tribal support for the MB on a regional level.

Other examples of transnational tribal initiatives are the many charities that were erected since 2011 by tribes to financially and materially support the victims of the Syrian war, and in particular Syrian tribesmen. Previously the domain of the urban notability, charities have now also become a means for tribes to strengthen their social standing within Kuwait. Examples are charities of the 'Ajman and Bani Yam tribes that organized various gathering in Kuwait attended by MPs, poets and notables to collect money for the people in Syria.[40] The Mutran tribe also organized a series of charity conferences for Syrian refugees creating dozens of centres offering food, clothes and blankets and hosting more than 150 families each.[41] While Kuwait is known to be the milk cow for regional (Islamic) charities, the creation of charities by tribes themselves is a rather new phenomenon. Though increasing the prestige of the tribe as a collectivity, it should be noted that many of these charities were set up by Islamist MPs and leaders (notably Salafis), relying on tribal solidarities to collect funding for Syria. Nonetheless, the fact that the charities were organized in the name of the tribe and not an Islamist movement shows the increased agility of branding strategies to mark themselves as full-fledged citizens of the nation, a status that requires gift-giving and charitable work in a small and personalized polity as Kuwait. A part of this authority-building also consisted in presenting themselves as the ones who take care of the affairs of the 'Umma', in an increasingly sectarian regional context in which these Salafi-oriented tribesmen present themselves as those of the Sunna who actively try to resist attempts by the Shi'a to dominate the region – the general discourse of Salafi preachers. As many of these preachers are of tribal background, they were able to attract tribesmen to fund their cause. Notable examples in this regard are Shafi al-'Ajmi, Hajaj al-'Ajmi and Hakim al-Mutairi; all *haraki* Salafis who employed tribal and social media networks to fund their cause in Syria.

It is essential to note that the quest for a place in Kuwait's nationhood has been marked by a search for authenticity, as authenticity is a prime value in Arabian societies and ingrained in a dominant culture that values most those who can count upon a traceable lineage and heritage rooted in Arabian tribalism in which purity of Arab blood (Qahtanites) is a sign of social standing, also among Kuwait's *hadar* elite. Here comes by that state-building in Kuwait has largely preserved the imaginary of continuity in social stratification and this – combined with a small population in which people know well the history of families – makes the search for authenticity even more important for these latecomers to the nation in search for a better integration into its polity. The material privileges that come along with citizenship in the rentier state naturally strengthen the anti-foreign rhetoric and reinforce the focus on authenticity to justify entitlement to these benefits.

Salafism – which is a modern phenomenon and a product of the region's interaction with globalization – has provided these tribesmen an identity which is perceived as authentic. In this regard, the spread of Salafism in Kuwait's peripheral regions is itself a manifestation of the reinvention of tribalism in a modern and globalized context. Returning to the practices of *Al-Salaf Al-Saleh* – who were Arabian nomads – is an ideology that therefore attracts particularly tribesmen in Kuwait as well as regionally. By presenting itself as a corrective interpretation of the Sunna – departing from the four dominant legal schools of Sunni Islam – and by refusing intercession (*tawassul*) or aid (*istighata*) – Salafism also empowers a new generation of preachers, who tend to defy the customs of seniority (*'asbaqiyya*) of Muslim clerics.[42]

As much as political entrepreneurs and the tribal social base rely upon tribalism as a reinvented concept to build social networks, the Kuwaiti regime itself also relies on tribal allegiances for the purposes of its survival. In this regard, it is interesting to note that during a rise in tensions between the Al-'Awazem tribe and the government of Shaykh Nasser al-Muhammad, the regime threatened the vocal oppositional shaykh of the 'Awazem – Falah Ben Jama'a – (one of the few oppositional tribal chieftains) that he might lose his position as shaykh of the tribe. At various moments during the crisis, the Emir invited the elder brother of Falah Ben Jama'a from Saudi Arabia, showing Ben Jama'a that he thanked his position to regime support. It was also meant to embarrass Ben Jama'a by showing that he was only recently naturalized and thus could be easily bypassed or replaced by others.[43]

From these anecdotal examples, we can see how tribalism has been strengthened, although in a reinvented form, as a consequence of its interaction with modernity and the modern tools of communication. Political entrepreneurs of tribal background have gradually replaced the tribal chieftains as new representatives and intermediaries for their constituencies. While focusing their speech acts on *'wataniyya'* (national feeling), transparency and a state of institutions (*dawla al-mu'assat*), these MPs rely upon tribal allegiances to gain political clout. Creating an identity of 'authenticity' to the nation and the region has been a key strategy for establishing authority and Salafism has been an identity par excellence to respond to this need in the identity search of young tribesmen. Yet this is a form of reinvented and cultural tribalism that serves political purposes. Officially shunning the return to *'Al-mashaikha'*, these tribal political entrepreneurs rely themselves upon semi-traditional identities to construct authority.

Discursive strategies to counter dominant *hadar* citizenship myths

We have seen that tribesmen have presented themselves as nationalists and staunch defenders of Kuwait's unique constitution, also out of the need to catch up with the *hadar* elite. In this regard, the attempts to reconstruct tribal identity within the context of the nation have been accompanied with speech acts that underline the tribes' contribution to Kuwait's nationhood and in comparison with the *hadar* elites.

In many cases, tribesmen have tried to appropriate earlier rhetoric of the *hadar* elites, who defended Kuwait's constitutionalism in the 1960s and until the 1980s, but today have witnessed waning popularity and are plagued by a void in political leadership. I will sketch these tribal narratives, relying on a compilation of newspaper articles and interviews I collected between 2012 and 2014.

The 'Awazem that is today among the largest tribes in terms of population (around 142,000 persons) is a tribe that – as we have seen – was present in the vicinities of the old town before the Battle of Jahra, comparable to the Rashaida. For a long time, the 'Awazem were loyal to the regime, but under the governments of Shaykh Nasser al-Mohammed (2006–11), its tribesmen took a stance against the government, and in particular against the corruption scandals. Contrary to other tribes in Kuwait, the 'Awazem's tribal chieftain – Falah Ben Jama'a – defied the government and supported the wishes of his tribal base that revolted against certain regime practices it deemed discriminatory vis-à-vis the tribe. The 'Awazem had a record number of seven MPs in the 2012 parliament, which was an oppositional parliament elected after the popular movement against the PM who resigned under pressure in November 2011. Subsequent gerrymandering by the regime that led to the cancellation of the 2012 Majlis – followed by an Emiri emergency decree (issued in the absence of a functioning parliament) – prompted the tribe under the leadership of Ben Jama'a to boycott the elections in December 2012 and support the Dignity of the Nation marches. The confrontational stance of the Al-'Awazem was also a reaction to the rise of anti-tribal rhetoric in the media by sections of society allegedly close to former PM Nasser al-Muhammad. This prompted members of the Al-'Awazem to mobilize against TV Channels with inflammatory declarations. An example in point was the attack on controversial Scope TV channel – owned by media tycoon Fajr al-Said – by members of the Al-'Awazem in 2008; following an interview in which the pro-government Shi'a MP Sayyid Hussayn al-Qallaf had criticized Ben Jama'a. It reportedly aroused criticism from neighbouring governments who denounced these media for stirring sectarianism.

In this context of rising tensions vis-à-vis the regime, the speech acts of Ben Jama'a are instructive for understanding both the resentment of the tribesmen vis-à-vis the regime and their strategies of justifying their entitlement and authenticity to the nation. One of these grievances has been the absence of names of public buildings or streets honouring the 'Awazem. The rhetoric goes that while the tribe has such a noble role and participated in the wars for Kuwait for over 300 years and counts around 2,000 academics, there is still not even one school or street named after the 'Awazem, as said by Ben Jama'a. The latter further emphasizes in his speeches the fact that the 'Awazem have participated in the Constitutional Assembly writing the Constitution, thereby implicitly comparing them with the *hadar* elite. He continues saying: 'Even those who were against Kuwait in 1967 (referring to nationalists) have schools in their name, and the 'Awazem don't. For example, why is there not one head of the armed forces, a dean of the university or an employee of the Emiri Diwan from the 'Awazem?' Interestingly, this comparison with the *hadar* is also voiced in Ben Jama'a's justification of the tribe's boycott of the December 2012 elections: 'We are not against the family (Al-Sabah), but against the forces of corruption and the 'Awazem boycotted the elections, just like the Ghanim, the Saqqar and a lot of people of Kuwait.'

The Mutran, the second largest tribe of Kuwait whose members have largely been naturalized, have voiced similar grievances. The tribe's social base today is largely oppositional vis-à-vis the government and particularly the previous government of Shaykh Nasser al-Mohammed. Unable to count upon a long history in the Emirate (apart from some individual members), the Mutran also resent the fact that they do not have any streets in their name, while the Rashaida have more than twenty reportedly.[44] Musallam al-Barrak, the uncontested leader of the Mutran also uses symbolic references to the *hadar* elites, appropriating their past causes and actions. During his lead role in the Dignity of the Nation Marches in November 2012, Musallam al-Barrak justified these marches to uphold the dignity of citizens who cannot accept regime corruption and compared these quests for dignity with the actions of those merchants who left Kuwait under Mubarak al-Sabah's reign, protesting the latter's rise in taxes on pearling. Among them was a Mutran merchant – Hilal al-Mutairi – and this reference to an *asli* member of the Mutran also adds to the tribe's attempts to assert and justify their entitlement to Kuwaiti citizenship.

Given the vocal opposition from the Mutran, the rise in anti-tribal rhetoric in the media (allegedly supported by the regime since the notorious victory of the tribal–Islamist opposition in 2008) often targeted the Mutran tribes. Media tycoon, MP and businessman Muhammad al-Juwaihal was allowed to create in 2009 his TV Channel *Al-Sur TV*. The name of the channel was symbolically chosen to strengthen the *hadar–badu* divide, as the Sur (Wall) evokes the imagery of Kuwait's founding myth that considers as original Kuwaitis those who had helped constructing the city wall against the Ikhwan zealots in 1920 (Battle of Jahra).[45] Media and society have rumoured about powerful backers behind the rise of Juwaihal such as former PM Nasser al-Muhammad and some merchants whom allegedly would have an interest in such anti-tribal rhetoric to strengthen societal voices critical of the tribal–Islamist opposition.[46]

The anti-tribal rhetoric of Al-Sur TV provoked the resentment of the tribes, leading to a series of violent clashes. A major topic raised by Al-Juwaihal was the issue of Kuwaitis having double passports, Kuwaiti and Saudi – *Al-muzdawijiin*. Already in 2009, thousands of tribesmen – among whom MPs – protested in front of Al-Sur TV, criticizing it for spreading racism in Kuwait and blaming the Ministry of Media for not shutting down the channel.[47] During the 2012 elections I witnessed how Mutran tribesmen had put the electoral tent of Al-Juwaihal in the third district on fire, enraged by his attacks on the Mutran tribe and MP 'Obeid al-Wasmi (*Mutran*).[48] Musallam al-Barrak and Mohammed al-Juwaihal were moreover engaged in ferocious battles in parliament and the media, leading to what some have considered a vulgarization of Kuwait's politics that increasingly took the turn of a soap opera without leaving much space for real debates.[49] In some regards, this plays to the interest of the regime, as it divides society and reduces interest association between *hadar* and *badu* citizens.

Another strategy is the appropriation of the strategies of the ancient *hadar* notability to acquire social standing via charities. In recent years many tribal charities have been set up in the name of a tribe and sometimes its leading figures. An example was the creation of the charity of the 'Awazem in March 2013, after alleged lobbying for such a charity for more than two years. Importantly, the initiative came from Falah Ben Jama'a and was accepted by the government in its willingness to approach itself to the tribes in a challenging context of tribal opposition and thereby co-opt tribesmen via gift-giving practices and patronage of leaders. Some of these charities focus on activities within Kuwait in the field of education/health/sports and culture and rely on regime support to provide aid to tribesmen.[50]

Interestingly too, an observed phenomenon among the tribesmen is the changing of their tribal names as a form of *passing* for a *hadar*.[51] Many such examples can be given for those tribesmen who relocated from Al-Sabahiyya to the inside (*hadar*) areas of Kuwait.[52]

From these examples, we can conclude that tribesmen and their leaders have tried to insert their struggle in a discursive strategy that compares themselves to the *hadar* elite of the past, appropriating their causes of constitutionalism and by reinventing their history and contribution to Kuwait's nationhood. Social media have provided new networks for such strategies of authority building and the creation of narratives.

Beyond tribalism: social dimensions of a broader middle-class struggle

Beyond the rise of these tribal voices in Kuwait looms a social struggle over existing logics of redistribution of oil-derived resources. In this regard, the tribal voices also represent the grievances of the average salaried public sector workers in Kuwait, frustrated with a dysfunctional welfare regime, high-level corruption scandals and with recent austerity measures such as cuts in subsidies. Their stance against corruption, austerity measures and the prerogatives of a merchant elite finds the support of a wider group of *hadar* citizens. The *hadar* are divided between those who have their interests directly aligned with the government and those who are taking a more oppositional and anti-corruption stance, such as urban Islamists or the youth. While led by tribesmen, the opposition movement that crystallized between 2011 and 2014 finds common ground in its middle-class representation which cuts across sects, sometimes families, and even the fundamental *hadar–badu* divide.

The real struggle is thus a social one that challenges the dominant social contract underpinning the Al-Sabah's authority system. As the regime-co-opted elites of the periphery are not anymore effective as channels with these constituencies, the regime faces a serious challenge to its authority system: a tribal power-sharing agreement with a merchant elite that since the inception of the dynasty was granted the privileged access to the major economic resources. This mode of politics is untenable as the regime cannot meet the demands of large groups in society without undermining this elite pact that attributes the bulk's share of rents to an *in-group* elite. The more diversified economy Kuwait needs would involve truly integrating the peripheral groups (including those outside the body politic: *Bidun* and expats) but would undermine the Al-Sabah's hegemony that relies upon the upholding of its pre-oil elite linkages.

While the grievances voiced by *badu* MPs are shared by a rising group of middle-income *hadar*, there is an engrained perception among some *hadar* as well as some Shi'a citizens that the Bedouins only want to deplete the welfare state of its resources without contributing to its development, comparable to anti-immigrant sentiments in other countries. From this fear stems the often-heard and mediatized expression in Kuwait 'Al-Badu Kalona' (the Bedouins ate us). This fear was also voiced in a book that was written in 2010 by Nasser Muhammad al-Fadhala; a *hadar* author whose book *al-halat wa al-hal* is replete with anti-*badu* bias. The book was banned in Kuwait (but is available on the web). The author points to the social dimensions of the struggle and some sections of the book are well researched. However, the argument fits in a rather larger bias among some Kuwaiti *hadar*, considering the *badu* not only a social group, but culturally distinct from the *hadar*, with different worldviews that would lead to a tribalization of politics and go against constitutionalism and development.

'Drop the consumer debts!' (*Isqat al-qurud*)

The rise in tribal opposition thus also led to a rise in confrontations with the government over issues of redistribution. One of such issues was the proposal to write off consumer debts (*isqat al-qurud*) on households. The issue was raised by a tribal MP – Daif Allah Burmiyya (Mutran) – but supported by other oppositional MPs. The argument was that the government had come to rescue banks and companies heavily indebted due to the economic crisis, but had failed to address the needs of middle-income households who were not any more capable of repaying their loans on houses, cars and other consumer products.[1] The proposal could not reach a parliamentary majority, as liberal MPs, Shi'a and the MB (*Hadas*) rejected it as populist.[2] It however generated mass support in the streets, also from regular *hadar* households, and the movement continued outside parliament via social media and street demonstrations. A Twitter campaign was initiated (*hamlat isqat al-qurud*). Despite various law proposals and a very long process of discussions between 2009 and 2014, no solution has been found and the government has so far refused to drop the interests on the loans, supported by the Central Bank.[3] In view of fiscal deficits for the government, dropping the consumer debts would be rather costly and therefore opposes it.[4] Instead, the government created a Defaulters Fund in 2011 to give financial aid to defaulters. The support the movement continues to receive from *hadar* groups (including some pro-regime MPs) is exemplary of the widely felt frustration of middle-class Kuwaitis over their material future and access to state resources, which they tend to attribute to bad governance and corruption. One of my interlocutors, an activist and lawyer close to the opposition movement says the following about it:

> If you take for example a genuine Kuwaiti who just finished college and is working in the public sector with a decent job, without fear of losing it, then you'll see that even for this ordinary middle-class Kuwaiti life is very expensive. Let's say he is married with two children. See how they live. For example, let's say he earns 1500 KD (around 5000 USD). Normally this would be a lot. However, you'll see that this does not cover the expenses of the family. Life in Kuwait is extremely expensive (the rent of the house, etc.). Also, society is very consumption-minded. So if the person has a medical problem and goes to the public hospital, you'll see that the waiting lists are long and treatment is bad. For this reason, he is almost obliged to go to a private clinic to get a treatment and this very expensive.[5]

Given the bad quality of state services (public hospitals, but also government housing), the costs of life have risen considerably for Kuwaitis over the past decade. The deficiencies of the welfare regime are also alluded to by Dr Ibrahim al-Shurayfi: 'Do not think that Kuwait is rich … the majority of Kuwaiti are indebted and until today, Kuwait is not advancing. There are no new projects and the government does not really build a lot … there are no new universities for example.'[6] Among Kuwaitis, there is a broad sentiment that the country has lost its prestige regionally and that the positive national feeling of development was destroyed in the 1970s as a consequence of regime policies.

'Allow us to build our diwaniyyas!'

As the movement to write off consumer debts was initiated in reaction to the government's help for companies and the merchant class, the same happened in the case of the Committee attributed to study property illegally built on government land (*lajna al-ta'diyyat 'ala amlak al-dawla*). The committee was created in 2008 following new government policy criticizing illegal building on government land. Whilst the law applied to different buildings (industrial/residential/chalets), the measure was said to target specifically diwaniyyas in middle-income neighbourhoods, where diwaniyyas were generally built as an extension to houses. The measure provoked great criticism from tribal constituents – as well as from middle-income *hadar* citizens – as they accused the government of turning a blind eye to the property of merchant elites in industrial areas and close to the seaside.[7] Questions were raised: 'What about the "industrial princes" (*shuyukh al-sina'a*) – who possess large parcels of land which they sell at extremely high prices or the merchant families occupying the seaside with their chalets?'[8]

Transparency and competition in attributing tenders (*munaqasat*)

Another issue that has been fiercely defended by tribal MPs is their call for more transparency in the attribution of lucrative government tenders (*munaqasat*), challenging the monopolies of the merchant elite in the private sector. Various calls have been made to propose new legislation to open the private sector for foreign competition and allow foreign companies to compete for the bidding for tenders, as the attribution of tenders is an opaque process based upon personal relations between Al-Sabah shaykhs and the merchants.[9] It might not be a coincidence that the 2012 oppositional parliament was dissolved just before passing these very important laws (such as the creation of a committee supervising tenders and transparency), which would seriously challenge the logic on which the Al-Sabah's authority has relied and paraphrased by the credo: '*al-tijara li-l-tujar wa al-hukm li al-Sabah*' (commerce for the merchants and governance for the Al-Sabah). Being assured almost exclusive rights in the private sector, the capitalist classes do not have a genuine interest in promoting democratization, which would challenge their status quo, especially since the rise of more populist demands that went along with the socio-political empowerment of the *badu* since the 1990s. This also explains why the five important newspapers in Kuwait owned by the merchants refused to publish the declaration of former speaker of Parliament, Ahmad al-Sa'dun and the opposition bloc, following the dissolution of parliament in which they plead for a 'chosen government' and a 'constitutional monarchy'. It also explains the alleged financial support of certain merchants for media outlets criticizing the tribes.

The dimensions of the social struggle that accompanies the political rise of the tribes become clearer when looking at some data on the composition of the private sector and the allocation of tenders. As shown by Al-Fadhala in his study, only 4.4 per cent of the registered shareholding companies in Kuwait have tribesmen on their boards. Moreover, they have a rather small share in these companies (out of 212 registered companies, there were only 9 companies in which tribesmen own more than 50 per cent of the shares).[10] Also in the field of the tenders, data show the marginalization of the *badu*. As latecomers to the nation, they do not have the same quality of ties to regime patrons and thus less '*wasta*' to receive government tenders. The regime upholds the attribution of tenders to a small elite that historically formed the nucleus of power-sharing. In the first quarter of 2010 only 11 per cent of the total direct tenders allocated went to *badu* Kuwaitis; while the *hadar* received 59 per cent and the Shi'a as a separate category 15 per cent (although representing only around 30 per cent of Kuwaitis).[11] As such, the *hadar* represent a 'market dominant minority'.

Given its marginalization in the private sector, the *badu* MPs have been the strongest opponents of the *hadar* elite's monopoly. This also explains why in 2009 *badu* MPs collectively attacked the 2009 law regarding 'Economic Stability' (*qanun al-istiqrar al-iqtisadi*), considering it a law to protect the *hadar*. It consisted of a set of provisions to protect the local economy against the pitfalls of the world financial crisis of 2008, including considerable financial support by the state to the local merchant class and the purchase of new loans that companies had taken from the Central Bank between 2009 and 2010.[12] This heightened regime support for the merchant class after 2008 made the latter even more dependent on the government. As such my interlocutor Khaled al-Fadhala says:

> They (merchants) have become in a certain sense the slaves of the government, as they also depended on it to get them out of their debts, caused by the world financial crisis. While they became the slaves of the government, the role of the Bedouins rose. In a certain way, the Bedouins are less dependent on the government, on its patronage, because as a lower middle-class, they have profited less from the oil wealth.[13]

After intense lobbying of youth groups and despite opposition from merchant groups, recognizing the challenge of absorbing youth into the job market, the government created in 2013 a National Chamber for small and medium-sized enterprises (SMEs). Its aim is to strengthen the role of new entrepreneurs in the private sector. More recently, in June 2019, an amended Tender Law (nr. 74) was promulgated that explicitly gives a role to SMEs in the attribution of tenders. As such, a contractor needs to give at least 10 per cent of the work for the project to an SME and 30 per cent of tenders need to go to local contractors to enhance local production. Although this law is a step into the direction of opening up the private sector and allowing stronger *badu* participation, its implementation remains a challenge and will only succeed if subject to independent oversight. Also, the National Chamber for SMEs is a top-down instrument (bestowed with a budget of 2 billion KD) in which SMEs remain dependent on government patronage and could therefore also face challenges to entrepreneurial initiatives that threaten the regime's interests.

'Waiting a House'

*This section was inspired by and for a great deal *verbatim* taken from an earlier co-authored article with Madeleine Wells-Goldburt entitled 'Contesting Welfare State Politics', published in *Middle East Report*, 272 (Fall 2014).

"A government poll in September 2013 showed that the housing shortage is a top concern of Kuwaitis. Over 106,000 Kuwaiti families (roughly one-third of all Kuwaitis) are currently on the waiting list for government-provided homes. Under Kuwaiti law, every married couple is entitled to a house built on a 400 square-meter plot or a 400 square-meter apartment. Once the plot of land is allocated, the government offers a 70,000 Kuwaiti dinar (approximately $209000) long-term, interest-free loan for home construction. With the current number of applicants for housing, an estimated 174,000 houses will be needed by 2020. In its sixty-year history, the public housing programme has financed a total of 93,040 homes." It therefore seems unlikely the government will be able to answer the demands for housing and in view of austerity measures cannot bear the high welfare spending it was accustomed to.

Many Kuwaitis blame the housing crisis not on waning government resources but more on the intransparent use of available resources through corruption. Although allegations of corruption might be manipulation and are often employed to denounce those one opposes, the inefficient use of resources cannot be denied. Only 8 per cent of Kuwait's land is developed but construction projects have been backlogged, not at least due to a critical parliament using its legislative power to delay or deny development projects out of fear such tenders would unduly enrich members of the business or ruling elite.

"The Emir's call for the Kuwait Conference on Housing in March 2014 elicited bitter reactions on social media, an important public forum considering Kuwait is the most Twitter-connected country per capita. A Twitter account, @na6er_bait (digital rendering of *natir bayt*, 'waiting for a house'), accuses the government of fabricating the crisis. The account has almost 20,000 followers" – about two-thirds of all Kuwaiti Twitter users.[14] "Critics of the government's response to the housing shortage also decry plans to offer dense urban housing instead of stand-alone homes that state loans have typically funded."

"Land is and has been a key currency for the government to use in cultivating political alliances. Housing policy in particular has allowed the regime strategically to divide Kuwaiti society while at the same time encouraging a sense of national belonging through the ownership of land.[15] Merchant families profited most from the land acquisition programme of the 1950s. They were granted large parcels of land and profited much from government rent distribution, as the latter purchased land from the townspeople at inflated prices to facilitate the relocation of urban families and to buy their loyalty. Housing policies also contributed to the segregation between the urban and tribal populations, as the nearly naturalized *badu* were generally placed in housing on the outskirts of Kuwait City or in other remote cities. *Badu* also received lower quality state services, especially in the size and quality of housing.[16]

Critics of the government argue that the current housing shortage stems from the vested financial interests of a group of powerful actors. Here too, the *badu* MPs have been the staunchest defenders of the housing campaign. As such, the Islamist–*badu* allied opposition was among the first to plead for measures to supervise the opaque process of distributing tenders and allowing foreign companies to compete for home construction bids. Musallam al-Barrak, icon of the opposition and general coordinator of the Popular Action Movement (known by the acronym HASHD that was created in 2014 and in essence is a rebranding of the Popular Action Bloc), blames Kuwait's political paralysis on a 'suspicious alliance between the merchants of corruption and the merchants of power'.[17] Others point directly to the owners of apartment buildings in the city centre – known as 'real estate princes' to their critics – whose profits depend on the 100,000-tenant rental market with little competition from government-funded housing.'

Kuwait's housing crisis is exemplary of the social struggle going on in Kuwait's society, with the frustration of wider middle classes – with the *badu* as the most vocal voicers of this frustration – about the shortcomings of Kuwait's welfare regime. Mounting populism and anti-elite political voices have challenged existing mechanisms of rent redistribution and brought to the fore the dysfunctions of the welfare regime that its detractors attribute to the corruption of the Al-Sabah–merchant elite alliance.

Challenges to its social contract: austerity and Kuwait 2035

The abundance of welfare spending on which Kuwait's rentier regime was built is not anymore sustainable and combined with the unequal distribution of rents – a consequence of alliance-building strategies with a privileged urban elite – the state is trapped in a dynamic of welfare redistribution it created. Citizens feel they have a stake in the state's assets (oil) and expect the state to manage it in the best way possible and voice their demands through parliament.

In 2014 a global decline in oil prices led to a budget shortfall with major economic and political ramifications. In 2015–16 and for the first time in sixteen years Kuwait witnessed a budget deficit of 4.6 billion dinars, which amounted to almost 16.5 per cent of GDP.[18] This led to the announcement of austerity measures such as cuts on commodity subsidies and on public sector employment. The cuts in fuel subsidies in August 2016 sparked outrage among the public and parliament and seven months later the Emir dissolved the government (for the seventh time in ten years). By dissolving parliament, the likely intention was to consolidate support in parliament for government measures through new elections. However, contrary to expectations, this time opposition forces that had previously boycotted elections since the issuance of an Emiri decree changing electoral law in 2012 decided to participate. Despite internal divisions they converged in their opposition to austerity and thereby succeeded in winning nearly half of the seats in parliament.[19]

The regionally unprecedented high ratio of public spending to GDP combined with the volatility of oil prices and a burgeoning youth population created a massive hole in the country's budget. Unemployment has been on the rise and particularly among the youth (in 2019, 14,37% of the Kuwaiti youth were unemployed). One of the reasons behind this rise is population growth and the arrival on the labour market of a large group of young graduates most of whom are waiting for the much sought after government jobs, thereby increasing the financial burden on the state. IMF estimates that Kuwait might need up to over $100 billion over the next five years. While boasting significant resources (including its sovereign wealth funds, the largest in the region), Kuwait must repay considerable debt in the coming years and has to fund its structural reform plans. Kuwait has cushioned itself against the impact of lower oil prices by saving annually at least 10 per cent of government revenue in the Future Generations Fund. In 2017 Kuwait launched its development plan New Kuwait, envisioning a radical shift from an oil-dependent economy to transform the country into a regional and financial hub by 2035 in a series of five-year development plans to strengthen the private sector and build a knowledge economy.[20]

Austerity measures have so far focused on subsidy cuts and reducing the costs of a bloated and inefficient public sector. One major measure was the cut in fuel subsidies, heavily resented by Kuwait's public and parliament. Other measures have included cuts in public sector spending by reducing unnecessary costs such as travel costs and allocations for all categories in society. Many of such measures (such as electricity and water price increases) have been scaled back by parliament and approval of a GCC-wide value-added tax (VAT) and a new debt law proposal have been delayed due to opposition in parliament, leading to the resignation of four ministers in December 2018.[21] The group most affected by budgetary cuts has so far been the expats as they do not have a voice in parliament and as society tends to support such measures, typical of a rich welfare regime creating boundaries between insiders and outsiders. Kuwaitization policies have led to cuts in employment of foreigners in both private and public sectors. In the first year of its programme (2017–18) 3,000 foreigners were laid off in public sector jobs and parliament discussed measures such as a tax on expatriates' salaries before they send home remittances and strengthening the scrutiny over the skills of foreign labour.[22] Other measures against foreigners include more restrictive access to public hospitals and to apply for a driver's license. The long-brewing crisis of the stateless (*Bidun*) in Kuwait also suffers from a rhetoric of those opposing the *Bidun*'s integration focusing on the costs it would entail for future generations. While populist anti-immigrant measures encounter little opposition among citizens, they will not contribute much to lowering Kuwait's high public wage bill. This would require a strengthening of the private sector relative to the public sector and the transfer of Kuwaitis to private sector jobs but often the skills lack among the local population to take up jobs expats hold in education, healthcare and technical sectors.

In its effort to reform its economy away from oil dependency, the regime finds itself confronted with multiple and contradictory challenges. The deficiencies of state services and welfare (such as housing, healthcare, transportation) require the opening up of the private sector to allow for competition and thereby reduce costs in delivering much-needed projects. This implies more transparency in attributing tenders, opening the private sector to new economic elites from outside the Najdi nucleus of families and further democratizing Kuwait's polity. The much-needed austerity measures to make Kuwait sustainable for future generations have found political backlash among opposition MPs – often *badu* – backed by the middle class frustrated with the deficiencies of the welfare regime. By targeting the privileges of an economic elite in a social struggle, this middle-class movement deflects however attention from the necessity to sacrifice some of its welfare entitlements as masses to secure the welfare of younger generations. Having to accept that it will not anymore receive the welfare privileges of previous generations, the new generation of Kuwaitis will inevitably want something in return. The calls for representation, accountability and transparency the opposition voices will have to go beyond a relative quest for entitlement vis-á-vis a privileged hadar elite and internalize a new form of citizenship and accompanying social contract. In this conundrum citizens will have to contribute actively to the economic development of their country and on that premise are entitled to a say in the managing and allocation of resources. The road to renegotiate the social contract will have to be gradual, inclusive and inevitably contribute to the modernization of the monarchical pact. The old elite bargain upon which the Al-Sabah House was established, relying on a periphery for support, has been accompanied with personalized and segmented rent distribution between the ruler and clients. Clientelism is pervasive and ubiquitous in Kuwait and other GCC political economies but strong institutions and the rule of law will have to prime and lead to more equal and impersonal dynamics of redistribution and representation that characterize modern welfare states and presupposes taxation.

Splits in the regime's 'asabiyya: royal infighting and succession

*This section is heavily inspired by and mostly verbatim taken from an earlier co-authored article with Claire Beaugrand, entitled 'Limits of political clientelism: elites' struggles in Kuwait fragmenting politics', *Arabian Humanities*, 4 (2015).

Introduction

Socio-political change among the *badu* – which carries in it the dimension of a social struggle of the masses as public sector workers against the privileges of a merchant elite – coincided with intra-family feuds within the Al-Sabah House. These dynastic feuds dominated political life in Kuwait between 2011 and 2014 with competing princes supporting and manipulating political and economic factions to weaken each other, with allegations of corruption – a particularly common tactic.[1] Elite rivalry started in 2006 after the appointment of Shaykh Sabah al-Ahmad as Emir and the subsequent end to the implicit rotation of power between the Al-Jabir and Al-Salim branches. With the Al-Salim branch marginalized, ambitious shaykhs within the Al-Jabir started to construct their own power bases in the hope of aspiring to the throne one day. A constitutional provision and the separation of the provision of CP from that of PM explained the importance for ambitious shaykhs to have allies in parliament as the latter needs to approve with absolute majority the Emir's choice of CP.

Both dynamics reinforced each other as princes and societal actors tapped into burning regional issues to reinforce their political ambitions. Elite rivalry between a second generation of princes – notably between Shaykh Nasser al-Muhammad and Shaykh Ahmad al-Fahd – divided politics in Kuwait and corrupted parliament. It reached its apogee in December 2013 when allies of Ahmad al-Fahd claimed to possess tapes purportedly demonstrating that Nasser al-Muhammad was plotting against the government. After a revival of such coup allegations in 2014, the government imposed total media ban on the topic and in 2015 Ahmad al-Fahd issued a public apology on state television in which he renounced the coup allegations. Ever since he has been much outside of Kuwait and many of his supporters have been targeted and arrested by Kuwaiti authorities. Since 2015 a fragile political calm has descended again upon

Kuwait although the succession question is looming with an ageing Emir of ninety years old. An orderly succession will determine much the capacity of the Al-Sabah to transition the country towards a knowledge economy and to renegotiate the terms of a new social contract. Maintaining internal 'asabiyya will be a crucial resource for the Al-Sabah in its efforts to deal with the challenge of weakening clientelist ties to its periphery, a consequence of the emancipation of the *badu* and the unsustainability of welfare redistribution dynamics.

The aim of this chapter is to highlight the regime's mechanisms of rule, focusing on the shifting sociological role of elites in terms of their utility for the regime as well as the sources underlying their power. It is crucial to differentiate regime intentions from regime outcomes. As we see throughout this chapter, the intentions the regime attributes to certain policies do not necessarily lead to the outcomes it wishes for. An example is the growing independence of actors who are initially regime loyalists – having profited from its co-optation – but over time strengthen their autonomous stance, often a consequence of changing demands of the social base, the electorate.

The declining utility of these regime-dependent elites is the manifestation of a broader phenomenon of political emancipation of the masses and reinforces the need to renegotiate the premises of the social pact between the regime and society by further democratizing Kuwait's political sphere and ultimately modernizing its monarchical pact beyond its Khaldunian nature.

Breaking the balance of power: the consolidation of the Jabir branch[2]

"The year 2003 was a pivotal year in Kuwaiti politics: due to the bad health of the then CP Sa'd al-'Abdallah, Emir Jabir al-Aḥmad decided to separate the position of CP from that of PM. Consequently, the PM lost his constitutional immunity and became subject to parliamentary scrutiny, setting the stage for parliamentary grillings. In 2003, Shaykh Ṣabaḥ al-Aḥmad officially became PM after having been the de-facto leader of government since 2001. As acting PM, Shaykh Sabah was particularly apt at forging alliances with MPs and his appointment in 2006, endorsed by Parliament, consolidated the power of the Al-Jabir."

"In order to better understand the rise of elite struggles within the second generation of princes, one has to go back to when Shaykh Ṣabaḥ was PM, as it was his role as premier which set the stage for his accession to the throne and for new dynamics within the royal family. Shaykh Ṣabaḥ's ambitious personality and the weak health of contending members of the Al-Salim branch led to him actively forge alliances with MPs, as well as within the royal family, particularly with the second-generation princes. This second generation had become more ambitious since the Iraqi Invasion, and Shaykh Ṣabaḥ's rise to government coincided with these princes playing a greater role in governance. In 2001, five of them were appointed as ministers."[3]

"Emir Jabir al-Aḥmad was not successful in arbitrating disputes between the two competing branches pitting Shaykh Ṣabaḥ against the remaining contenders to the throne, CP Sa'd and Shaykh Salim al-Salim (then Minister of Defence). To complicate matters further, this competition also included members of the second generation supported by powerful patrons. Shaykh Aḥmad al-Fahd, with the support of Shaykh Ṣabaḥ, competed with Shaykh Muḥammad al-Khalid al-Ḥamad (ex-Minister of Interior), allied to the Al-Salim branch – a competition which transpired clearly during the 2003 elections."[4]

"Upon the death of Emir Jabir al-Aḥmad, these alliances with MPs and young princes played out in favour of Shaykh Ṣabaḥ. As PM he had already succeeded in eliminating one other contender to the throne, Shaykh Salim al-Salim (leaving only CP Saʿd as competitor). This explains why parliament picked him when it chose to intervene – in a historic *impeachment* – to decide over a difficult succession struggle. Only nine days after Emir Jabir's death, it held an extraordinary session and voted unanimously for Saʿd's destitution. Shaykh Ṣabaḥ who was officially third in line for succession, invoking article 4, was instead chosen as Emir. Adding insult to injury for the Al-Salim, Shaykh Ṣabaḥ appointed, against all expectations, his full brother, Nawaf al-Ahmad al-Jabir, as CP, and his nephew, Naṣser al-Muḥammad al-Aḥmad as PM."

"While this ended the immediate succession struggle between the two competing branches by excluding the Al-Salims and consolidating power in one branch, it opened a Pandora's Box for new elite rivalry, as it paved the way for a second generation of princes, including descendants of other sons of Mubārak the Great to aspire to the throne one day, now that succession rules had been discarded."

The rise of a second generation of princes

"Since 2001, the composition of governments has reflected the greater role of princes from the second generation. This generation refers to the great-grandsons of Mubarak Al Sabah (1896–1915) the children of only four of his seven sons: Jabir, Salim, Ḥamad and ʿAbdallah. While competition centred primarily on the Al-Jabir and Al-Salīm branches, princes of the Al-Ḥamad and Al-ʿAbdallah branches have also claimed the throne in recent years, referring to article 4 of the Constitution which makes them de jure eligible.[5] Former PM, Jābir al-Mubārak, as well as the MFA are from the Al-Ḥamad branch."

"Following the Iraqi Invasion of Kuwait, these princes started increasing their public visibility and voicing their ambitions. On 13 July 1992, seventeen young princes – under the lead of Shaykh Nasser Sabah al-Aḥmad, the son of the current Emir – presented a petition to Emir Jabir al-Ahmad, in which they announced the need for profound political reforms and constitutional amendments, and expressed the widespread malaise and the public's lack of confidence in their rulers. The petition called *Al-Wathīqa* was published in *Al-Zamān*, a newspaper belonging to Shaykh Nasser Sabah al-Aḥmad. This open criticism coming from within the ruling family revealed a deep generational divide within the ruling elite."

"Breaking the tacit rule of alternation between the Jaber's and the Salim's had increased these princes' ambitions, as they wanted to be eligible for the throne one day. Competing princes and their fathers co-opted societal forces and particularly MPs in the ensuing years. A constitutional provision in article 4 is the reason why having allies in parliament is so important for royal contenders. Article 4, regulating succession matters, stipulates that the Emir's choice for CP needs to be approved by an *absolute majority* of parliament. If a new CP fails to win parliament's approval, the Emir submits the names of three eligible members of the family to parliament, which then selects one of them."

"Although there were more than two contenders who were well placed to secure the Al-Sabah family's acquiescence for the position of CP, the worst fight pitted former PM Shaykh Nasser al-Muḥammad against Shaykh Aḥmad al-Fahd. The politics of alliance-building contributed in the period between 2011 and 2014 to a polarization of political life, which each prince striving to create alliances. These patron–client games impacted society and both coincided and reinforced a protest movement instigated by an educated youth, largely tribal, calling for a modernization of political life and the end of corruption scandals."

Nasser al-Muhammad al-Ahmad al-Sabah and the Shi'ite alliance

Sectarianism as a chance: 2008 and the forging of an alliance with the Shi'a

"As the PM appointed by the Emir in 2006, Shaykh Nasser al-Muḥammad was traditionally seen as having Emir Sabah al-Aḥmad's trust, all the more so as he had served as Minister of the Royal Court from 1991 to 2006 under the two Emirs and brothers Jaber (1977–2006) and Sabah al-Aḥmad (from 2006 on).[6] A career diplomat, he served as Ambassador to Iran from 1968 till 1979 and as the Dean of the Diplomatic Corps from 1971 to 1979; he is seen as close to the Shi'a."[7]

"His experience means he is on good terms not only with elites from the Shah's regime but also of the Islamic Republic, which was reflected in his visits to Iran as a PM, outnumbering his official visits to all GCC countries combined, while he did not even visit Saudi Arabia a single time as head of government. In addition to this factor, the government's policy towards the Shi'a cannot be understood without taking into account the fact that tribal MPs and their electorate have increasingly become opposition forces. The trend predates Shaykh Nasser's coming to power in February 2006, coinciding rather with the early 2000s and the rise of charismatic tribal MPs, such as Musallam al-Barrāk, united in the Popular Action Bloc. Since the 2008 general elections, relations between the government and the tribes turned markedly confrontational, after the government banned a practice that it had tolerated before, namely tribal primaries (*fari'yyāt*), which led to violent clashes between tribesmen and security forces."

"With the government incapable of placating tribal constituencies, Shaykh Nasser resorted to the Shi'a. It is important to understand that by allying himself to the Shi'a, he also tried to support factions hostile to Shaykh Aḥmad al-Fahd, who had entered the government in 2001 and was one of the main princes of the second generation, and thus Shaykh Nasser's main rival. Shaykh Nasser managed to rally the ethnically and religiously heterogeneous group of Kuwaiti Shi'a behind the government, following a divide-and-rule strategy. He did so through the tactical favouring of an emerging Shi'ite business elite and, with their support, by uniting the Shi'a and turning them into a cohesive pro-government voting group." These loyal merchants and co-opted MPs served as informal mediators and community brokers between the government and the wider group of Kuwaiti Shi'a.

The culmination of these regime strategies to co-opt the Shi'a as a loyal minority in the wake of tribal–Islamist opposition happened in 2008, at a time of rising sectarian tensions in Kuwaiti society, as a result of the commemoration of the assassination of Imad Mughniyeh by a group of *Al-Tahaluf* members.[8] In this context, sectarian tensions were exploited by the regime – the government of Nasser al-Muhammad – to rally this minority behind its rule by relying upon a group of new merchants and loyal MPs. Here, the rentier nature of the state – coupled with a historical memory of this non-core group's support for the monarchy – allowed it to resort to newly created mediators as channels of the state's informal power. However, it was the consent of the social base here – the Shi'a feeling threatened by a hostile society (in analogy to the 1938 events) – which allowed these regime strategies to be effective. Yet, the nature of the patronage and intercession of these new semi-notables is rather circumstantial and short term, as they owe their position directly to the regime and therefore tend to lack local social embeddedness, although over time their investment in charities, media and political life can contribute to a growing role within communities. In all cases, the social base is crucial in understanding the utility and role of intermediary elites. The Bahraini crisis demonstrated the limits of these policies of co-optation, as the assertiveness of the Shi'a rose, their growing assertiveness also being the consequence of their loss of the patron in government, Shaykh Nasser al-Muhammad (23 November 2011).

The emergence of new Shi'ite business elites as semi-notables[9]

As mentioned, in order to reach Shi'a masses in a context of heightened opposition, the regime relied upon a limited group of 'new' Shi'a merchants who were incorporated into the highest political 'asabiyya around the House of Al-Sabah and particularly the person of Shaykh Nasser. These Shi'a merchants belong to the wealthiest families in the emirate and differ from the old families in the sense that their wealth has only been created since the early 1990s. The rentier nature of the state enabled it to revive with relative ease a form of notable politics through a policy of political patronage in the private sector.[10]

One of the newly prominent Shi'a merchants is Jawaad Bukhamseen, who belongs to the *shaykhi* community. Coming from an old clerical family from Al-Hasa, the Bukhamseen family only settled in the emirate at the start of the twentieth century. Having no prior social capital as a merchant, Jawaad Bukhamseen started as a small broker on the Kuwaiti stock market and benefitted in the 1980s from state incentives to invest in the then-booming real estate sector; a sector which benefitted from a policy of state patronage aimed at weakening the Sunni mercantile opposition. Currently, the *Bukhamseen Holding* represents a conglomerate of economic activities, with a concentration on real estate and contracting. Moreover, the merchant is in the executive board of the *International Bank of Kuwait,* which – being presided by merchant Abdelwahhab al-Wazzan – is often referred to as a Shi'a bank. The charitable activities of Jawaad Bukhamseen are considerable and differ from the old merchant families in the sense that his activities transcend the *shaykhi* community and include all political Shi'a movements, including *Al-Tahaluf*.[11] We could argue that his exorbitant charitable activities are a means for this 'new' merchant to buy social prestige in the Shi'a community, which will also enhance his position as an intermediary between the various Shi'a movements and the central power. Furthermore, contrary to the old elite of Shi'ite merchants who have largely lost their community power, the Bukhamseen family has been actively involved in Shi'a politics. An example was the alliance between his son, Anouar Bukhamseen, and Saleh Ashour in the 2008 elections when they decided to work together for *Al-Adala wa-Salam*.[12] However, *Al-Adala wa-Salam* only succeeded in having one representative in parliament, the leading political figure of the movement: Saleh Ashour. As a merchant, Anouar Bukhamseen, despite massive financing of his campaign, could not mobilize enough popular support and lost against the *Al-Tahaluf* deputies in the first district, which led the Bukhamseen family to criticize Saleh Ashour, accusing him of having used the family's money to get into parliament. In the elections of May 2009, Jawaad Bukhamseen, like the other new merchants, publicly insisted on the need to unify the Shi'a and has actively supported the unification efforts between the representatives of the main Shi'a political currents, namely *Al-Tahaluf, Al-Mithaq* and *Tajamu' al-Risala al-Insaniyya* (the latter, 'Assembly of the Human Message' was created in 2006 and emanates from the shaykhi community[13]).[14] This position reflected the regime strategy towards the Shi'a minority that culminated in 2008, although the Bahraini crisis (2011) marked the limits of these sectarian-based policies and of personal co-optation.

It is also in this logic that we should understand the creation in 2007 of Bukhamseen's personal daily newspaper, *Al-Nahar,* which is characterized by its pro Al-Sabah stance and which – although not officially presented as a Shi'a newspaper – serves largely a Shi'a audience. This investment in the media by new elites – that paralleled a more open role of Al-Sabah members in the media – was favoured by a new press, publication and TV law in 2006 that broke the monopoly of the five daily newspapers and legalized private TV channels. It had a considerable impact on the polarization of Kuwait's political life, with royal feuds and societal ones being fought out via these media channels.[15]

On the regional level, Jawaad Bukhamseen has played an important role in Kuwait's soft-power diplomacy towards its new Shi'a neighbour: Iraq. He is particularly known in Shi'a society for his economic alliances with business families in Iraq. Moreover, Jawaad Bukhamseen was the first to use the direct flight to Najaf airport, built in 2008 by the *Al-Aqeelah* group: a Kuwaiti company that specifically invests in the Shi'a shrine cities in Iraq and Syria and which is essentially financed by the Shi'a merchants in Kuwait.[16] His economic investments in Iraq have gained him prominence in top political and religious circles, through which he can play an indirect role in the reinforcement of Kuwait's diplomatic ties to its neighbour.[17]

Another merchant who gained prominence over the past decade is Ali al-Matruk, belonging to the Baharna Shi'a. One of my interviewees has described him as follows:

> Ali al-Matruk and Mahmud Haider, they aren't from the old merchant families, they are really new. There is a very rich old Al-Matruk family, but Ali al-Matruk he is not from the same family. He didn't have any money, but the government supported him and wanted to give him the image of an old family. So that is why most of the Shi'a think he is an old merchant.

Being from a modest family, Ali al-Matruk started his career as a bureaucrat for the Ministry of Finance and gained his riches in the 1980s through the policy of state land allocation. Instead of being invested in commercial activities, Ali al-Matruk is a rich landlord and has profited from government patronage through land distribution.[18] As a poet and columnist for *Al-Watan* newspaper (owned by Shaykh Ali 'al-Khalifa), Al-Matruk presents himself as an enlightened person and considers himself neutral among what he considers to be a fragmented Shi'a landscape in Kuwait. It is interesting to note that Ali al-Matruk as the other new Shi'a merchants has since 2004 been on board of the International Bank of Kuwait.

As is the case with Jawaad Bukhamseen, Al-Matruk presented himself as a merchant who transcends the ethnic Shi'a 'asabiyya and supports all sections of the Shi'a community.[19] Moreover, in the aftermath of the 2008 Mughniyeh affair, in which he played a crucial role as mediator, Al-Matruk has supported the pro-Iranian *al-Tahaluf* movement, which is remarkable if we consider that he had fiercely criticized this movement in the past in his columns. Like the other new merchants, Ali al-Matruk is considered in Shi'a society as a close friend to the Emir himself. Furthermore, at the start of the uprising in Bahrain, Ali al-Matruk together with other Shi'ite notables has had a key role in the Kuwaiti delegation to mediate in the conflict between the opposition group *Al-Wefaq* and the Bahraini government.[20]

Finally, there is another 'new' merchant who became one of the wealthiest persons of Kuwait: the Iranian merchant Mahmud Haider who has gained his wealth after the 1990 Invasion. The companies Mahmud Haider presides over, such as 'Mahmud Haydar and Sons Trading Company' and 'Zumorrodah Holding Company', represent capital of approximately two billion dollars each. Telecommunications and real estate constitute the bulk of the family's activities.[21] Rumours are widespread in Kuwaiti society that the merchant cannot have gained his wealth in a proper way. It is important to note the hatred that exists in the group of old merchant families vis-à-vis those whom they consider to be newcomers, as reflected in the following statement: 'Mahmud Haider is very young. He is not a merchant and he was never a merchant. He started his life dirty.'[22] This is exemplary for the general rivalry within the group of Shi'a merchants and shows the strength of ascriptive and weakness of class-articulated identities in Kuwait's rentier institutional context.

Even more than the other new merchants, Mahmud Haider embodied the will of Nasser al-Mohammed's government to unify the Shi'a population behind its rule. He owned a daily newspaper, *Al-Dar* (2007–12), which was shutdown in 2012 during the Bahraini crisis and heightened sectarian tensions in Kuwait. The newspaper was explicitly Shi'a in tone and during my fieldwork in 2009 I noticed the omnipresence of stickers of *Al-Dar* and Bukhamseen's *Al-Nahar* in neighbourhoods with a high concentration of Shi'a such as *Al-Da'iyya* and *Al-Dasma*. In terms of charity work, Mahmud Haider supports all Shi'a branches and has enhanced his visibility in the public space through the establishments of medical centres in his name. It is important to note that the merchant has good relations with Sayyid Mohammad Baqer al-Mohri, a politicized Shi'a cleric who regularly publishes fierce statements against the Salafists and who maintains close ties with prominent pro-government personalities, such as the former speaker of parliament, late Jasem al-Khorafi (1940–2015). Although

Mohammed Baqer al-Mohri presents himself as the official spokesmen of Shi'a *'ulema*, he is not considered as such by most of them. These new merchants became part and parcel of the government's strategy to unify its minority as a loyal bloc in the face of rising opposition.

One of the regime's top-down measures with regard to the Shi'a has been the creation of a Shi'a Awqaf Department at the Ministry of Religious Endowments in 2004. Despite various previous attempts to regularize the husayniyyas and to control the financing of religious affairs, it was only in the post-2003 context that the project was implemented. As in other GCC countries with Shi'a minorities, the Shi'a' accession to power in Baghdad was initially accompanied by state-led anti-discriminatory policies in the religious sphere to better control their minorities.[23] In this context the initiative to establish an Awqaf Department came from the Emir himself without prior parliamentary approval, which explains the opposition of the *Al-Tahaluf* movement to the project.[24] However, the pro-government Shi'a movements such as *Al-Mithaq* and the *Shiraziyyin*, supported by the old merchant families, were in favour of the project which they considered to be a means to control the flow of Islamic funds that could potentially be used for non-nationalist causes. During my interviews the resentment of *Shi'a 'ulema* towards the Awqaf Department was particularly pronounced, considering it a violation of the principle of financial independence from the state.[25]

Various attempts have also been made to unify the Shi'a diasporas and movements in the political domain. The merchant Abdelwahhab al-Wazzan has played an important role in this process, notably since 2003. The alliances in 2003 and 2006 (*'Itilaf al-Tajammu'at al-Watani*) comprised all the Shi'a political movements except the oppositional *Al-Tahaluf* movement. However, because of their weak social base, these unions did not succeed in vanquishing the *Al-Tahaluf* deputies in parliament. *Al-Tahaluf* presented an obstacle in the new government's policy aimed at rallying the Shi'a behind its rule.

It is in this context that we should understand the reaction to the events of 12 February 2008, when members of *Al-Tahaluf* came together to commemorate the assassination of Imad Mughniyeh, one of the leading figures of Lebanese Hezbollah. The act (*ta'bin*) provoked widespread indignation in Kuwaiti society, since Mughniyeh was considered to be the mastermind behind the terrorist attacks of the 1980s, including the assassination attempt on the Emir. Vocal accusations in the media – notably from radical Sunni Islamists – against the deputies revived sectarian tensions. The event also divided the joint opposition platform along sectarian lines and the Shi'ite MPs were expelled from the main parliamentary group of the Popular Action Bloc. Shi'a generally refer to this episode as a period of societal hostility towards them, comparing it to the tense interlude of the 1980s. This context of sectarian tensions has enabled the state – through the intermediation of the new Shi'a merchants – to come closer to its minority. As in 1938, the context of a society considered to be hostile towards the Shi'a was a crucial factor explaining the reshaping of Shi'a politics after the Mughniyeh incident.

Following the incident, the government and high personalities close to the Emir tacitly supported the Shi'a. The speaker of Parliament, Jasem al-Khorafi, appeased tensions by saying that no final proof existed on the implication of Mughniyeh in the attacks. However, the merchants Ali al-Matruk and Mahmud Haider were the ones who presented themselves as crucial mediators in the conflict by organizing meetings between *Al-Tahaluf* and government representatives in their diwaniyyas.[26] It is here where a tacit agreement was made: the government reopened the *Jam'iyyat al-Thaqafah Wa al-Ijtima'iyya* – the old bastion of Al-Da'wa activists, most of whom had adhered to the Imam Line after 1979 – in exchange for political compliance with the government. Furthermore, the government appointed Fadhal al-Safar, from *Al-Tahaluf*, as a Minister of Public Works and Municipal Affairs; the first time ever an *Al-Tahaluf* deputy has been appointed minister. On 26 May 2011, the government released the Kuwaiti Shi'ite author of the attacks on the Emir's convoy, the French and American embassies and several cafes in the 1980s.

Since the Mughniyeh affair, the Shi'a became a rather loyal voting bloc for Nasser al-Muhammad's government; supporting the PM in the various grillings he faced from 2008 until the end of the cabinet in November 2011.[27] This alliance transpired in the election results: in 2009, the number of Shi'ite MPS more than doubled (from 4 to 9), whereas Sunni Islamist groups lost one-third of their deputies.[28]

How should we interpret the co-optation of the Shi'a and the utility of the new merchants that brokered this alliance? As we will see in subsequent sections, the utility of these elites depends largely on the demands of the social base – the electorate – vis-à-vis the regime. Pure material patronage is not what explains the utility of these rent-generated elites. This is also the case in rich rentiers – as Kuwait – and rentier state theory has tended to obliterate the importance of other another factor of rule common in Arab monarchical systems: a relative continuity in social hierarchies and elites who were not dethroned as opposed to what happened to them in the Arab republics. Monarchical regimes had been relatively apt at upholding the support of their respective periphery, but forces of globalization have uprooted hierarchies within the rural and tribal peripheries throughout the region. For the Shi'a – whose loyalty to the regime was part and parcel of its founding story – their minority status has made them rather supportive of monarchy in view of hostile societal forces. Yet, this rallying behind the flags of the Al-Sabah depends on the consent of the social base.

While family reputation and money continue to play a role in constructing networks (although superseded by more horizontal communication networks), the agency of the social base is crucial in making or breaking intermediaries – regime-generated ones but also more independent ones. In effect, patron–client relations are always ones of mutual obligations and never of coercion, with both actors profiting from the alliance. The Shi'a' feeling of being threatened in a hostile society of largely tribal–Islamist voices made them accept the regime's outreach to them, via new intermediaries. Patronage here is twofold: from the intermediary vis-à-vis his constituencies and from the royal backer vis-à-vis the intermediary elite agent, playing the role of broker. In all cases, mutual interests bind these groups together and when the interests decline, the utility of the patronage weakens. This happened after the ouster of Shaykh Nasser from the government in 2011, strengthened by a regional context of the Bahraini uprising (2011) that provoked the sympathy of Kuwaiti Shi'a for their Bahraini coreligionists.

Ahmad al-Fahd al-Ahmad al-Sabah: 'opposition' supporter[29]

"When Aḥmad al-Fahd entered the government in 2001, he was in a position of strength: a strong ally to the current Emir Sabah al-Aḥmad, at the time PM, against the Salim branch, and himself a powerful second-generation prince, he was considered a potential CP supported by the United States before the choice fell on Nawaf in 2006. Yet, while the Emir is said to be close to the *ḥaḍar*, Shaykh Aḥmad himself fell out of grace with the business elites and then – cause or consequence – became close to the MB current (*Hadas*, as abbreviated in Arabic), the backing of which turned him into a very different contender for power and put him *in* an original and strategic position for the future."

"On a personal level, Aḥmad al-Fahd inherited a legacy, namely the Arab nationalist tendency, which differs completely from Shaykh Nasser al-Muḥammad's line. He is the son of Shaykh Fahd al-Aḥmad, a staunch supporter of the Palestinian cause – who actually served during the 1967 war – and a Kuwaiti royal martyr, shot at the outset of the 1990 Iraqi Invasion. Shaykh Aḥmad al-Fahd also inherited a 'family' involvement in sports, particularly in Olympic committees, football and handball,[30] through which he wields an increasing amount of power, as sports have risen to a prominent place not only in business terms worldwide but also in terms of Gulf diplomacy and control over its young population."[31]

Rivalries with the *hadar* in Kuwaiti sports and parliament

"Shaykh Fahd's activities in sports have created some tensions with the *hadar* commercial elites that have also been historically involved in the management of sports clubs (*andiyya*). Being the chairman of a sports club is a good springboard to politics. In particular, Fahd al-Ahmad and his sons after him ran against the merchants to be chairman of the board of the Al-Qādisiyya sporting club.[32] The downside of this is that these conflicts of interest were transposed to the national parliament where *ḥaḍar* MPs would vote against him, yet at the same time it constituted a great asset for the Shaykh as it proved to be an incredible tool for building international networks as well as an image of himself different from that of other princes."

"Shaykh Aḥmad made his political debut in 2001 under Emir Jaber's rule as Minister of Information (2001–3). Afterwards, he occupied the positions of Deputy Minister of Oil and Minister of Energy (2003–6) and, after some years out of government, was appointed Deputy PM for Economic Affairs and Minister of State for Development and Housing Affairs (2009–11). As a result of his strained relations with the Sunni *ḥaḍar* liberal current, Aḥmad al-Fahd tried, upon entering government, to reach out to the tribal forces – particularly Al-'Awāzīm – and the Sunni Islamist currents (with less success). He was said to have found allies among the Salafi MPs staunchly opposed to the pro-Shi'ite tendency of Nasser al-Muḥammad, particularly the scientific Salafists led by MP Walid al-Ṭabaṭaba'i."[33]

"This alliance was reflected in the stance several MPs took in favour of Aḥmad al-Fahd during his stints in government: when in June 2011 MPs of liberal persuasion requested to investigate Shaykh Aḥmad's finances, his role in the Kuwait Olympic

Committee and his performance as a Minister of Development, the heterogeneous coalition of MPs supporting him voted against any parliamentary interpellation.[34] Shaykh Aḥmad eventually chose to resign rather than face the grilling, after government members and parliamentary supporters of the PM withdrew their backing." Although at first Shaykh Aḥmad seemed to build short-term and individualized alliances – often with so-called 'service deputies' – he gradually emerged as the main supporter of the opposition movement since 2011" – and this, until an escalation of overt competition with Shaykh Nasser prompted a strong government response and led to a public apology of Shaykh Ahmad in 2015, after which he largely retreated from public life. This has restored a relative calm in Kuwait's politics although the question of succession looms.

Media battles: airing the opposition's ideas

In 2006, Shaykh Ahmad left the government, following the discovery of various corruption scandals in which he was involved as Minister of Oil. Following his ouster, he became very active in the media, enabled by a new press, publication and TV law "that contributed to the flourishing of the Kuwaiti press scene" according to Azoulay and Beaugrand. "Many TV channels of relatively poor quality by media standards opened for the sake of either supporting or opposing the government by means of hour-long talk shows. Shaykh Ahmad and MPs of the Popular Action Bloc opposing the government found a common enemy in PM Shaykh Nasser and coordinated attacks against him", both in parliament and in the media. The Popular Action Bloc was established in 1999 and represents a populist view, defending the salaried middle classes. While it explicitly aimed to run on a non-tribal and non-sectarian ticket – including *hadar, badu*, Shi'a and Sunna – the bloc is considered by its detractors as the mouthpiece of the tribes. Since the ouster of the Shi'a in 2008 and the rise of the young and tribal-led anti-corruption movement, the Popular Action Bloc has relied even more on a tribal electorate. This is also due to the prominence of Musallam al-Barrak (*Mutran*) within the movement, in addition to many other tribesmen.[35] Its *hadar* founder, veteran Ahmad al-Sa'dun, also counts in large upon this young and tribal support.[36] Since 2014, the Popular Action Bloc has become HASHD and has its similar anti-merchant elite stance, a position that resonates well within the tribal electorate that challenges this elite pact.

In media, "Al-Watan TV was said to work extensively to support Shaykh Ahmad al-Fahd against the PM, who in turn was suspected to state-sponsor channels that would mention him favourably. The same could be said about several newspapers: the short-lived *Āwān* newspaper (2007–10) earned itself a reputation of being pro-PM, while Aḥmad al-Fahd is said to be supportive of *Al-Kuwaytiyya, Al-'Ālam al-Yawm* and the TV channel Qanat al-Yawm, all of them mouthpieces of social groups, particularly the tribes, willing to challenge the current privileges of the business and political elites." Many of these media outlets linked to Ahmad al-Fahd and the opposition have been shut down by the government and numerous associates of his have been targeted, detained or stripped of their citizenship. Those actions have weakened his support base, although the opposition to government policies continues to exist as its roots reflect structural changes in Kuwait's society.

The opposition has used these media platforms (the most vocal of which have now ceased to exist) throughout the crisis and during anti-corruption mobilization to disseminate its ideas and accusations. "For instance, Musallam al-Barrāk, a former MP of the Popular Action Bloc who boycotted the 2012 elections, launched a virulent attack against Nasser al-Muḥammad without naming him on the satellite channel Al-Yawm on 21 April 2014.[37] In this ninety-minute TV show, Al-Barrāk urged people, in a dramatic fashion, to protect Kuwait against the thieves and accused Nasser al-Muhammad, in thinly veiled terms by mentioning a 'former high-ranking official', of embezzlement of public funds amounting to billions of dollars, claiming he had evidence to support his claims. The very timing of these corruption allegations coincided with another climax in the intra-dynasty struggle for power."

"The situation of royal feuds reached its climax after December 2013, when an anonymous tweet claimed that Shaykh Ahmad al-Fahd possessed a compromising recording in which a senior member of the royal family – understood to be Nasser al-Muhammad – was plotting against the Emir and the CP, together with Jāsim al-Khurāfī (the former speaker of parliament, 1999–2012, from a very well-to-do merchant family), as well as with other businessmen (such as Mahmud Haider), and with alleged Iranian backing. In early April 2014, a few weeks before Al-Barrak's TV show, the scandal was revived thanks to social media buzz, when Shaykh Aḥmad was heard in the general prosecution's offices as a witness in the 'tape scandal'. This audition, furthermore, coincided with an important tactical move of the opposition which had just formed a coalition, officially presenting its National Reform Project on 11 April 2014. The Coalition included ḤASHD or the Constitutional Popular Movement created in 19 May 2013 by the leaders of the parliamentary group Popular Action Bloc; *Ḥadas*, the MB's Islamic Constitutional Movement, in Kuwait since 1999; and Ḥadam, the Civil and Democratic Movement, stemming from youth movements and created in February 2012. The project, largely presented and explained on Al-Waṭan TV, proposed thirty-six amendments to the 1962 Constitution in order to better ascertain the principle of the people's sovereignty as the source of all power and to establish an absolute (*muṭlaq*) parliamentary regime with an elected government emanating from the ranks of the parliamentary majority. Its promoters did not hide that they saw in Shaykh Aḥmad al-Fahd the best placed among the royals to implement their vision."[38]

Qatar and the international sports' connection

"Finally, one of Ahmad al-Fahd's network resources lied in his international sports connections, especially in football and handball, two sports in which Doha has invested heavily. These links made him publicly close to Qatar. While international relations are usually the prerogative of the Emir and then members of the government, sports diplomacy has become a powerful tool for international leverage, and with influence that carries enough weight, to a certain extent, to build domestic support." Because of this proximity to Qatar, Ahmad al-Fahd was considered as being backed by Qatar's ideological line in terms of soft-power diplomacy: supporting Sunni Islamist movements and particularly those related to the MB current and – more broadly –

those that are hostile to Saudi Arabia and its state Salafism (as a reference for quietist Salafism in Kuwait). This fits in a pattern of rising competition between Saudi Arabia and Qatar over regional leadership in the aftermath of the Arab revolts and support to local groups that saw their rise in the context of power vacuums in countries such as Syria, Libya, Egypt, Tunisia and Yemen. Within the GCC, however, Saudi Arabia has been a leader and influencer of the GCC's common political actions as well as of internal affairs in countries such as Bahrain, which has become a de-facto dependence of the Kingdom.

"The elite group of royals, aristocrats, CEOs and Olympians who constitute the 115 members of the International Olympic Committee (IOC) counts among its members Shaykh Aḥmad but also Emir Tamīm bin Ḥamad Al Thānī (since 2002). In his capacity as president of the Olympic Council of Asia, Shaykh Aḥmad has strongly supported Qatar's sport policy. Although he has no position in the international football organizations, his close ties to the Bahraini head of the Asian Football Confederation allowed him to defend Qatar against the British *Sunday Times'* accusations of bribery to obtain the 2022 FIFA World Cup. Shaykh Aḥmad's indignation was very vocal, particularly visible in the Qatari press and TV, like the popular Qatar-based Al-Kās TV sports channel.[39] Finally, Shaykh Aḥmad presides over the Asian Handball Federation, a sport in which Qatar has made significant headway by reviving a worldwide handball competition and by hosting the International Handball Federation's showpiece, the World Men's Championship, in 2015."

"This proximity, compounded with obvious ideological affinities between the Kuwaiti Sunni Islamist movements and Qatari regional foreign policy led to widespread rumours in Kuwait accusing the opposition of being supported if not bankrolled by Qatar. On 4 December 2011, the 'tabloid' daily newspaper *Al-Shahīd* broke the news of an alleged payment made to the account of the then MP al-Barrak by former Qatari PM Ḥamad B. Jasim. This was firmly denied by Doha, where the Emir of Qatar summoned the representative of the newspaper *Al-Shahīd* and of Scope TV for spreading false information."[40] It is important to note that Scope TV – owned by media tycoon Fajr al-Said – represented an anti-tribal and anti-Islamist line that was part of the government line of Shaykh Nasser al-Muhammad.

Limits of political patronage vis-à-vis non-core elites (2011–14)

These princely feuds that spilled over into parliamentary life, media and society impacted the coherence of the regime in its capacity to act as one bloc vis-à-vis the opposition. While there has been a tacit alliance between opposition forces and their royal backer, it would be misguided to think of the opposition purely in terms of a 'created opposition' (*mu'arada mustana'*), given the changing demands of the social base it aims to represent. In the following, I will demonstrate how regime survival strategies vis-à-vis non-core groups have proved ineffective, therefore obliging the regime to resort to more repressive measures to quell these voices for change and discipline royal family members whose ambitions challenged the 'asabiyya of the Al-Sabah House.

The tribal volte-face: interdicting the *far'iyyat* (primaries)

The aforementioned changes in the perception of the young tribal electorate came to fruition in the period between 2005 and 2007 that witnessed a volte-face in terms of regime–tribal relations with the emergence of a tribal parliamentary opposition. This rise also led to a growing number of interpellations against members of the ruling family. While between 1962 and 1976, of the six interpellations only one concerned a prince, this number rose to twenty-seven interpellations in the period 2006–11, with twenty-one targeting members of the ruling family. This was also accompanied by rising instability of Kuwait's parliamentary life. Until Shaykh Nasser's resignation, seven governments had been formed, two of which were formed before elections were due: the result of parliamentary dissolutions in 2008 and 2009.[1]

The tribal volte-face coincided with a broader youth movement in 2006 – inspired by the Orange Movement in the Ukraine – that pleaded for the redrawing of electoral constituencies, from twenty-five to five (*Nabiha khamsa*: we want five). In some ways, the movement marked a new form of politics, as the youth groups acted largely outside existing parliamentary blocs and succeeded where MPs had failed in previous years. A novelty was the widespread use of mobile phones and internet to create social networks. The period saw the rise of personal blogs by activists that had an important impact on youth constituencies (Kuwait is one of the biggest social network users in the Arab world, along with Bahrain, Saudi Arabia and Egypt).

While the 2005 campaign clearly aimed to cross-cut *hadar–badu* and sectarian cleavages, it was largely instigated by a small group of liberal-minded *hadar* youth, such as Khaled al-Fadhala, former secretary-general of the National Democratic Alliance (*Al-tahaluf Al-watani Al-dimoqrati)*, a liberal political bloc. The implication of the tribal youth in political activism really started with the legislative elections of 2008. Fearing rising tribal assertiveness in parliament and the Islamist–tribal opposition that had been growing since the millennium, the regime forbade the illegal, but hitherto tolerated practice of the tribal primaries. For the first time, the government used violence in interdicting them, with security forces staging raids in diwaniyyas where it suspected primaries to be organized. Most violent clashes occurred in the *Sabahiyya* district, in front of the diwan of former MP Ghanim al-Mi'a, accusing the 'Awazem of holding primaries in his diwaniyya. Teargas and sticks were used against civilians present in the diwaniyya and various people were arrested. According to my interlocutors, the Sabahiyya events were considered as the first real moment of a confrontational stance vis-à-vis the regime. From this moment on, the 'Awazem (historically loyal to the Al-Sabah) became rather oppositional, led by their shaykh, Falah Ben Jama'a, who contrary to other chieftains has maintained his standing within the tribe, a consequence of his more independent stance vis-à-vis the government. In reaction, many of the 'Awazem entered police stations to steal information on the primaries.[2]

The violent nature of the confrontation between security forces and tribesmen marked a turning point in the relation between the tribes and the government. In the following parliament, tribal MPs and even those who had previously been loyal to the government were now mandated to voice opposition to the government and harboured deep resentment against the Minister of Interior. The outcome of the 2008 elections – following the reduction in electoral districts to five – reflected major gains for tribal forces, especially those linked with the Salafi current.[3] Tribes showed themselves even more effectively than in the past able to organize primaries in the now larger five districts. The rise of Islamists was also the consequence of the government's clumsy handling of the Mughniyeh crisis, steering sectarian tensions and the rise of more radical Sunni Islamist forces. In an attempt to appease the tribes, the PM (with Emiri backing) appointed members of the four largest tribes to the cabinet, all related to the Salafi current.[4] Nonetheless, the tribal MPs became more and more confrontational in the 2008 parliament, defending their constituents' political interests, such as the forgiveness of consumer debt (*isqat al-qurudh*) that until today continues as a powerful plea.

As a consequence of the more confrontational stance of the tribes, the government strengthened other societal forces and particularly those hostile to the tribes. An important phenomenon since 2008 has been the rise of anti-tribal rhetoric in the media. The case of media tycoon, MP and businessman Mohammed al-Juwaihal and his TV station Al-Sur (Wall) is particularly instructive in this regard. His TV channel, Al-Sur, refers to the old wall of Kuwait, constructed during the Battle of Jahra (1920), which has become the national symbol of the *hadar* populations, to whom are referred the townspeople who have helped constructing the wall of Kuwait as a protection against the *Ikhwan* troops.[5] His programmes on Sur TV have turned out to be ferociously anti-tribal in tone, considering the tribes non-Kuwaitis with dubious loyalty, and raising the issue of Kuwaitis who allegedly possess two passports, Kuwaiti and Saudi

(*Al-muzdawijin*). Especially the case of double passports has provoked strong debates in Kuwait and the resentment of tribesmen. At various times this resulted in violent clashes with tribesmen attacking Juwaihal and the office of Sur TV. Already in 2009, thousands of tribesmen, among them MPs, protested in front of Sur TV criticizing it for spreading racism in Kuwait and denouncing the Ministry of Media for not shutting down the channel.[6] During the 2012 elections, Mutran tribesmen had put the electoral tent of Juwaihal in the third district on fire, enraged by Juwaihal's attacks on their tribe and MP Obeid al-Wasmi (*Mutran*).[7] Al-Sur TV was shutdown in 2014 following accusations of raising sectarianism in Kuwait and Muhammad Juwaihal, facing judicial procedure against him, left to Egypt.

Tribesmen from the 'Awazem – symbolized by their charismatic leader Shaykh Ben Jama'a – have vehemently criticized these anti-tribal declarations by media outlets. In 2014, tribesmen of the 'Awazem attacked the building of the controversial Scope TV channel, following an interview with pro-government Shi'a MP Sayyid Hussayn al-Qallaf, in which the latter had criticized Shaykh Ben Jama'a. Scope TV – owned by media tycoon Fajr al-Said – has provoked criticism from neighbouring governments such as Qatar and Bahrain over its coverage of political issues.[8]

These examples show the extent of the anger among tribesmen towards those media outlets and public figures spreading anti-tribal rhetoric. In December 2010, relations took a dramatic turn when state security forces entered the diwaniyya of MP Jumu'an al-Harbasch in Sulaybikhat, where a crowd of MPs and civilians gathered in and outside the diwaniyya for a conference on the constitution and the denunciation of the measures taken to lift parliamentary immunity for MP Faisal al-Muslim after his discovery of corruption scandals reportedly said to originate from the person of the PM himself. Various people were beaten, including MPs such as Faisal al-Muslim and Abdelrahman al-Anjeri. The event sparked widespread indignation among the activists, as it demonstrated the government's capacity to use force to which it rarely resorted in the past. Shaykh Mishal al-Ahmad – Head of the National Guard and half-brother to the Emir – has been held responsible for the event and accused of heading a 'secret government' by opposition MPs. Following the event, tensions between the parliament and the government rose, resulting in grillings from tribal and Islamist MPs around the alleged transfer of money to certain MPs and public figures.[9]

The crystallization of the anti-corruption movement (2009–14)

Two successive scandals led to the resignation of PM Nasser al-Muhammad in November 2011. Already in 2009, tribal Islamist MP Faisal al-Muslim (*'Utban*) brought to fore the alleged discovery of money laundering scandals supposedly originating from the PM. It followed the release of a report by the Audit Bureau (*Diwan al-Muhasaba*), revealing discrepancies amounting to 23 billion KD; an amount not justified in terms of expenditures. Al-Muslim accused certain MPs of having received cheques on their bank accounts with exorbitant amounts of money and was the first MP to grill the PM in 2009, for a case of an MP that would have received 700,000 KD on his account. In subsequent years, various other discoveries of corruption followed. In September 2011, the oppositional bloc accused fifteen MPs of having accepted bribes by the government; hitherto branded as the *nuwab al-qabida*.[10] In October 2011, MP Musallam al-Barrak (*Mutran*) exposed at a public what he claimed to be secret evidence of millions of dinars being transferred from Kuwait's Central Bank to the PM via the Ministry of Foreign Affairs. It led to a major grilling against the PM by three MPs, of whom two were *badu*, under the name 'Al-tahwilat wa al-idaʿat al-milioniyya' (the million's cheques and deposits). Considerable collateral damage was caused, including the resignation of the last remaining member of the Al-Salim branch in a senior government position, Foreign Minister Shaykh Muhammad al-Sabah al-Salim. A parliamentary committee was also formed, presided by Al-Barrak, which summoned various individuals (bank representatives, MPs, businessmen and princes) to appear in front of parliament. Its work was obstructed by the reluctance of the government to provide any documents.[11]

These events of political corruption stirred the anger of an already frustrated young population. The next day, clashes occurred with police forces during a public rally of tens of thousands of demonstrators in front of parliament – branded Will Square (*Sahat al-Irada*) in analogy to the squares and roundabouts that became the chief rallying points during the Arab uprisings of 2011. These demonstrations were unprecedented in their number, as they gathered during their peaks around 20,000 people, mostly youth. On the night of 16 November, demonstrators and several opposition MPs stormed the Abdallah al-Salim Hall of parliament, chanting slogans calling for the departure of the PM. The seventy activists who stormed the Assembly included nine MPs who were almost all tribal and represented together six different tribes.[12] While summoned by the Constitutional Court that threatened to imprison them for five years, they were finally judged innocent by the Criminal Court.[13] During this tense period, some political commentators issued the threat of a 'revolution of the tribes'.[14]

Given the extent of the mass demonstrations assembling thousands of protestors, on the 23rd of November PM Nasser resigned and the cabinet stepped down. It was an unprecedented event in the GCC and provoked the ire of the Saudi regime, bothered by Kuwait's vocal parliament. The resignation happened in the agitated context of the Shiʿa-led uprising in Bahrain (February–March 2011) that was violently repressed by a Saudi-led GCC Peninsula Shield Force (14 March 2011). This fear of a spillover of popular unrest to the GCC and to Saudi Arabia's domestic scene is what spurred the lead role of the Saudi kingdom and its attempts to strengthen the unity of the GCC, accompanied by a reasserted authoritarianism internally vis-à-vis dissent.

When analysing the MPs accused of bribes from the government, one finds a variety of MPs, including Shiʿa, liberals, Islamists and some tribesmen.[15] These were all MPs close to the PM who supported him in the various grillings he faced, which were predominantly issued by *badu* MPs. The search for allies outside the tribal constituencies can be seen as a regime survival strategy as it lost control over its periphery. Controversial media outlets that flourished and that tended to be anti-tribal in tone have been accused of being supported by Al-Sabah shaykhs and influential merchants.[16] Shiʿa businessman Mahmud Haider has also been accused of bribing MPs.

The February 2012 oppositional Majlis

Following Nasser's resignation, new elections were announced for February 2012. They saw a landslide victory for the opposition forces that were largely tribal and Islamist. It was a historical moment with thirty-five oppositional MPs elected; unprecedented in Kuwait's modern politics, as for the first time, the opposition dominated the legislature: a dangerous situation for the political regime.

Sunni Islamists saw their return, with twenty-three MPs, compared to only nine in the previous parliament. All of those who had participated in the storming of the Assembly were re-elected and for the first time the primaries were not a good indication of electoral results. Many tribal MPs of the Opposition Bloc (*Al-Kutla al-Mu'arada*) did not run on a tribal ticket and presented themselves outside the primaries, although – as we have seen – they relied on tribal solidarities to win. Apart from the first district where Shi'a and *hadar* candidates dominated, tribal candidates received the highest number of votes in all other districts and some counted on the support of the *hadar*.[17] An example is Faisal al-Muslim who received 16,383 votes in the third district, while the tribe to which he belongs ('*Utban*) has only 4,000 members in that district. The same is true for Jumu'an al-Harbasch ('*Anezi*), who received 8,475 votes in the second district, which is largely a *hadar* district in which his tribe has around 2,295 members and where the MP has historically enjoyed the support of the *hadar* members of *Hadas* (the MB current to which he belongs). Musallam al-Barrak was the uncontested leader of the opposition, as he received the highest number of votes for an opposition MP: 30,118 in the fourth district.

Consequently, the February 2012 parliament was entrusted with a clear popular mandate for change and acted accordingly. Since its early inception, the parliament proved far more assertive than any parliament Kuwait had known. One of the first projects of the opposition was to propose a law guaranteeing the independence of the courts. Not much later, the oppositional majority worked on a draft law challenging the attribution of lucrative tenders to the merchant elite, by demanding more transparency and opening the private sector for foreign competition in the bidding for tenders.

It might not be a coincidence that the 2012 parliament was dissolved just before passing these very important laws (such as the creation of a committee supervising tenders and transparency) which would seriously challenge the social contract upon which Kuwait's political order was built since its establishment ('commerce for the merchants and governance for the Al-Sabah'). This also explains why the five important newspapers in Kuwait owned by the merchants refused to publish the declaration of former speaker of parliament – Ahmad al-Sa'dun – and the opposition bloc, following the dissolution. In the declaration, they pleaded for a 'chosen government' and a 'constitutional monarchy'.

Fearing this scenario, the Emir announced an unprecedented one-month suspension of parliament, which was officially dissolved on 16 June 2012 by the Constitutional Court. It stated that the February 2012 parliament was unconstitutional, as the elections were allegedly flawed. The 2009 pro-regime parliament was reinstated, but only three months later (3 October 2012) was dissolved by the Emir, as more than two-thirds of the MPs refused to reconvene. Consequently, new elections were scheduled for December 2012.

'We will not allow you!' Dignity of the Nation marches

Fearing the power of the tribal and Islamist forces on the ground it might not be a coincidence that the Emir resorted to electoral measures, in a logic of regime survival. On 13 October 2012, the Emir announced his intention to change by Emiri decree the election laws from four-votes-a-person to one-vote-a-person. While justified by the regime as a measure that would strengthen the 'democratic' nature of Kuwait's polity (as the one-vote-a-person system was the dominant one worldwide), the opposition considered the measure as sheer gerrymandering. The proposed decree clearly targeted the Islamist–tribal alliance that had been so effective in the landslide oppositional victory earlier, under which Islamists and tribesmen could support each other in campaigns, leading their electoral base to vote for each other's candidates.

The measure prompted the anger of the opposition, which started to raise its tone vis-à-vis the Al-Sabah in a series of demonstrations and public rallies that would break the implicit sanctity of the Emir, as opposition MPs started to direct their speeches directly at the person of the Emir. The opposition announced its boycott of the December elections as long as the new voting law would exist. It resulted in a series of mass demonstrations at Will Square and processions led by members of the defunct 2012 parliament under the guidance of Musallam al-Barrak. Meanwhile, government loyalists (mostly Shi'a and some liberals) supported the measure, divisions the regime was happy to exploit. In an unprecedented strong speech (15 October 2012) anticipating the law, Musallam al-Barrak addressed himself directly to the Emir: 'We will not allow your highness to take Kuwait into the abyss of autocracy ... We are not scared of your new batons or the jails you have built', hitherto branded in Kuwait as the '*lan nasmakh lek*' (we will not allow you) speech. This was the first of its kind in Kuwait, as the constitution prohibits criticizing the Emir. Apart from Al-Barrak, other members of the defunct 2012 parliament spoke in equally strong terms. These were Khaled al-Tahous, Falah al-Sawagh and Badr al-Dahoum; all tribesmen, two of them from the 'Awazem. This led the chieftain of the 'Awazem – Falah Ben Jama'a – to strengthen his voices against the regime, approving demonstrations he earlier disapproved of.[18] While the Constitutional Court ordered their arrest on charges of 'undermining the status of the Emir' (but later released them on bail as is so common in Kuwait), mass demonstrations continued and this time were organized in different locations and in the form of processions.[19]

During the months between October and December, relations between the regime and the opposition became overtly confrontational. Both parties used the constitution and constitutionalism in their discursive strategies vis-à-vis the public. The Emir appeared at various times on state television in speeches in which he – as often – played upon the threat of 'tribal and sectarian forces' undermining national unity and underlined that the regime would react strongly against those 'breaching the constitution'. In other speeches, government representatives said it had no choice but between 'chaos and applying the constitution'. Trying to give more credibility to his intentions, the Emir – inviting prominent Kuwaiti personalities – underscored that the Law would be applied to all Kuwaiti citizens, including members of the ruling family. Also, the usual paternalistic tone was applied in his speeches in which the Emir represents himself as a father figure who punishes his 'children' when needed, but also shows his clemency. Consequently, opposition members were liberated, referring to them as 'the children who were incarcerated'. From its part, the opposition also used the constitution as a justification for its actions. It opposed the electoral law out of respect for the constitution and said that only an acting parliament could vote on such a law. Meanwhile, constitutionalism – as we have seen – has been a prime referent in the speech acts of tribal MPs; mimicking the previous role played by *hadar* elites in this regard.

After the issuance of the Emiri decree (19 October 2012), the opposition bloc organized weekly gatherings as processions from Will Square (*Sahat al-Irada*) in front of parliament to Saif Palace (housing offices of the Emir, the CP and the PM). These marches were called the 'Dignity of the Nation' (*Karamat al-Watan*) marches, for which the 'Conscience of the Nation', Musallam al-Barrak, became the spiritual reference.[20] The aim of the marches was to annul the election law and convince people to boycott the elections. The first march on 20 October was organized from three different locations (Kuwaiti Towers, coastal area and Will Square) and gathered thousands of people. Although peaceful, marchers were harshly met by security forces as the Ministry of Interior had forbidden demonstrations to take place outside the circumscribed area of Will Square.[21] Despite the warning of the government that it would repress any marches, the second procession took place on 4 November, in the Mishrif area, and was equally met with teargas and stun grenades. The next day, the Emir appeared on television and reiterated his intention to continue with the electoral law. On 11 November, a new gathering was organized that took place simultaneously with the 50th anniversary of the Constitution of Kuwait. While the Emir was celebrating the anniversary of the Constitution, the opposition rallied with speeches focusing on its violations under Nasser al-Muhammad's government, branding the celebrations the 'celebrations of the death of the Constitution'.

Over time, a growing repressive stance of the regime impacted the opposition and contributed to the waning of mass mobilization, leading to a growing gap between opposition figures and their social base, largely young and tribal. Reasserted authoritarianism by the regime proved the only means to reduce political threat, as the more conventional strategies of soft-authoritarianism (resorting to intermediaries and divide-and-rule tactics) proved inefficient. In the midst of the crisis, the Emir also resorted to help from powerful allies, notably Saudi Arabia and Great Britain. For the first time in seventeen years, the Emir left for a five-day official visit to the UK, a move that was considered to gather the UK's support for the Al-Sabah in case of an escalation of the crisis. Saudi Arabia's role was largely manifested in growing attempts of coordination and union between GCC states.

Growing repression of dissent fitted in a larger GCC-coordinated initiative to crack down on any form of political dissent, in real life, but also in virtual public space. Internet and media freedom were significantly curtailed since 2012, with various news channels (temporarily) suspended and hundreds of Twitter activists arrested on charges of 'undermining the authority of the Emir', the Constitution or the royal system. A new media law known as the 'unified media law' was passed that specifically targeted social media.[22]

Growing repression also targeted the street demonstrators. At various times, the regime interdicted the gathering of more than twenty people (following in Bahrain's footsteps) and warned opposition to heavy-handedly crack down on unlicensed processions. As a consequence, the Dignity of the Nation marches slowly attracted less people, as the opposition was divided about whether or not to participate. Youth groups and the tribes largely supported the continuation of the marches, while some members of the opposition entered into dialogue with the government.[23] This led to a growing gap between the social base, largely tribal, and the semi-organized groups that saw their rise since 2012, such as the Front to Protect the Constitution (*Jabhat Himaya al-Dustur*) and the Majority Bloc (*Al-Kutla Al-Aghlabiyya*).[24] This became apparent during the fourth Dignity March, organized on the eve of the 1 December elections (30 November), that received a last-minute green light by the government, on the condition that it would be peaceful and take place between 3 and 5 pm, but attracted less people. Numbers would only decrease in subsequent marches.

December 2012 elections and the election boycotts

Given the opposition's rejection of the election law, the 1 December elections led to a rubber-stamp parliament of largely pro-regime MPs. The fourth and fifth districts almost entirely boycotted the elections, leaving some commentators to argue that it was a tribal boycott. Opposition leaders chanted that they would defend their dignity in a series of gatherings that celebrated the boycotts.[25] The large tribes – 'Awazem, Mutran and 'Ajman – had all boycotted the elections, together with a large number of Sunni Islamists (*Hadas, haraki* Salafis and independent Salafis).[26] The Rashaida tribe – known for its historical role of *fidawiyyin* –participated in the elections and had four seats in parliaments.[27] Given the larger tribes' boycott, smaller tribes fared relatively well. An example is the case of the Dhafir, who succeeded in having two seats, while it had been out of parliament since 1992 (with Ahmad al-Shari'an). The Shi'a and liberal-minded *hadar*, on the contrary, voted en masse in favour of the new law. This explains the unprecedented number of Shi'a in the December 2012 parliament that reached a record of seventeen MPs, a third of parliament, making cynics refer to it as the 'Iran majlis'. Contrary to their usual concentration of votes in the first district, this time they gained seats in each of the five districts, even in the tribal fourth and fifth, where their demographic presence is weak. The parliament also comprised a number of the candidates of the '*qabida*' scandal; accused of having received bribes under the government of Shaykh Nasser. Those Salafists who backed the government (purists) were awarded with a ministerial post: Minister of Awqaf and Justice. While the regime appointed tribal Ministers – as in the past – no Mutran minister was appointed, as this tribe formed the core of the opposition.[28]

The opposition continued its protests on the streets and in social media against the law and the parliament. Yet, over time these street protests waned in number and activism, a consequence of growing fissures within the opposition movement, as well as a certain fatigue of the social base. The sleep-in at Will Square organized just after the inauguration of the new parliament only gathered around 300 people, compared to the thousands present at the first demonstrations. Spontaneous night demonstrations of the youth in residential areas such as Kayfan, Fayha, Al-Jahra and Farwaniyya moreover were criticized by residents in the *hadar* areas. The sixth Dignity of the Nation march in the Sabah al-Nasser area – largely inhabited by the Mutran – also received much smaller crowds than previously. The seventh that took place in the tribal area of Sabahiyya – at which Musallam al-Barrak was present – was met with teargas and stun grenades.

The decision of the Constitutional Court (16 June 2013) to endorse the new voting law gave a lease of legitimacy to the Emir's decree despite the questionable autonomy of the Court. It revived the Dignity Marches – after a period of silence – with the organization of the eighth March under the slogan 'The people want to cleanse the judiciary'.[29] The march that was started at the Grand Mosque proceeded to the Palace of Justice, but met with strong violence from security forces. While the Constitutional Court endorsed the new voting law, it also annulled the reinstated 2009 parliament (that had been resurrected due to this very law) and called for new elections that were held on 27 July, the third legislative elections in a period of only seventeen months.

This time, the opposition was more divided about whether or not to boycott the elections. Members of the liberal Bloc of National Action (*Kutla al-'Amal al-Watani*) decided to participate this time, although it had been part of the anti-corruption movement since 2011.[30] The Salafi movement (*haraki*) and the political wing of the Ikhwan (*Hadas*) boycotted the elections. Meanwhile the purist stream of Salafism – the Salafi gathering – participated in elections, considering it an Islamic and national duty. This time there was a larger participation of tribesmen too.[31] As previously, the small tribes fared well and the role of the lineage (*fikhd*) rather than the tribe became more prominent. In the past, the big tribes all had four or five winners, now their lineage had two on average (leading some to conclude that politics has become even more tribal under the new law). The success of the small tribes was also the result of policies of co-optation by the regime preceding the elections in a logic of divide-and-rule. Having previously been marginalized by the large tribes in their constituencies, they now profited from the latter's boycotts and regime support. Smaller tribes, such as the Rashaida and the Dhafir, thus fared well, at the expense of the larger ones that boycotted the elections ('Ajman, Mutran). The 'Awazem decided largely to participate, contrary to previous elections, the result of a successful charm offensive of the Emir vis-à-vis the tribe and its vocal leader, Shaykh Falah Ben Jama'a. Also, given a stronger campaign of Sunni *hadar* groups in the first and second districts, the Shi'a this time lost seats and only won eight, which is their usual average number of seats in parliament.

Reasserted authoritarianism and Saudi regional leadership

As a result, the new parliament was also rather pro-government and able to pass many laws strengthening the regime. It validated the new one-vote-a-person system that had triggered the anti-regime demonstrations. It also passed a controversial media law –

'Unified Media Law' – that was proposed as early as April 2013 and endorsed by an outright majority in parliament in May 2014. The law however was widely slammed by the opposition and human rights activists, as it gave the regime considerable leeway to crack down on online dissent.[32] Vaguely termed, article 70 was particularly worrisome, allowing to incarcerate for up to two years and fine over $17.700 anyone who with 'any means of communication threatens, insults or harms the reputation of others'.[33] The law thus allowed the regime to prosecute Twitter activists that had been incarcerated widely since 2011 under a veneer of legality.

These crackdowns on civil liberties fit in a regional context in which Saudi Arabia has reasserted its leadership role within the GCC since 2003. Forced regime change in Iraq in 2003 strengthened the fear of a Shi'a crescent and Iranian regional influence, prompting Saudi support for anti-Iranian forces in countries such as Iraq and Yemen. The Arab Revolts of 2011 were another shock to the Saudi leadership and the GCC monarchies, fearing their spillover effect to the domestic context. Internally, repression of dissent was accompanied by the usual rentier gift-giving practices. Externally, the regime – together with the UAE – intervened in transitioning countries such as Egypt, Tunisia, Libya and Syria to support groups that were hostile to the MB. Frustrated with American inaction vis-à-vis Syria, Saudi Arabia (in parallel to Qatar) supported many Syrian 'rebel' groups with money and weapons that also reached jihadi groups.[34] Furthermore, it intensified its support for the poorer GCC states – Bahrain and Oman – via the establishment of a fund in which the richest GCC states help the two countries financially, essentially to buy social peace (pledging $10 billion over a decade for each).[35]

This reasserted regional role was accompanied with initiatives to strengthen the security, intelligence and defence coordination between GCC members. In this context, Saudi Arabia led the proposal to create a 'Common Defense and Security apparatus'.[36] In December 2013, GCC members decided to create a Unified Military Command structure to coordinate air, land and marine forces under one structure and strengthen the rather weak military structures of member states. The deployment of the Saudi-led Peninsula Shield Force in Bahrain was a clear manifestation of this GCC-coordinated military action. Another Saudi-led initiative is the 'GCC Security Pact'. The pact was initially signed in 1994 and endorsed by three of the six GCC states (Saudi Arabia, Bahrain and Oman; Qatar joined in 2009). Yet, on 14 November 2014, an amended version was presented and approved by the government of Kuwait, indicating its hardened stance vis-à-vis the opposition as it had previously refused to endorse it. The pact however has not been ratified by Kuwait's parliament and even pro-government MPs have been wary of it, as it would contradict certain clauses of Kuwait's constitution. Kuwait so far is the only GCC member that has failed to ratify it.[37] The pact would allow for the exchange of intelligence information (related to cyber criminality) and for the pursuit of wanted people regardless of their nationality that can be extradited to any GCC state asking for their extradition. Also, Kuwait could theoretically face a direct military intervention by a GCC neighbour in case GCC security was threatened, along the Bahraini model. Given these far-reaching powers undermining Kuwait's legislative privileges, the Kuwaiti public has so far refused the ratification of the security pact.

However, Kuwait's sole abstention from ratification made it subject to increasing pressures from Saudi Arabia. In general, Saudi Arabia has been wary of Kuwait's democratic experience and within Kuwaiti society it is widely known that Saudi Arabia has resorted to tacit diplomacy at various times to intervene when Kuwaiti politics became too vocal threatening its interests.

One such example was the organization of the Youth Renaissance Forum (*Multaqa al-Nahda al-Shababi*) that was cancelled last minute in 2012 by the Ministry of Interior, as Salafi groups and the Saudi government had purportedly put pressure on the Al-Sabah to cancel the forum fearing the vocal youth groups. The threat of the youth was not referred to officially and instead the argument was that the presence of radical members of a Hezbollah cell in the Hijaz explained the Saudi stance.[38] Similarly, Saudi Arabia was rather displeased with Shaykh Nasser al-Muhammad's (2006–11) government's stance vis-à-vis Iran and co-optation of its domestic Kuwaiti Shi'a. Both Saudi Arabia and the Bahraini media criticized in this regard Shi'a merchant Mahmud Haider – and so-called Kuwaiti offenders – for their unfavourable covering of the Saudi intervention in Bahrain in 2011.[39] Another example is the volte-face made by Salafi Muhammad Hayef (*Mutran*) in 2013 – who together with Obeid al-Wasmi – was lured by the Kuwaiti regime to depart from the oppositional bloc and engage in dialogue with the regime. According to my interlocutors, this was also the consequence of Saudi pressure, notably from the Wahhabi state 'ulema pressuring Hayef, himself an 'alim, to change his political line. The fact that he is from a new family, later naturalized, was further used by the Kuwaiti regime as a tool to pressure him (as it has done in other cases too).[40] Finally, a salient case was the volte-face of Shaykh Falah Ben Jama'a – chief of the 'Awazem – who after a charm offensive of the Emir convinced his tribe to participate in the elections and to even present a unified voice against the idea of a constitutional Emirate or elected government, arguing that this would be revolution against the state, a very different position from his previous role in the opposition movement (*Al-hirak*). In this context, the brother of Ben Jama'a – older in age – was invited by the Emir, a move supported by the Al-Saud, to come to Kuwait and pressure his brother to participate in the elections. The move was also a clear warning to Ben Jama'a and also an embarrassment, as the regime underlined Ben Jama'a's Saudi roots and the fact that he was only recently naturalized (and thus could easily bypass him by inviting his brother).[41]

Where Saudi Arabia has been the supporter of the pro-regime Sunni forces and has tried to exert its informal diplomacy vis-à-vis the Al-Sabah in the political crisis (2006–13), its regional rival Qatar has had a discrete role in supporting oppositional groups in Kuwait and often those that opposed the Saudi regime (such as *haraki* Salafis, the MB current and the various youth groups). This paralleled the royal feuds between Shaykh Nasser and Shaykh Ahmad al-Fahd, the latter reportedly being close to Qatar. While some of the accusations of foreign backing might be manipulation and disinformation, the various travels of opposition figures to Qatar during the crisis at least point to an influence of the Qatari regime on these domestic actors. Ahmad al-Sa'dun travelled regularly to Qatar and Tareq al-Mutairi – founding members of *Hadam* and leading youth activist – also often travelled to Qatar and to Turkey. Other allegations in the tabloid media – some sheer rumours – accused Musallam al-Barrak of having received money on his account from former Qatari PM Hamad Bin Jasim. The news was firmly denied by Doha, summoning the representative of the Kuwaiti tabloid and Scope TV for spreading false information.[42]

The demise of traditional intermediaries and reasserted authoritarianism

Leadership void among the *hadar*

Realizing the loss of political leadership within the *hadar* – and thus of effective channels of mediation – the regime tried to resurrect new leaders. This would also allow the regime to canalize a part of the *hadar* middle class towards political elites still loyal to the regime, to prevent them from switching to supporting the tribal MPs who have become so successful in the streets. One of the persons designated to take this role was Jasem al-Khorafi. Although from a merchant family, the Al-Khorafi family did not participate in the 1938 Majlis movement or earlier power-sharing agreements with the Al-Sabah; and is thus a family outside the inner Najdi 'asabiyya.[43] Al-Khorafi started as a Minister in 1986, but only became important as a speaker of parliament (1999–2011), benefitting from the patronage of Shaykh Sabah al-Ahmad al-Jabir. His proximity to the Emir and political role also made him close to Shaykh Nasser and his allies, mostly Shi'a and some liberals. Yet, Al-Khorafi never succeeded in becoming a new leader for the *hadar*, considered as too much a government client, and never played the community role that was assumed among Shi'a by Mahmud Haider, whose circles he also frequented. One of my interlocutors phrases it as follows:

> In 2009, when Nasser al-Muhammad allied with the Shi'a, the idea was the following ... the Sunna hadar have lost their political power over the people. They always used to represent a strong movement, with popular backing and had their symbols, Ahmad al-Khatib, Abdallah al-Nibari. But these have lost their popularity and this was realized. And no new leaders emerged within these Sunna hadar class constituencies. For this reason, the person of Jasem al-Khorafi appeared in politics. His father is "new", in the sense that he appeared in the 1960s. The Al-Khorafi family never had this old role in politics, like the merchants. He only became important as a speaker of parliament and had very good relations with Sabah al-Ahmad.[44]

The loss of leadership within the *hadar* community has been a topic raised by many of my interlocutors. Persons like Abdallah al-Nibari or Ahmad al-Khatib still have a symbolic power as historical leaders of the leftist and nationalist movements; however, they themselves cannot mobilize the streets anymore. This also became apparent during the Dignity of the Nation marches, in which some liberal groups participated. In case they called upon people to demonstrate, they only succeeded in gathering not more than around 100 people, whereas the tribal MPs were able to mobilize thousands.[45] This is also paraphrased by my interlocutor, Khaled al-Fadhala, youth activist, 'In the past, if Muhammad al-Saqqar (former head of the Kuwait Chamber of Commerce) said something, everyone was listening. Today, his impact is practically zero. Ten years ago, he still had an impact'.[46]

The Bahraini crisis emboldening regime patrons within the Shi'a community[47]

Another example of the decline in the utility of state-induced intermediaries is the case of Kuwaiti Shi'a. While co-opted by the regime, under the governments of Nasser al-Muhammad, they started to raise their voice which, according to Azoulay and Beaugrand, happened" during the 2011 Bahraini uprising and its violent repression by the Saudi-led GCC Peninsula Shield Force. Their reaction illustrated the limits of these sectarian-based policies and of personal co-optation. During the Mughniyeh crisis, the Shi'a, feeling threatened, rallied behind the government that offered protection. "Yet, witnessing the overt repression of their Bahraini coreligionists emboldened them – even those new intermediary elites closest to the royals – to use their power in the media and parliament to defend the cause of the Bahrainis, acting independently and *transgressing* the limits of the alliance. With identity politics becoming more important than the fear of a hostile political environment, the Shi'a took more vocal and less unified stances on the Bahraini crisis." The fact that they lost their major patron in government – since the resignation of Shaykh Nasser (23 November 2011) – gave them more leeway to voice independent political demands."

"At the start of the crisis in Bahrain, the then still acting government of Shaykh Nasser tried to maintain a certain distance from the crackdown in Bahrain and took a moderate stance, favouring a mediating role. It did so by sending a delegation of Kuwaiti notables (among whom the new Shi'ite merchants) as possible mediators between the Bahraini government and the opposition; because of 'their experience in dealing with the Shi'ite opposition in Kuwait'.[48] Among them were merchants Ali al-Matruk and Mahmud Haider, who had played a crucial role in appeasing the tensions in 2008 and brokered the rapprochement between *Al-Tahaluf* and the government. Another sign of its moderate stance within the GCC was the government's decision not to contribute troops to the Saudi-led force that on 14 March 2011 entered Bahrain to protect the 'Al-Khalifa monarchy. Though moderate by GCC standers, this drew criticism from the Kuwaiti Shi'a, even among the regime's most loyal clients. Concerns were also raised about the government's decision to send naval forces as part of the military intervention and as early as March 2011 Shi'ite MP Salah Ashur asked to question the Foreign Minister on this matter, while pointing to an end of the Shi'a–regime alliance in his speeches."

"During and after the fall of Nasser al-Muhammad, the merchants who had previously been instrumental in mediating between *Al-Tahaluf* and the government were raising support through their media outlets for the Bahraini Shi'a and their pro-Shi'ite voice. Mahmud Haider was the most prominent in this; his Al-Dar newspaper, although loyal to the Emir and the former PM, was suspended for the strong pro-Shi'a tone of its articles under reported pressure from the Saudi and Bahraini regimes. In February 2012, the newspaper's operations were ordered to cease for two weeks for creating sectarian strife. According to its editor-in-chief, the Ministry of Information had brought 133 cases against the newspaper, one of which led to a fine of 2000 KD for writing 'unfavourably' about the Saudi-led intervention. The Bahraini media had also launched a campaign against Haider and 'other Kuwaiti offenders' who were subsequently denied entry into the Kingdom."[49]

Again, one sees that the consent of the social base is crucial in understanding the utility of regime-endorsed elites as semi-intermediaries with broader constituencies. Patron–client ties always involve a sense of mutual obligations and interests, and the strengthening of sectarianism – coupled with the loss of their patron Shaykh Nasser – emboldened the Shi'a, even the state clients, to defend their interests. Though initially bolstered by the regime, elites such as Mahmud Haider over time developed a semi-community role which required them to defend the interests of their constituencies if they wanted to maintain their social position.

Failed attempts at recreating tribal intermediaries and reasserted authoritarianism

During the political crisis (2006–14), the Al-Sabah regime tried to reach out the tribes and regain the support of its important constituency. This was done by an attempt by the Emir and Al-Sabah members to revive the role of the old tribal chieftains, who had largely lost their power since the Invasion. The usual gift-giving strategies of co-optation were accompanied by divide-and-rule tactics, aimed at fragmenting tribes and the opposition movement. This carrot-and-stick approach took place in a wider regional context, with the regime resorting to its Saudi neighbour and transnational tribal allegiances as mechanisms of rule.

In this regard, the regime gave favours to tribal chieftains, trying to confer upon them the role of new intermediaries. As such, they became again the crucial figures with *wasta* to make regime services available, such as jobs, driver's licenses, medical care abroad or travels.[50] When these policies were revealed by famous 'Ajman commentator, Muhammad al-Washehi, on Al-Youm channel (a voice of tribesmen) – including alleged attempts by former PM Nasser to co-opt the tribes – the programme was taken off the air.[51] The provision of *wasta* was usually the domain of the tribal MPs, who were in the capacity to threaten the government or government officials with opening files of ministries (as they had access to these files via the clerks supporting the MP). Yet, their oppositional stance and boycott of the elections since 2012 made them lose this *wasta*, with the regime trying to confer this role upon the old chieftains. These chieftains were given a house, an enormous car, sometimes a plot of land and direct access to the Emiri Diwan. This was explained by my interlocutor, a professor at Kuwait University: 'So the tribal men once again find themselves in the necessity to go through the shaykh al-qabila, to go with the pro-regime shaykh and to bypass the "democratic shaykh" (referring to oppositional tribal leaders).'[52] In many cases however, these policies proved inefficient and only effective when the tribal leader showed a rather independent stance vis-à-vis the regime and could convince his tribesmen that he would first defend their interests, rather than being seen as a regime crony.

The only successful example of such a policy is the volte-face made by Shaykh Faisal Ben Jama'a – leader of the 'Awazem – since early 2013. Initially a staunch participant of the anti-corruption movement against the former PM, he changed his position in early 2013, when the Emir engaged in a charm offensive vis-à-vis the tribes to convince them to participate in the elections under the new voting system. A meeting with the Emir resulted in the granting of a large plot of land that was used by Ben Jama'a to build a new diwaniyya. Also, the brother of Ben Jama'a – Habeeb Ben Jama'a – was invited by the Emir from Saudi Arabia to put pressure on Falah to change his stance, a move supported by the Saudi regime. Following this, Ben Jama'a changed his discourse and supported the regime, although in a way that still showed some level of independence, as he complained about the marginalization of the tribe in various domains. In May 2013, he called upon members of his tribe to present a unified voice against the often-cited idea among the opposition of a 'Constitutional Emirate' and an 'Elected Government', considering it a revolt against the state. He also argued against political parties. Meanwhile, he expressed his resentment about the marginalization of the 'Awazem in leadership positions despite their 'noble history' in participating in wars in Kuwait for already 300 years and resented the fact that not even one school or street was named after his tribe.

When asking my tribal interlocutor about what made the tribe support Ben Jama'a he says:

> This was not because of the land they gave him … If the tribe had felt that he has received money from the government to change his position, then the tribe would not want him anymore. However, if they feel he has a point and supports their interests, then they will support him and this is what happened. He says he wants to give gains and profits to his tribe.[53]

The capacity to serve one's constituency has been frequently mentioned as a factor explaining the popularity and success of local elites and intermediaries vis-à-vis the regime. In a context of corruption scandals, local popularity goes to those leaders who show they are honest and want to serve their constituency (which also helps to explain the popularity of Salafi Shaykhs with their modest style).

The Emirs of the Mutran, the 'Ajman and the Rashaida have, however, proved rather weak as leaders of their tribes and my interviews with these chieftains pointed to their general loss of power. Many of them criticized the young generation and the fact that today their diwaniyyas were not frequented anymore as before and that Twitter and the mobile phones have come to substitute the more personal contacts between them.[54] Between 2012 and 2013, newspaper articles were full of references to dinners and meetings organized between tribal heads and the Emir, PM and CP. In the context of the new election law of one-vote-a-person, the Emir received the tribal heads, who tended to express their support for the law and for 'baba' Emir. In this context, the leader of the Mutran said that he was in favour of the electoral law and that it would lead to stronger social justice.[55] However, the Mutran have become largely oppositional to the regime and do not really listen to their shaykh, who has merely become a symbolic figure incapable of mobilizing his tribesmen. Musallam al-Barrak has become the uncontested Mutran leader. Each time Al-Barrak was arrested, masses of Mutran gathered to demonstrate against the regime, some even carrying their own machine guns and, in some cases, called upon members of the Mutran in Saudi Arabia to join their ranks in a call for tribal disobedience (*Tanga*).[56]

Given the widespread opposition from the Mutran, the regime had also tried to co-opt this tribe's members, sometimes via the creation of new elites. An example in point is the new merchant Saud Sahoud al-Mutairi. He was active in real estate and construction and had profited from regime patronage in the private sector. One of the few prominent tribal merchants, he had increased his role in community affairs, yet remained still mostly a merchant lacking strong social support. During the crisis with the opposition and the Mutran in 2013, he organized a celebration in honour of the Mutran in Kuwait, Saudi Arabia and the region; entitled 'Mutran ... the red caretakers'.[57] It was a huge celebration and the first of its sort in the whole Gulf region that was attended by Western diplomats. During the gathering, promises were made to create an investment fund for the tribe, with the Emir of the Mutran in Saudi Arabia saying it would contribute 400,000 Saudi riyal each year to the fund to remove any form of poverty among the tribe. Conferring upon him this role of semi-notable was in the interest of the regime. Yet, it could not appease the movement led by Musallam al-Barrak.

Now what can we conclude from these examples? While the regime continues its paternalist modes and still views society in terms of its classical ascriptive categories (*badu/hadar*/Shi'a), society seems increasingly in search of new ways to fill the void of political leadership and representation. Regime-endorsed elites have been largely rejected by the tribal social base that searches for new leaders that can represent its demands, including a fairer inclusion into the nation state, better access to its resources and an end to the privileged position of the *hadar* in the private sector. Where it worked – such as in the case of the Shi'a in 2008 – this was only possible because of the consent of the Shi'a that the best option was to support the regime in the face of what was perceived as a hostile society. Old leadership and authority patterns have been disintegrating and the youth is in search of new leaders and identities to fill this void. Some have been disappointed with their leaders – even with some of the opposition leaders – who have displayed a tendency for opportunism whenever the regime extends a hand to them. One can think here of the accusations against Mutran opposition figures, such as Muhammad Hayef or Obeid al-Wasmi, who entered in 2013 in dialogue with the regime and whose oppositional stance was therefore considered as compromised by the tribesmen they represented.

As to the regime, it has found it increasingly difficult to have effective channels of communication and interaction with society and therefore has resorted to more overt repression, departing from its usual 'soft-authoritarianism'. One of the most powerful measures it resorted to was the stripping of nationality of protestors and those opposing the government. Such measures were a powerful message to others and to the families of the protestors to end their opposition to the government. Citizenship is granted through inheritance rather than birth, thus many relatives were also denaturalized as a consequence of these measures. Many of such crackdowns and the stripping of citizenship happened in 2014 during the heydays of the protest movement.[58] Revoking citizenship was justified by the regime on claims of 'undermining the country's security and stability, bringing harm to institutions' by invoking article 13 of Kuwait's Nationality Law 15/1959 that says that under certain circumstances and in case of the undermining of the 'social or economic system of the country or belonging to a foreign political party' citizenship may be revoked.[59] It has been reported that between 2014 and 2016 at least 120 people were arbitrarily deprived of their nationality and it remains unclear today how many individuals remain without nationality and how many have been stripped of their nationality since 2016.[60] As Nationality Law was promulgated before the Constitution, the Al-Sabah's stance is that nationality is a sovereign matter and no referral to court is possible, therefore giving it leeway to use it rather arbitrarily towards political dissidents.

These citizenship revocations included protestors but also aimed public figures active in the opposition movement. Owner of Al-Yawm TV and newspaper (Ahmad al-Shammari) lost his citizenship as his newspaper had a vocal role in the publication of the alleged coup attempt against the monarchy. Not soon after protests flared up in the summer of 2014 the spokesman of Musallam al-Barrak, Sa'd al-'Ajmi, was stripped of his nationality along with dozens of others.[61] Furthermore Musallam al-Barrak was sentenced to prison for his critical comments on the Emir during the Dignity of the Nation marches and served a two-year sentence from which he was released in April 2017. Not soon after he was sentenced again to seven years in prison for 'using force and inciting unrest' for his role in the storming of parliament (*iqtiham al-majlis*) in 2011 and he handed himself to authorities after a short self-exile in Saudi Arabia.[62] After an initial acquittal Kuwait's appeal court sentenced in 2017 Al-Barrak along with dozens of others to prison sentences of one to five years in prison.[63] To avoid serving his prison sentence, Al-Barrak fled to Turkey in 2018, which has reduced his direct influence in society.

With these sentences the prominent symbols of the tribal–Islamist opposition have been incarcerated, sending a clear message to political activists and symbols of the opposition not to overstep the boundaries in criticizing the Al-Sabah. Tougher media laws such as a cyber crime law (passed in 2016) have restricted the freedom of the press. Combined with electoral law changes all these measures have contributed to the weakening of the opposition movement. Many of those who had boycotted elections since the 2012 change in election law participated in the November 2016 elections. Contrary to expectations, however, opposition figures managed to win nearly half of the seats in parliament converging in their opposition to austerity and corruption. Austerity measures were widely resented by Kuwait's public. The withdrawal of gas subsidies and salary cuts in 2016 represented a significant retrenchment, triggering a backlash in parliament and a revival of the country's labour movement through a series of strikes by workers in the state oil company union.[64]

Having lost its capacity to exercise soft-power control over its population during the 2011–14 political crisis, the government has resorted to more overt forms of repression ever since to still the tribal–Islamist opposition movement that reveals deeper societal change. Practices such as vote rigging, the co-optation via intermediary elites and gerrymandering have either failed or backfired. Failing to address the root causes of the opposition's frustration however might lead to a greater political impasse for the decades to come. It is only by modernizing and renegotiating its monarchical pact to allow for a more equal distribution of resources and representation that a new social contract can be negotiated that draws upon the acceptance of broad strata of society.

The Royal aura of respectability erodes, the Emir intervenes

One of the aspects I consider crucial for regime resilience is the coherence of the regime's 'asabiyya; meaning its capacity to act as one bloc and maintain a certain balance between competing regime elites by monopolizing or dominating the highest state offices. This argument was coined by Michael Herb in his book *All in the Family*, in which he considers this capacity of dynastic rule as one of the reasons as to why monarchical rule in the Middle East is resilient. In Khaldunian terms this refers to 'those with tribal solidarity lead' (*Al-ri'asa fi ahl al-'asabiyya*).[65] Yet, in Kuwait the royals' aura of respectability has been threatened, a result of the infighting between royals that has become public and sets Kuwait apart from other GCC states where – with the partial exception of Bahrain – palace politics remain hidden. Consequently, not only the institutional equilibrium of the Emirate, but in fine the reputation (*hiba*) of the Family was affected.

The princely feuds between Shaykh Ahmad al-Fahd and Shaykh Nasser al-Muhammad with mutual accusations of corruption scandals and their escalation in the alleged coup attempts "revealed the degree to which intra-family struggles had expanded out of the family council. Parliament was brought into the picture and with it the press and the judiciary". As a result of the tapes scandal about the alleged plot pointing fingers at Shaykh Nasser, "two opposition newspapers, *Al-Watan* and *'Alem al-Youm*, were closed down. The judiciary had to step in to arbitrate in the matter".[66]

The culmination of the opposition movement demonstrated the erosion of the Al-Sabah's reputation. Until today this is revealed in multiple interpellations that do not shun to target Al-Sabah members. "The Emir's status of being 'immune and inviolable' (art. 54 Constitution)" was challenged in the Dignity of the Nation marches whose spokesmen have been arrested for offending the Emir. "Shaykh Sabah gradually appeared as a partisan if not divisive figure – along with other Al-Sabah princes – and despite his calls for unity."[67]

As a consequence of both growing societal opposition and the escalation of royal infighting – intersecting with the first – the Emir stepped in and disciplined dissident voices within the Al-Sabah. It argued that the law would be applied to all citizens, including members of the royal family. Shaykh Ahmad al-Fahd was sidelined facing various legal proceedings in connection with corruption scandals that have embroiled the International Football Association and presented a public apology on state TV in 2015 in which he said that he had been 'misinformed' and does not anymore leverage MPs as he once did.

This reasserted grip on both society and the royal family has contributed to the return of a fragile political calm in Kuwait. The Emir disciplined vocal and dissident members of the royal family who faced prison sentences thereby sending a message that the law would apply to everyone including dissident shaykhs.[68] Ahmad al-Fahd lost much of his power as his support of oppositional MPs made him lose the sympathy of the Emir, the CP and other powerful members within the family.[69]

Yet, the question of succession looms with an Emir who reached 90 and is in frail health. CP Shaykh Nawaf is in his eighties and rather uncontested as a choice for Emir, although his old age might lead him to only serve for a short term. Also, there are chances that given Shaykh Nawaf's easy-going personality, real politics might fall in the hands of other powerful members within the Al-Sabah. With Shaykh Nasser al-Muhammad's and Ahmad al-Fahd's reputation were tarnished due to their divisive role during the political crisis and with Jaber al-Mubarak being from the minor Al-Hamad branch, there might be a stronger role envisioned for the oldest son of the Emir in the future of the country, Shaykh Nasser al-Sabah. Shaykh Nasser al-Sabah was catapulted into his first top government job in December 2017, appointed by his father as deputy PM and Minister of Defence after having served a decade as Minister of Emiri Diwan Affairs (2006–17) during which he developed a reputation for his business-like approach to development by reviving the Silk Road through greater trade and investment with Asia and bringing to completion major construction and infrastructure projects. He embodies the will to diversify Kuwait's economy and leads the Supreme Council for Planning and Development (SCPM) which is invested with the execution and implementation of Kuwait's Vision 2035 initiative. However, Shaykh Nasser al-Sabah's role in steering economic reforms might make it difficult for him to build political alliances as measures such as austerity are resented by the broader public.

It is therefore still unclear how the future reshuffling of cards within the Al-Sabah will proceed, although it will be crucial to maintain coherence in the ruling family in order to guide the country as one bloc through its much-needed economic reform process. During the tense interlude of intra-family struggles (2006–12) the ruling elite's 'asabiyya was weakened, contributing to its loss of social control over different groups in society. The cross-cutting dimension of opposition from society towards austerity and high-level corruption however makes it more complicated for power contenders to draw upon sufficient support within parliament and might favour those who are less inclined to push for such painful reforms, slowing down Kuwait's transitioning towards a knowledge economy in which costly measures such as taxation will have to be compensated with growing public accountability and representation.

Conclusion

Since the unfolding of the Arab revolts in 2011, we have witnessed the rise and revolts of marginalized communities at the periphery of power everywhere in the MENA region. Kuwait too has witnessed since the start of the millennium the rise of its periphery, its naturalized tribesmen, latecomers to the nation's fabric.

The core argument of this book is that the support of the periphery is the condition without which Arab authoritarianism cannot survive. The periphery has been broadly defined, referring to rural and tribal communities as well as to minorities in the context of hybrid authoritarian and specifically Arab regimes. The support of the periphery is crucial to such non-inclusive regimes, as it is more prone to patronage politics. This is not as much the consequence of the less 'modern' nature of these constituencies, but more of their relative marginalization vis-à-vis the political centre, creating a greater need for intermediaries in the deliverance of services and having stronger group solidarities as a consequence of a lesser and later exposure to the forces of globalization.

The legacy of the lineage mode has made the Arab regimes – and particularly the Arabian monarchies – prone to this logic of relying on non-core groups outside the tribal ruling 'asabiyya. Yet, it also applies to hybrid authoritarian regimes that basically rely on more dependent, less politicized forces to govern against the more independent, urban forces that tend to be the carriers of political ideologies and movements and incubators of opposition. This argument was placed in its broader regional context of distinct political trajectories of Arab regimes – the military-backed republics and the traditional monarchies. It shows the legacy of early state-building in understanding the position of social elites and their role within the regime's patronage networks. Although tangential to the core argument, the monarchies relied on the periphery without much social engineering, while traditional elites where dethroned in the republics constrained by populist ideologies. The first chapter demonstrated tentatively how the neoliberalizing Arab republics lost the crucial support of their peripheries, with disintegrating patronage networks, and how the Arab revolts were started from the periphery.

I argue that two factors are crucial in understanding the salience of hybrid authoritarian regimes or their fragmentation and correspond to Ibn Khaldun's theory on the lifecycle of dynasties. The first factor is the internal cohesion of ruling elites – the regime's 'asabiyya and capacity to act as one bloc. The second relates to the ties between the ruling elite and the periphery: the ruling elite relying on the support of the periphery – as clients and followers. Pointing to these crucial factors in upholding the regime's 'asabiyya, this book also argued that the nature of globalization since the 1990s uprooted existing hierarchies in the periphery and led to the rise of the periphery that was the last and minimal remaining support structure upon which Arab authoritarians rely. These forces of globalization were felt strongest in the periphery, exactly because these communities were governed by strict hierarchies and codes of conduct, consequently leading to strong generational divides and the uprootedness of a young generation. It is the tragedy of this anomic youth frustrated about its future in our interconnected world which is the main driver of political change in the decades to come in the region.

This argument provided the analytical framework to apprehend the empirics: a case study of political order and development in Kuwait, since its inception until 2018. Part One provided a historical account of the fundamentals of the Al-Sabah's authority structure in Kuwait, analysed through the prism of the ruling elite's relations with the traditional social categories of the pre-oil community, living both within and outside the walls of the old city, namely the *hadar* (urban dwellers), Shi'a and *badu* population. Emphasis was laid on the impact of socio-economic transformations that went along with the rise of British direct interest in Kuwait and changed the authority system since the mid-nineteenth century. It explicitly provided an alternative reading of Kuwait's modern political history, by focusing on the role played by *non-core* elites in Kuwait's pre-oil community, i.e. elites outside the in-group of the Sunni Najdi aristocracy. The role of these elites as clients of the Al-Sabah – as was the case of the Shi'a *'Ajam* merchants – is indicative of the high degree of stratification within the group of Kuwaiti merchants, a factor that has been overlooked in existing literature on pre-oil Kuwait.[1] This segmentation along identity and occupational lines played a key role in consolidating an authoritarian shaykhdom, first in 1896 and later with the discovery of oil.

I demonstrated how a *hadar* narrative of a pre-oil political community dominates Kuwait's foundation myth and nationhood, as well as the academic literature. In these accounts, the history of the Shi'a and the role of the desert tribes in the high politics of pre-national times are downplayed. It also showed how what used to be a tribal shaykhdom in which the ruler acted as primus inter pares over a plural society (where real power lay with the Najdi merchants) was transformed into an authoritarian shaykhdom under Mubarak al-Sabah. It revealed how the British supported the coup of Mubarak against his half-brothers to advance their interests in the region against the Ottomans and their allies (such as the Emirate of Al-Ha'il). Small rulers such as Mubarak profited from this, flirting with foreign powers to avoid absorption by a great Islamic power. As tribalism determined relations of production and power, these regional dynamics strengthened existing fault lines in Kuwaiti society and favoured alliance-building with the non-core groups: Shi'a and the tribesmen. British economic penetration curtailed the independent power of the indigenous Najdi merchants, who had developed into autonomous forces of production. The Shi'a merchants were not similarly affected, as their ethnicity and sect had excluded them from the lucrative business of pearling. This, coupled with the Sunni identity of the Ottoman

Empire, had made them allies of Mubarak and the British, while the Najdi merchants embraced Arab nationalism against the authoritarian ruler and his tutelary backers. Not surprisingly, the Shi'a merchants would be instrumental in signing the Protection Agreement (1899) and sided with the ruler during the outbreak of nationalist agitation in 1938. Meanwhile, Mubarak allied with tribesmen, who helped him in seizing the throne in 1896 as subservient guardians of the Al-Sabah shaykhs. In 1938, Ahmad al-Jabir resorted to these private tribal guardians – *fidawiyyin* – to crush the movement. Consequently, the 1938 *Majlis* events where the Najdi merchants revolted against the ruler and pleaded for Kuwait's annexation by Iraq marked the crystallization of the Al-Sabah's alliance-building strategies with non-core elites. This dimension of alliances with non-core elites has been overlooked in existing literature, but would lay the basis for contemporary regime relations with these groups.

Part Two of this book analysed regime–ruled relations in Kuwait following independence and its consolidation into an oil state until the Invasion (1961–90). It demonstrated how Kuwait's liberal *Sonderweg* was the consequence of an involuntary condition, the repeated threats of Iraqi irredentism. It also demonstrated how the Al-Sabah regime used its oil wealth in a segmented way to reproduce pre-oil elite linkages and stratification patterns. As the major threat in this period still stemmed from the *hadar* elite, rulers resorted to the co-optation of contending groups and ideologies. As such, Sunni Islamism was supported and this study underlined the social foundations of this current. It demonstrated how second-tier elite strata from outside the Najdi aristocracy (e.g. Qina'at) or lower to middle class pre-oil *hadar* groups (e.g. Persian Sunni merchants) composed the bulk of the early *hadar* elite of Sunni Islamist movements. The support for Sunni Islamism coincided with the political naturalizations of thousands of southern tribesmen by the Al-Sabah regime since the 1960s to counterbalance the *hadar* opposition. The Islamist current was particularly successful in tribal areas, where it proved to be an important resource for the socio-political emancipation of young tribesmen. Yet, until the Invasion Islamists and tribesmen still remained rather supportive of the regime and the status quo upon which Kuwait's political order was built was not challenged: an elite bargain between the merchants and the Al-Sabah, in which the masses are upgraded as state-dependent middle-class actors but do not challenge the prerogatives of this inclusive elite. The regime's violent crackdown of Monday diwaniyya gatherings in the tribal zones in 1989 proved an effective deterrent warning the *badu* not to join the *hadar* in their movement protesting the dissolution of parliament. Then still effective, a similar display of force in 2008 would not quieten the tribesmen, who had now become the core of the opposition.

Part Three analysed the rise of the tribal periphery in politics in Kuwait from the Invasion until roughly 2018. It contends that this period has led to a fragmentation of the two components of regime 'asabiyya: the coherence of the ruling elite and its ties to the periphery. The first trend is the rise of a young generation of *badu* in search of new modes of politics and better access to state resources; breaking away from previous clientelist modes of rule that were based upon traditional tribal hierarchies mediated via elites as service deputies. New forces of globalization and its communication revolution played a crucial role in empowering this young tribal generation, just as everywhere in the region. The second trend has been the rise in elite rivalry since 2006 as a consequence of the breaking of the implicit rotation of power with the coronation of Sabah al-Ahmad as Emir. This move opened a Pandora's Box for ambitious princes to struck alliances in society and parliament in the hope to be able to aspire to the throne one day as article 4 of the constitution stipulates that the Emir's choice of CP needs to be approved by an absolute majority in parliament. As a consequence, parliament has been an important leverage for princes in their bid for succession.

In 2014 a global decline in oil prices led to a budget shortfall with major ramifications in Kuwait. This combined with a growing youth population has compelled the regime to introduce austerity measures and to gradually reform its economy away from oil dependency. Austerity measures such as cuts in fuel subsidies and wages sparked outrage in parliament and society as these measures added fuel to the fire for Kuwaitis who have become increasingly dissatisfied with deficiencies in welfare distribution which many attribute to the misuse of public money more than to dwindling state resources. Parliament so far has contributed to the slowing down of much-needed reforms to diversify and privatize the economy and strengthen the private sector. This frustration cuts across sect and the important *hadar–badu* cleavage, marking the start of a social struggle which presents a real challenge for the regime as it directly attacks the privileges of an oligarchic urban elite in the private sector; an alliance upon which the Al-Sabah's authority was built.

Increasingly incapable of controlling its restless periphery via the co-optation of its elites and gift-giving during the 2011–14 crisis, the regime resorted to more repressive methods to deal with societal opposition. New media laws, incarcerations and the arbitrary revocations of citizenship of political activists stripped the movement of its leadership and sent a strong signal to others not to overstep the boundaries of their criticism of the Al-Sabah. Failing to address the root causes of the opposition's frustration however might lead to a greater political impasse for the decades to come. It is only by modernizing and renegotiating its monarchical pact to allow for a more equal distribution of resources and representation that a new social contract can be negotiated that draws upon the acceptance of broad strata of society. This would imply the opening up of the private sector to competition with new entrants, the growing participation of Kuwaiti citizens in private sector jobs who would have to be taught the technical skills required for such jobs and accept more competitive salaries based upon performance rather than privilege. In order to accept such sacrifices including cuts in subsidies and the introduction of taxation, citizens would like to see something in return: transparency, public accountability and representation; central themes of the opposition movement which reflects deeper social change with calls from a large group in society – notably those with the least access to state patronage, its *badu* citizens – to find new modes of politics and representation based upon a modern state of law and institutions rather than networks of privilege. Such a renegotiation of the social contract is only possible if both regime and society will accept the painful concessions they have to make while securing Kuwait's survival through the modernization of its monarchical pact (absolute parliamentary regime, an elected government from the ranks of a parliamentary majority).

Surrounded by a rather divided and volatile regional environment with powerful neighbours – notably Saudi Arabia – Kuwait's independent future depends much on the capacity of the Al-Sabah to successfully renegotiate social pact with their citizens, thereby upholding its authority firmly in a region of strong, influential neighbours and power blocs (Saudi Arabia/UAE; Qatar/Turkey; Iran) vying for regional influence.

Notes

Introduction

1   Observations of a nineteenth-century British naval officer Slade on the modern Middle East. See Lewis, B., *Notes on a century: reflections of a Middle East historian*, New York: Penguin Group, 2012.

2   Abd al-Rahman Ibn Khaldun, *Muqaddimah (Introduction to history)*, Beirut: Centre of Arab Unity Studies, 1369/1983, pp. 119, 120, 147.

3   Herb, M., *All in the family: absolutism, revolution and democracy in the Middle Eastern monarchies*, New York, State University of New York Press, 1999, p. 235.

4   Ibid., p. 235.

5   Ibid., p. 9.

6   Tönnies, F., *Community and society: Gemeinschaft und Gesellschaft*, translated and edited by C. P. Loomis, Michigan: Michigan State University Press, 1957.

7   Scott, J., 'Patron-client politics and political change in Southeast Asia', *The American Political Science Review*, Vol. 66, No. 1 (1 March 1972).

8   Erdmann and Engel, 'Neo-patrimonialism revisited: beyond a catch-all concept', GIGA working paper 16, Hamburg, 2016.

9   Al-Nakib, F., 'Revisiting Hadar and Badu in Kuwait: Citizenship, Housing and the Construction of a Dichotomy', *International Journal of Middle East Studies* 46/1, Feb. 2014.

10 Moore, B., *The social origins of dictatorship and democracy: lord and peasant in the making of the modern world*, Boston, MA: Beacon Press, 1966, pp. 420–426.

11 See Batatu, H., *Syria's peasantry: the descendants of its lesser rural notables and their politics*, Princeton, NJ: Princeton University Press, 1999. Also see Batatu, H., *The old social classes and the revolutionary movement in Iraq*, Princeton, NJ: Princeton University Press, 1978.

12 Ayubi, N., *Overstating the Arab State: politics and society in the Middle East*, London: I.B. Tauris, 1995, p.121.

13 Remy Leveau in his classic work on rural elites in Morocco and their relation to the Palace considers the support of the rural periphery as the 'groupe stabilisateur' limiting the expansion of the urban bourgeoisie. Leveau, R., *Le fellah marocain: défenseur du trône*, Presses de la Fondation Nationale des Sciences Politiques, 1976.

14 An example is the Party for Authenticity and Development (PAM) that was created by the regime as a party essentially relying on rural notables, reacting to earlier failed regime strategies to rely on old leftist intellectuals (in a landscape of local notables). Boussaid, F., 'The rise of the PAM in Morocco: tramping political scene or stumbling into it?', *Mediterranean Politics*, Vol. 14, No. 3, pp. 413–419.

15 This corresponds to the theory of relative deprivation. Ted Robert, G., *Why Men Rebel*, Princeton, NJ: Princeton University Press, 1970.

16 King, S., *The new authoritarianism in the Middle East and North Africa*, Bloomington: Indiana University Press, 2009.

17   Binder, L., *In a moment of enthusiasm: political power and the second stratum in Egypt*, Chicago, IL: Chicago University Press, 1978.

18   Al-Khalaf, S., 'Shaykhs, peasants and party comrades: political change in northern Syria', in Mundy and Musallam (eds), *The transformation of society in the Arab East*, Cambridge: Cambridge University Press, 2000. The author analyses the case of the Meshrif family – a rural elite family of shaykhly descent – that was able to reinsert itself into the Ba'ath system and produce many of its local elites, notably a consequence of the high level of education of its younger members.

19   Hinnebusch, R., *Authoritarian power and state formation in Ba'athist Syria: army, party and peasants*, San Francisco, CA: Westview Press, 1990.

20   See Dukhan, H., 'Tribes and tribalism in the Syrian uprising', *Syria Studies Journal*, Vol. 6, No. 2 (2014), p. 5. The regime called for the assistance of some tribes (especially the Hadidiyin) in the countryside of Hama to check the flow of guns from Iraq to Hama and to prevent the Muslim Brotherhood members fleeing to the desert.

21   As a consequence of the building of the Euphrates Dam, many tribesmen from Al-Raqqa Governorate were encouraged to settle in the northeast in Kurdish lands to challenge the status quo of the region that was historically inhabited by a Kurdish majority. Since 1982, tribal representation in Syria increased from 7 per cent to 10 per cent and Bedouins started to occupy important posts in the Ministries of Interior and Agriculture and certain branches of the security apparatus. Bashar al-Assad relied on tribal clients to suppress the Kurdish uprising in 2003.

22   Wolf, E., *Peasant wars of the 20th century*, Norman: University of Oklahoma Press, 1969, p. 282. Wolf considers Western capitalism as the main cause behind the social dislocations in the countryside that preceded peasant-led revolutions. This would create more exploitative relations between peasants and their landlords and tribal chiefs. Meanwhile, it created opportunities for new elites (political brokers, intellectuals, credit merchants). Out of this transitional situation did peasant revolutions emerge.

23   Mulderig, M., 'An uncertain future: youth frustration and the Arab Spring', *The Pardee Papers*, No. 16 (April 2013).

24   In comparison, population growth in India in this period was 290 million (34 per cent), in Europe 26 million (5 per cent) and in China 92 million (17 per cent). See IEA (OECD/World Bank), *Population 1971–2010*, 2010, p. 89.

25   In 2005, 73.3 per cent of the deputies entered for the first time the People's Assembly and only 40 per cent of them had previous experience serving in the Consultative Council or in a local popular council. In 2000, 70 per cent of the deputies were new, whereas this number was only 45 per cent in 1995. It was the consequence of the grand failure of former PND deputies to have themselves re-elected – a symptom of the fragmentation of existing notabilities. Patrick Haenni demonstrates how this phenomenon relates to the growing independence of 'intermediaries' and their autonomization in his analysis of the suburb of Inbaba adjacent to Cairo. Vannetzel, M., *Freres eligibles: etude de la mobilisation electorale islamiste en Egypte: le cas des elections leigslatives de 2005'*, MPhil thesis, Sciences Po Paris, 2006–07, p. 67.

26   For a comparative overview of the hollowing out of populist coalitions of Arab republics, see King, *The new authoritarianism in the Middle East and North Africa*. The author analyses how structural adjustment policies favoured the creation of rent-seeking urban and rural economic elites and a state bourgeoisie seeking their fortunes by entering into the private sector. The author – who wrote the book in 2009 – only failed to draw the important implications of this phenomenon in terms of the fragmentation of these regimes. Instead, he focused on how economic

liberalization led to a new form of authoritarianism, in the then popular literature of so-called authoritarian resilience.

27　See Dukhan, 'Tribes and tribalism in the Syrian uprising'.

28　His appointment followed the assassination of his predecessor – on 18 July 2012 – Dawood Rajiha in a car bombing in Damascus.

29　http://world.time.com/2012/10/10/syrias-tribes-will-rise-again-an-exiled-chief-remains-unbowed/#ixzz2C8Wp8mCs. (accessed 20 February 2020). Also see Dukhan, 'Tribes and tribalism in the Syrian uprising', p. 11.

30　The political and social marginalization of tribesmen since the access to power of the Ba'ath regime was according to Syrian researcher Haian Dukhan a major impetus for creating enough support among displaced tribesmen in Syria's most resistant cities to organize an activist network (relying on tribal networks) as part of the protest movement. The Baba Amr district that was heavily bombed by the Syrian regime was mainly inhabited by tribesmen who had organized a mass anti-Assad protest.

31　http://www.syriadeeply.org/articles/2014/10/6299/hassan-hassan-uproot-isis-deir-ezzor/ (accessed 19 September 2019). Also see Azoulay, R., 'Islamic State franchising: tribes, transnational jihadi networks and generational shifts', *Clingendael, Netherlands Institute of International Relations*, CRU Report (April 2015).

32　For more on the rural and agricultural roots of the Tunisian revolution, Gana, A., 'The rural and agricultural roots of the Tunisian revolution', *International Journal of Sociology of Agriculture and Food*, Vol. 19, No. 2 (2015), pp. 201–213.

33　Krugman, P., *The role of geography in development*. Paper prepared for the Annual World Bank Conference on Development Economics, Washington, DC, April 1998, pp. 20–21.

34　https://www.aljazeera.com/indepth/opinion/sudan-protests-people-revolution-led-periphery-190127061619964.html (accessed 1 November 2019).

35　Skocpol, T., 'What makes peasants revolutionary?', Review article, *Comparative Politics*, Vol. 14, No. 2 (April 1982), p. 358.

36　Moore, *Social origins of dictatorship and democracy*.

37　Migdal, J., *Peasants, politics and revolution: pressures toward political and social change in the third world*, Princeton, NJ: Princeton University Press, 1974; Scott, J., 'Hegemony and the peasantry', *Politics and Society*, Vol. 7, No. 3 (1977), pp. 267–296; Wolf, *Peasant wars of the Twentieth Century*; Paige, J., *Agrarian revolution: social movements and export agriculture in the underdeveloped world*, New York: Free Press, 1975.

38　See Skocpol, 'What makes peasants revolutionary?', p. 353.

39　Skocpol, T., *States and social revolutions: a comparative analysis of France, Russia and China*, Cambridge: Cambridge University Press, 1979.

40　Other conditions would be dependent on the capacity for collective action by peasants. This itself depends upon inter-peasant relations, local class relations and the degree of communalism of peasant communities.

41　See Skocpol, 'What makes peasants revolutionary?', p. 368.

42　Lerner, D., *The passing of traditional society*, New York: Glencoe, 1958; Levy, M., *Modernization and the structure of societies: a setting for international affairs*, Princeton, NJ: Princeton University Press, 1965; Inkeles, A., 'The modernization of man', in M. Weiner (ed.), *Modernization: the dynamics of growth*, New York: Basic Books, 1966, pp. 138–150. Also see Eisenstadt's study on social change and modernization in developing countries: Eisenstadt, S., *Tradition, change and modernity*, New York: Wiley, 1973.

43　The Ba'ath Party was explicitly modernist and Arab nationalist in its agenda and sought to create a modern, totalitarian party-state that mirrored the Soviet Union and would supplant ethnic leadership, tribal chiefs and religious orders and implement policies along a developmentalist-nationalist agenda.

44 In his study, Faleh al-Jabir demonstrates how the Ba'ath regime in a logic of 'etatist tribalism' incorporated tribes into its institutions and especially military and policing institutions by integrating them into the highest state ranks. The favoured clan groups gained access to family 'asabiyyas, as a result of growing competition over oil-derived state wealth. Al-Jabir, F., 'Shaykhs and ideologues: detribalization and retribalization in Iraq: 1968–1998', *Middle East Report*, No. 215 (Summer 2000), p. 30.

45 Family continuity can be observed in both Syria and Iraq. Khalaf, S. 'Shaykhs, Peasants and Party Comrades: Political Change in Northern Syria', in *Arab Society: class, gender, power and development* (eds. Hopkins, N. and Ibrahim S.E.), New York, the American University in Cairo Press, 2006, pp. 311–325. For the case of Iraq, see Baram, A., 'Neo-tribalism in Iraq: Saddam Hussayn's tribal policies 1991–1996', *IJMES*, Vol. 29, No. 1 (February 1997), p. 4. Baram notes that more than half of the families who were regarded as tribal elites in the 1990s were the same as those who were regarded as such in the 1950s.

46 For more on the rehabilitation of the tribal shaykh, see Baram, 'Neo-tribalism in Iraq'.

47 Al-'Ajmi, A., 'A nomadic logic; an intellectual image: divergent meanings on the concept of the state in Kuwait' (unpublished working paper).

48 Leveau, R., *Le fellah marocain, défenseur du trône*, Presses de la Fondation Nationale des Sciences Politiques, 1985.

49 As argued by Hammoudi, the tenets and ritual practices of Islam are paramount in peasant life and thus leave little room for a coherent system of ideas and concepts. Hammoudi, A., *Master and discipline: the cultural foundations of Moroccan authoritarianism*, Chicago, IL: University of Chicago Press, 1998, p. 41. The author – an anthropologist – argues that the politics of notables are engrained in Morocco's political culture and thus likely to last for some time.

50 Liddell, J., 'Notables, clientelism and the politics of change in Morocco', *The Journal of North African Studies*, Vol. 15, No. 3 (September 2010). Also see Barwig, A., 'The new Palace guards: elections and elites in Morocco and Jordan', *The Middle East Journal*, Vol. 66, No. 3 (Summer 2012).

51 Bergh, S., 'Inclusive neoliberalism, local governance reforms and the redeployment of state power: the case of the national initiative for human development (INDH) in Morocco', *Mediterranean Politics*, Vol. 17, No. 3 (October 2012). The author argues that neoliberal reforms increased the power of the regime, mediated via local (appointed) regime elites and at the cost of local public accountability.

52 The Moroccan political landscape is characterized by a relatively high degree of ideological flexibility of local elites that change parties rather easily dependent upon their interests. Also, in general the focus within parties is more upon charismatic leaders rather than ideological programme as part of parties' electoral strategies. See Liddell, 'Notables, clientelism and the politics of change in Morocco'.

53 Lucas, R. E., *Institutions and the politics of survival in Jordan: domestic responses to external challenges*, New York: SUNY Series, 2012, p. 21. Also see Massad's interesting discussion of the role of tribes in Jordan's state- and nation-building: Massad, J., *Colonial effects: the making of national identity in Jordan*, New York: Colombia University Press, 2001.

54 In November 2009, the government established a particular system dividing electoral districts in 'zones' composed of undefined sub-districts. This strengthened the local support structure of candidates. Earlier in 1993 the regime had introduced a one-vote system that naturally led to the selection of those candidates with the highest vote totals. And in 2012, the monarchy introduced a new electoral law of a mixed

system to allow for greater representation for some constituencies, preserving the parliament as the domain of traditional elites. Ryan, C., 'The implications of Jordan's new electoral law', *Foreign Policy* (13 April 2012).

Part I

Chapter 1

1   Abu Hakima, *The modern history of Kuwait 1750–1965*, London: Luzac, 1983. Also see Rush, A., *Al-Sabah: history and genealogy of Kuwait's ruling family 1752–1987*, London: Ithaca Press, 1987.

2   Various authors have used system theory as a heuristic tool for understanding processes of social change. See, for example, Bailey, G. *Strategems and spoils*, New York: Schocken Books, 1969, p. 10; Boudon, R., *La logique du social*, Paris: Haschette, 1997.

3   See Crystal and others. See Ayubi, *Overstating the Arab State*, p. 231. See Peterson, J. E., 'Tribes and politics in Eastern Arabia', Middle East Journal, Vol. 31, No. 3 (Summer 1977), pp. 297–312.

4   Beaugrand, C., Statelessness and transnationalism in Northern Arabia: Biduns and state-building in Kuwait (1959–2009), LSE, PhD thesis, 2010, p. 87.

5   Ibid.

6   Al-Mazeini, A., *Ansab: al-usar wa al-qaba'il fi al-kuwayt (Lineage: the families and the tribes of Kuwait)*, Dat al-Salasil, 1994, pp. 202–205. Also see https://wikileaks.org/cable/1989/08/89KUWAIT3922.html (accessed 20 February 2020)

7   Since this current combines legal reasoning with the insistence on *mystical illumination* as guidance towards salvation, shaykhism has been criticized by traditional *Usuli* scholars who consider it to be a deviant sect of Shi'ism. Cole, J. R., 'Shaykh Ahmad al-Ahsa'i on the sources of religious authority', in L. S. Walbridge (ed.), *The most learned of the Shi'a: the institution of the Marja' Taqlid*, Oxford: Oxford University Press, 2001.

8   The first shaykhi marja' who settled in Kuwait was Mirza 'Ali al-Ihqaqi, who left the shaykhi community in Al-Hasa because of a conflict with local ulema. Until today, the descendants of Mirza 'Ali al-Ihqaqi live in Kuwait and continue to lead the religious affairs of the community.

9   *Akhbari* scholars reject the *Usuli* current that considers the deductive reasoning (*'aql*) and the consensus (*'ijma*) of the mujtaheds as legitimate sources for elaborating Islamic law and complementing the Quran and the Akhbar.

10 The term 'serf tribes' refers to the fact that these tribes were landless and were grazing on the territory of other tribes, in this case the 'Ajman and Mutran: both noble Arabian tribes.

11 Al-Nakib, F., 'Revisiting Hadar and Badu in Kuwait: Citizenship, Housing and the Construction of a Dichotomy', *International Journal of Middle East Studies 46/1*, Feb. 2014.

12 Beaugrand, C., Statelessness and transnationalism in Northern Arabia: Biduns and state-building in Kuwait (1959–2009), LSE, PhD thesis, 2010, p. 135.

13 As quoted in Beaugrand (2010), p. 137. Assiri estimates the rise in citizens between 1965 to 1980 to be from 220000 to 680000. Ghabra calculates the number for this period to reach 220000. Assiri, A., The government and the politics in Kuwait: principles and practices, Kuwait, Al-Watan Printing Press, 1996, p. 139. Ghabra, S., 'Kuwait and the dynamics of socio-economic change', Middle East Journal, Vol. 51, No. 3, Summer 1997, p. 364.

14   Beaugrand, C., Statelessness and transnationalism in Northern Arabia: Biduns and state-building in Kuwait (1959–2009), LSE, PhD thesis, 2010, p. 137.

15   Beaugrand, C., Statelessness and transnationalism in Northern Arabia: Biduns and state-building in Kuwait (1959–2009), LSE, PhD thesis, 2009, p. 137.

16   Al-Nakib, F., 'Revisiting hadar and badu in Kuwait: citizenship, housing and the construction of a dichotomy', *IJMES*, Vol. 46 (2014), pp. 5–30.

17   Beaugrand, C., Statelessness and transnationalism in Northern Arabia: Biduns and state-building in Kuwait (1959–2009), LSE, PhD thesis, 2010, p. 137.

18   Interview with an old Shi'a member of the Tarakma community, Kuwait City, April 2009.

19   Ismail, J., *Kuwait: social change in historical perspective*J., Syracuse: Syracuse University Press, 1982, p. 23.

20   Crystal, J., *Oil and politics in the Gulf: rulers and merchants in Kuwait and Qatar*, Cambridge: Cambridge University Press, 1992, p. 20. Also see Beaugrand, *Stateless and transnationalism in Northern Arabia*, pp. 92–101. Beaugrand discusses the role of the tribes in the high politics of pre-oil Kuwait, as their alliances would determine the cause of regional wars, whilst the merchants were the moneylenders.

21   As Ismail already remarks, there is very little to document as to the Al-Sabah's role in the caravan trade, and references are made to it only tangentially. An example is Al-Rushaid, *Tarikh al-Kuwayt (History of Kuwait)*, pp. 54 and 121. Abu Hakima, *History of Eastern Arabia: The Rise and Development of Bahrain and Kuwait*, notes the wealth of the Al-Sabah, probably a consequence of zakat income from the caravan trade. Ismail, *Kuwait: social change*, p. 27.

22   Crystal, J., *Oil and politics in the Gulf: rulers and merchants in Kuwait and Qatar*, Cambridge: Cambridge University Press, 1992, p. 20.

23   Al-Ebraheem, H. A., *Kuwait: a political study*, p. 25. Also see Rush, *Al-Sabah: History and genealogy of Kuwait's ruling family: 1752–1987*, p. 2; Crystal, *Oil and politics in the Gulf*.

24   Lorimer, J.G., *Gazetteer of the Persian Gulf, Oman and Central Arabia*, Vol. I, pt. 1B, p. 1006.

25   Ismail, *Kuwait: social change*, p. 22.

26   Ismail, *Kuwait: social change*, p. 23. Khaz'al, *Tarikh al-Kuwait al-siyasi (Political history of Kuwait)*, 1922, Vol. I, p. 42.

27   Crystal, *Oil and politics in the Gulf*, p. 22.

28   Peterson, J. E., 'The nature of succession in the Gulf', *The Middle East Journal*, Vol. 55, No. 4 (Autumn 2001), pp. 586–589.

29   Moore, P., *Doing business in the Middle East: politics and economic crisis in Jordan and Kuwait*, Cambridge: Cambridge University Press, 2004; Carter, J., *Merchant families of Kuwait*, London: Scorpion Books, 1984.

30   Ismail, *Kuwait: social change*, p. 35. Following the pact between the Al-Saud and Muhammad Bin Abd al-Wahhab in 1744, the Al-Saud were able to expand their territory considerably, as Wahhabism provided the religious legitimacy for their tribal conquests, becoming an 'ideology of conquest'. In 1792, the Saudi Emirate expanded its territory by unifying Central Arabia and conquering parts of Eastern Arabia, Hijaz and even Bahrain which they controlled for a few years (1810–11). The smaller coastal emirates, like Kuwait were spared absorption by the Saudis only by establishing protection agreements with the British.

31   Khaz'al, *Tarikh al-Kuwait al-siyasi*, p. 35. Khaz'al notes four crucial moments in the hijra of Najdi merchants to Kuwait: 1676, 1748, 1767 and 1775.

32   Ibid.

33   These merchants imported goods from the desert hinterland (Najd, Jabal Shammar, but also in the north on the route to Zubayr and Basra), while they would export notably dates from date plantations in Iraq and since 1890 thrived on the smuggling of arms

for the desert hinterland. Import consisted of cloths, rice, sugar and tobacco, while the export (apart from some desert products) was essentially centered around dates. Beaugrand (2010), p. 91.

34   Khaz'al, H.K. Al-Shaykh, *Tarikh al-kuwayt al-siyasi*, Vol. I, p. 154; Salame, G., 'Small is pluralistic' (p. 140) also refers to Yusuf al-Ibrahim as a "meteque" (foreigner) who was not part of the 'asabiyya of Bani Utub founding fathers, but had acquired his 'citizenship' and political influence on account of his wealth, allowing him also intermarriages with the daughters of the Al-Sabah.

35   The Shi'a were engaged in this activity in Kuwait.

36   Ismail, *Kuwait: social change*, p. 20/21. See Aarts, Eisenloeffel, G. and Termeulen, J., 'Oil, money and participation: Kuwait's *Sonderweg* as a rentier state', *Orient*, Vol. 32, No. 2 (June 1991), p. 210.

37   Ismail, *Kuwait: social change*, p. 21.

38   Interview, Walid al-Nusf, Kuwait, April 2009. Various other interviews confirmed this perception.

39   'Al-nukhba al-tijariyya. Dhamir al-Kuwait al-tarikhi' (The merchant elite. Conscience of historical Kuwait), *Al-Zaman*, 34, Kuwait, 29 May 1999.

40   Lorimer, J. G., *Gazetteer of the Persian Gulf, Oman and Central Arabia*, Vol. I: *Historical*, Calcutta: Superintendent Government Printing, 1915.

41   Abu Hakima, A., *History of Kuwait*, Kuwait: Kuwait Government Press, 1967/1970.

42   Salame, G., 'Small is pluralistic: democracy as an instrument of civil peace', in G. Salame (ed.), *Democracy without democrats? The renewal of politics in the Muslim World*, p. 84–111. London: I.B. Taurus, 1994.

43   The prime values characterizing the classic polis are solidarity, unity, participation, political deliberation and highly restricted citizenship. Held, D., 'The Exclusivity of Ancient Democracy', in Models of Democracy, Stanford, Stanford University Press, 2006, pp. 19-23.

44   Beaugrand, C., Statelessness and transnationalism in Northern Arabia: Biduns and state-building in Kuwait (1959–2009), LSE, PhD thesis, 2010, p. 89.

45   Pure Arab blood refers in popular parlance to the Qahtanites; those Arabs who originate from the southern region of the Arabian Peninsula, especially from Yemen. They oppose to Adnanites, the Arabized Arabs who descended from Adnan. This classification continues to play a role in social stratification in the region.

46   Crystal, *Oil and politics in the Gulf*.

47   https://wikileaks.org/cable/1989/08/89KUWAIT3922.html (accessed 19 September 2019).

48   Personal interviews with the heads of the families, Kuwait City, April 2009.

49   Claire Beaugrand makes this argument in her Ph.D. analyzing the historical role played by tribes in the high politics of the region. Beaugrand, C., Statelessness and transnationalism in Northern Arabia: Biduns and state-building in Kuwait (1959–2009), LSE, PhD thesis, 2010, pp. 92–101.

50   These families were the self-appointed members of the twelve-member consultative council of 1921 following the death of Salim al-Mubarak. While its immediate goal was to forestall factionalism within the Al-Sabah over succession, its broader goal was to restore the political influence of the merchant elite.

51   Khuri, F., *Tribe and state in Bahrain*, Chicago, IL: University of Chicago Press, 1980, p. 2.

52   Various interviews with members of the Shi'a merchant elite, Kuwait, March/April 2009 and Kuwait 2012/2013.

53   Other tribes considered 'arib dar were the 'Adawin, Hawajir, Sb'an (Sbay'i) and the Suhul – the Suhul mostly worked as ironmongers and smiths. Beaugrand, C.,

Statelessness and transnationalism in Northern Arabia: Biduns and state-building in Kuwait (1959–2009), LSE, PhD thesis, 2010, pp. 88–89.

54 Ibid.

55 Al-Rasheed, M., *Politics in an Arabian oasis*, London: I.B. Tauris, 1997, pp. 17, 117.

56 Al-Shamlan, *Pearling in the Arabian Gulf*, p. 108.

57 Beaugrand, C., *Statelessness and transnationalism in Northern Arabia*, pp. 91–92. Al-Rasheed, M. -Rasheed, M. Politics in an Arabian Oasis: the Rashidis of Saudi Arabia. London: I.B. Tauris, 1991.

58 Beaugrand, C., *Statelessness and transnationalism in Northern Arabia*, p. 96.

59 Beaugrand, C., *Statelessness and transnationalism in Northern Arabia: Biduns and state-building in Kuwait* (1959–2009), LSE, PhD thesis, 2010, pp 96–97.

60 Al-Shamlan, *Pearling in the Arabian Gulf*, p. 59.

Chapter 2

1 Al-Rasheed, *Politics in an Arabian oasis*, p. 117.

2 Beaugrand, *Statelessness and transnationalism in Northern Arabia*, p. 123.

3 Hourani, A., 'Ottoman reform and the politics of notables', in W. Polk and R. L. Chambers (eds), *Beginnings of modernization in the Middle East in the 19th century*, Chicago, IL: University of Chicago Press, 1968, pp.

4 Shaul Yanai explicitly compares the political transformation in these three tribal states from the perspective of the role played by the commercial elites in the early phases of state-building and parliamentary politics. See Yanai, S., *The political transformation of the Gulf tribal states: elitism and the social contract in Kuwait, Bahrain and Dubai: 1918–1970*, Sussex: Sussex Academic Press, 2014.

5 Crystal, *Oil and politics in the Gulf*.

6 Segal, E., 'Merchant networks in Kuwait: the story of Yusuf al-Marzuk', *Middle Eastern Studies*, Vol. 45, No. 5 (September 2009), p. 711.

7 Interview with Ahmad Bin Barjas, Kuwait City, March 2014.

8 Nakash, Y., *Reaching for power: the Shi'a in the modern world*, Princeton, NJ: Princeton University Press, 2006, p. 57.

9 Ibid.

10 Fromherz, A., *Qatar: a modern history*, Washington, DC: Georgetown University Press, 2013, p. 118.

11 In Oman, for example, during Sultan Said Bin Taimur's rule until the 1970s, tribal shaykhs acted as political intermediaries on behalf of communities, while the role of the 'walis' appointed by the ruler was often sidelined by the much more effective power of the tribal shaykhs. In Saudi Arabia, the Rashaida dynasty in Ha'il was a powerful opposition to the Al-Saud and could only be 'encapsulated' by the latter after the discovery of oil, making it difficult for tribal leaders to compete with the hydrocarbon state for the loyalty of followers.

12 Potter, L., *The Persian Gulf in modern times: people, ports and history*, New York: Palgrave Macmillan, 2014.

13 Khuri, *Tribe and state in Bahrain*, p. 197.

14 This is a quote by anthropologist, Furnivall, when describing the type of society he found in European colonies of Southeast Asia before the Second World War. See Furnivall, J., *Colonial policy and practice*, Cambridge: Cambridge University Press, p. 304. Also see Longva, *Walls built on sand: migration, exclusion and society in*

Kuwait, New York: Routledge, 1997. Longva alludes to the importance of pluralism for understanding Kuwait.

15 Longva, *Walls built on sand*, p. 6.
16 See Hakima, *The modern history of Kuwait 1750–1965*.
17 See Khaz'al, who explicitly names the Al-'Awazem and the al-Rashaida as two separate neighbourhoods. Khaz'al, p. 17.
18 Khuri, *Tribe and state in Bahrain*, p. 80.
19 Beaugrand, C., *Statelessness and transnationalism in Northern Arabia*, p.87.
20 Interview, Hassan Jowhar, Al-Da'iyya, March 2009.
21 Various interviews with Dr Sami al-Khalidi, February–March 2014.
22 Fuccaro, Nelida (2005) 'Mapping the Transnational Community: Persians and the Space of the City in Bahrain, c. 1869-1937.' In: Al-Rasheed, M., (ed.), Transnational Connections and the Arab Gulf. Routledge, p. 45.
23 *Khaz'al, Tarikh al-kuwait*, p. 37.
24 Among the important farij of the Al-Wasat neighbourhood, one finds farij al-Qina'i, farij al-shuyukh (referring to the Al-Sabah), farij al-Adsani, as well as the farjan of some of the original tribes present in Kuwait, such as farij al-Rashaida, farij al-'Awazem and farij al-'Anza. http://www.kuwait-history.net/vb/showthread.php?t=3076 (accessed 16 February 2017).
25 http://www.alqenaei.net/, http://www.ansab-online.com/phpBB2/showthread.php?549-%D3%C4%C7%E1-%DA%E4-%DA%E6%C7%C6%E1-%C7%E1%DE%E4%C7%DA%C7%CA-%BF (accessed 19 September 2019).
26 http://wikileaks.org/cable/1989/08/89KUWAIT3922.html (accessed 20 September 2019).
27 http://www.alqabas.com.kw/node/176414 (accessed 20 September 2019).
28 http://www.kuwait-history.net/vb/showthread.php?t=4880 (accessed 19 September 2019).
29 Beaugrand, *Statelessness and transnationalism in Northern Arabia*, p. 122.
30 Ibid., p. 135.
31 Ibid, p. 88.
32 Al-Haddad, *The effect of detribalization and sedentarization*, p. 44.
33 Beaugrand, C., *Statelessness and transnationalism in Northern Arabia*, pp. 88–89.
34 Bin Barjas, A., *Al-'Awazem: Khilal Elf Sanat (The 'awazem during 1000 years)*, Kuwait, Maktaba al-'Ajeiri, p. 69.
35 Dickson, H.R.P., *Kuwait and Her Neighbors*, London, 1956, p.51.
36 The Batin plain was located to the south of Kuwait; in the Kuwaiti desert that represented the end of many caravan trade routes, from Najd, Jabal al-Shammar, but also from northern Basra and Zubayr. See Beaugrand, *Statelessness and transnationalism in Northern Arabia*, p. 91.
37 Bin Barjas, *Al-'Awazem*, p. 68.
38 Lorimer, J. G., *Gazetteer of the Persian Gulf, Oman and Central Arabia*, Vol. 2, London: Archive Editions, 1986.
39 Beaugrand, C., *Statelessness and transnationalism in Northern Arabia*, p.121.
40 Bin Barjas, *Al-'Awazem*, p. 71.
41 Ibid. Also see Wikileaks cable https://wikileaks.org/plusd/cables/09KUWAIT244_a.html (accessed 20 September 2019).
42 Kuwait, Maktaba Afaq, 2013, p. 88.
43 Ibid.
44 Lorimer, *Gazetteer*, p. 188.
45 Ibid., p. 188.

46 Beaugrand, *Statelessness and transnationalism in Northern Arabia*, p. 93. Also see personal interview with Mubarak al-Duwaila. Also see personal interview with Mubarak al-Duwaila, Kuwait City, March 2014.

47 These were the Awna, Muhaymazat, Ajarma, Siyad. See Al-Muzaini, *Ansab: al-Usur wa al-Qabail fi al-Kuwayt*, p. 97.

48 Ibid., p. 95, http://www.alaan.cc/pagedetails.asp?nid=44662&cid=30 (accessed 21 September 2019).

49 http://www.sudaneseonline.com/aarticle2005/nov26-98927.shtml (accessed 19 September 2019)

50 http://www.nationalkuwait.com/forum/index.php?threads/96070/ (accessed 19 September 2019).

51 http://www.annaharkw.com/annahar/Article.aspx?id=305154 (accessed 12 March 2018). Also see Gavrieldes, N., 'Tribal democracy: the anatomy of parliamentary elections in Kuwait', in L. Layne (ed.), *Elections in the Middle East: implications of recent trends*, Boulder, CO: Westview Press, 1987, pp. 187–213.

52 One can think of the Al-Wazzan and Al-Qattan families who lived in Al-Murqab.

53 Beaugrand, C., *Statelessness and transnationalism in Northern Arabia*, p. 89.

54 Al-Mazeini, *Ansab: al-usar wa al-qaba'il fi al-Kuwayt*, p. 171.

55 Beaugrand, C., *Statelessness and transnationalism in Northern Arabia*, p.135. Also see: Ebrahim, *Problems of nomadic settlement in the Middle East with a special reference to Saudi Arabia and the Haradh project*, p. 66.

56 Beaugrand, *Statelessness and transnationalism in Northern Arabia*, p. 201.

Chapter 3

1 Tetrault, *M., Stories of Democracy: Politics and Society in Contemporary Kuwait*, Columbia, Columbia University Press, 2000.

2 One can think of the extensive biography of Slot, B. J., *Mubarak al-Sabah: founder of modern Kuwait (1896–1915)*, London: Arabian Publishing, 2005. Also see Anscombe, F., *The Ottoman Gulf The creation of Kuwait, Saudi Arabia and Qatar*, New York: Columbia University Press, 1997. And see the biography by Al-Ghanim, S., *The reign of Mubarak al-Sabah: Shaykh of Kuwait 1896–1915*, London: Bloomsbury, 1998.

3 Onley, J., 'British informal empire in the Gulf: 1820–1971', *Journal of Social Affairs*, Vol. 22, No. 87 (Fall 2005).

4 Ibid. Also see Kelly, J. B., *Britain and the Persian Gulf: 1795–1880*, New York: Oxford University Press, 1968.

5 Shanavaz, S., *Britain and Southwest Persia 1880–1914: a study in imperialism and economic dependence*, London: Routledge Curzon, 2005, p. 145. Ali Salman, I. M., *Hukm Shaykh Khaz'al fi Ahwaz 1897–1925 (The reign of Shaykh Khaz'al in Ahwaz)*, Baghdad: Maktaba Dar al-Kendi. http://www.arabistan.org/books/alsheekh_khazaal.pdf

6 Ibid.

7 Khaz'al's possessions in Iraq on the banks of the Shatt al-'Arab were so considerable that the number of his tenants on Iraqi soil amounted to around 30,000 families or individuals. See Shanavaz, *Britain and Southwest Persia 1880–1914*, p. 143.

8 http://www.alqabas.com.kw/node/742195 (accessed 19 September 2019).

9 Al-Ghanim, *The reign of Mubarak al-Sabah*, p. 3.

10 Slot, *Mubarak al-Sabah*, p. 65, p. 100.

11 Ibid., p. 65.

12 Among the notables who assembled in Yusuf al-Ibrahim's house to plead for Mubarak's cause were Sayyid Khalaf Pasha al-Naqeeb, Fahad al-Khalid, Sulayman Abdel Jalil, Fahad al-Duwirij and Abdel Aziz al-Sumayt. See Al-Rushaid, *Tarikh al-Kuwayt*, p. 140.

13 Ibid., p. 75.

14 Ismail, *Kuwait: social change in historical perspective*, p. 35.

15 See Khaz'al, H. K. Shaykh, *Tarikh al-Kuwayt al-Siyasi (the political history of Kuwait)*, 1922, Vol. I, p. 35.

16 Ismail, *Kuwait: social change*, p. 35. Following the pact between the Al-Saud and Muhammad Bin Abd al-Wahhab in 1744, the Al-Saud were able to expand their territory considerably, as Wahhabism provided the religious legitimacy for their tribal conquests. In 1792, the Saudi Emirate expanded its territory by unifying Central Arabia and conquering parts of Eastern Arabia, Hijaz and even Bahrain which they controlled for a few years (1810–11). The smaller coastal emirates, like Kuwait, were spared absorption by the Saudis only by establishing protection agreements with the British.

17 The report of the French consul in Bagdad (4 June 1896) refers to Muhammed's alleged alienation of the tribes and his ambitions to confer power exclusively upon his branch of the family.

18 Khaz'al, *Tarikh al-Kuwayt al-siyasi*, pp. 146–147. Lorimer, *Gazetteer*, p. 1016 and Anscombe, F., *Ottoman Gulf*, p. 93.

19 Al-Nakib, F., 'The lost two-thirds: Kuwait's territorial decline between 1913 and 1922', *Journal of Arabian Studies*, Vol. 2, No. 1 (June 2012), p. 3. In 1892, a branch of the Al-Mutran attacked Kuwait and the same year Muhammed asked Mubarak al-Sabah to militarily support a Dhafir leader against a rivalling leader within his tribe. And in 1894, Kuwait was attacked by members of the Bani Hajir, apparently a retaliation for a raid in which the tribe had lost livestock and men.

20 Slot , *Mubarak al-Sabah*, p. 172. By the 1890s, Arabia was under the domination of the Al-Rashid of Jabal Shammar. The Emirate was established in 1836 and was led by a tribal elite in Najd that relied exclusively upon the support of the Al-Shammar tribe. The leaders had strong independent power, but were close to the Ottomans and very hostile to British encroachment and their local trustees, Mubarak and later the Al-Saud.

21 See Slot, *Mubarak al-Sabah*, p. 84.

22 See Slot in his description of Dickson's account of Muhammad al-Sabah, Slot, *Mubarak al-Sabah*, p. 62. Also see Khaz'al, Vol. I, p. 152.

23 Lorimer, *Gazetteer*, p. 1290 (Section: Mutran).

24 Personal interviews Kuwait City, February–March 2014. Interviews with historian, author and specialist of tribal affairs, Ahmad Ben Barjas, Kuwait City, February 2014.

25 Ibid.

26 Lorimer, *Gazetteer*, p. 1291 (Section: Mutran).

27 Al-Ghanim, *The reign of Mubarak al-Sabah*, p. 87.

28 Al-Ghanim, *The reign of Mubarak al-Sabah*, p. 1.

29 Slot, *Mubarak al-Sabah*, p. 172.

30 'Rakan Bin Huthlayn settled in Kuwait asking for British protection against the Al-Rashid and incited Mubarak to kill his brothers and usurp power, which happened in 1896. And he was among the strongest agitators inciting Mubarak to fight against the Ibn Rashid, who threatened Bin Huthlayn with a raid if he wouldn't stop inciting Mubarak against them.' Personal interview, Ahmad-Bin Barjas, Kuwait City, October 2014.

31 Beaugrand, C., *Statelessness and transnationalism in Northern Arabia*, pp. 96–97.

32   Beaugrand, *Statelessness and transnationalism in Northern Arabia,* pp. 96–97.

33   Interview with Mubarak al-Duwaila, March 2012, Kuwait City.

34   Khaz'al, Vol. I, p. 160.

35   These sons were Saud and Sabah Bin Muhammad and Hamud Bin Jarrah. They asked the *wali* of Basra, Hamdi Pasha, for help. Yet, the latter was reluctant to help and Mubarak had the support from the commander-in-chief of the Ottoman Empire, the far more powerful *Mushir* of Baghdad.

36   Khaz'al, Vol. I, p. 162.

37   Slot, *Mubarak al-Sabah,* p. 78.

38   Khaz'ali, S., *al-jama'at al-Kuwaytiyya al-siyasiya fi qarn al-jadid 1910–2007 (the Kuwaiti political groups in the new century 1910–2007),* Kuwait: Dar al-Qurtas, p. 321. Also see Jamal, A. M., *Lamahat min Tarikh al-Shi'a fi al-Kuwayt (remarks on the history of the Shi'a in Kuwait),* Kuwait: Dar al-anba li-l nashr wa tawzi', 2005.

39   Jamal, *Lamahat min tarikh al-Shi'a fi al-kuwayt (min nashat al-Kuwayt ila al-istiqlal),* p. 71.

40   Husayniyya refers to a congregation hall for Shi'a religious ceremonies, particularly those that are associated with the remembrance of the month of Muharram, in which the Shi'a commemorate the martyrdom of Imam Hussayn in Karbala in 680 AD, on the day of Ashura.

41   See Salih, K. O., 'The 1938 Kuwait legislative Council', *Middle Eastern Studies,* Vol. 28, No. 1 (January 1992), p. 98.

42   Louër, L., *Transnational Shia Politics: Religious and Political Networks in the Gulf,* Columbia, Columbia University Press, 2008, p. 62.

43   Salih, 'The 1938 Kuwait legislative Council', p. 86.

44   Slot, *Mubarak al-Sabah,* p. 275, also see pp. 275–286.

45   http://www.alqabas.com.kw/Articles.aspx?ArticleID=769266&CatID=567 (accessed 19 September 2019).

Chapter 4

1   I.e. Crystal, *Oil and politics in the Gulf;* Carter, *Merchant families of Kuwait;* Moore, P., *Doing business in the Middle East: politics and economic crisis in Kuwait and Jordan,* Cambridge: Cambridge University Press, 2009.

2   Ismail (1982), p. 68. Moore, *Doing business in the Middle East,* p. 38.

3   Ismail (1982), p. 75.

4   Ibid.

5   Crystal, *Oil and politics in the Gulf;* Carter, *Merchant families of Kuwait;* Moore, *Doing business in the Middle East.*

6   Interviews with historian Ahmad Bin Barjas, specialist and historian of tribal Gulf history, Kuwait City, April 2012.

7   Interview with Ahmad Bin Barjas, Kuwait City, April 2014.

8   Khuri, *Tribe and state in Bahrain,* p. 80.

9   Personal interview, Kuwait City, March 2009.

10 Jamal *Lamahat min tarikh al-Shi'a fi al-kuwayt (min nashat al-Kuwayt ila al-istiqlal),* p. 45. Personal interview with Al-Wazzan elders, Kuwait City, April 2009.

11 Personal interview with Jasem Qabazard, Kuwait City, April 2009.

12 Personal interview with Al-Kadhemi family (Zaid al-Kadhemi and his grandson), March 2009.

13   https://wikileaks.org/cable/1989/08/89KUWAIT3922.html (accessed 19 September 2019).
14   One can think here of the families that were elected for the pre-parliamentary
     councils in 1921 and 1938, such as the Al-Marzuq, Al-Khudayr, Al-Saqqar, Al-Adsani,
     Al-Ghanim, Al-Humaidi, Al-Khamis, Al-Uthman and Al-Hilal. At the time of the
     merchant agitation, they were in their twenties and thirties and formed a politicized
     youth. For more information on their background, see Rush, A., *Records of Kuwait
     1899–1961*, Internal Affairs: Cambridge Archive Editions, 1989, pp. 266–267.
15   Tribal relations were an important factor in these merchants' regional ties. A case in
     mind is Hilal al-Mutairi, one of the wealthiest pearl merchants in Kuwait's history
     who had close relations to leaders in Najd and the leader of the Ikhwan rebellion,
     Faisal al-Duwaish, both belonging to the same tribal section of the Al-Mutran tribe.
     Gazetteer of Arabian Tribes, Vol. 10 Mutair-Qumarah: Archive Editions, p. 212.
16   Personal interview with tribal affairs historian Ahmad Bin Barjas, Kuwait City,
     February 2014.
17   This itself was the result of the difficult Interbellum period in which trade with Najd
     was closed by the Al-Saud, hurting many of these merchants, who diversified their
     financial role by expending to investment in date plantations in Iraq. See Ismail,
     Kuwait: social change, p. 68.
18   The movement was truly Iraqi Arab, with Sunnis, Shi'a, urbanites and tribes
     cooperating together against British rule and for the establishment of an Arab
     government. During the revolt, Ayatollah al-Shirazi issued a fatwa, stating it was
     permitted to make use of defensive force against the British. The revolt led to British
     to drastically reconsider their strategy towards Iraq and decided to focus on indirect
     rule, by appointing Faisal Ibn-Husayn as King of Iraq.
19   For this reason, Iranian residents of Iraq were obliged to have a mentioning on their
     identity card of their Iranian nationality, while Arab nationals from neighbouring
     countries were easily granted Iraqi nationality and reach high positions in politics.
     See Louër, 'Transnational Shi'a politics', pp. 63–64. Also see Cleveland, W., *The making
     of an Arab nationalist: Ottomanism and Arabism in the life and thought of Sati al-
     Husri*, Princeton, NJ: Princeton University Press, 1977.
20   Kha'zal, Vol. 5, p. 13; Ismail (1982), p. 72.
21   Rush, *Records of Kuwait 1899–1961*, p. 118.
22   Salih, 'The 1938 Kuwait legislative Council', p. 86. After a long twist-and-turn, the
     Emir dismissed Salih, but instead appointed his son 'Abdallah.
23   Marr, P. and al-Marashi, I., *The Modern History of Iraq*, London, Routledge, 2017, p. 78.
     The author claims this was the first time that an Iraqi ruler claimed sovereign rights
     over Kuwait. Crystal also places the beginning of the Iraqi efforts to annex Kuwait to
     the early 1930s, with a campaign to convince the ruler to voluntarily accept to merge in
     the face of the Saudi threat, See Crystal, *Oil and politics in the Gulf*, pp. 52–53.
24   Al-Naqeeb, K., *Al-Mujtama' wa al-Dawla fi al-Khaleej wa Jazeera al-'Arabiya*, Beirut,
     Markaz dirasat al-wahda al-'arabiyya, 2008, p. 117.
25   Rush, *Records of Kuwait 1899–1961*, p. 146.
26   The British Archives describe Abdallah al-Salim rather negatively, as an ambitious
     prince who wants to concentrate power in his hands, while Ahmad al-Jabir was naïve
     and lacked the capacities of a strong ruler.
27   These were Shiyan al-Ghanim, Abdullah al-Hamad al-Saqr, Yusuf Ben Issa al-Qina'i,
     al-Sayyid al-Ali al-Sulayman, Yusuf Marzuq al-Marzuq, Salih al-Uthman, Mishan al-
     Khudayiral-Khalid, Abdul Latif Muhammad al-Uthman, Sulayman Khalid al-Adsani,
     Yusuf Salih al-Humayd, Muhamad al-Dawud al-Marzuq, Sultan Ibrahim, Mishari

Hasan al-Badr, Khalid al-Abd al-Latif. Al-Adsani (1947), K. M., *Nisf Am lil hukm al-niyabi fi al-kuwayt*, pp. 5–6. Ismail (1982), p. 73.

28 Rush, *Records of Kuwait 1899–1966*, p. 252.

29 Ibid., p. 186.

30 Personal interview with Habeeb Hayaat, Kuwait City, April 2009.

31 Personal interview with Humud al-Nisf, Kuwait City, April 2009.

32 Salih, 'The 1938 Kuwait legislative Council', p. 61. Also see Louër, *Transnational Shi'a politics*, p. 62.

33 The British estimates are the following: Baharna: 983, Hasawis: 37, Iranians less than ten years in Kuwait: 170, Iranians in Kuwait up to 120 years and more than 10 years: 3457. Rush, *Records of Kuwait*, p. 202.

34 Khuri, *Tribe and State in Bahrain*, p. 198.

35 Personal interview with historian Ahmad Ben Barjas, Kuwait City, February 2014.

36 See Beaugrand, *Statelessness and transnationalism in Northern Arabia*, p. 99. Also see Tétrault, M. A., *Stories of democracy: politics and society in contemporary Kuwait*, New York: Colombia University Press, 2000, p. 66.

37 Beaugrand, C., *Statelessness and transnationalism in Northern Arabia*, p. 99.

38 As quoted in Beaugrand, C., *Statelessness and transnationalism in Northern Arabia: Biduns and state-building in Kuwait (1959–2009)*, LSE, PhD thesis, 2010, p. 99.

39 Ibid.

40 This dual set-up gave rise to elite struggles within the ruling family over the control of these important fiefdoms. Between 1939 and 1959, Shaykh Sabah al-Salim al-Sabah (r. 1965–77) was in charge of the Police Department. Between 1942 and 1961, Public Security was headed by Shaykh Abdallah al-Mubarak (the last son of Mubarak) who was very powerful in the 1950s and could count upon the support of the Rashaida. This powerful position made him a serious contender to the throne; he tried to seize power in the 1950s, but Shaykh Abdallah al-Salim al-Mubarak was enthroned. See Beaugrand (2010), p. 100.

41 Herb, *All in the family*.

42 https://cy.revues.org/2827

Part II

Chapter 5

1 Ayubi, *Overstating the Arab State*, p. 34.

2 This argument was developed by Ghassan Salame, who compares Kuwait's exceptionalism within the Gulf to that of Lebanon in the Levant. Salame, G., 'Small is pluralistic: democracy as an instrument of civil peace', in G. Salame (ed.), *Democracy without democrats*, London and New York: I.B. Tauris, 1994, p. 93. Also see Michael Herb who develops the argument about the threat of Iraqi irredentism in explaining Kuwait's opting for democracy: Herb, M., *The wages of oil*, Ithaca, NY: Cornell University Press, 2014.

3 In 1973 Bahrain had ratified a rather liberal constitution which resembled in spirit and wording Kuwait's constitution. However, only two years later, in 1975, the ruler would disband parliament, replace it with an appointed council. In 2002, a new constitution was promulgated, promised by the new ruler, Hamad Bin Issa, upon his succession to the throne in 1999. Yet, this constitution was hardly comparable to the earlier one. It was enacted unilaterally and provided for a Consultative Council of appointed

members that had equal legislative powers as the elected Chamber of Deputies, therefore only allowing for a very minor legislative role for the public. Electoral gerrymandering and press censorship further curtailed political and civil liberties.

4   Herb quoting Zahlan. Herb, *The wages of oil*, p. 80.

5   Ahmad al-Jabir was also accused of usurping the public budget for private purposes and depriving others within the Al-Sabah of their share in wealth and power, explaining the rise of the dissident faction led by Shaykh Abdallah al-Salim. Also, the violent confrontation between the Al-Malik branch of the Al-Sabah and the rest of the family that erupted in 1957 was over an issue of allowances. Al-Najjar, G., *Decision-making process in Kuwait: the land acquisition policy as a case study*, PhD thesis, Exeter University, January 1984, p. 127.

6   Crystal, *Oil and politics in the Gulf*, pp. 63–64; Herb, M., *All in the Family: absolutism, revolution and democracy in Middle Eastern monarchies*, New York: SUNY Press, 1999.

7   For Bahrain, the direct impetus to adopt a constitution was internal threat immediately after Independence, emanating from the increased activism of a cross-sectarian nature of its Shi'a population, labour (most of which was Shi'a) and merchant nationalists. As Bahrain had lost its direct backer – Great Britain – with independence, the 'Al-Khalifa needed a new form of legitimacy in order to secure their rule. Political opening was thus a means to secure its political survival, but soon proved counter-productive given the demographic weight of opposition. In Kuwait, the main impetus for parliamentarianism was the direct threat of Iraq, enabling the creation of the constitution in 1962 and the reinstatement of parliament in 1981 which allowed its survival in the aftermath of Saddam Hussayn's Invasion, despite the ruler's intention to restore full authoritarianism. Herb, *The wages of oil*, 2015.

8   See Davidson, C., 'Arab nationalism and British opposition in Dubai, 1920–1966', *Middle Eastern Studies*, Vol. 43, No. 6, 2007, p. 890. As Davidson recalls: 'Indeed, it is no coincidence that some of the biggest and wealthiest of Dubai's family trading empires today were the recipients of these licenses in the 1960s and most tellingly featured prominently among the described proponents of the National Front in the 1950s.'

9   While Abu Dhabi's popular Shaykh Zayed al-Nahyan favoured a more liberal design inspired by the Kuwaiti model, Dubai's ruler, Rashid al-Maktoum, was vociferously against this, as he would know it would lead Dubai to play second fiddle. Ultimately, the latter's intransigence combined with a tense regional context of the Iranian Revolution convinced Shaykh al-Nahyan to drop the initiative and abide by an illiberal constitution, with no real popular accountability. Allegedly, Kuwaiti officials had warned the UAE rulers of the dangers of a democratic constitution, as they were facing the difficulties of dealing with opposition groups acting through parliament. Taryam, A., *The establishment of the UAE 1950–1985*, London: Croom Helm, 1987, pp. 242–243.

10   Assiri, *The government and the politics in Kuwait*, pp. 20–24. A Soviet client, Iraq had an army of 60,000 and modern Soviet air and land equipment whereas Kuwait had between 2,000 and 3,000 soldiers.

11   The timing of events makes the argument of external threat as a crucial factor more convincing. Kuwait was one of the first Gulf shaykhdoms to declare independence from Britain (22 June 1961). Despite the Iraqi claim, the Arab League granted Kuwait membership on 20 July 1961 and offered military support to repel the Iraqis without relying totally on the British. Shortly thereafter, the Emir appointed a Constitutional and Elections Law Committee (26 August). Arab League forces arrived a couple of weeks later (10 September) and the British withdrew by 10 October. By the time Kuwait's constitution was promulgated (11 November 1962) and the first elections held (23 January 1963), the immediate threat to Kuwait was

foregone. Things had changed in Iraq. The Ba'ath overthrew Qasim (9 February) and the Arab League could depart from Kuwait (19 February). Most importantly, Kuwait had secured itself as a sovereign state, by adopting modern institutions and allowing for a regionally unprecedented degree of legislative oversight.

12 The private sector is still very much state-dependent in resource-rich Gulf States. This is the consequence of the fact that for these rich rentiers a major part of income is derived from oil wealth and the private sector contributes relatively little to national capital formation and employment, nor does it have a role in the delivery of public services or welfare. The private sector is largely invested in non-productive sectors (real estate, contractors and agents for foreign companies) that are directly or indirectly dependent on oil rents. As the ruling family controls oil, successful actors in the private sector depend on the goodwill of the Al-Sabah. See, for example, Hertog, S., Luciani, G. and Valeri, M., *Business politics in the Middle East*, London: Hurst University Press, 2013.

13 I refer hereby to the definition of notable employed by Max Weber in his essay 'Politics as a vocation'. In this, he distinguishes between those who do politics to defend their interests, but who have other sources of income and activists on the side, and those for whom politics is a vocation and who have specialized in the profession of doing politics. Relatedly, the first refers to those who do politics on account of their wealth and inherited status, while the professionals of politics (political entrepreneurs) have other qualities that make them do politics, based upon charisma, ideological programme and general political leadership. See Weber, M., 'Politics as a vocation', translated and edited by H. Gerth and C. W. Mills, New York: Free Press, 1946.

14 I borrow this term 'extra-legal' from Claire Beaugrand, who explains in her PhD how the naturalization of thousands of southern tribesmen in Kuwait occurred outside the legal framework of the Nationality Law (1959). Given the fact that it was promulgated before the Constitution, it gives the ruling family leeway to use it rather arbitrarily. The official stance of the Al-Sabah is that nationality is a sovereign matter and no referral to court is possible. Beaugrand, *Statelessness and transnationalism in Northern Arabia*, pp. 137–139.

15 Herb was the first to develop this argument of class-inspired politics in rich rentier states. See Herb, M., 'A nation of bureaucrats: political participation and economic diversification in Kuwait and the UAE', *IJMES*, Vol. 41 (2009), pp. 375–395.

16 Al-Najjar, *Decision-making process in Kuwait*, p. 61.

17 Then, voting excluded women (granted the right to vote in 2006) and all those who came to Kuwait after 1920, presumably those who had not fought in the Battle of Jahra. See Beaugrand, *Statelessness and transnationalism in Northern Arabia*, p. 17.

18 Al-Najjar, *Decision making in Kuwait*, p. 374.

19 These were Abdullatif al-Thunayyan, Humud al-Zaid, Ya'qub al-Humaidi, Saud al-Abdulrazzaq. The CC was elected by the Constitutive Council (*al-Majlis al-Ta'sisi*). See Al-Jasem, M. A., *al-Kuwayt mathalat al-dimoqratiyya (Kuwait represented a democracy)*, Kuwait: Dar al-Qurtas, 2007, p. 54.

20 Al-Najjar, *Decision making in Kuwait*, p. 50.

21 Al-Najjar, *Decision making in Kuwait*, p. 49.

22 Only Bahrain's short-lived 1973 constitution resembled the Kuwaiti one in word and spirit. Other Gulf states issued constitutions by decree (i.e. Oman, Saudi Arabia and Bahrain in 2002) or by committees directly appointed by rulers.

23 See Brown, N., *Constitutions in a non-constitutional world: Arab Basic laws and the prospects for accountable government*, Albany: SUNY Press, 2002, pp. 54–61. This

potential was first shown in a broad constitutional movement of 1989–90, when much of the agitation for a full restoration of constitutional life took place within the diwaniyyas, in the Monday gatherings organized as part of the movement (*Al-diwawein al-ithnayn*).

24 That is, free education, public sector jobs, public housing, rent and utility subsidies for water, electricity and monthly family allowances.

25 This contradiction is most clearly apparent in two constitutional articles that are contradictory in nature. Art. 4 stipulates that Kuwait is a hereditary Emirate in the line of the descendants of Mubarak al-Sabah, while art. 6 stipulates that governance in Kuwait is democratic, with the sovereignty of the people as the source of all powers. Kuwaiti lawyer and activist Abdelqader al-Jasem discusses in his book the deliberations within the CA about the political system to adopt. A parliamentary system was chosen as the presidential system was considered in contradiction with Kuwait's hereditary Emirate as it would allow for criticism of the person with the highest executive power (Emir and the ruling family). See Al-Jasem, *al-Kuwayt mathalat al-dimoqratiyya*, p. 63.

26 Parliament has influence over the composition of government (despite the Emir's appointment of the executive) by voting by majority vote that it cannot cooperate with the PM, which will require the Emir to appoint a new cabinet. A vote of no-confidence in a minister by a majority of parliament will lead to his immediate resignation from cabinet (art. 101).

27 According to the constitution, this should be done within a two-month period after parliament's suspension. Kuwait's rulers violated this principle twice – in 1976 and 1986 – by dissolving parliament without calling for new elections in a context of rising opposition.

28 Two-thirds of parliament needs to approve a draft law for it to be adopted. It will then need to be sanctioned and promulgated by the Emir within a thirty-day period (art. 66). The final power here lies with the Emir, who can also reject legislation adopted by parliament.

29 http://www.servat.unibe.ch/icl/ku00000_.html (accessed 19 September 2019).

30 These decrees have the force of law although a future parliament can veto them and retrospectively revoke their law status. In September 2012, Kuwait's Emir issued an emergency decree changing the electoral system from four votes a person to one vote a person in each of the five electoral districts. This measure was considered gerrymandering by the opposition forces, as it reduced the capacity of Islamists and tribes to coordinate votes in a political alliance that had been so successful in the 2012 elections.

31 Cabinet ministers have the same rights as elected deputies, with two exceptions: (1) they cannot vote in the case of interpellations against ministers, and (2) they do not participate in parliamentary committees.

32 Azoulay R. and Wells, M., 'Contesting welfare state politics in Kuwait', *Middle East Report*, Vol. 272, Fall 2014.

33 https://www.lawfareblog.com/how-long-can-deadlock-kuwaits-parliament-last (accessed 21 September 2019).

34 http://www.kt.com.kw/ba/tawareth.htm (accessed 22 September 2019).

35 Given the fact that parliament used its prerogatives in 2006, ambitious princes now hope that it will do so again when a new CP or even a new Emir is appointed, by using its veto power and choosing a contender to the throne it considers more favourable to its interests.

36   https://storify.com/kuwaitstory/kuwait-s-constitutional-mess (accessed 19 September 2019).

37   Judges who are citizens are appointed for life. Judges who are not citizens (a significant number) have one- to three-year contracts. The Supreme Judiciary Council (SJC) administers the judiciary.

38   See Goldenziel, J., 'Veiled political questions: Islamic dress, constitutionalism and the ascendance of courts', *The American Journal of Comparative Law*, Vol. 61, No. 1 (Winter 2013), p. 31. In major political cases, such as the suspension of parliament, press censorship and the structure and procedures of the judiciary, it has tended to support the regime, for example by sidestepping key political issues by dismissing them on technicalities.

39   https://cy.revues.org/2827

40   In 1976 upon the dissolution of parliament the Emir issued a decree in which he called for the creation of a committee to look into the amendment of the constitution. The committee was created in 1980, composed of a wide spectrum of social actors, but its proposals were immediately rejected by the opposition when it forwarded them to the parliament of 1981. For a compilation of the reasons enumerated by the government to suspend parliamentary life, see Al-Jasem, *al-Kuwayt mathalat al-dimoqratiyya*, pp. 80–81.

Chapter 6

1   I refer hereby to the terminology advanced by Enver Khoury on the structure of power in Saudi Arabia, whereby he uses the concept of *halaqat* (groups, branches and clans) organized in concentric circles that are linked to the ruling elite. See Khoury, E., *The Saudi decision-making body*, Hyattsville, MD: Institute of Middle Eastern Affairs, 1978.

2   Ayubi, *Overstating the Arab State*, p. 228.

3   Al-Naqeeb, K., Bin'a al-mujtama'a al-'arabi: b'ad al-furud al-bahtiya (The building of Arab society: some research hypotheses), Al-Mustaqbal al-'Arabi, 8th year, No. 79, September 1985, 4–41, especially pp. 26–28.

4   Al-Najjar, *Decision making in Kuwait*, p. 122.

5   Crystal, *Ruler and merchants*, p. 68.

6   In April, he resigned from the post as commander-in-chief and deputy ruler and went into exile to Beirut, later Paris and Cairo. His ouster was one of the issues that received full consensus within the family, as Al-Mubarak's power politics had left him with many enemies.

7   Crystal, *Rulers and merchants*, p. 71.

8   The Al-Malik branch claimed to be distant members of the Al-Sabah that had moved to Saudi Arabia, where Fahad al-Malik had been a bodyguard of Ibn Saud. In Kuwait, the latter came to act as a shaykh, using similar flags on his car as the Al-Sabah's and began claiming desert. When Al-Malik defied a request of the ruler to leave Kuwait, he was met with a violent crackdown. Fahad and his brother Salim, a storekeeper, were executed. Crystal., *Rulers and merchants*, p. 66.

9   Crystal, *Rulers and merchants*, p. 70.

10   In this regard the British Foreign office said: 'While it has been our declared policy over the past two years to increase our influence in the internal affairs of Kuwait, to achieve a close hold over our moral and material interests, it has been equally the firm determination of the ruler and his family to resist us in doing so; and the ruler has in great part succeeded.' Crystal, *Rulers and merchants*, p. 73.

11   See Michael Herb's overview of government positions since 1962. http://www2.gsu. edu/~polmfh/database/govt38.htm (accessed 10 October 2018).

12   https://www.youtube.com/watch?v=mNgnFWmPhQo (accessed 20 September 2019). The National Cultural Club was created after Abdallah al-Salim's coming to power which marked a period of growing political tolerance vis-à-vis the opposition forces.

13   This is recalled in Ahmad al-Khatib's memoirs. Beirut, al-markaz al-thaqafi al-'arabi, 2007. p. 192.

14   The United Arab Republic was a short-lived political union between Egypt and Syria and lasted from 1958 until 1961, when Syria seceded following a coup d'état in Syria.

15   In 1954, a group called the Kuwait Democratic League had issued a pamphlet in which it criticized certain shaykhs who 'think of himself as an independent ruler and demands absolute obedience to his wishes and insists that particular schemes must be carried out'. It continued by stating that in these circumstances, the only solution would be power to the people. Crystal, *Rulers and merchants,* p. 80.

16   Abdallah al-Mubarak went so far to attack and ridicule the ruler, Abdallah al-Salim, openly in his diwaniyya. He was also known for his extravagant lifestyle and had built the Mishrif palace for himself.

17   Ibid., p. 192.

18   Crystal, *Rulers and merchants,* p. 82.

19   The British had assisted the Pahlavi in their coup against the Qajar dynasty in 1925, just as they had assisted coups by leaders in the Gulf to support their interests regionally and in Iran's oil industry. The British initially tried to use Iran as a springboard to reverse the Russian Revolution of 1917. The Pahlavi dynasty (1925–79) was a British ally, a situation reversed after the popular Islamic Revolution in 1979. Also see Al-Najjar, *Decision making in Kuwait,* pp. 32–33.

20   http://www.nbk.com/aboutnbk/management/boardofdirectors_en_gb.aspx (Khaled, Bahar, Saqqar, Khorafi, Hamad, Fulaij) (accessed March 2011).

21   Al-Najjar, *Decision making in Kuwait,* pp. 68, 472.

22   On 25 December 1965 eight MPS resigned. They represented the nationalist bloc. These were Dr Ahmad al-Khatib, Jasim al-Qatami, Rashid al-Tawhid, Sami al-Munayes, Ali al-Umar, Sulaiman al-Mutawa', Abdulrazzaq al-Khalid and Ya'qub al-Humaidi.

23   Crystal, *Rulers and merchants,* p. 76.

24   Al-Najjar, *Decision making in Kuwait,* p. 108.

25   Ibid., p. 110.

26   This group was composed of the bureaucrats that were directly involved in the land acquisition programme, working in the Development Board, the Municipality and the Expropriation Department. As they had access to information about future development projects, they were capable of using it for private purposes and could purchase land in advance without the owner of the property knowing about the development plan for his land. They often gave rather advantageous prices to the owners, as they knew they would make money out of it later. They generally allied with influential merchants in deals advantageous for both parties. Al-Najjar, *Decision making process in Kuwait,* pp. 122–125.

27   Expatriates were banned entirely from banking and finance. Moreover, the 1960 Commercial Companies Law required that 51 per cent of all companies belong to Kuwaitis and that only Kuwaitis could own businesses or property outright. Kuwaiti companies receive far-reaching preferential treatment at the cost of foreigners.

28   This blurring of the separation between private and public interests is one of the main reasons behind the high level of corruption in Kuwait's administration.

29 Sabah al-Salim was appointed by Abdallah al-Salim in 1962 as CP. Doing so he passed power to another Salim. Low key, Sabah al-Salim had served as head of police, health and public works and upon independence as deputy PM and MFA.

30 On 25 December 1965 eight MPS resigned. They represented the nationalist bloc. These were Dr. Ahmad al-Khatib, Jasim al-Qatami, Rashid al-Tawhid, Sami al-Munayes, Ali al-Umar, Sulaiman al-Mutawa', Abdulrazzaq al-Khalid and Yaʿqub al-Humaidi.

31 Al-Najjar, *Decision making process in Kuwait*, p. 57.

32 The merchant group was known as the 'Chamber' group (referring to the KCC) led by Adel Aziz al-Saqqar. The nationalists were led by Ahmad al-Khatib and Jasem al-Qatami.

33 This same policy of naturalizing, arming and electing 'Ajman tribesmen was contested by Saudi Arabia, which preferred the 'Ajman to settle on Saudi territory. Crystal, *Rulers and merchants*, p. 93.

34 Kuwait, Dar al-Qabas, 2010, p. 31.

35 Crystal, *Rulers and merchants*, p. 84.

36 Al-Ghaz'ali, S., *al-Jamaʿat al-kuwaitiyya al-siyasiyya fi qarn 1910–2007 (The political groups in Kuwait in the period of 1910–2007)*, p. 69.

37 This is the interpretation of Jill Crystal to the event. See Crystal, *Rulers and merchants*, p. 87.

38 http://www.almoslim.net/node/218070 (accessed 23 September 2019).

39 In this parliament, the leftist and nationalist forces were close to Jaber al-'Ali, which Ahmad al-Khatib – icon of the leftists – himself confessed and considered one of their biggest mistakes. Other alliances were those with the 'Ajman, who were personally loyal to Jaber al-'Ali, as he had naturalized them.

40 Personal interviews with Kuwaiti historian and specialist of tribal affairs Ahmad Bin Barjas, 2012–14.

41 Al-Najjar, *Decision making process in Kuwait*, p. 56.

42 Al-Saʿidi, *al-Sulta wa tajarat al-siyasiya fi al-kuwait*, p. 31.

43 The statement was issued on 27 January 1967. Thirty-eight candidates, among whom six incumbent MPs, had issued a statement criticizing the electoral results. The MPs resigned in protest, among them one elected minister. They were Khaled al-Masoud (Minister), Rashid al-Farhan, Abdel Razzaq Khaled al-Zaid, Abdel Aziz al-Saqqar, Muhammad Abdel Mohsin al-Khorafi, Muhammad Yusuf al-Adsani, and Ali al-Amar. See Al-Saʿidi, *al-Sulta wa tajarat al-siyasiya fi al-kuwait*, p. 32.

Chapter 7

1 Haddad, Y., 'Islamists and the problem of Israel: the 1967 awakening', *Middle East Journal*, Vol. 46, No. 2 (1992).

2 In views of the defeat of 1967 regionally, the movement radicalized and took a more Marxist-Leninist stance, supported by South Yemen, China and the USSR. Although the rebels were defeated, the state of Oman had to modernize and reform in order to cope with the uprising.

3 Others were Nashi al-Ajmi, Rashid al-Muharab, Naser al-Ghanim and Husayn al-Yuwha. Al-Saʿidi, *al-Sulta wa al-tayarat al-siyasiya fi al-kuwait*, p. 37.

4 Al-Najjar, *Decision making process in Kuwait*, pp. 62–63.

5 In October 1973, members of the OAPEC – consisting of the Arab members of the OPEC together with Egypt, Syria and Tunisia – proclaimed an oil embargo. By the

end of the embargo, in March 1974, the price of oil had risen from 3 USD a barrel to nearly 12 USD, with major effects on the global economy.

6   Crystal, *Rulers and merchants*, p. 98.

7   https://wikileaks.org/cable/1989/08/89KUWAIT3922.html (accessed 20 September 2019).

8   The Society for Social Reform was established in 1963 as a consequence of a growing democratic opening in reaction to independence and the Iraqi threat which had prompted Abdallah al-Salim to open up politically. Its creation took place in a context of the reopening of other cultural societies by the government. Al-Mudairis, F., *Jama'at al-Ikhwan al-Muslimin fi al-Kuwayt (The MB in Kuwait)*, p. 34.

9   Islamic reformism developed by the end of the nineteenth and start of the twentieth centuries in reaction to the decay of Ottomanism, Islamic civilization and the penetration of Western modernism and colonialism. The idea was that the stagnant situation could only be resolved by embracing Western scientific taught and adapting to these changes, while staying faithful to Islamic faith and culture. The main ideologues of Islamic reformism were Muhammad Abdu (1849–1905), Rashid Ridda (1865–1935) and Jamal-al-Din al-Afghani (1839–97). Their ideas also led to the reform of educational curricula, introducing modern science.

10   One can think here of Shaykh Muhammad Amin al-Shanqiti, Shaykh Muhammad al-Ghazali or Rashid Rida, the intellectual of the MB, who all spent time in Kuwait. Lahoud-Tatar, *Islam et politique au Koweit*, p. 51.

11   Among those belonging to the Najdi elite, one can think of Humud al-Rumi and Yusuf al-Haji.

12   Muhammad al-Adsani is from the al-Adsani family that historically gave many judges to Kuwait. Muhammad al-Adsani was head of the municipal council and member of the Kuwaiti Ikhwan. Khaled al-Adsani was Minister of Trade and Industry and Suleiman Khaled al-Adsani member of the 1938 Council.

13   The sociology of transnational movements has concluded that face-to-face diffusion of movement ideas still seems to be the strongest means for transmission, despite modern means of communication. Tarrow, S., *The new transnational activism*, Cambridge: Cambridge University Press, 2005.

14   Al-Mudairis, F. *Jama'at al-ikhwan al-muslimin fi al-kuwayt*, p. 31. The first wave of expats arrived in Kuwait between 1948 and 1950. Among the Ikhwan teachers in Kuwait were Abdelaziz Ahmad al-Jalal (Egyptian professor of English), Muhammad Yusuf al-Najjar, Khalil al-Wazir and Khalid al-Hassan (Palestinians who would later become leading members of Fatah). Apart from Egyptians, the Iraqi Ikhwan had a major influence on Kuwait's Ikhwan, via its intellectuals as well as the spread of its ideas through the printing houses in Basra. Lahoud-Tatar, *Islam et politique au Koweit*, p. 52.

15   Falah al-Mudairis further details how the movement then failed to gain more support from workers and from merchants. The former (although not so established as a group) largely supported the nationalists, while the latter had a general liberal and nationalist inclination. Al-Mudairis, F., *Jama'at al-ikhwan al-muslimin fi al-kuwayt*, pp. 18–19.

16   This was also the consequence of splits within the organization between a more moderate elite of businessmen and young men who wished for more radical stances and closer ties to the Egyptian movement. It resulted in 1954 in the departure of Abdelaziz al-Mutawa'a and his replacement by Abdelrazzaq al-Mutawa'. The departure of Abdelaziz al-Mutawa' led to the departure of many intellectuals and influential members of the movement, some of whom opted instead for the nationalist current. Lahoud-Tatar, *Islam et politique au Koweit*, p. 57.

17 Pall, Z., *Salafism in Lebanon: local and transnational actors*, PhD thesis, Anthropology, Utrecht University, 2012, p. 63.

18 Ibid., p. 64.

19 Abdelaziz al-Mutawa'a was the leading figure in transplanting Ikhwani thought to Kuwait's society via his personal contacts with Hassan al-Banna and members of the movement in the Arab world. In 1953 the Irshad Society was created by a group of devout merchants and shaykhs: Muhammad Yusuf Abdelwahab al-Adsani, Abdelrazaq al-Askar, Ali al-Jassar, Abdelaziz Ali Abdelwahab al-Mutawa', Abdelrazzaq al-Saleh al-Mutawa' and Khaled Issa al-Saleh al-Qina'i. Shaykh Yusuf al-Qina'i was appointed head of the society. Ghaz'ali, *al-Jama'at al-siyasiya al-kuwaitiyya*, p. 186.

20 For more on this generational change Lahoud-Tatar, *Islam et politique au Koweit*, pp. 66–76.

21 Already in the 1950s did young men in what then still was Al-Irshad oppose the centralizing and conservative tendencies of the organization's dignitaries and notably its leader, the merchant Abdelaziz al-Mutawa'a. As a result of these internal clashes and a context that was then unfavourable to Islamism, the society gradually waned and ceased to exist in 1960. Remaining activities of the members continued either on an individual basis or in coordination with non-Kuwaiti Islamic groups. Lahoud-Tatar, *Islam et politique au Koweit*, p. 67.

22 Al-Ghaz'ali, *al-Jama'at al-siyasiya al-kuwaitiyya*, p. 201.

23 This structure created by Abdel Wahab 'Aman consists of: (1) an Emir who supervises a (2) Consultative Council that supervises (3) Emirs of regions who supervise (4) Neighbourhood Observers who supervise (5) Neighbourhood Officers who supervise (6) soldiers. See Lahoud-Tatar, *Islam et politique au Koweit*, p. 68.

24 It was the idea of the mother organization to diffuse its ideology from Kuwait, given its relative open press climate. Lahoud-Tatar, *Islam et politique au Koweit*, p. 75.

25 The name was chosen in analogy to the Jami'yat al-Islah of Zubayr in Iraq.

26 Lahoud-Tatar, *Islam et politique au Koweit*, p. 70. Al-Mudairis, *al-Jama'at al-Ikhwan al-Muslimin fi al-Kuwayt*, p. 31.

27 It was a legal right of recognized societies to receive government support in the building of their offices Al-Zumai, F., *The intellectual and historical development of the Islamic movement in Kuwait: 1950–1981*, PhD thesis, Exeter University, 1988, p. 187.

28 Until 2003, the Kuwaiti Central Bank did not have any oversight on the Kuwait Finance House, which fell directly under the authority of the Ministry of Commerce. Things would change in 2003 when the government opened the Islamic finance sector for competition.

29 Al-Zumai, *The intellectual and historical development of the Islamic movement in Kuwait*, pp. 196–197.

30 One can think of Ahmad al-Dabbous, Hamid Falah here. Al-Zumai, *The intellectual and historical development of the Islamic movement in Kuwait*, p. 197.

31 Ghaz'ali, *al-Jama'at al-siyasiya al-Kuwaytiyya*, p. 188.

32 Ghabra, S., 'Voluntary associations in Kuwait: the foundation of a new system?', *Middle East Journal*, Vol. 45, No. 2 (Spring 1991), p. 206.

33 Al-Zumai, *The intellectual and historical development of the Islamic movement in Kuwait*, p. 199.

34 In 1981, the Society for Social Reform managed to control the board of the Society of Kuwaiti Teachers; from 1977 it controlled the Union of Kuwaiti Students.

35   For an idea, see this video of Kuwait University in the 1960s: https://www.youtube.
      com/watch?v=t-thHL1336o (accessed 10 November 2014).

36   These ministers were Yusuf Jasem al-Hajj and Abdallah al-Mufarrij who had
      previously served respectively as Ministers of Religious Affairs and Justice. Also see
      Crystal, *Oil and politics in the Gulf*, p. 103.

37   The place of Salafism in the Islamic world is part of a long theological debate that
      started in the early period of the Abbasid Caliphate (749–1258 AD) in which religious
      scholars diverged as to the role played by human reasoning (*'aql*) in analysing the
      sacred text (*nass*). The first group – the *Mu'tazila* – were of the opinion that reasoning
      should take priority when analysing the text. The second group – the *Ahl al-Hadith*
      or *Athari* stream – were against any form of reasoning, applying a strictly literal
      reading. While the Mu'tazila have disappeared, they were replaced by the *Ash'aris*
      (referring to their founder, Abu al-Hassan al-Ash'ari) who try to find a balance
      between reasoning and the text by allowing space for reasoning in the interpretation
      of Islamic law (*shari'a*). Although the Ash'aris have dominated Sunni Islam, there have
      always been literalists throughout its history, such as medieval scholar *Ibn Taymiyya*
      or eighteenth-century scholar *Muhammad al-Shawkani*. The current was revived
      with Wahhabism in Saudi Arabia since the eighteenth century and its exportation
      throughout the Muslim world financed by Saudi Petrodollars that skyrocketed since
      the oil boom in the 1970s. As a second source of Salafism (apart from the Athari
      stream), there is the practice of *ijtihad* developed by Islamic reformers on which
      Salafis rely. Rather than relying on the four dominant legal schools, ijtihad refers to
      the making of legal decisions on the basis of the independent interpretation of legal
      sources. However, while Islamic reformers and the Shi'a rely on reasoning to come
      to ijtihad, the Salafis instead rely on analogies (*qiyas*) in the Qur'an and the Sunna
      for ijtihad. *Shaykh Nasser al-Din al-Albani* (1914–99) was a major source behind
      the revival of ijtihad and inspiration for Salafism. For an elaborate discussion of the
      origins of Salafism and its creed, see Pall, *Salafism in Lebanon*, pp. 27–34.

38   The veneration of saints is a rather common practice everywhere in the Islamic
      world, despite the fact that it is considered by literalists as a grave violation of the
      oneness of god. Their very literal interpretation of the Qur'an and the Sunna makes
      practically all beliefs and practices that transcend this strict line as innovation (*bid'a*)
      which are therefore rejected by Salafism.

39   Prior to the Syrian revolution, the controversial leader of the Salafi Umma Party
      (Hakim al-Mutairi), for example, voiced his interest in working with the Shi'a. The
      movement which calls for the establishment of political parties is rather marginal
      within the Salafi field in Kuwait and this is one of the reasons explaining his stance.
      Another reason is that before the Syrian revolution, he advocated the idea of unifying
      the Umma, as was the case under the Caliphate too, when different schools of
      thought were allowed. However, I believe that his main motive was pragmatic, as his
      stance in the Syrian revolution clearly showed a sectarian bias and anti-Shi'a rhetoric.

40   The Shi'a venerate the descendants of the prophet in the line of Ali as the rightful
      successors who are not only the temporal leaders of the *Umma* but do also have
      access to the hidden (divine), meaning of the Qur'anic message, and are thus
      considered religiously infallible. In this they differ from the Sunna, who do not
      believe the prophet explicitly designed 'Ali and his descendants as his rightful
      successors. Mainstream Shi'ism is Twelver Shi'ism that considers Ali (656–661) as the
      first in a line of twelve imams. The last imam disappeared in Samarra (northern Iraq)
      in 874 under mysterious circumstances and is believed to be occulted by god as the

awaited imam – the *Mehdi* – who will return by the end of times to restore justice and truth in this world. Ever since, Shi'ism became messianic and gave an increasingly important role to the delegates of the imams in the management of the Shi'a' daily affairs. Since the nineteenth century, Shi'a religious authority has been increasingly centralized in Iraq and Iran via the system of the *marja'iyya* and the person of the marja' al-taqlid (the referent for emulation). Salafis staunchly oppose *taqlid* that could eventually lead to the veneration of humans. They sometimes refer to the *surat* al-Tawba 31: 'They take their rabbis and monks as lords'. Salafis insist on the direct relation between a human and the Scripture. A religious authority's (mufti) can only be accepted by Salafis as long as there is proof (*dalil*) in the Qur'an and the Sunna for his reasoning.

41   With pure they mean an Islam corrected for what they considered the deviances of other movements in Kuwait, the Ikhwan and the *Jama'at al-Tabligh* in particular.

42   Pall, *Salafism in Lebanon*, pp. 67–68.

43   Ibid., p. 66. Lahoud-Tatar, *Islam et politique au Koweit*, p. 93.

44   One quote of Ibn Taymiyya (the most important scholar of the Hanbalite school) goes: 'Sixty years of an unjust ruler (imam ja'ir) is better than a single night without a ruler (sultan)'. The purists converge as to their unconditional obedience to the ruler as long as the latter is not an open apostate. They consider that open criticism to the ruler could lead to internal strife and only allow secret advice to the ruler (*nasiha siriyya*). Yet, within the purists one can find those who allow for political participation for *da'wa* if sanctioned by the ruler and the Wahhabi establishment (i.e. *Ihya al-Turath* and the Islamic Salafi gathering in Kuwait) and those who reject any form of political participation (i.e. *Madkhalis*).

45   The targets are both foreign (French and American embassies) and Kuwaiti (airport, Ministry of Electricity and Water, cafes, industrial zones). In 1985, moreover, an attack was orchestrated against the person of the Emir – Jaber al-Ahmad – who escaped a car bomb on his motorcade. Responsibility for all attacks was claimed by *Islamic Jihad*; the predecessor of the Lebanese Hezbollah that was active in Lebanon's civil war during the 1980s. The movement was led by Imad Mughniey, a leading figure in Hezbollah, who was a Shi'a member of Palestinian Fatah's Force 17. In 2008, sectarian tensions would flare up again when Shi'a members in Kuwait would commemorate his murder.

46   According to Boghardt, between 1988 and 1990, approximately twenty Kuwaitis were involved in political violence against the Al-Sabah. The Saudi regime executed in 1989 sixteen Kuwaiti Shi'a who were allegedly involved in the Mecca bombings. See Boghardt, L., *Kuwait amid war, peace and revolution: 1979–1991 and new challenges*, Hampshire: Palgrave Macmillan, 2006, pp. 124 and 133.

47   These were Jabir al-Jalahma and Abdellatif al-Dirbas. Also, the group to which Al-Utaybi belonged (the *Jama'at al-Salafiyya al-Muhtasiba*) had numerous followers in Kuwait, as elsewhere in the Gulf, and recruited mostly from tribesmen, profiting from the rather porous borders between Saudi Arabia and Kuwait. It is also in Kuwait that the letters of Juhayman were printed, surprisingly by the leftist journal, *Al-Tali'a*, belonging to Ahmad al-Khatib's group. These letters were widely dispersed in Kuwaiti Salafi circles. See Lahoud-Tatar, *Islam et politique au Koweit*, pp. 104–105.

48   Lacroix, S., *Awakening Islam*, Cambridge, MA: Harvard University Press, 2011.

49   Al-Mudairis, F., *al-Jama'at al-Salafiyya fi al-Kuwait (The Salafi Group in Kuwait)*, Kuwait: Dar al-Qurtas, 1999, p. 15.

50   Interview with the Al-Wazzan brothers, Kuwait City, April 2009.

51   For more on the origins of Jama'at al-Tabligh in Kuwait, see Lahoud-Tatar, *Islam et politique au Koweit,* p. 101.

52   The Salafi current was soon invested in the field of the student unions, both within Kuwait and via the networks of Kuwaiti students studying abroad. In 1980, the Salafi current entered the student elections on the separate list, called 'The list of the Islamist Union' as a competitor to the Ikhwan. The Salafis also entered the competition for the Teachers Society against the Ikhwan, but only won 306 votes against 1378 votes for the Ikhwan. Al-Mudairis, *al-Jama'at al-Salafiyya fi al-kuwayt,* pp. 17–18.

53   The Salafis were successful in these elections and able to dominate the boards of a number of cooperatives, such as the ones in Fayha, Kayfan, al-Nazha and al-Qadisiyya. The boards of these societies constitute an important means to develop patronage networks in neighbourhoods. For this reason, many of the heads of the cooperative societies are presented by these Islamist groups as candidates for the Municipal and Legislative elections. Al-Mudairis, *al-Jama'at al-Salafiyya fi al-kuwayt,* p. 18.

54   Pall, Z., Salafism in Lebanon: local and transnational actors, PhD thesis, Anthropology, Utrecht University, 2012, p. 63.

55   This corresponds to the general position of the purist Salafis, who have dominated Ihya' al-Turath in the aftermath of the Invasion and particularly since 1997, as a consequence of explicit government support. Pall, *Salafism in Lebanon,* p. 70.

56   While the political naturalizations have largely ended after the Invasion, article 5 continues to be invoked to grant nationality to important persons in Kuwait. As such, the regime naturalized in 2007 twelve members of the Al-Hazal family, paramount shaykhs of the 'Aneza tribe. Beaugrand, *Statelessness and transnationalism in Northern Arabia,* p. 128.

57   http://carnegieendowment.org/sada/?fa=43079 (accessed 21 September 2019).

58   http://www.bahrainrights.org/en/node/425 (accessed 20 September 2019).

59   The systematic use of foreign forces is a tradition that dates back to the British presence in the region in the nineteenth century. The 'Al-Khalifa – supported by the British – relied on individuals from Baluchistan and the Indian Subcontinent to fill the ranks of its defence and security forces.

60   Beaugrand, *Statelessness and transnationalism in Northern Arabia,* p. 137. Also see Gresh, A. and Vidal, D., *Les 100 cles du Proche-Orient,* Pluriel, 2011, p. 354.

61   In total, there are eight major tribal groups in Kuwait: Al-'Awazem, al-Mutran, al-Rashaida, al-Dhafir, al-Aneza, al-Uteibi, al-'Ajman and al-Shammar. The number of 53 per cent was the result of a government statistic about the number of voters in Kuwait that was published on 12 July 2008 in *al-Rai* newspaper. However, in reality the number might be higher for two reasons. Some of them were recently naturalized and were not yet entitled to vote (according to the Nationality Law) and others don't any more use the name of their tribe – in order to better 'fit in' society.

62   Shafeeq Ghabra gives a number of 220,000 between 1965 and 1981. Ghabra, S., 'Kuwait and the dynamics of socio-economic change', *Middle East Journal,* Vol. 51, No. 3 (Summer 1997), p. 364. Naser al-Fadhala comes with detailed statistics that also converge to around 220,000 naturalizations, but over a larger period, from 1965 until 1988. Al-Fadhala, N., *al-hala wa al-hal: fardhiyyat awaliyya li-taswib al-sira' al-siyasi ila itarhu al-ijtima'i (The situation and the solution: first hypotheses to straighten the political struggle to its social frameworks),* internet version (banned in Kuwait), pp. 31–34.

63   Ghabra (1997) and Assiri (1996) refer to 1980 and 1981 as an end date. Al-Fadhala analyses the naturalizations in three distinct waves: 1965–70, 1971–80 and 1981–8 and ends the analysis in 1988; implying that no such naturalizations took place

after the Invasion. According to Al-Fadhala, the highest number of naturalizations took place in the last phase (113,609 persons compared to the early numbers of 77,139 and 29,529 persons, respectively). Al-Fadhala relies on the reports of the Ministry of Planning but does not show these reports in his book. This is contested by others who say that most naturalizations took place in the earliest phase between 1965 and 1970 and were later strongly restricted as a consequence of the arrival to power of the new Emir, Jaber al-Ahmad, who was opposed to such naturalizations.

64 Nakash, Y., *The Shi'a of Iraq*, Princeton, NJ: Princeton University Press, 1994, p. 445.

65 Personal interview with Kuwaiti historian, Ahmad Ben Barjas, Kuwait City, February 2014.

66 Beaugrand, *Statelessness and transnationalism in Northern Arabia*, p. 116.

67 Personal interviews with Kuwaiti historian and specialist of tribal affairs, Ahmad Bin Barjas, 2012–14.

68 The 'Ajman have around 85,000 members to date, with around 50,000 in Saudi Arabia and the rest living in Kuwait. https://ar.wikipedia.org/wiki/%D8%A7%D9%84 %D8%B9%D8%AC%D9%85%D8%A7%D9%86 (accessed 24 September 2019).

69 He was also known to be a nationalist and had participated in the lobbying efforts for Kuwait's independence and was not very loved by the British who considered him too nationalist. http://www.alraimedia.com/Articles.aspx?id=510434 (accessed 14 February 2014).

70 Beaugrand, *Statelessness and transnationalism in Northern Arabia*, p. 100.

71 Interview with Ahmad Bin Barjas, Kuwait City, 2014.

72 Beaugrand, *Statelessness and transnationalism in Northern Arabia*, p. 117.

73 An example from my interview with a member of the prominent Shi'a merchant family, Jasem Qabazard: 'The merchants were the link between the common Shi'a and the ruling family. In order to reach the people, they would go through the merchants. Even in finding out where people were coming from. This became very helpful in organizing nationality. This minister would ask the merchants if they knew the person. So if you go back to the old files of each Kuwaiti, you will find the signature of my father (Mohammed Qabazard) of Mohammed Rafi Ma'rafi, etc.' Personal interview, Kuwait City, March 2009.

74 *Gazetteer of Arabian Tribes*, Vol. 10 Mutair-Qumarah, Archive Editions, p. 212. Also see historical part, p. 75.

75 This argument is supported by the statistics presented by Naser al-Fadhala on the waves of naturalizations in Kuwait. The author says that the largest number of naturalizations took place in the period between 1981 and 1988, around 113,609, compared to earlier numbers of respectively 77,419 and 29,529 persons.

76 Personal interviews, Kuwait City, December 2014. Interview with Sami al-Adwani, active member of *hadas*.

77 Al-Fadhala, *al-hala wa al-hal*, p. 40.

78 In 1963, there were eighteen tribal MPs. In 1971, nineteen tribal MPs and in 1975, twenty-two, whereas after the redistricting in 1979 the number reached twenty-six in 1981 and ever since stayed around an average of twenty-five, despite the redistricting that occurred in 2006 from twenty-five to five districts (which did not really reduce tribal power in the parliament).

79 For a good discussion of the literature of tribalism and politics, Picard, E., 'Les liens primordiaux, vecteurs de dynamiques politiques', in E. Picard (ed.), *La politique dans le monde arabe*, Paris: Armand Colin, 2006, pp. 55–77.

80   This bias is to be found in the English and Arabic literature. The latter is often written by Arab urban intellectuals with few ties to the tribal populations. For example, Al-Jabri, M., *al-'Aql al-siyasi al-'arabi*, Beirut: Center for Arab unity studies, 2011; Ibrahim, S., 'Urbanization in the Arab world: the need for an urban strategy', in Ibrahim and Hopkins (eds.), *Arab society: social science perspectives*, Cairo: American University Press, 1985, pp. 123–147; al-Naqeeb, K., *Sira'a al-qabaliah wa al-dimoqratiyya: halat al-Kuwayt*, London: Dar Assaqi, 1996.

81   Al-Boghaili, M., *al-Qabila wa al-Sulta al-hirak al-siyasi al-qabali fi al-Kuwayt*, 2012, p. 60.

82   See ibid., pp. 61–62. The author refers to authors as Ibn Khaldun and Gholoob Pasha who would consider the Bedouin values as opposed to the ideals of Islam, such as moderation and the abhorrence of the ego. Bedouin communities would instead have a tendency for personality cults and not shy away from the display of a certain arrogance and ostentatious behaviour.

83   Personal interviews, Ahmad Ben Barjas, Kuwait City, December 2013. http://www.nationalkuwait.com/forum/index.php?threads/246192/page-2 (accessed 18 September 2014).

84   Gown worn by Gulf men.

85   Lindholm, C., 'Kinship structure and political authority: the Middle East and Central Asia', *Comparative Studies in society and history*, Vol. 28, No. 2 (1986), p. 349.

86   A cross-cousin marriage is marriage from a parent's opposite-sex siblings, while a parallel cousin marriage is from a parent's same-sex siblings.

87   Descended from the male's or father's side.

88   Lindholm, 'Kinship structure and political authority', p. 344.

89   The pivotal role of lineage groups rather than the tribe in the economic and political organization of nomadic life has been demonstrated in the literature on Arabian tribes. See Al-Zo'abi, A., 'Tribe and tribesmen in Kuwait: a historical study of the tribal structure' (unpublished working paper), p. 4; Lindholm, 'Kinship structure and political authority', p. 343. In this regard, also see the theory on segmented lineage, in which this competition between agnatic rivals is further detailed: Sahlins, M., 'The segmentary lineage model: an organization of predatory expansion', *American Anthropologist*, Vol. 63, No. 2 (1961), pp. 322–344.

90   Sharara, W., *al-Ahl wa al-ghanima* (Kin and the booty: the foundations of politics in the Kingdom of Saudi Arabia), Beirut: Dar al-Tali'a, 1981, pp. 23–24.

91   Al-Ajmi, 'A nomadic logic; an intellectual image', p. 9.

92   Al-Boghaili, *al-Qabila wa al-Sulta*, p. 61.

93   Ibid.

94   Because oil companies were in short of cheap labour, Bedouins were given loans to settle around these companies. The government itself also encouraged them to seek work in road, construction, police and armed forces. See Al-Naqeeb, F., 'Revisiting hadar and badu in Kuwait: citizenship, housing and the construction of a dichotomy', *IJMES*, Vol. 46 (2014), 5–30, p. 6.

95   Al-Naqeeb, 'Revisiting hadar and badu in Kuwait', p. 15.

96   See Al-Naqeeb who has made a similar argument, ibid.

97   The Emirs of the Rashaida and 'Awazem tribes were among the original population of Kuwait. Faisal al-Duwaish was living in the area of Dasman palace. Interview with Ahmad Ben Barjas, July 2015.

98   Personal interview, Dr Tiql al-'Ajmi, Kuwait City, March 2012.

99 Al-'Ajmi, 'A nomadic logic: an intellectual image', pp. 28 and 29. This also explains, according to Al-Ajmi, why many tribal shaykhs have increasingly shunned the arena of tribal primaries, as it would be an embarrassment for them in case they lose.

100 The primaries help avoid tribes to split their votes and to concentrate their votes instead on one or two candidates to strengthen their seats in parliament. In 1975, the first primaries were organized by the Al-'Ajman tribe in the Ahmadi area, to strengthen its power vis-à-vis the 'Awazem tribe that dominated the region. While officially penalized in 1998 by the regime, tribal primaries continue to be organized and the government has tended to turn a blind eye to them (with some exceptions). Osman Salih, K., 'Kuwait primary (tribal) elections: 1975–2008: an evaluative study', *British Journal of Middle Eastern Studies*, Vol. 38, No. 2, pp. 141–167.

101 In 1964, a new urban housing scheme was developed to rehouse the residents of the villages of Salmiyya, Jahra, Farwaniya and the southern coastal Adan district who had recently been naturalized. While the *hadar* were allocated houses in the new suburbs between the first and fourth ring roads, the *badu* could only acquire housing in the same village in which they had previously acquired their property, limiting their ability to move to the central urban areas. Many of them came to live initially in the shanty towns in the areas close to the oil and industry centres (Maqwa and Wara close to Ahmadi, Jleeb al-Shuyukh close to Shuwaikh and Shamiya). In the 1970s and 1980s, many were relocated to newly constructed areas, but well beyond the fifth and sixth ring roads (i.e. Riqqa, Umariyya, Sabahiyya and Jahra). The fact that the *sur* served as the basis of Kuwait's ring road system inadvertently strengthened the divide between the *hadar* and *badu* in Kuwait. See Al-Naqeeb, 'Revisiting hadar and badu in Kuwait', pp. 5–30.

102 Interview with Muhammad al-'Oteibi, Kuwait City, December 2014.

103 Interview with Sami al-Adwani, tribal young member of hadas (MB), Kuwait City, December 2014.

104 See also Al-Ajmi, 'A nomadic logic; an intellectual image', p. 20.

105 See also the memoirs of Dr Ahmad al-Khatib in which he criticizes this tendency of personality politics within movements and arguments that he witnessed similar problems with his movement, Al-Minbar al-Dimoqrati that was created in 1990, as well as in the movement's attempts to reach out to other actors on the national level. Al-Khatib, *al-Kuwait min al-Imara ila al-Dawla*, p. 14.

106 Al-Zumai, *The intellectual and historical development of the Islamic movement in Kuwait*, p. 181.

107 Ibid., p. 197.

108 Ibid., p. 218. As the Jama'at came to Kuwait via the Indian expatriate workforce living and working in the Ahmadi area, it was here that the movement first spread among tribesmen.

109 In 1992 – for example – the Salafi movement gained more than 50 per cent of its votes in *hadar* areas and then was described by sociologist Khaldun al-Naqeeb as a *hadar* phenomenon. See Al-Naqeeb, K., *Sira'a al-qabila wa al-dimoqratiyya: halat al-Kuwayt (Struggle between tribe and democracy: the situation of Kuwait)*, London: Dar al-Saqi, 1996, p. 217.

110 See historical part of this thesis, p. 40.

111 Lahoud-Tatar, *Islam et politique au Koweit*, p. 70; al-Mudairis, *al-Jama'at al-Ikhwan al-Muslimin fi al-Kuwayt*, p. 31.

112   One can also think here of the participation of certain tribal MPs in the interpellation
      against the Minister of Oil and Finance (Abdulrahman al-'Uteibi); the interpellation was
      led by members of the leftist group of Ahmad al-Khatib but supported by 'Ajman MPs.

Chapter 8

1   An example is the case of Jasem al-Khorafi, former speaker of parliament and
      merchant with strong ties to the current Emir, Sabah al-Ahmad. According to my
      interlocutors, Al-Khorafi was allowed a political role by the Al-Sabah to fill up the
      leadership vacuum of the *hadar* since the early 2000s, as the leftist and nationalist icons
      (such as Al-Khatib and Al-Nibari) had largely lost their popularity. Although from a
      family active in business, the Al-Khorafi are not part of the Najdi core that participated
      in the 1938 events and the family made its fortune in the 1960s and later. Al-Khorafi
      became an important figure under Nasser al-Muhammad's government, although the
      two were initial foes. Interview with Abdelqader al-Jasem, Kuwait City, 8 May 2012.
2   https://cy.revues.org/2827#tocto2n4
3   In his analyses on political modernization, Max Weber defines the political
      entrepreneur in opposition to the notable. The political entrepreneur is considered
      to be specialized in politics as a profession. Social position and economic resources
      are not anymore indispensable for succeeding in politics. The political entrepreneur –
      acting in a competitive environment – needs to mobilize other capacities (i.e.
      political program, political ideas) in order to gain the votes of the electorate. Weber,
      M., *Economie et Société II: l'organisation et les puissances de la société dans leur
      rapport avec l''économie*, Paris: Librairie Plon, 1971.
4   Khuri, *Tribe and state in Bahrain*, pp. 179–180.
5   Weber, M., *Economy and Society: an outline of Interpretative Sociology*, edited by
      Guenther Roth and Claus Wittich, New York: Bedminster Press, 1968. Max Weber
      distinguishes social relations on the basis of the orientation of social action. If social
      action is based upon a subjective feeling of belonging together – either affective or
      traditional – the social relation is called 'communal formation' *(Vergemeinschaftung)*.
6   With its accession to power (1926), the Pahlavi dynasty enacted a number of reforms,
      like land reform and mandatory military service, which severely hit the poor Iranians
      from rural backgrounds in the southern regions. See Reza Ghods, M., 'Government
      and society in Iran, 1926–1934', *Middle Eastern Studies*, Vol. 27, No. 2 (April 1992),
      pp. 223–226.
7   Since this current combines legal reasoning with the insistence on *mystical
      illumination* as guidance towards salvation, shaykhism has been criticized by
      traditional *usuli* scholars who consider it to be a deviant sect of Shi'ism. Cole, J. R.,
      'Shaykh Ahmad al-Ahsa'i on the surces of religious authority', in L. S. Walbridge
      (ed.), *The most learned of the Shi'a: the institution of the Marja' Taqlid*, Oxford: Oxford
      University Press, 2001, pp. 82–93.
8   The first shaykhi marja' who settled in Kuwait was Mirza 'Ali al-Ihqaqi, who left
      the shaykhi community in Al-Hasa because of a conflict with local 'ulema. Until
      today, the descendants of Mirza 'Ali al-Ihqaqi live in Kuwait and continue to lead the
      religious affairs of the community.
9   *Akhbari* scholars reject the *usuli* current that considers the deductive reasoning (*'aql*)
      and the consensus (*'ijma*) of the mujtaheds as legitimate sources for elaborating
      Islamic law and complementing the Quran and the Akhbar.

10 See Louër, L., *Transnational Shi'a politics: religious and political networks in the Gulf*, London: Hurst, 2008, p. 122.

11 Personal interview, Kuwait City, March 2009.

12 The term 'marja'iyya' means reference in Arabic and refers to the centralization of religious authority in Shi'a Islam around the person of the marja' al-taqlid (the source of emulation). Ordinary scholars having not reached the level of ijtihad should follow the opinions of a senior living mujtahed on a wide range of issues falling within the realm of religious law. The marja' al-taqlid is considered to be the most learned by the community of religious scholars of the *hawza*; a religious school for training Shi'a 'ulema. Since the nineteenth century, religious authority has become increasingly centralized around the Shi'a shrine cities in Iraq and Iran, whereby the marja' relies on a set of representatives (*wukala*) acting as his delegates in main centres of leaning. Nowadays the marja'iyya is a form of centralized religious authority with transnational networks.

13 An example is Ali al-Korani, a Lebanese activist of Al-Da'wa who, through his virulent speeches, would have an important impact on a young generation of Kuwaiti Shi'a. He was replaced by Sh. Mohammed Mahdi al-Asefi, an Iraqi of Iranian descent. The latter's arrival in Kuwait marked the arrival of political exiles to Kuwait following growing repression by the Ba'athist regime. See Louër, *Transnational Shi'a politics*, pp. 110–120.

14 The system of the marja'iyya, whilst centralizing religious authority, does not recognize undisputed rules for designating a marja' and is hence characterized by continuous factional struggles opposing contenders for religious authority. Al-Shirazi's claim to the marja'iyya was not recognized by the mujtahed of Iraq, Muhsin al-Hakim, because of his circumvention of several unwritten rules related to the marja'iyya. He was too young and did not frequent the Najafi seminars, being mostly educated in Karbala. For a detailed account of the problems within the centralization of clerical leadership in contemporary Shi'ism, see Amanat, A., 'In between the madrasa and the marketplace: the designation of clerical leadership in modern Shi'ism', in S. A. Arjomand (ed.), *Political authority and political culture in Shi'ism*, Albany: SUNY Press, 1988, pp. 98–132.

15 These Shi'a designated themselves as the Young Men (*Shabab*), in order to distinguish themselves politically from the older generation of notables and organized in the diwaniyya of the Young Men. See Al-Khaldi, S. N., *al-ahzab al-islamiyya fii al-kuwayt: al-shi'a, al-ihwan wa al-salfiyyun (The Islamic movements in Kuwait: the Shi'a, the Ikhwan and the Salafists)*, Dar al-Naba'li alNashra wa al-Tawzi', 1999, pp. 102–104.

16 In countries where traditional 'asabiyyat prevail, the structure of society tends to be 'articulated' rather than 'stratified'. The literature on neo-patrimonialism analyses these phenomena of weak horizontal integration from a systemic point of view; arguing that patronage and clientelism are at the heart of the neo-patrimonial state and enables the state to maintain its patriarchal domination over society.

17 The Social Society for Culture was established in 1963 by the dominant Shi'a merchant families, notably Qabazard, Ma'rafi, al-Kadhemi and Assiri. See Al-Khaldi, *al-ahzab al-islamiyya fii al-kuwayt*, p. 105.

18 The dominant Shi'a merchant families, who also occupied positions in parliament, did all have a substantial part of their business concentrated in sectors relatively dependent on government patronage, such as real estate/lands and contracting. Some examples: the Ma'rafi family is specialized in a broad range of activities, varying from trade to services, but concentrates on construction and real estate. The Al-Wazzan family is the main contractor in foodstuff with the ministries of Interior, Social Affairs and Health. Next to contracting, most of the notables became commercial agents for foreign companies: Mercedes (Al-Kadhemi), Panasonic (Al-Youssefi), Porsche (Behbahani).

19 Al-Khaldi, *al-ahzab al-islamiyya fii al-kuwayt.*
20 Although playing a de-facto leadership role within al-Mithaq Abdelwahhab al-Wazzan does not have a formal role in the movement. The secretary general of the movement is 'Abd al-Hadi Saleh (ex-vice president of the Social Society for Culture in the 1980s).
21 Personal interview, Kuwait City, March 2009.
22 Personal interview with Abdullilah Ma'rafi, Kuwait City, March 2009.
23 For more information on the various terrorist attacks that swept the country in the 1980s, see Boghardt, L. P., *Kuwait amid war, peace and revolution: 1979–1991 and new challenges*, Hampshire: Palgrave Macmillan, 2006, p. 89.
24 Ibid.
25 The two pro-government Shi'a deputies were Ya'coub Hayati (liberal and close to the Shiraziyyin) and Abbas Hussayn Khudari (a 'service deputy'). The only Shi'a pro-Iranian Islamist who succeeded to have a seat in parliament was Nasr Sarkhu. Other Islamist deputies like Adnan Abdelsamad and Abdelmohsin Jamal lost in the competition against other, government-supported candidates, like Abbas Khudari. See Layne, L. L. (ed.), *Elections in the Middle East: implications of recent trends*, Boulder, CO, Westview Press, 1987, p. 179.
26 Boghardt, *Kuwait amid war, peace and revolution*, p. 133.
27 See in this context the concept of 'corporatism' as employed by Khaldoun al-Naqeeb in his analysis of state–society relations in the Gulf region. Al-Naqeeb, K., *State and society in the Gulf and the Arab Peninsula*, London: Routledge, 1990.
28 Several authors (Shambayati, Ayubi, Ross) have argued that the nature of the rentier state inhibits the crystallization of class-based politics, thus leaving more space for the emergence of social movements based on moral (ascriptive and cultural) considerations.
29 See the study of E. Lust-Okar on elections and the role of MPs in authoritarian MENA regimes, comparing to a situation of 'competitive clientelism'. Lust-Okar, E., 'Competitive clientlism in the Middle East', *Journal of Democracy* (2009), 203, 122–135.
30 See in this context the distinction – formalized by Maurice Duverger – between 'parties of cadres' and 'parties of masses' related to the nature of the legitimacy of political parties. Duverger, M., *Les partis politiques*, Paris, Le Seuil, coll. 'Points Essais', 1992, p. 84.
31 Adnan Abdelsamad, Abdelmohsin Jamal, Nasr Sarkhu.
32 For more on the role of the diwaniyya for the new middle classes created since the inception of the modern state, see Dazi Heni, F., *Le diwaniyya: entre changement social et recompositions politiques au Koweit au cours de la decennia 1981–1992*, PhD thesis Sciences Po, Ph.D thesis (unpublished), 1996.
33 As such, the shaykhi Shi'a are likely to vote for deputies of *Tajammu'a al-Risalat al-Insaniyya (The Assembly of the Human Message).*
34 We can think of Ahmad Lari (Al-Tahaluf), Adnan Abdelsamad (Al-Tahaluf), Hassan Jowhar (independent, but close to Al-Tahaluf), Saleh Achour (Al-Adala Wa-Salam) and Abdelmohsin Jamal (Al-Tahaluf). This information was collected during our fieldwork in Kuwait (March–April 2009).
35 The Shi'a deputies who are considered to be descendants from the Prophet: Sayyid Adnan Abdelsamad (Al-Tahaluf), Sayyid Hussayn al-Qallaf (independent, pro-government) and Sayyid Youssef al-Zilzalla (Al-Mithaq).
36 The ideological principles of the movement are justice, peace, Islamic unity, and consultation. Interview with AbdelHussayn al-Sultan, secretary-general of the Shiraziyyin, Kuwait City, March 2009.

37   After the death of Mirza al-Ha'iri al-Ihqaqi, a split occurred with the shaykhi-hasawi community in Kuwait. One group recognizes his son, Abdallah al-Ihqaqi, as their new marja' and is associated with the *Imam al-Sadiq* mosque. Another group, not recognizing Abdallah al-Ihqaqi as their marja', is associated with *Majlis Abadar*, under direction of the merchant Hussayn al-Qattan (Abu Bachar). Personal interviews, Kuwait City, March/April 2009.

38   The charitable associations of the Shiraziyyin are *Ahl al-Beyt, Sayyid al-Shuhada, Mohammed al-Ameen* and *Jama'iyyat AlTaqalin*. Interview with Ibrahim al-Gholoom, director of the Shiraziyyin library 'Rasol al-Azam', Kuwait City, March 2009.

39   *Al-Anwar* (The Lights) was created in 2003 and broadcast its programs for the first time in 2005. The project of Mohammed AlShirazi and his son, Mortadha al-Shirazi, seems to have profited from the financial support of affluent Shi'a merchants in Kuwait and in Saudi Arabia. Interview with AbdelHussayn al-Sultan, Kuwait City, April 2009.

40   In 2013, following the boycott of December 2012, the Shi'a had a record representation of seventeen MPs.

Chapter 9

1   The term 'competitive authoritarians' was introduced by Levitsky and Way to describe regimes in the post–Cold War era that combine the holding of multiparty elections with significant democratic abuse. See Levitsky, S. and Way, L., *Competitive authoritarianism: hybrid regimes after the Cold War*, New York: Cambridge University Press, 2010.

2   Al-Khatib, *al-Kuwait min al-Imara ila al-Dawla*, p. 14.

3   http://www2.gsu.edu/~polmfh/database/portfolio10.htm (accessed 29 September 2019).

4   Here the 1967 defeat and death of its symbol Gamal Abdel Nasser in 1970 presented a blow to the secular nationalist ideology and gradually replaced the nationalist focus on constitutionalism in the defence of middle class and public money.

5   Al-Sa'idi, S., *al-sulta wa al-tajarat al-siyasiya fi al-kuwayt: bidayat al-ta'awun wa al-sira'* (The (political) power and the political movements in Kuwait: the start of the cooperation and the struggle), Kuwait: Dar al-Qabas, 2010, p. 41. Also see: Al-Khatib, A., *al-Kuwait min al-Imara ila al-Dawla*, p. 20.

6   Al-Sa'idi, S., *al-sulta wa al-tajarat al-siyasiya fi al-kuwayt*, p. 43.

7   1974 FCO 8/2190, 'National Assembly Elections', 8 December 1974, Report by P.R. M Hinchcliffe, PRO: BNA, Richmond, UK. Al-Najjar, *Decision-making process in Kuwait*, pp. 66–67.

8   Al-Najjar, *Decision-making process in Kuwait*, p. 67.

9   Ibid., p. 68. Also see Ghabra, 'Voluntary associations in Kuwait', 1991, p. 205.

10   Ibid.

11   Al-Ghabra, 1991, 205.

12   Al-Najjar, *Decision-making process in Kuwait*, p. 114.

13   The most important example of this was Afghanistan and the support given to mujahedeen to fight against the Soviets, a policy supported by the Americans and officially endorsed by the Saudi Wahhabi authorities. US troops in 'holy' territory infuriated the jihadis, leading to a call by Bin Laden of global jihad against impious regimes and their apostate backers, the House of Al-Saud.

14 The conflict started as a conflict between Maronite and Palestinian forces in Lebanon. Later, left-wing, pan-Arabist and Muslim Lebanese forces joined the Palestinians. The Maronites had dominated the Lebanese political system as a minority – a consequence of the colonial structure – and allied with the United States in the Cold War.

15 In the districts considered their fiefs, the nationalists represented by the groups of Al-Khatib and Al-Qatami did not succeed, losing the competition against pro-government merchants, Islamists or tribal groups. Meanwhile, the general decline of nationalism as a postcolonial ideology also had its impact on Kuwait, where Islamism filled the void.

16 Rising sectarianism in elections was observed and for the first time, the Sunni majority population held a primary in the *da'iyya* district that also had an important Shi'a population. This strategy reportedly followed the Shi'a semi-primary elections in this district, resulting previously in Sunni candidates losing. The Shi'a candidates winning in these elections were all educated members of Iranian origin, from middle-class background, supportive of the Iranian Revolution. They won in their districts against Shi'a merchants (i.e. Habib Hayat lost against Sarhu in district 2; Abdelmutalib al-Kazemi against Al-Samad in district 1).

17 These were Jasem al-'Awn (Salafi current), Humud Saleh al-Rumi (Ikhwan), Khaled al-Sultan (Salafi), Saleh al-Fadhala (support for Ikhwan/independent) and Issa al-Shahin (Ikhwan).

18 One can think here of Jasem al-'Awn or Khaled al-Sultan. Both were previously active members of Al-Islah. See Al-Mudairis, Al-Sultan was elected as head of the administrative committee of Ihya. Al-Turath, F., *al-Jama'at al-Salafiyya fi al-Kuwait: al-Nash'at wa al-fikr wa al-tatawur 1965–1999 (The Salafi movement in Kuwait: origins, thought and development 1965–1999)*, Dar al-Qurtas, 1999, p. 9.

19 Crystal, *Oil and politics in the Gulf*, p. 104.

20 Al-Sa'idi, *al-Sulta wa al-tajarat al-siyasiay fi al-kuwait*, p. 52.

21 Lahoud-Tatar, *Islam et politique au Koweit*, p. 119.

22 Competition between the two groups was fiercest in the fifth (Qadisiyya) and seventh (Kaifan) districts. In the fifth, Abelaziz al-Mutawa'a opposed Ahmad al-Baqer and Abdallah al-Khalib (Salafis). In the seventh, fief of the Salafis, Jasim al-'Awn opposed Adel al-Subayh and Muhammad al-Adsani (the latter two representing the Ikhwan).

23 Tribal seats in parliament rose from nineteen in 1963 to twenty-seven in the 1985 parliament as a consequence of the naturalization of thousands of southern tribes in this period. Osman Salih, K., 'Kuwait primary (tribal) elections: 1975–2008', *British Journal of Middle Eastern Studies*, Vol. 38, No. 2 (2011), p. 148. It also marked the increased professionalization of the tribal vote via the process of organizing tribal primaries (*far'iyyat*), reducing the number of candidates. Both phenomena explain the rise in the electoral base by 35 per cent and the decline in the number of candidates from 447 to 231 in 1981 compared to the previous elections in 1975.

24 For details on the MPs, see http://www2.gsu.edu/~polmfh/database/maj198500.htm (accessed 27 September 2019).

25 See overview of interpellations, compilations of Al-Qabas archives: *Tarikh Istijwabat al-wuzara fi al-hukumat al-Kuwaitiyya 1963–2011*. The interpellation against 'Al-Khalifa was presented by Abdallah al-Nafisi (Ikhwan) and Jasem al-Qatami (nationalist). While the bombings of the embassies in 1983 and the assassination attempt on the life of the Emir were largely carried out by foreign Shi'a militias, the 1986 attacks on Kuwait's oil installations were perpetrated by radicalized Kuwaiti Shi'a.

26 Crystal notes that the interpellated Ministers of Education (Hasan al-Ibrahim) and Communication (Isa al-Mezidi) were known for their proximity to Sa'd. Crystal, *Oil and politics in the Gulf*, p. 105.

27 Various reasons explain this decision: failure of parliament to co-opt effectively dissenting voices, the strong attacks against members of the royal family and a regional context in which GCC members (Saudi Arabia foremost) criticized the vocal opposition of Kuwait's parliament.

28 Among the thirty-two former deputies, there were twenty new ones who only had their first parliamentary experience in 1985. They were mostly from a new generation of young, educated Kuwaitis who had been educated abroad. One can think here of Ahmad al-Baqer (Salafi), Ahmad al-Rubi'i (liberal), Ahmad al-Shari'an (tribal) and Mubarak al-Duwaila (tribal and Ikhwani).

29 In total, the founding members of this movement comprised around eighty-five persons from different socio-economic, socio-cultural and confessional background. They had organized popular committees in each electoral district entrusted with the election of general secretaries, supervising the area and serving as an intermediary in communication between the movement's leadership and the people. Dazi-Heni, F., *La diwaniyya*, PhD thesis, Sciences Po Paris, 1996, pp. 368–369.

30 On 4 July 1989, the merchants Abdelaziz Hamad al-Saqqar, Humud Yusuf al-Nusuf and Abdelrahman al-Badr met with Shaykh Jaber al-Ahmad, the Emir, to present their petition.

31 In total, six of such meetings were organized. The first was organized in the diwaniyya of Jasem al-Qatami (4 December 1989) that saw a presence of around 700 people. The second was held in the diwaniyya of Masharia al-'Anjari (11 December 1989). The diwaniyya was closed by the police. The third was held in the Fatima Mosque, without the holding of a speech, to protest in silence about the closure of the previous meeting in which 3,500 people participated. The fourth meeting was held in the diwaniyya of Muhammad al-Rashid (25 December) in Khaldiyya. The fifth meeting was held in the tribal area of Al-Jahra, in the diwaniyya of Ahmad al-Shari'an (8 January 1990). It was this meeting which was met with strong government repression. Reportedly, thousands of people were present, some of whom were met with violence by security forces (Muhammad al-Rashid was beaten himself). This incident resembles an incident that would occur in 2008 in the diwaniyya of tribal MP Jumu'an al-Harbash. The sixth was held in the diwaniyya of Faisal al-Sani'a (15 January 1990) and the last in the diwaniyya of 'Abbas Habib al-Musailem (22 January 1990).

32 Such as the ones of Mubarak al-Duwaila (Rashaida), Ahmad al-Shari'an (Dhafir), Rashid al-Hajilan ('Awazem) and Da'ij al-Jerri ('Ajman).

33 On one of these occasions, Ikhwan member, Mubarak al-Duwaila, presented a lecture in the diwaniyya of Abbas al-Munawar entitled *'Mada ahd al-fidawiyya'* (*The time of the fidawi is gone*), in which he called upon tribesmen to emancipate themselves and come up for their rights as full citizens, referring to their historical role as loyal guards for the Al-Sabah. Personal interview Mubarak al-Duwaila, Kuwait City, March 2012. This was in December 1989.

34 Saudi Arabia has become a dominant power in the region ever since the 1973 war, upgrading OPEC to a body capable of influencing international politics. Throughout the 1980s it was able to expand its influence, via its alliance with the United States, in the context of the Cold War and the support given to *mujahedeen*, exported by the KSA to foreign contexts (Afghanistan and Bosnia). Following American's intervention in Iraq in 2003, it supported Sunni insurgent groups in Iraq, stepping up its rivalry with Iran for regional dominance. In the context of the Arab revolts of 2011 and their aftermath, Saudi Arabia's role has strengthened even more within the GCC and in the wider MENA, although contested since

the 1990 Gulf War by radicalized Sunni Islamists. Out of American inaction and intending to profit from the power vacuums and the reshuffling of cards in the region, it asserted its role in Syria, Yemen, Bahrain and Egypt. Within the GCC, Saudi Arabia has been a leading player and has pressured rulers of small states with vibrant societies (Kuwait and Bahrain) to crack down on popular movements and Shi'a activism.

35   Abdallah al-Nafisi and Ahmad al-Baqar stayed loyal to the opposition, despite the general change in tone by Al-Islah 's members (Ahmad al-Jasar, Yusuf al-Hajji and Abdallah al-Mutawa') and the members of Jam'iyyat al-Turath (Khaled al-Issa and Muhammad al-Rumi).

36   For a full picture of the members of the National Council: http://www2.gsu. edu/~polmfh/database/maj199000.htm (accessed 25 September 2019).

Part III

Chapter 10

1   Personal interview, Mubarak al-Duwaila, Kuwait City, March 2012.

2   While some tribesmen presented themselves on a non-tribal ticket – generally linked to the Islamist movement – most still won on a tribal ticket, via the so-called primaries (fari'yyat). In 1992, twenty-two tribal candidates were elected and were rather loyal to the regime. See Al-Naqeeb, K., *Sira'at al-qabila wa al-dimoqratiyya: halat al-Kuwayt (A struggle between the tribe and democracy: the situation of Kuwait)*, Kuwait: Dar al-Saqi, 1996, p. 217.

3   Lahoud-Tatar, *Islam et politique au Koweït*, p. 172.

4   Al-Boghaili, M., *al-Qabila wa al-sulta: hirak al-siyasi al-qabali fi al-Kuwayt (The tribe and the power: the political tribal movement in Kuwait)*, Kuwait: Maktabat Afaq, 2012, p. 122.

5   Osman Salih, K., 'Kuwait primary (tribal) elections 1975–2008: an evaluative study', *BRISMES*, Vol. 38, No. 2 (2011), pp. 149–150.

6   Al-Sa'idi, S., *al-Sulta wa al-tajarat al-siyasiya fi al-Kuwayt: bidayat al-ta'awun wa al-sira' (The [political] power and the political movements in Kuwait: the start of the cooperation and the struggle)*, Kuwait: Dar al-Qabas, 2010, p. 90.

7   Al-Ghabra, S., *al-Kuwayt: dirasat fi aliyat al-dawla wa al-sulta wa al-mujtama' (Kuwait: a study in the mechanisms of the state, of the power and of the society)*, Kuwait: Dar al-Afaq, 2012, pp. 151–156.

8   A characteristic of Ibn Baz's doctrine was his open animosity towards Christians and Jews, both considered as polytheists. He also promoted a new type of jihad, economic jihad (*jihad bi'l-mal*). This meant by petro-dollars-funded dispersion of the Wahhabi creed throughout the world. Meanwhile, Ibn Baz – as the Grand Mufti – was supportive of the Ruling House and issued fatwas in line with the government's policies. As such, he authorized the presence of foreign armies on Saudi soil in the 1990s, a position which was fiercely denounced by radical (jihadi) Salafi groups (i.e. Usama Ben Laden, Al-Maqdisi). Ibn Baz contributed to the institutionalization, by the Saudi regime, of a Salafi-Jihadi ideology that was propagated outside Saudi borders, whilst repressed from within, leading to contradictory stances (i.e. support of Muslim resistance in Iraq, but the condemnation of Al-Qaeda in the Peninsula).

9   Pall, Z., *Salafism in Lebanon: local and transnational resources*, PhD thesis, University of Utrecht, 2014, p. 80.

10 See Al-Boghaili, *al-Qabila wa al-sulta: al-hirak al-siyasi al-qabali fi al-Kuwayt*, p. 113.

11 Osman Salih, 'Kuwait primary elections 1975–2008', pp. 148–149.

12 This is how our interlocutor, Jamal al-Nafasi (former Kuwaiti Ambassador and member of the Rashaida tribe) describes this: 'They are not with and not against the primaries. They cannot be against, because themselves, they rely on this tribal support. No one can really be against: Al-Barrak lives within his tribe, the same is the case for Al-Harbasch. Thus, their criticism vis-à-vis the primaries is a very shy criticism and they do it indirectly, because themselves, they are dependent on the tribal vote.' Interview, Kuwait City, September 2013. It is important to note here that of the twelve former MPs who constitute the core of the defunct oppositional bloc since 2009, one finds six who participated in primaries. See Al-Fadhala, S. N., *al-halat wa al-hal*, p. 81.

13 Personal interview, Kuwait City, September 2013.

14 Interview with Muhammad al-Uteibi in his law office in Al-Riqa'i, Kuwait, October 2013.

15 Personal interview, HQ of the Social Reform Society, Kuwait City, October 2013.

16 The law No. 9/81 imposed a three-year imprisonment and a fine of 1000 KD on those who participate in primary elections. While it deterred many tribesmen from conducting primaries prior to the 1999 elections (which explains the poor performance of tribesmen then), in subsequent years primaries were reorganized and tolerated by the regime.

17 In 1992 tribesmen running exclusively on a tribal ticket had eight seats, while this increased to twenty in 2003 and 2006 and nineteen in 2008; in addition to the other tribesmen running on non-tribal (Islamist) tickets, but relying on tribal support. See Osman Salih, 'Kuwait primary elections 1975–2008', p. 152 (Table 6).

18 See Al-Boghaili, *al-Qabila wa al-sulta*, p. 131. This was for example done by the Rashaida tribe. Also see Osman Salih, 'Kuwait primary elections: 1975–2008', p. 156.

19 Personal interview, Sami al-Adwani, HQ of the Social Reform Society, Kuwait City, October 2013.

20 Personal interview with Jamal al-Nasafi, Kuwait City, September 2013.

21 This corresponds to the previously detailed concept of 'political tribalism' as developed by late Kuwaiti sociologist Khaldun al-Naqueeb. In this perspective, the Arabian monarchies deal with societal groups via the reinvention of traditional corpus of sectarian and tribal groups that are dealt with via elite representatives of these groups. This system would stimulate tribal groups to reinvent themselves into the modern state to advance their interests and opposes ideals of democracy. Al-Naqueeb, K., *Sira' al-qabila wa al-dimoqratiyya: halat al-Kuwayt*, Dar al-Saqi, 1996.

22 Personal interviews, Kuwait City, 2012–14.

23 http://news.kuwaittimes.net/youth-ministry-launches-initial-national-strategy/ (accessed 28 September 2019).

24 https://goo.gl/LO9q4S (accessed 25 September 2019). The first Youth Renaissance Forum was organized in Bahrain 2010 and the second in Qatar. The third was the one that was to be organized in Kuwait, but it was cancelled on the first day by the Ministry of Interior.

25 Personal interview with Muhammad Abdelqader al-Jasem, prominent lawyer, Kuwait City, 8 May 2012.

26 Personal interview with Ahmad Bin Barjas, historian of Arabian tribalism, Kuwait City, September 2013.

27　Personal interview with a former member of Hadam. A liberal member of hadam, my interlocutor left the movement in 2013 out of dissatisfaction with the internal election procedures and what he considered a lack of transparency regarding the source of financing for the movement. Personal interviews, Kuwait City, March 2012 and September 2013.

28　https://www.youtube.com/watch?v=tqG9y0qDGR4 (accessed 24 September 2019).

29　Personal interviews, Ahmad Bin Barjas, Kuwait City, September 2013. Al-Fadhala, N., *al-halat wa al-hal*, pp. 56–62.

30　Personal interview with Khaled al-Fadhala, Kuwait City, 27 February 2012.

31　See Al-Fadhala, N., *al-halat wa al-hal*, pp. 66, 67. One can think here of veteran politician Ahmad al-Sa'dun, who clearly identified with the *hadar* liberal current, but is a founder of the Popular Action Bloc that represents the middle classes and counts upon significant support from tribesmen (not the least because of the presence of Musallam al-Barrak as a leading member). Other examples are Ali al-Doqbasi (Rashaida/Popular Action Bloc) who supported the government during the crisis about electoral redistricting in 2005. Other examples are Khaled al-Adwa ('Ajman/Islamist), Sa'dun Hamad (Uteibi/formerly part of the pro-regime National Council) or Hussayn Mezid (Mutran).

32　Personal interview with Sami al-Khalidi, Kuwait City, 8 October 2013.

33　Personal interview with Muhammad Abdelqader al-Jasem, Kuwait City, 19 November 2012.

34　Personal interview with Dr Badr al-Nashi, former SG of *Hadas*, Kuwait City, April 2012. When asking him about why they lost so many members in 2009, he replies: 'Because we did not support the tribes during the "isqat al-qurud" issue. For them, it felt as if we betrayed them. However, we had done a study on this and came to the conclusion that it would be better not to support the question. The demands were populist. This is the reason why we lost our votes in 2009 within the outside areas, because we depend on these votes'.

35　Some examples: the website of the Al-'Awazem tribe, the Mutran tribe or the 'Ajman tribe. These tribes also have their own Twitter accounts.

36　Interview with Ahmad Ben Barjas, 13 February 2013.

37　Al-Boghaili, *al-Qabila wa al-sulta*, p.132.

38　*Al-Shahid*, 16 December 2012, '*Hiwarat twitiriyya taba'aha al-kathirun wa addat il taskhin al-sahat: al-shammari: Musallam al-Barrak yaziif al-hawadith kei yahut min qudar shammmar*' (Twitter debates followed by many and that led to stirring up the arena: shammari: Musallam al-Barrak falsifies events to degrade the capacities of the Shammar).

39　http://www.alaan.cc/pagedetails.asp?nid=44662&cid=30 and http://www.youtube.com/watch?v=GVpYyx0-tjk and http://www.nationalkuwait.com/forum/index.php?threads/96070/ (accessed 1 October 2019).

40　*Al-Anba*, 27 March 2013, '*Multaqi qabilat al-'Ajman wa qabail yam tadai l-jam'a al-tabaru'at li-saleh al-sha'b al-suri al-shaqiq*' (Forum of the 'Ajman and the Yam tribes calls to collect finds for the brotherly Syrian people).

41　*Al-Qabas*, 15 March 2013, '*Qadamatha qafila qabilat mutair ardiyya wa malabis wa bataniyyat li al-lajiin al-suriyyin* (A bus of the Mutair has donated food, clothes and blankets to the Syrian refugees).

42　This generational shift can be found everywhere in the Sunni Islamist field (from purists to jihadis). The Islamic State itself represents a third generation of jihadis that defy the customs of seniority and the consensus of jihadi scholars.

43   Personal interview with Ahmad Ben Barjas, Kuwait City, 13 February 2013. Also
      see Al-Hayat, 22 May 2013. http://www.alhayat.com/Details/516093 (accessed
      19 September 2019).

44   Personal interview with Ahmad Ben Barjas, Kuwait City, 13 February 2013.

45   Upon the creation of his TV Channel, Al-Juwaihal explained that the goal would be
      to 'reinforce the true unity of the country for the children of Kuwait and through
      reviving the original Kuwait consisted of that elite of children and grandparents who
      have constructed and who are taking care of Kuwait'.

46   Media have accused former PM Nasser al-Mohammed and certain merchants to be
      the main backers of Juwaihal. In 2011, *Al-Anba* newspaper accused some merchants
      (such as Nasser al-Khorafi) of having large shares in the company. http://www.alaan.
      cc/pagedetails.asp?nid=71274&cid=30 (accessed 3 October 2019).

47   http://www.alwatanvoice.com/arabic/news/2009/12/21/144897.html (accessed 12
      September 2018).

48   These attacks came after Juwaihal had publicly declared that 'those who describe the
      Kuwaitis as dogs, to them I would say, you are you are the ....your tribe (Mutair)'.
      Following the incident various MPs asked the government to incarcerate Juwaihal.
      See: *'Elaf min shabab mutair dahamu maqar al-juwaihal wa awqadhu al-nar fi-hi
      ihtijajan 'ala ilfath rawan anna hum al-ma'niun biha', al-Watan,* 21 January 2012.

49   An example here is a video in which Musallam al-Barrak allegedly discovers
      names of princes who support Al-Juwaihal, https://www.youtube.com/
      watch?v=A03Hx3DI9xQ (accessed 3 October 2019).

50   Al-Qabas, 28 March 2014, *'Fi Ihtifal ishar mubarrat al-'Awazem bin Jama'a: lan uqabal
      'ala al-qabila ai musawamat aw tanazulat' (During the celebration of the opening
      of the 'Awazem charity. Falah Ben Jama'a says he will not accept any bargaining or
      concessions).*

51   Many examples are to be given and I can refer to the case of Dr Faris al-Waqian; who
      does not refer anymore to his tribe, but instead uses Al-Waqian, which is also the
      name of a famous *asli hadar* family.

52   Personal interview, Dr Muhammad al-Wohaib, Professor of Political Philosophy,
      15 March 2012.

Chapter 11

1   Between 1994 and 1998, these families had profited from the easy lending conditions
     existing in Kuwait, against very low interest rates, a policy of the Central Bank
     stimulating people to take large loans.

2   All the tribal MPs voted in favour of the proposal. Among the *hadar* MPs, twelve out
     of fifteen voted against it. Al-Fadhala, *al-halat wa al-hal,* p. 48.

3   http://www.hasanews.com/6219882.html (accessed 28 November 2015).

4   https://www.aljazeera.net/news/ebusiness/2018/12/10/القروض-إسقاط-الكويت-البنكية-القروض
     مجلس-الأمة-ماجد-المطيري (accessed 7 October 2019).

5   Personal interview, Kuwait City, 19 November 2012.

6   Personal interview, Ibrahim al-Shurayfi, Kuwait City, November 2012. Al-Shurayfi is
     a professor of political science at the Open University of Kuwait.

7   During the voting in Parliament (11 December 2008), all the tribal MPs voted
     against the government's law proposal, while most *hadar* (apart from Salafi Walid
     al-Tabtaba'i, relying on the tribal vote). Al-Fadhala, *al-halat wa al-hal,* p. 49.

8   'Lajna Badr', *al-Nahar*, 28 June 2010, Zayed al-Zaid.

9   http://www.alaan.cc/pagedetails.asp?nid=113323&cid=30# (accessed 28 November 2015).

10 Al-Fadhala, *al-halat wa al-hal*, pp. 56–57. These companies are: (1) Network Holding Company (*sharika al-shabaka al-qabidha*) 40 per cent is owned by Nayef Abdelaziz al-'Anezi and 12 per cent by Bandar Ayed al-Thafiri; (2) Our Holding (*Mana al-qabidha*): 24 per cent is owned by Mubarak al-Duwaila and others, 10 per cent by Muhammad Naser al-'Ajmi and others, 6 per cent by Jumu'an al-'Azemi and Tareq Issa al-Sultan; (3) National Company for Consumable Industries: 11 per cent for Faiz Mut'ab al-Thafiri and Nawf Mut'ab al-Thafiri and 22 per cent for Walid Manahi al-'Asemi and others; (4) Grain Company for Petrochemicals: 12 per cent to Walid Manahi al-'Asemi; (5) Salbukh Trading Company: 10 per cent for Falah Abtihan al-Rashidi; (6) Safat Global Holding Company: 5 per cent for Yusuf al-Thafiri; (7) Financing of Housing Company: 9 per cent for Naser Manahi al-'Asemi; (8) Dalqan Real Estate Company: 51 per cent for Muhammad Saud al-Mutairi; (9) Food Festival Company: 51 per cent for Muhammad Saud al-Mutairi (one of the most affluent and rather new *badu* merchants).

11 I refer hereby to the conclusions of the study of Nasser al-Fadhala on the attribution of tenders to different sections of Kuwaiti citizens in the first quarter of 2010. Al-Fadhala, *al-halat wa al-hal*, pp. 60–61.

12 http://www.alyaum.com/article/2668251 (accessed 28 November 2015).

13 Personal interview, Khaled al-Fadhala, Kuwait City, 27 February 2012.

14 Delia Monacu, Andrea Baronchelli, Nicola Perra, Bruno Gonçalves, Qian Zhang et al., 'The Twitter of Babel: mapping world languages through microblogging platforms', *PLos ONE*, Vol. 8, No. 4 (April 2013).

15 Azoulay and Wells, 'Contesting welfare state politics in Kuwait'.

16 Al-Nakib, 'Revisiting hadar and badu in Kuwait: citizenship, housing and the construction of a dichotomy'.

17 HASHD was created in April 2014 by Musallam al-Barrak and Ahmad al-Sa'dun, leading figures of the defunct oppositional bloc of the 2012 Parliament that was dissolved the same year. It is in essence a rebranding of the Popular Action Bloc. As its predecessor, the movement has a strong anti-corruption position and sharply criticizes the privileges of the merchant class. It also calls for an elected government. See http://goo.gl/qTt7o2 (accessed 28 November 2015).

18 https://www.alanba.com.kw/ar/economy-news/740184/24-04-2017-هل-توقف-الكويت-خطط-التقشف-وخفض-الإنفاق/ (accessed 11 October 2019).

19 Weiner, S., 'How long can the deadlock in Kuwait's parliament last', *Lawfare*, 24 May (2017). https://www.lawfareblog.com/how-long-can-deadlock-kuwaits-parliament-last (accessed 10 October 2019).

20 https://kif.kdipa.gov.kw/wp-content/uploads/khalid-mahdi-english.pdf (accessed 12 October 2019); https://www.arabianbusiness.com/kuwait-launches-new-plan-transform-economy-by-2035-661652.html (accessed 12 October 2019).

21 'Kuwait', *IMF Country Report No. 19/95*, April 2019.

22 https://worldview.stratfor.com/article/kuwait-shifts-burden-reforms-expatriates (accessed 12 October 2019).

Chapter 12

1   Al-Wuhaib, M., 'Kuwait: the crisis and its future', *Arab Reform Bulletin*, Vol. 63 (2012), p. 3.

2   The section below (into quotation mark) is reproduced verbatim from an earlier co-authored piece, referenced as Rivka Azoulay and Claire Beaugrand, 'Limits of political clientelism: elite struggles' fragmenting politics in Kuwait', *Arabian Humanities*, Vol. 4 (2015).

3   In 2001, five of them were appointed as ministers. These are Aḥmad al-Fahd al-Jabir (see below), Aḥmad 'Abdallāh al-Ṣabāḥ, (Minister of Communications, then Minister of Oil until 2011 Muḥammad Khālid al-Ḥamad (former Minister of Interior in 2001, then adviser for the Emiri Diwan in 2003 and in 2009 Head of the National Security apparatus), Muḥammad al-Ṣabāḥ al-Sālim (MFA until 2011 when he left over a corruption scandal), and Jābir al-Mubārak al-Ḥamad (Current PM).

4   *Dazi-Heni, F.,* 'Coups de théâtre à Koweït-City', *Outre-Terre*, Vol. 1, No. 14 (2006), pp. 281–294.

5   Article 4 of the 1962 constitution states that the rule of the hereditary Emirate should remain among the descendants of the late Mubārak al-Ṣabāḥ.

6   See his biography http://www.da.gov.kw/eng/diwnamiri/nasser.php (accessed 18 October 2019).

7   For a more complete sociology of the Shi'a in the Kuwaiti context, see Louer, L., *Transnational Shi'a politics: religious and political networks in the Gulf*, Colombia, NY: Hurst, 2008. Also see my own work Azoulay, R., 'The Politics of Shi'i Merchants in Kuwait', in St. Hertog, G. Luciani and M. Valeri (eds), *Business politics in the Middle East* (April 2013), pp. 67–99.

8   For more on *Al-Tahaluf*, see Part Two of this book, entitled 'Socio-political change within Kuwait's Shi'a population'. *Al-Tahaluf* is a pro-Iranian political bloc in Kuwaiti politics, supporting the wilayat al-faqih of Khamenei and previously Khomeini.

9   A notabe part of this part was verbatim taken from an earlier published article. Azoulay, R., 'The Politics of Shi'i Merchants in Kuwait', in Business Politics of the Middle East (eds. S. Hertog, G. Luciani, M. Valeri), London: Hurst, 2013, pp. 67–99.

10 Personal interview, Kuwait City, March 2009.

11 In the elections of May 2008, an alliance was formed between Saleh Ashour, Anwar Bukhamseen and Khalil al-Saleh. The three deputies decided to work together in the first district for al-Adala Wa-Salam.

12 Tajamu' al-Risala al-Insaniyya is the first political movement of the shaykhi community in Kuwait. The movement is organized around the Imam al-Sadiq mosque, led by the merchant Hussayn al-Qattan. The group represents a couple of hasawi families, related through intermarriages (such as Al-Sayegh, Al-Arbasch and Al-Qattan). Among the political figures related to the movement are Ali al-Baghli (former Minister of Oil) and Abdel Azizi al-Qattan, both of liberal persuasion.

13 Participation in electoral campaign of *al-I'tilaf al-Islami al-Watani (The National Islamic Coalition)*, uniting Al-Tahaluf, Al-Risalat al-Insaniyya and Al-Mithaq. During the conference, Jawaad Bukhamseen insisted on the need for the Shi'a in Kuwait to be united and called upon the audience to support this national coalition in a 'patriotic spirit'. Kuwait City, April 2009.

14 Selvik, K., 'Elite rivalry in a semi-democracy: the Kuwaiti press scene', *Middle Eastern Studies*, Vol. 47, No. 3 (May 2011), pp. 477–496.

15 Al-Aqeelah was created by Hamad Khaaja in 2006. The investments of Al-Aqeelah are multi-billion-dollar projects in the shrine cities of Najaf, Karbala and Sayyida

Zeinab in Syria. In 2008 the Najaf airport was opened, a project which includes the building of villas, schools and hotels in the city. The same is true for Sayyida Zeinab which is transformed into a touristic pilgrimage hub.

16   The statement of Nouri al-Maliki is telling in this context: 'We will never forget what Bukhamseen has done for Iraq through his investments and his dialogue with important Iraqi personalities.' Dar al-Nahar, 22 July 2007, *'al-Maliki: baladuna maftuhan amama al-Kuwaytiyiin Lil-istithmar'* (*Al-Maliki: our country is open for Kuwaitis for investments*).

17   Personal interview, Kuwait City, March 2009.

18   In the policy of land allocation, parcels of state land are distributed or 'sold' at symbolic prices to select citizens, to be subsequently repurchased by the state at a much higher price. It has been a very important policy for creating state clienteles. See also Al-Najjar, *The decision-making process in Kuwait.*

19   'I am someone neutral in the midst of all these people. I am original from Bahrain, but I support all the Shi'a movements and I am very close to the Emir. You know, they seem to be unified, but they are very dispersed, the Shi'a. At this moment we are trying to unite them.' Personal interview, Kuwait City, March 2009.

20   'Kuwait to mediate in Bahrain crisis', 27 March 2011.

21   The Haider family holds 28 per cent of shares in the 'Pearl of Kuwait Real Estate Company'. See IPR Strategic Business Information Database, *Kuwait: holding of Mahmud Haydar Family in the Kuwait Pearl Real Estate Company,* 21 September 2003.

22   Personal interview, Kuwait City, March 2009.

23   See Louër, *Transnational Shi'a politics,* p. 249.

24   Al-Rai al-Aam, 14 December 2001, *'al-Tahaluf al-Islami 'an al-waqf al-ja'fari: nuhadhdhiru al-hukuma min al al-istijabati li al dhughut al-kharijiyya'* (*The Islamic Coalition with regards to the Ja'fari waqf: we warn the government and we ask the government not to cede to external pressures*).

25   They underlined that most of the *'ulema* have not accepted to receive a government salary. Hence, instead of representing a policy of religious recognition responding to grassroots demands, the creation of the Shi'a Awqaf should be understood as a top-down measure by the state, aimed at better controlling its religious minority. Personal interviews of Shaykh Hashem al-Hashemi, Shaykh Bin Nakhi, Shaykh Hussayn al-Ma'atuq and Shaykh Ali al-Saleh.

26   Various personal interviews, Kuwait City, March/April 2009.

27   Shi'a were all the more supportive when the PM was attacked on sectarian questions, like in November 2008, when Salafis MPs filed a request to grill the PM for allowing prominent Iranian Shiite cleric Mohammad Bāqir al-Fālī to enter Kuwait despite a legal ban.

28   In 2008 the Sunni Islamists still represented twenty-one seats, whereas they only got eleven seats in the May 2009 elections. http://www2.gsu.edu/~polmfh/database/database.htm (accessed 11 September 2016), Kuwait Politics database, compiled by Michael Herb, Georgia State University.

29   The section below (into quotation mark) is reproduced verbatim from an earlier co-authored piece, referenced as Rivka Azoulay and Claire Beaugrand, 'Limits of political clientelism: elite struggles' fragmenting politics in Kuwait', *Arabian Humanities*, Vol. 4 (2015).

30   Like his father, he was president of the Kuwait National Olympic Committee (KOC) (1990–March 2001) and member of the International Olympic Committee (since 1992) as well as president of the Kuwait Football Association (1990–2004 and since

January 2009) and president of the Kuwait-based Olympic Council of Asia (OCA, since September 1991). Moreover, he has chaired the Asian Handball Federation since 1992.

31 Dorsey J. M., 'Soccer: a Middle East and North African battlefield', unpublished manuscript, November 2011, pp. 1–32. DOI: 10.2139/ssrn.1955513.

32 Shaykh Fahd al-Aḥmad was the president from 1969 till 1979, a position also occupied by Ṭalāl al-Fahd, his son and brother of Aḥmad al-Fahd, who has also been chairman of the Union since 1997.

33 Dazi-Heni, F., 2006.

34 Aḥmad al-Fahd was accused of corruption for using his position as head of the Ministry of Oil and Energy from 2003 to 2006.

35 One can think of Khaled al-Tahous, Ahmad al-Shari'an, Mishan al-'Azmi and 'Ali al-Doqbashi.

36 Al-Sa'dūn was many times Parliament Speaker in 1985, 1992, 1996 and 2012.

37 https://www.youtube.com/watch?v=2FGJFoeXVCQ (accessed 6 November 2017).

38 Interview with Tāriq al-Mutayrī, one of the leaders of Hadam, Kuwait, conducted by Claire Beaugrand, 27 April 2014.

39 Shaykh Aḥmad is an important powerbroker in Olympic circles: his comments came after the IOC decided to wait for the results of the FIFA Ethics Committee inquiry before launching its own investigation into two of its members implicated in the scandal. http://www.olympic.qa/en/NewsCenter/Pages/Shaykh-Ahmad-al-Fahad–We-will-face-racism-and-stand-with-Qatar-for-hosting-the-2022-World-Cup.aspx (accessed 6 December 2014).

40 *Arab Times*, 'Probe call on "Barrak cash" – deposits form Qatar', 4 December 2011. http://www.arabtimesonline.com/NewsDetails/tabid/96/smid/414/ArticleID/176905/reftab/69/Default.aspx (accessed 8 December 2014).

Chapter 13

1 Dazi-Heni, F. , 'The Arab Spring Impact on Kuwaiti "Exceptionalism', *Arabian Humanities* 4, 2015.

2 http://www.annaharkw.com/annahar/Article.aspx?id=63398&date=12042008. *'Mudahama diwan ghanim al-mi'a bi-l-qanabil al-musila' (Raid in the diwan of Ghanim al-Mi'a with the use of teargas)*. Also see the reaction of the 'Awazim: http://www.h-alali. net/j_open.php?id=87cfad70-5aa0-102b-943e-0010dce2d6ae (accessed 12 October 2019).

3 In the 2008 elections, Islamists won twenty-four out of fifty seats and twenty-five candidates out of fifty were tribal MPs. Most of the tribal MPs were linked to the Islamist current, either independently or affiliated to the Islamist movements (particularly the Salafis).

4 These ministers were from the Mutairi, 'Ajmi, 'Azmi and Rashaida tribes. Ali Mohammed al-Barrak (Minister of Health; 'Ajmi), Bader al-Duwaila (Minister of Social Affairs and Labor; Rashaida, independent Islamist), Hussayn al-Huraithi (Minister of Justice, of Awqaf and Islamic Affairs; 'Azmi, independent Islamist), Mohammed Abdullah al-Olaim, Minister of Oil and Minister of Electricity and Water; ICM, Al-Mutairi tribe).

5 Upon the creation of his TV channel in 2009, Al-Juwaihal explained that the goal would be to 'reinforce the true unity of the country for the children of Kuwait

and through reviving the original Kuwait consisted of that elite of children and grandparents who have constructed and who are taking care of Kuwait'.

6   http://www.alwatanvoice.com/arabic/news/2009/12/21/144897.html (accessed 10 April 2010).

7   Following the incident various MPs asked the government to incarcerate Juwaihal. See: *'Elaf min shabab mutair dahamu maqar al-juwaihal wa awqadhu al-nar fi-hi ihtijajan 'ala ilfath rawan anna hum al-ma'niun biha'*, al-Watan, 21 January 2012.

8   Bahraini premier Khalifa criticized Scope TV and *Al-Dar* newspaper for stirring up sectarian tensions in the region. The Emir of Qatar summoned Scope TV, *Al-Shahed* newspaper and *Al-Watan* for spreading false information about the bribing of MP Musallam al-Barrak with a cheque worth of 200 million Qatari riyals.

9   In this year, eight grillings were issued of which most against PM Nasser al-Mohammed, accusing him of corruption and the co-optation of MPs through the use of political money. See Al-Qabas summary *'Tarikh Istijwabat al-wuzara fi al-hukumat al-kuwaytiyya min 1963–2011'*.

10 These MPs received very bad media attention, shown in videos as the following: https://www.youtube.com/watch?v=s1h7OAfJpNU (accessed 10 October 2019).

11 Shaykh Nasser al-Muhammad – prime suspect in the scandals – refused to appear before the committee.

12 These MPs are Waleed al-Tabtabai, Musallam al-Barrak, Khaled al-Thahous, Faisal al-Muslim, Jumu'an al-Harbasch, Falah al-Sawagh, Mubarak al-Wa'alan, Mohammed al-Matar and Salem al-Namlan. Most of these MPs defend an Islamist view on politics.

13 http://alwatan.kuwait.tt/articledetails.aspx?id=322934 (accessed 6 December 2015).

14 Kuwaiti lawyer, writer and political activist Mohammed Abdel Qader al-Jasem (who has publicized these corruption scandals). Personal interview, Kuwait City, May 2012.

15 One can think of Sa'ad al-Zunayfir, Muglit al-Azemi, Husayn al-Huraythi, Galf Dumaythir, Khaled al-'Awda, Hussayn Mazid and Ali al-'Amir.

16 An example is the case of Mohammed al-Juwaihal and his al-Sur TV Channel. In 2011 *Al-Anbaa* newspaper claimed to have discovered the sourcing of funding of the channel, mentioning merchants such as Nasser al-Khorafi and Fahd Salem al-Humaydi for having shares. http://www.alaan.cc/pagedetails.asp?nid=71274&cid=30 (accessed 14 October 2019).

17 See the list of results of the February 2012 elections: http://voteforkuwait.com/?page_id=9155 (accessed March 2012).

18 Falah Ben Jama'a asked the government to apologize for the way it treated these two 'Awazem MPs, considering it a direct assault against the tribe. He added that if the 'Awazem would get angry, he wouldn't blame them and that he now supported demonstrations against the government. 'We are no criminals … we did not engage in explosions of refineries and did not kill ….there are others who defamed the authority, but were not dealt with in a similar way'. With the oil refineries, he refers to the bombings by Shi'a radicals during the Iran–Iraq War, when Kuwait became the scene of Hezbollah-led violence.

19 al-Barrāk was first sentenced to five years in jail for insulting the Emir in April 2013 but after a court appeal that cancelled the verdict, the court handed down two years jail in February 2015. The very popular former MP and leader of the opposition ended up spending only two months in jail after being freed on a KD 1,000 bail by the Court of Cassation on 21 April 2015 (*al-Qabas*, 21 April 2015). Following another Court appeal, security forces arrested the former MP in his farm on Saturday,

12 June 2015 and put him in jail in order to serve out his two years prison sentence (*al-Qabas*, 16 June 2015).

20 http://reliefweb.int/report/kuwait/lift-protest-ban-respect-right-demonstrate-peacefully (accessed 12 October 2019)

21 Dozens were wounded by bullets and teargas and various activists (among whom many former MPs) were arrested. One can think of Walid al-Tabtaba'i, Khaled Shahir and Saifi al-Saifi, along with liberal activist Khaled al-Fadhala (spokesman of the National Front).

22 See Tetrault, M., 'Eroding civil liberties in Kuwait', *Atlantic Council*, 30 April 2013. http://www.atlanticcouncil.org/blogs/menasurce/eroding-civil-liberties-in-kuwait (accessed 12 October 2019).

23 One can think here of Obeid al-Wasmi (*Mutran*) and Muhammad Hayef (*Mutran*), who were lured by the regime – allegedly in combination with Saudi pressure in the case of Hayef – to engage in a dialogue. The same was true for Dr Walid al-Tabtabai' (Scientific Salafi) who was also invited to engage in dialogue with the government. Ahmad al-Sa'dun, former parliamentary speaker and leader of the movement, also called for calm in this period and the need to find 'new formula for political opposition'.

24 http://goo.gl/wfdyFl (accessed 7 December 2015).

25 Musallam al-Barrak chanted: 'the committees of Jalib and Sabah al-Nasser will remain empty because they won't be satisfied with disgrace and shame'. Obeid al-Wasmi said "For dignity is a price …. It is not allowed that the executive is abusing its powers al-Barrak added "I am proud to say that I haven't betrayed you and haven't assembled money in banks" and added that the regime had tried to attack the Mutran and the media'. Personal collection of archives, *Alem al-Youm*, 2 December 2012.

26 The fifth district even celebrated that it had the highest number of electoral boycott within Kuwait. As such, a celebration was organized by a prominent Salafi leader – Dr Badr Majid al-Mutairi – that was attended by Musallam al-Barrak in Al-Sabahiyya. It was also attended by members of the defunct Majority Bloc and other tribal heads. During the meeting, speakers argued that the Mutran was the foremost tribe that had faced discrimination at the hands of the regime under the governments of Shaykh Nasser. Personal collection of archives, *Al-Qabas*, 6 December 2012.

27 These went to Dhikra al-Rashidi (appointed the first tribal Minister), Mubarak al-Kharinj, Sa'd al-Ghanfur and Muhammad Nasser al-Barrak.

28 The Cabinet was composed of two Rashaida ministers, one 'Ajman and one belonging to the 'Awazem.

29 https://www.youtube.com/watch?v=eNwFylc8rG8 (accessed 8 December 2015). Also see the speech given by Musallam al-Barrak on this occasion: https://www.youtube.com/watch?v=brjfiWQOzAg (accessed 8 December 2015).

30 The Bloc of National Action was created in 2006 as a liberally inclined bloc formed by eight former MPs. These are Abdallah al-Rumi, Saleh al-Fadhala, Muhammad al-Saqqar, Ahmad al-Mulaifi, Ali al-Rashid and Faisal al-Sha'iji. http://www.alqabas.com.kw/Articles.aspx?ArticleID=209083&CatID=307 (accessed 10 December 2015). Also see the declaration of the Bloc demanding a new PM and a new government: http://www.q8ow.com/vb/threads/40537/(accessed 10 December 2015).

31 http://studies.aljazeera.net/reports/2013/07/201373110162733491.htm#e3 (accessed 7 December 2015).

32 Comprising 93 articles, it establishes a Commission for Mass Communications and Information Technology to oversee all technical matters related to mobile phone

services and internet providers (a role previously carried out by the Ministry of
Communications).

33 http://www.aljazeera.com/news/middleeast/2014/07/kuwait-activists-social-media-2014727111219709724.html (accessed 8 December 2015).

34 http://www.arab-reform.net/saudi-arabia-political-implications-new-regional-policy-and-jihadist-challenge (accessed 8 December 2015).

35 http://www.thenational.ae/news/world/middle-east/gcc-to-set-up-20bn-bailout-fund-for-bahrain-and-oman (accessed 8 December 2015).

36 For the full text: http://www.almeezan.qa/AgreementsPage.aspx?id=1527&language=ar (accessed 8 December 2015).

37 Qatar ratified it on 29 August 2013. Saudi Arabia on 16 September 2013. The UAE on 21 October 2013. Bahrain on 27 November 2013 and Oman on 14 January 2014. The articles 2, 4, 9, 10 and 14 allegedly contradict constitutional laws. See 'Sovereignty Concerns in GCC Security Pact', *Arab Times*, 27 May 2013.

38 http://www.almqaal.com/?p=2032 (accessed 8 December 2015).

39 http://mirror.no-ip.org/news/24714.html (accessed 8 December 2015).

40 Personal interview with specialist of tribal history, Ahmad Bin Barjas, Kuwait City, 13 February 2013.

41 Personal interview, Ahmad Ben Barjas, Kuwait City, 13 February 2014. Personal interview, Muhammad al-Boghaili, Kuwait City, December 2013.

42 *Arab Times*, 'Probe call on "Barrak cash" – deposits from Qatar', 4 December 2011. http://www.arabtimesonline.com/NewsDetails/tabid/96/smid/414/ArticleID/176905/reftab/69/Default.aspx (accessed 10 November 2012).

43 Personal interview Kuwait City, 8 May 2012. Also see a Wikileaks document confirming the 'recent' nature of the Al-Khorafi, arriving to Kuwait in the twentieth century only. https://wikileaks.org/plusd/cables/89KUWAIT3922_a.html (accessed 10 October 2019).

44 Personal interview, Kuwait City, December 2013.

45 Personal interviews. Muhammad Abdelqader al-Jasem, Kuwait City, 19 November 2012. Khaled al-Fadhala, Kuwait City, November 2012.

46 Personal interview, Khaled al-Fadhala, Kuwait City, November 2012.

47 The section below which is into quotation mark is reproduced verbatim from an earlier co-authored piece, referenced as Rivka Azoulay and Claire Beaugrand, 'Limits of political clientelism: elite struggles' fragmenting politics in Kuwait', *Arabian Humanities*, Vol. 4 (2015).

48 BICI, 2011, p. 98.

49 https://cpj.org/2012/03/kuwaiti-daily-suspended-for-creating-sectarian-str.php (accessed 9 December 2015).

50 *Wasta* is an Arabic word that translates as nepotism, referring to the necessity to have a *wasit*, a mediator or broker to get access to services (i.e. government services).

51 He alluded to these meetings as being not for free (*ghair majaniyya*). *Al-Hayat*, 22 May 2013.

52 Personal interview, Kuwait City, 15 March 2012.

53 Personal interview with Ahmad Ben Barjas, Kuwait City, 13 February 2014.

54 Interview with Faisal al-Duwaish, chieftain of the Mutran, Kuwait City, February 2014.

55 *Al-Qabas*, 22 October 2012 (Personal archives). Leader of the Khwalid tribe said: 'The meeting is a meeting between a father and his children'. Leader of the Al-Utan

said: 'We were asked to discuss with the Emir the elections and found a positive and good answer and we are obedient to the Emir'.

56 http://ladieswhodolunchinkuwait.blogspot.nl/2013/04/commandos-raid-barraks-home-as-standoff.html (accessed 8 December 2015).

57 Al-Siyasa, 16 March 2013 (personal archives).

58 https://www.bbc.com/arabic/middleeast/2014/08/140812_kuwait_citizenship_revoke (accessed 12 October 2019).

59 https://www.hrw.org/news/2014/08/10/kuwait-5-critics-stripped-citizenship (accessed 11 October 2019).

60 https://www.economist.com/middle-east-and-africa/2016/11/26/to-silence-dissidents-gulf-states-are-revoking-their-citizenship (accessed 12 October 2019).

61 https://pomed.org/kuwait-revokes-citizenship-of-18-nationals/ (accessed 14 October 2019).

62 https://www.thenational.ae/world/mena/former-opposition-mp-surrenders-to-kuwaiti-authorities-1.697304 (accessed 13 October 2019).

63 https://www.alaraby.co.uk/english/news/2017/11/27/kuwait-opposition-figure-musallam-al-barrack-gets-nine-year-prison-term (accessed 12 October 2019).

64 Boodrookas, A., 'Crackdowns and coalitions in Kuwait', *MERIP*, 6 August 2018. https://merip.org/2018/06/crackdowns-and-coalitions-in-kuwait/ (accessed 11 October 2019).

65 Ibn Khaldun, *Muqqadimah,* pp. 119–120.

66 Rivka Azoulay and Claire Beaugrand, 'Limits of political clientelism: elite struggles' fragmenting politics in Kuwait', *Arabian Humanities*, Vol. 4 (2015).

67 Ibid.

68 http://mubasher.aljazeera.net/news/آخر-وسجن-الكويت-في-الحاكمة-الأسرة-أفراد-أحد-إعدام (accessed 11 October 2019).

69 https://www.neilpartrick.com/blog/kuwait-the-struggle-for-leadership-and-reform (accessed 13 October 2019).

Conclusion

1   For example, Crystal, *Oil and politics in the Gulf.* Ismael, J. S., *Kuwait. Social change.*

Bibliography

Al-'Ajmi, A. 'A nomadic logic: an intellectual image: divergent meanings on the concept of the state in Kuwait' (unpublished paper).

Ayubi, N. (1995), *Overstating the Arab state: politics and society in the Middle East*, London: I.B. Tauris.

Azoulay, R. (2015), 'Islamic State franchising: tribes, transnational jihadi networks and generational shifts', *Clingendael, Netherlands Institute of International Relations*, CRU Report, April.

Baram, N. (1997), 'Neo-tribalism in Iraq: Saddam Hussayn's tribal policies: 1991–1996', *International Journal of Middle Eastern Studies*, Vol. 29, No. 1, February. pp. 1–31.

Barwig, A. (2012), 'The new palace guards: elections and elites in Morocco and Jordan', *The Middle East Journal*, Vol. 66, No. 4, Summer.

Batatu, H. (1978), *The old social classes and the revolutionary movement in Iraq*, Princeton, NJ: Princeton University Press.

Batatu, H. (1999), *Syria's peasantry: the descendants of its lesser rural notables and their politics*, Princeton, NJ: Princeton University Press.

Bergh, S. (2012), 'Inclusive neoliberalism, local governance reforms and the redeployment of state power: the case of the national initiative for human development (INDH) in Morocco', *Mediterranean Politics*, Vol. 17, No. 3, October. pp. 410–426.

Binder, L. (1978), *In a moment of enthusiasm: political power and the second stratum in Egypt*, Chicago, IL: Chicago University Press.

Al-Boghaili, M. (2012), *Al-Qabila wa al-sulta: Al-hirak al-siyasi al-qabali fi al-Kuwayt*, Kuwait: Maktabat Afaq.

Boussaid, F. (2009), 'The rise of the PAM in Morocco: tramping political scene or stumbling into it?', *Mediterranean Politics*, Vol. 14. No. 3, pp. 413–419.

Al-Dakhil, K. (2011), 'al-Malakiyyat wa al-jumhuriyyat: hel tudi'a al-fursa maratan ukhra', *al-Hayat*, 27 November.

Dukhan, H. (2014), 'Tribes and tribalism in the Syrian uprising', *Syria Studies Journal*, Vol. 6, No. 2, pp. 1–28.

Eisenstadt, S. (1973), *Tradition, change and modernity*, New York: Wiley.

Eisenstadt, S. (1977), 'Convergence and divergence of modern and modernizing societies: indications from the analysis of the structuring of social hierarchies in Middle Eastern societies', *International Journal of Middle Eastern Studies*, Vol. 8, pp. 1–27.

Erdmann, G. and Engel, U. (2006), 'Neo-patrimonialism revisited: beyond a catch-all concept', GIGA working paper 16, Hamburg.

Fukuyama, F. (2011), *The origins of political order: from prehuman times to the French Revolution*, New York: Farrar, Straus & Giroux.

Gana, A. (2012), 'The rural and agricultural roots of the Tunisian revolution', *International Journal of Sociology of Agriculture and Food*, Vol. 19, No. 2, pp. 201–213.

Gramsci, A. (1971), *Selections from the prison notebooks of Antonio Gramsci*, New York: International Publishers.

Gurr, T. (1970), *Why men rebel*, Princeton, NJ: Princeton University Press.

Haenni, P. (2005), *L'ordre des caids: conjurer la dissidence urbaine au Caire*, Paris: Karthala.

Hagopian, F. (1996), *Traditional politics and regime change in Brazil*, Cambridge: Cambridge University Press.

Hajnal, J. (1965), 'European marriage patterns in perspective', in D. V. Glass and D. E. C. Eversley (eds), *Population in history: essays in historical demography*, Chicago, IL: Aldine Publishing Company.

Hammoudi, A. (1987), *Master and discipline: the cultural foundations of Moroccan authoritarianism*, Chicago, IL: University of Chicago Press.

Herb, M. (1999), *All in the family: absolutism, revolution and democracy in the Middle Eastern monarchies*, New York: Hurst University Press.

Hinnebusch, R. (1990), *Authoritarian power and state formation in Ba'thist Syria: army, party and peasants*, Boulder, CO: Westview Press.

Huntington, S. (1968), *Political order in changing societies*, New Haven, CT: Yale University Press.

Ibn Khaldun, A. (1369/1983), *Muqaddimah (Introduction to history)*, Beirut: Dar wa Maktabat al-Hilal.

Inkeles, A. (1966), 'The modernization of man', in M. Weiner (ed.), *Modernization*, New York: New York University Press.

Al-Jabir, F. (2000), 'Shaykhs and ideologues: detribalization and retribalization in Iraq: 1968–1998', *Middle East Report*, No. 215, 28–48.

Kepel, G. (1985), *The Prophet and Pharaoh: Muslim extremism in Egypt*, London: Saqi Books.

Khalaf, S. (2000), 'Shaykhs, peasants and party comrades: political change in northern Syria', in M. Mundy and B. Musallam (eds), *The transformation of society in the Arab East*, Cambridge: Cambridge University Press, pp. 110–122.

Khuri, F. (1980), *Tribe and state in Bahrain: the transition of social and political authority in an Arab state*, Chicago, IL: Chicago University Press.

King, S. (2009), *The New Authoritarianism in the Middle East and North Africa*, Bloomington, Indiana University Press.

Lerner, D. (1958), *The passing of traditional society: modernizing Middle East*, New York: Glencoe.

Leveau, R. (1976), *Le fellah marocain: défenseur du trône*, Paris: Presses de la Fondation Nationale des Sciences Politiques.

Liddell, J. (2010), 'Notables, clientelism and the politics of change in Morocco', *The Journal of North African Studies*, Vol. 15, No. 3, September, pp. 315–331.

Lindholm, C. (1986), 'Kinship structure and political authority: the Middle East and Central Asia', *Comparative Studies in Society and History*, Vol. 28, No. 2, pp. 334–355.

Lucas, R. E. (2005), *Institutions and the politics of survival in Jordan: domestic responses to external challenges*, New York: SUNY Press.

Mann, M. (1986), *The sources of social power, Volume 1: a history of power from the beginning to AD 1760*, Cambridge: Cambridge University Press.

Massad, J. (2001), *Colonial effects: the making of national identity in Jordan*, Colombia, NY: Colombia University Press.

Migdal, J. (1974), *Peasants, politics and revolution: pressures toward political and social change in the third world*, Princeton, NJ: Princeton University Press.

Moore, B. (1966), *Social origins of dictatorship and democracy: lord and peasant in the making of the modern world*, Boston, MA: Beacon Press.

Mulderig, M. (2013), 'An uncertain future: youth frustration and the Arab Spring', *The Pardee Papers*, No. 16, April.

Mylonis, H. (2013), *The politics of nation-building: making co-nationals, refugees and minorities*, Cambridge: Cambridge University Press.

Page, J. (1975), *Agrarian revolution: social movements and export agriculture in the underdeveloped world*, New York: Free Press.

Ryan, C. (2012), 'The implications of Jordan's new electoral law', *Foreign Policy*, 13 April.

Sahlins, M. (1961) 'The segmentary lineage model: an organization of predatory expansion', *American anthropologist*, Vol. 63, No. 2, pp. 322–344.

Scott, J. C. (1972), 'Patron-client politics and political change in Southeast Asia', *The American Political Science Review*, Vol. 66, No. 1, 1 March, pp. 91–113.

Sidel, J. (1999), *Capital, coercion and crime: bossism in the Philippines*, Stanford, CA: Stanford University Press.

Skocpol, T. (1979), *States and social revolutions: a comparative analysis of France, Russia and China*, Cambridge: Cambridge University Press.

Skocpol, T. (1982), 'What makes peasants revolutionary?', Review article, *Comparative Politics*, Vol. 14, No. 2, April.

Tilly, C. (1975), *The formation of national states in Western Europe*, Princeton, NJ: Princeton University Press.

Vannetzel, M. (2007), *Frères éligibles: étude de la mobilisation électorale islamiste en Egypte: le cas des élections législatives de 2005*, MPhil thesis, Sciences Po Paris.

Wittfogel, K. (1957), *Oriental despotism*, New Haven, CT: Yale University Press.

Wolf, E. (1969), *Peasant wars of the 20th century*, Oklahoma: University of Oklahoma Press.

Wolf, E. (1982), *Europe and the people without history*, Berkeley: University of California Press.

Al-Zo'abi, A., 'Tribe and tribesmen in Kuwait: a historical study of the tribal structure' (unpublished working paper).

Part I: Traditional politics and the pre-oil authority system of the Al-Sabah (1716–1938)

Abu Hakima, A. M. (1983), *The Modern History of Kuwait, 1750–1965*, London: Luzac.

Adsani, K. (1947), *Nusf Am li-l hukm al-niyabi fi al-kuwayt*, Kuwait.

Anscombe, F. (1997), *The Ottoman Gulf: the creation of Kuwait, Saudi Arabia and Qatar*, New York: Colombia University Press.

Bin Barjas, A. (2012), *Al-'Awazem: khilal elf sanat*, Kuwait: Maktaba al-'Ajeiri.

Beaugrand, C. (2010), *Statelessness and transnationalism in Northern Arabia: Biduns and state-building in Kuwait 1949–2006*, PhD thesis, London School of Economics.

Crystal, J. (1990), *Oil and politics in the Gulf: rulers and merchants in Kuwait and Qatar*, Cambridge: Cambridge University Press.

Crystal, J. (1992), *Kuwait: the transformation of an oil state*, Boulder, CO: Westview Press.

Dazi-Heni, F. (1992), *La diwaniyya : entre changement social et recompositions politiques au Koweït au cours de la décennie 1981–1992*, Paris: Institut d'Etudes Politiques.

Dickson, H. R. P. (1949), *The Arab of the desert: a glimpse into Badawin Life in Kuwait and Saudi Arabia*, London: George Allen & Unwin Ltd.

Ebrahim, M. (1981), *Problems of nomadic settlement in the Middle East with a special reference to Saudi Arabia and the Haradh project*, PhD thesis, Cornell University.

Fromherz A. (2014), *Qatar: a modern history*, Georgetown, DC: Georgetown University Press.

Furnivall, J. (1948), *Colonial policy and practice*, Cambridge: Cambridge University Press.

Al-Ghanim, S. (1998), *The reign of Mubarak al-Sabah: founder of modern Kuwait 1896–1915*, New York: I.B. Tauris.

Habib, M. (2013), 'Al-Shi'a fi ma'rakat al-Jahra: qira'at watha'iqiyya jadida', *Al-dawriyyya al-kuwaytiyya*, Vol. 19, March.

Al-Haddad, M. S. (1981), *The effect of detribalization and sedentarization on the socio-economic structure of the tribes of the Arabian Peninsula: 'Ajman tribes, a case study*, University of Kansas.

Ismael, J. S. (1982), *Kuwait: social change in historical perspective*, New York: Syracuse University Press.

Jamal, A. M. (2005), *Lamaht min tarikh al-shi'a fi al-Kuwayt*, Kuwait: Dar al-Naba' li-l-nashr wa al-tawzi'a.

Kelly (1968), *Britain and the Persian Gulf: 1795–1880*, Oxford: Oxford University Press.

Khaz'al, H. (1922), *Tarikh al-Kuwayt al-siyasi*, Kuwait: Manshurat Dar al-Hayat.

Al-Khaz'ali, S. (2008), *Al-jama'at al-siyasiya al-kuwaytiyya fi qarn 1910–2007*, Kuwait: Dar al-Qurtas.

Lorimer, J. G. (1908), *Gazetteer of the Persian Gulf, Oman and Central Arabia*, Vol. I, II, London: British Royal Archives.

Al-Mazeini, A. (1994), *Ansab: Al-usar wa al-qaba'il fi al-Kuwayt*, Kuwait: Dath al-Salasil.

Al-Nakib, F. (2012), 'The lost two-thirds: Kuwait's territorial decline between 1913 and 1922', *Journal of Arabian Studies*, Vol. 2, No. 1, June, pp. 19–37.

Onley, J. (2005), 'British informal empire in the Gulf: 1820–1971', *Journal of Social Affairs*, Vol. 22, No. 87, Fall, pp. 29–45.

Peterson, J. E. (2001), 'The nature of succession in the Gulf', *The Middle East Journal*, Vol. 55, No. 4, Autumn, pp. 580–602.

Potter, L. (2014), *The Persian Gulf in modern times: people, ports and history*, New York: Palgrave Macmillan.

Al-Rasheed, M. (1991), *Politics in an Arabian oasis: the Rashidis of Saudi Arabia*, London: I.B. Tauris.

Al-Rasheed, M. (2003), 'Tribal confederations and emirates in Central Arabia', in F. A. Jabar and H. Dawod (eds), *Tribes and power: nationalism* Al-Rushaid, *Tarikh al-Kuwayt*, Kuwait: Manshurat Dar al-Hayat.

Rush, A. (1989), *Records of Kuwait: 1899–1961*, Cambridge: Cambridge Archive Editions.

Salih, K. O. (1992), 'The 1938 Kuwaiti Legislative Council', *Middle Eastern Studies*, Vol. 28, No. 1, January, pp. 66–100.

Segal, E. (2009), 'Merchant networks in Kuwait: the story of Yusuf al-Marzuk', *Middle Eastern Studies*, Vol. 45, No. 5, September, pp. 709–719.

Al-Shamlan, S. (2001/translation), *Pearling in the Arabian Gulf: a personal memoir*, translated by P. Clark, London: The London Center of Arab Studies.

Shanavaz, S. (2005), *Britain and Southwest Persia: 1880–1914; a study in imperialism and economic dependence*, London: Routledge Curzon.

Slot, B. J. (2003), *Mubarak al-Sabah: founder of modern Kuwait 1896–1915*, Leidschendam: Arabian Publishing.

Al-Tamimi, A. (1992), *Al-Kuwayt wa al-khalij al-'arabi al-mu'asir: abhath tarikhiyya*, Kuwait: mu'assat al-shir'a al-'arabi.

Al-Tamimi, A. (2006), *Abhath fi tarikh al-Kuwayt*, Kuwait: Dar al-Qurtas.

Tétrault, M. A. (2000), *Stories of democracy: politics and society in contemporary Kuwait*, New York: Colombia University Press.

Yanai, S. (2014), *The political transformation of the Gulf tribal states: elitism and the social contract in Kuwait, Bahrain and Dubai: 1918–1970*, Sussex: Sussex Academic Press.

Part II: Oil and the consolidation of a tribal authoritarian shaykhdom: ruler–ruled relations 1961–90

Assiri, A. R. (1990), *Kuwait's foreign policy: city-state in world politics*, Boulder, CO: Westview.

Brown, N. (2002), *Constitutions in a non-constitutional world: Arab basic laws and the prospects for accountable government*, New York: SUNY Press.

Davidson, C. (2007), 'Arab nationalism and British opposition in Dubai, 1920–1966', *Middle Eastern Studies*, Vol. 43, No. 6, pp. 879–892.

Ghabra, S. (1997), 'Kuwait and the dynamics of socio-economic change', *Middle East Journal*, Vol. 51, No. 3, pp. 358–372.

Herb, M. (2014), *The wages of oil: parliaments and economic development in Kuwait and the UAE*, Ithaca, NY and London: Cornell University Press.

Hertog, S. (2011), *Princes, brokers and bureaucrats: oil and the state in Saudi Arabia*, Ithaca, NY: Cornell University Press.

Al-Jasem, A. (2007), *Al-Kuwayt mathalat al-dimoqratiyya*, Kuwait: Dar al-Qurtas.

Al-Khatib, A. (2007), *Al-Kuwayt min al-imara ila al-dawlat: dikrayat min a-'amal al-watani wa al-qawmi*, Beirut: al-Markaz al-thaqafi al-'arabi.

Lahoud, C. (2011), *Islam et politique au Koweit*, Paris: Presses Universitaires de France.

Louer, L. (2008), *Transnational Shi'a politics: religious and political networks in the Gulf*, London: Hurst.

Luciani, G. (1990), 'Allocation vs. production states: a theoretical framework' in G. Luciani (ed.), *The Arab State*, Berkeley: University of California Press.

Al-Najjar, G. (1984), *Decision-making process in Kuwait: the land acquisition policy as a case study*, PhD thesis, Exeter University.

Al-Nakib, F. (2014), 'Revisiting hadar and badu in Kuwait: citizenship, housing and the construction of a dichotomy', *IJMES*, Vol. 46, pp. 5–30.

Al-Naqeeb, K. (1985), 'Bina'a al-mujtama' al-'arabi: b'ad al-furudh al-bahatiyya', *Al-Mustaqbal al-'arabi*, No. 79, September.

Al-Naqeeb, K. (1996), *Sira' al-qabialiya wa al-dimoqratiyya halat al-Kuwayt*, London: Dar al-Saqi.

Pall, Z. (2012), *Salafism in Lebanon: local and transnational resources*, PhD thesis, Utrecht University.

Plotkin-Boghart, L. (2006), *Kuwait amid war, peace and revolution 1979–1991 and new challenges*, London: Palgrave Macmillan.

Salame, G. (1994), 'Small is pluralistic: democracy as an instrument of civil peace', in G. Salame (ed.), *Democracy without democrats*, London: I.B Tauris, pp. 90–95.

Taryam, A. (1987), *The establishment of the UAE: 1950–1985*, London: Croom Helm.

Weber, M. (1946), *Politics as a vocation*, New York: Free Press.

Part III: New forces of globalization and the rise of the tribal periphery in Kuwait (1990–2014)

Azoulay, R. (2013), 'The politics of Shi'i merchants in Kuwait', in S. Hertog, G. Luciani and M. Valeri (eds), *Business politics in the Middle East*, London: Hurst & Co, pp. 67–99.

Azoulay, R. and Beaugrand, C. (2015), 'Limits of political clientelism: elites' struggles in Kuwait fragmenting politics', *Arabian Humanities*, 4.

Azoulay, R. and Wells, M. (2014), 'Contesting welfare state politics in Kuwait', *Middle East Report 272*, Fall, pp. 43–47.

Davidson, C. (2012), *After the shaykhs: the coming collapse of the Gulf monarchies*, London: Hurst.

Diwan, K. (2014), 'Breaking taboos: youth activism in the Gulf states', *Issue Brief, Atlantic Council*, March.

Al-Jasem, M. A. (2006), *Akher shuyukh al-hiba*, Kuwait: Jam'iyyat al-huquq makhfudha li-l-mu'alef.

Maisal, S. (2015), 'The resurgent tribal agenda in Saudi Arabia', *Arab Gulf States Institute*, 30 July.

Matthiesen, T. (2013), *Sectarian Gulf: Bahrain, Saudi Arabia and the Arab Spring that wasn't*, Stanford, CA: Stanford University Press.

Index

www.ingramcontent.com/pod-product-compliance
Lightning Source LLC
Chambersburg PA
CBHW050411280326
41932CB00013BA/1821